Other Books by Michael A. Cusumano

MICROSOFT SECRETS: How the World's Most Powerful
Software Company Creates Technology, Shapes Markets,
and Manages People *(with Richard W. Selby)*

COMPETING ON INTERNET TIME: Lessons from Netscape
and Its Battle with Microsoft *(with David B. Yoffie)*

PLATFORM LEADERSHIP: How Intel, Cisco, and Microsoft
Drive Industry Innovation *(with Annabelle Gawer)*

JAPAN'S SOFTWARE FACTORIES: A Challenge to U.S. Management

STRATEGIC THINKING FOR THE NEXT ECONOMY
(with Costas Markides)

THINKING BEYOND LEAN: How Multi-Project
Management Is Transforming Product Development at
Toyota and Other Companies *(with Kentaro Nobeoka)*

THE JAPANESE AUTOMOBILE INDUSTRY: Technology and
Management at Nissan and Toyota

The Business of Software

What Every Manager,

Programmer,

and Entrepreneur

Must Know to

Thrive and Survive

in Good Times and Bad

Michael A. Cusumano

Free Press
New York London Toronto Sydney

FREE PRESS

A Division of Simon & Schuster, Inc.

1230 Avenue of the Americas

New York, NY 10020

For information regarding special discounts for bulk purchases,

please contact Simon & Schuster Special Sales at 1-800-456-6798

or business@simonandschuster.com

Designed by Karolina Harris

Manufactured in the United States of America

10   9   8   7   6   5   4   3   2   1

Library of Congress Cataloging-in-Publication Data

Cusumano, Michael A., 1954–

  The business of software : what every manager, programmer, and entrepreneur must
know to thrive and survive in good times and bad / Michael A. Cusumano.

     p.   cm.

  Includes bibliographical references and index.

  1. Computer software industry.   2. Computer software industry—Management.

I. Title.

HD9696.63. A2C87   2004

005.3'068—dc22   2003063147

ISBN 0-7432-1580-X

For Robbie and Cristen,

and what their futures might bring

Contents

Acknowledgments ix

Preface xiii

1: The Business of Software: A Personal View 1

2: Strategy for Software Companies: What to Think About 24

3: Services, Products, and More Services: How Software
Became a Business 86

4: Best Practices in Software Development:
Beyond the Software Factory 128

5: Software Entrepreneurship: Essential Elements
of a Successful Start-up 195

6: Start-up Case Studies: Software Products, Services,
and Hybrid Solutions 215

7: Conclusion: The "Ideal" Versus "Realistic" Software Business 272

Appendix 283

Notes 303

Index 321

Acknowledgments

The idea for this book goes back to 1997, when I first put together a course on "The Software Business" at MIT's Sloan School of Management. In August 2000, I proposed the book to my publisher. Many thanks go to Bob Wallace, my longtime editor at the Free Press, and to others at the parent company Simon & Schuster, for taking on the project and sticking with me. I began writing in mid-December 2001, starting with the strategy chapter. Nearly two years later, much has changed in the fast-paced software business. The Internet bubble has peaked and burst. The software business has gone through remarkable highs, frightening lows, and now a modest recovery. I have done my best to follow the changes and incorporate what I learned. Hence the subtitle "in good times and bad."

Many people helped me write a better book. Bob Wallace especially helped me focus on the best new material and balance a personal view with a tone appropriate for general readers. Xiaohua Yang was the first person to read any part of the manuscript. She provided many comments on several chapters and started me on what I believe is the right track for tone and content. She has been a constant source of encouragement and support for many years, and I cannot thank her enough. Charlie DeWitt, my ex-student and a former veteran of i2

Technologies, read the entire original manuscript and provided detailed, frank comments throughout. He, Bob, and Xiaohua were a wonderful sounding board in the final writing stages and helped me improve the book significantly.

Many other people commented on specific parts of the book and were extremely helpful. At Sloan, Eleanor Westney read numerous drafts of what are now the first two chapters and encouraged me to position the book more as a "personal story." Her enthusiastic suggestions greatly helped me move forward. Ed Roberts read several chapters and provided excellent advice, especially on the entrepreneurship chapter and the conclusion. JoAnne Yates provided expert comments (and corrections) on the history of software as a business. Michael Scott Morton also read the entire manuscript and helped me refine plans for the final draft.

Alan MacCormack of Harvard Business School gave me meticulous and very useful editing suggestions on the software development material now in Chapter 4. Ted Schadler of Forrester Research provided comments on the first two chapters and the business models. Suresh Shanmugham of Boston Millennia Partners pushed me in what is now Chapter 5 to find a smaller number of points to characterize the essential elements of a software startup. Alessandro Narduzzo of the University of Bologna provided comments on the first three chapters and helped me refine the arguments. Tracy Eiler of Business Objects provided some corrections on Chapters 1 and 2. Finally, I need to thank the students of "The Software Business" course in spring 2003 for patiently reading an early version of the manuscript and providing many comments that I incorporated into the last revision.

Many people gave their time for interviews or provided other useful comments and opportunities for me to develop the material in this book. My thanks especially to Bernard Liautaud of Business Objects and Sanjiv Sidhu of i2 Technologies for recent opportunities to work with their companies. I also thank the many entrepreneurs (and a couple of venture capitalists) interviewed for the entrepreneurship chapter, some of whom I have also worked with closely over the years. They are Jim Moskun, Frank Grosman, Tom Herring, Yannick Loop, Garth Rose, Ron Schreiber, Gaurav Rewari, Navaid Farooqi, J. P. Singh, Imran Sayeed, Ennis Rimawi, Brad Miller, Campbell Stras, O. Emre Eksi, Neil Crabb, Sina Hakman, David Schwedel, and Nicolas Economou.

Since the late 1980s, I have given many presentations on software development, beginning with Japanese software factories and more recently on approaches used at firms such as Microsoft and Netscape. The questions I received helped me refine my thoughts and arguments. My special thanks to Frances Paulish of Siemens in Germany for providing a transcript of a March 2001 talk that provided the basis for the chapter on software development. I have also spoken about all the material in the book while teaching at MIT and need to thank in particular the 190 or so students who have participated in "The Software Business" course since 1997.

I gave numerous seminars on the strategy material, and they all provided valuable feedback. In particular, in June 2002, my colleagues at the Institute for Innovation Research at Hitotsubashi University in Japan encouraged me to highlight what is unusual about strategy for software companies. In October 2002, my colleagues in the Strategy and International Management Group at the MIT Sloan School of Management helped me figure out the best way to approach the product versus services debate. In January 2003, Professors Michael Jacobides and Fernando Suarez of London Business School provided important feedback on interpreting the data I was collecting. Patrick Kremer, a Sloan Fellow at LBS, sent useful comments by e-mail. I also benefited from comments by Professor Jyrki Konti and his colleagues at the Helsinki University of Technology, where I presented at another seminar in January 2003. Other helpful suggestions came from students during a February presentation in the MIT Business and Technology Lecture Series.

In addition, I thank my colleagues in the software process study described briefly in Chapter 4. Along with Alan MacCormack, they are Chris Kemerer of the University of Pittsburgh and Bill Crandall of Hewlett-Packard, as well as former MIT students Pearlin Cheung and Sharma Upadhyayula. Of course, I also need to thank many managers around the world for participating in the surveys, on which we plan to report in more detail. My thanks in particular go to Kouichi Kishida of SRA in Japan for his help with the Japanese data.

Funding for much of my research on software development and the software business over the past several years came from MIT's Center for Innovation in Product Development. The Center for eBusiness at the MIT Sloan School provided some funding for the platform leadership study. The Entrepreneurship Center provided inspiration for me to record what I was learning about start-ups and venture capitalists. My thanks also to the MIT Sloan School and Dean Richard Schmalensee for funding part of my sabbatical year during 2001–2002, which I used to write a first draft of this book.

Michael A. Cusumano
Groton and Cambridge, Massachusetts
November 2003

Preface

My goal in this book is to provide an overview of the software business for managers who are already working in the business, programmers who would like to be managers, and anyone who would like to be a software entrepreneur. I focus mainly on firms selling what we can call "enterprise software" to other companies and large organizations, although much of what I say about products, services, and software development also applies to companies selling software to individual consumers. My primary concerns are with strategy and business models, a historical look at software entrepreneurship, best practices in managing software development, and the do's and don'ts of founding a software start-up. The examples and topics reflect my personal experiences as a researcher, teacher, consultant, director, and company founder. I have used a version of this book in my MIT class "The Software Business." The material should also be a useful reference for investors and analysts who follow software companies and for anyone else interested in how high-tech firms deal with problems of strategy and product development in rapidly changing markets.

Chapter 1 starts out with a personal sketch of my involvement in the software business and how the business seems to differ around the world. I also sketch out the experiences of two firms that I have worked with recently and that demonstrate many of the strategic and business-model issues that I take up in subsequent chapters: Business Objects in France and i2 Technologies in the United States.

Chapter 2 focuses on strategy for software companies—the most important things that managers and entrepreneurs, as well as programmers, should think about. I begin with the most fundamental question: Do you want to be mainly a *products company* or a *services company*? I also talk in more detail about a third alternative: *hybrid solutions*. Other key issues are the kinds of customers and markets (enterprise, consumer, mass-market, niche, vertical, or horizontal) that the company will target, as well as platform versus complementor decisions.

Chapter 3 probes these issues of strategy, management, and entrepreneurship in more depth. I use history to suggest where most opportunities in the business have come from and how the industry has evolved from services to products and now back, to some extent, to a renewed emphasis on services, especially in bad economic times, when customers are reluctant to buy more software products. I also examine the history of IBM and end with a discussion of open-source and "for free" software.

Chapter 4 presents what I have learned about how to manage the most fundamental technical activity in a software company: *software development*. The discussion is not specifically for programmers, but is more for managers of programmers and general managers who need to know what goes on in software projects and how best to deal with issues ranging from architecture and teams to project management and testing. I begin with basic problems in software development and how organizations introduced "software factories" and process improvement initiatives from the Software Engineering Institute (SEI). I then discuss practices that provide an effective balance of structure and flexibility. In particular, I review "synch-and-stabilize" techniques that have characterized software products companies such as Microsoft and Netscape, and how managers can apply these concepts in different settings. I also include some preliminary observations from survey data on the practices and performance of software companies in the United States, Japan, India, Europe, and elsewhere.

Chapters 5 and 6 apply ideas about the software business to startups. I give my view of how to interpret entrepreneurship in times of boom and bust and reflect on what the most important elements in a successful software venture are. I then evaluate ten case studies of start-ups I have been involved with since the mid-1990s. I also use these examples to illustrate strategic issues as well as differences among the three main business models for software companies: products, services, and hybrid solutions.

Chapter 7, the conclusion, offers some final thoughts on the three basic models and the different capabilities they require, and contrasts the "ideal" software business with a more realistic business model. I also make some suggestions on how to run a successful software business, whether you are a products company, a services company, or something in between.

1

The Business of Software:

A Personal View

If the software business were like other businesses, there would be no need for this book. But *software is not like other businesses*. First of all, the technology consists of a digital "soft" good—usually English-like programming commands eventually translated into zeros and ones—that provide instructions to a computer. These instructions form products that companies can standardize for many users, customize for individual users, or do something in between. Companies that rely on this highly malleable technology for their livelihoods must be unique in many ways, particularly in how they deal with business models, product strategy, people (especially software engineers), and management of a core activity: software development.

There are many examples of how software technology and software companies differ from what we see in traditional manufacturing and service industries. In how many businesses does making *one* copy or *one million* copies of your product cost about the same? How many businesses have up to 99 percent gross profit margins for their product sales? In how many businesses do many products companies eventually become services or hybrid companies (that is, providing some customization of product features and technical services such as system integration and maintenance), whether they like it or not? In

how many businesses is there frequently a ten- or twentyfold difference in productivity between your best employee and your worst one?
How many businesses tolerate some 75 to 80 percent of their prod-
uct-development projects routinely being late and over budget, with
"best practice" considered to be 20 percent on time? How about a
company where the people who build products often consider themselves artists rather than scientists or engineers and have the mercurial
temperament to go with it? In how many businesses are customers
"locked in" to a particular vendor because of product decisions someone made a decade or two ago that can't easily be reversed?

The software business also differs from conventional industries because it is not really one kind of business. Software becomes whatever
function or application it addresses. This means that the range of possible products and services is almost infinite. Software can help you
write a report, calculate your taxes, build a bridge, navigate an automobile, control the space shuttle, or dial your telephone. Not surprisingly, there are many categories and even layers of software products
and customized programs that work with one another to form complete systems (such as networking software with operating systems,
and operating systems with applications). The definitions of these categories and layers are relatively well accepted, though Microsoft and
other companies have been blurring the traditional distinctions for
many years.

These and other observations describe aspects of software technology, software companies, and the software business. They also describe some other high-tech markets, such as telecommunications and
various types of businesses heavily dependent on information systems
and digital content. But surely these observations describe an unusual
type of business.

As I discuss in Chapters 2 and 3, get the strategy and the management side right, and the software business can be like having a license
to print money. Just ask Bill Gates of Microsoft or Larry Ellison of
Oracle, among many other software billionaires and multimillionaires around the world. But get the business model wrong, and—to
borrow a metaphor from Frederick Brooks's *The Mythical Man-
Month*—software companies can resemble dinosaurs futilely trying to
escape the death grip of an ancient tar pit.[1] The more you struggle—
that is, the more time, money, and people you pour into product development, sales, and marketing in the hope of a turnaround—the

deeper you sink and the quicker you die. In the software business, this is not only because the more people you add to a late software project, the later the project can become—a rule of thumb now described as "Brooks's law" (and not always true). But the broader downward spiral can accelerate for a whole company and become self-fulfilling as present and potential customers flee from software producers unlikely to survive long enough to deliver, support, and upgrade their products.

In bad economic times, or when there is bad corporate news, we can see the sales of once high-flying software companies suddenly drop as if they had fallen off a cliff. Billion-dollar companies can shrink to half their peak size (e.g., i2 Technologies), declare bankruptcy almost overnight (e.g., Baan), or turn suddenly from modern-day gold mines into investment nightmares. SAP, Oracle, Siebel Systems, Business Objects, and many other blue-chip software companies lost 80 to 90 percent of their value at one time or another during 2000–2002, depending on when an investor bought the stock—despite having solid products and businesses. Even Microsoft dropped about two thirds of its value during this period of boom and bust. We have seen this phenomenon of rapid growth and dramatic decline as well in the telecommunications equipment and services industries (e.g., Lucent and WorldCom), businesses that are also heavily based on software technology but even more distressed in terms of profits and sales.

Since software technology, software companies, their people, and their markets have unique challenges and opportunities, I believe that the business requires a unique approach to strategy and management. For example, software managers, programmers, and entrepreneurs need to encourage innovation wherever and whenever they can, but they have a special need to contain it as well; otherwise projects and plans can spin out of control. Perhaps most important, a large number of software companies—those selling "enterprise software" to other companies and large organizations—have to be nimble enough to tailor their products and their strategies to the needs of individual users and particular kinds of customers. Often they must survive the transition from selling high-margin products to selling low-margin services, especially in bad economic times and as their products and customer bases age.

This last idea—that many software companies need to sell *both* products and services to maintain a successful business—is a central theme throughout this book. I argue in Chapter 2 that there are basically three business models that fall along a spectrum: On one end are *software products companies,* which get all or most of their revenues from new product sales (called "software license fees"). On the opposite end are *software services companies,* which get a majority of their revenues from IT consulting, custom software development, integration work, technical support, systems maintenance, and related activities. In the middle are what I call *hybrid solutions companies*—software firms that have some new product sales but derive as much as 80 percent of their revenues from services and "maintenance" (incremental product updates or special enhancements sold through long-term contracts to the purchasers of the initial software license).

I also argue that even companies trying to emphasize products eventually end up selling more services and incremental maintenance upgrades to their existing customer base than new products to new customers. *They often fall unwittingly into the services or hybrid business models and are not prepared for the change.* Bad economic times can accelerate this transition as customers postpone purchases of new software products. It also seems an almost inevitable transition for software companies that sell to corporate customers (enterprises): their revenues increasingly consist of sales of services and maintenance upgrades to existing customers, rather than new product sales to new customers. It can be devastating to a software company to find its new-software-product sales collapse, but it happens frequently. This is why managers, programmers, and entrepreneurs need to understand what the future usually holds for enterprise software companies, and how to manage and adapt to that future as effectively as possible. Accordingly, because of the potential for rapid change in the marketplace, software companies must combine extraordinary levels of *structure* with *flexibility.* Companies must pay constant attention to strategies and business models as well as continuously evolving their technical skills and core technologies. They must often experiment with new-product development while preventing projects from running years behind schedule or devolving into chaos.

SOFTWARE AS A TECHNOLOGY

How a software firm manages the technology to create and deliver products and services is usually central to its long-term success. Almost any firm can have a onetime hit product. But following this first product with multiple versions for different customer segments or with compelling updates and new services that meet future customer needs requires thought and careful management. But what does "managing the technology" mean in the context of a software producer? In this book, I treat the question in fairly straightforward terms, separating "the technology" from "technology management."

Technology Versus Management

Software technology is many things. I have already described it most directly as code—programming instructions or algorithms, eventually translated into zeros and ones. But for practical reasons, we must also include system architectures, program designs, the data or digital content that computer programs need to do anything useful, user interfaces, application programming interfaces, programming support and testing tools, test cases, documentation, and other physical and nonphysical artifacts. Software technology also includes the effects of what programs do—how one module of code interacts with other programs, modules, and computers, and what the whole system enables users to do.

Managing the technology in a software business primarily refers to overseeing the process of designing a software product or information system for a particular customer need and then building, testing, delivering, supporting, and enhancing that software product or system over its lifetime of use. Chapter 4 contains a lot of what I have learned about managing this chain of activities. In addition, though I do not talk much about managing the science, managing the technology should include facilitating communication between scientists pushing the state of the art and engineers building real-life applications.

From a business point of view, managing software technology well should imply knowing how to go through the phases from design to delivery at a cost that is less than the revenues generated from selling the resulting product or service. This may be common sense, but it is not always common practice. Here is where marketing and sales—and financial discipline—become as important as anything else in the software business. Managers, programmers, and entrepreneurs need to understand how to build or package technology *and price it* in a way that both makes people want to buy it and earns them a profit. Selling software and services at enormous losses (and I will discuss many examples of this, ranging from start-ups to established firms) is *not a business.* Many software companies waste millions and billions of dollars on development efforts, acquisitions, or marketing campaigns that generate no profitable results.

As a researcher and consultant, I have found that managing the technology well becomes a serious problem at one time or another in the lifetime of nearly all software businesses, including dedicated software companies and firms that do a lot of software development for in-house use. As I discuss in Chapter 3, IBM went through the pain of building OS/360 in the 1960s and eventually created a structured process that worked, despite a great deal of variation within the company and without much concern for flexibility or innovation. The Software Engineering Institute (SEI) at Carnegie Mellon University, to a large degree, has disseminated the best practices of IBM for large-scale systems development. The Japanese also attempted to solve problems in large-scale systems development by incorporating many practices similar to IBM's approach into their software factories of the 1970s and 1980s. Microsoft struggled mightily in the 1980s and came up with more flexible but still structured "synch-and-stabilize" techniques that worked well during the 1990s and early 2000s. Another giant, Oracle, in the early 2000s was still figuring out how to build high-quality applications the first time around. And these firms are all success stories! There are many other examples of start-ups and established firms wasting years and millions of dollars on software development, with little or nothing to show for it.

I also know of many cases (such as some of the start-ups described in Chapter 6) where the software engineers knew very well what they were doing but still failed anyway. They were able to create a prototype or small-scale system without spending too much time or money. But then problems almost always set in as these firms tried to build a commercial-grade product with more sophisticated features, or as they took on hybrid-solutions projects that rose quickly in complexity and then overwhelmed their management skills or financial resources. And even where managing development of the technology was not a major problem, understanding how to market and sell the technology they were creating was a major factor in their struggles or demise. As Chris Peters of Microsoft once said, it is just as important in software development to decide what you are *not* going to do as it is to decide what you *are* going to do.[2]

Because software can perform an almost infinite number of functions, the challenges of managing the technology well continue to be enormous, especially for inexperienced start-ups or established firms where software development is not the primary business. Managers, programmers, and entrepreneurs have to accommodate different kinds of projects and customer requirements, as well as anticipate changes in the technology and market needs. What do you have to think about if you are working on software for the space shuttle? It is very different from what you must think about if you are working on a video game. What software producers must do well may be the same at a high conceptual level—they need to design, build, test, deliver, support, and maintain a product or a custom-built system. But the demands vary considerably depending on how customers will deploy the software technology in their particular applications or markets. In short, the requirements of managing software as a technology vary with the requirements of managing software as a business.

MY INVOLVEMENT WITH THE SOFTWARE BUSINESS

This book is very much a personal view of the software business, seen through the lens of nearly two decades of research on the industry, professional involvement with dozens of software companies and organizations, and teaching a class titled "The Software Business" at MIT since 1997. I am not a programmer, but I have been fascinated by computers since first using an IBM mainframe in college during the mid-1970s. But my first recognition that software was a special *business* with special problems in strategy and management came in 1985. That is when I started studying how Japanese companies built large-scale industrial software systems and were trying to add sophisticated software skills to their already formidable hardware skills. Since the late 1970s, I had been studying Japanese production and quality management techniques, particularly in automobile design and manufacturing.[3] But I had tired of looking at this one industry and thought that the next great challenge for Japan after automobiles would be computer software.

I began the new research by reading about the history of the computer industry in Japan as well as some articles on Japanese software engineering practices. One fact immediately got my attention. Since 1969, the major Japanese computer manufacturers had been concen-

trating their people with software expertise in relatively large facilities and had been trying to apply the same disciplined approach to
software production and quality management as they had done in
"hard" manufacturing businesses. I then began to write case studies
and conduct surveys of software projects and development practices
at Hitachi, Toshiba, NEC, Fujitsu, NTT, and several other Japanese
firms. I also studied IBM, DEC, System Development Corporation,
and Andersen Consulting, among other U.S. firms, for comparisons.
I learned a great deal about process and organization in mostly custom or semicustom software development for mainframe computers.
But I ended up wondering why process excellence and "zero defects"
did not necessarily make a company successful in software as a *business.*

I remember giving a press conference for the American Electronics
Association's Tokyo chapter in February 1991 to announce the results of my research on Japanese software. I began with the statement
that the "$60-billion-dollar question" people had been debating for
years was whether or not the Japanese could write software. I said
that I finally had an answer, though I divided this into "good news"
and "bad news" from the point of view of American firms.[4]

The bad news was that the Japanese *could* write software. In fact,
they wrote *a lot* of software, and they wrote it as well as or better
than U.S. firms in terms of reliability (few "bugs" or defects) and
crude measures of productivity (code output per programmer, including large amounts of reused and semiautomatically generated code).[5]
The "factory-like" approach that the Japanese computer manufacturers used for software development also differed from the approaches
common in the United States. The Japanese emphasized incremental
innovation in feature design, standardized development techniques,
common training programs, reusable component libraries, computer-
aided support tools, rigorous quality assurance techniques, and statistical data to manage projects. The Japanese also tended to staff
projects with a combination of experienced people and relatively low-
skilled programmers who had merely a few months of training.

But there was also good news, again, from the perspective of U.S.
firms: the Japanese approach seemed well suited for building certain
kinds of software systems but not others. Moreover, Japanese companies didn't seem to know much about *how to make money* from software or compete outside Japan, except for software embedded in

products such as programmable machine tools, VCRs, and microwave ovens. The Japanese were focused mainly on labor-intensive custom or semicustom information systems built to sell mainframe computers and targeted to Japanese customers. They had limited innovation capabilities and ambitions, although Fujitsu, NEC, and Hitachi routinely beat U.S. competitors in the Japanese market because of their quality, service, and reliability. The Japanese economy would continue to modernize through the introduction of more computers and new PC-based or workstation-based information systems. But there was no dominant global software player likely to come from Japan, except perhaps in niches such as the video game industry. (This was an area of software that the Japanese excelled in, perhaps because of their fascination with comic books from childhood through adulthood.)

After studying Japanese software factories, I decided to "follow the money," so to speak. I decided to look at the company that made the most money and seemed to care the least about the process of product development: *Microsoft*. As it turned out, I soon learned that Microsoft managers and programmers did care *a lot* about process. But compared to the approaches followed by traditional U.S., Japanese, and European software organizations, they cared in a way that was much better suited to the fast-paced and somewhat unpredictable world of PC software and, later, the Internet. Microsoft people also cared more about strategy and money than they did about following textbook processes. They were interested in dominating markets— albeit *too* interested at times, so much so that the company ran afoul of antitrust laws. My new interest in Microsoft turned into another book published in 1995 with Richard Selby. In subsequent research, I continued to follow the evolution of Microsoft through the Internet age and competition with Netscape as well as into the world of .NET and Web services.[6]

My research also created opportunities to work with approximately fifty software producers in Europe and Asia as well as the United States, beginning in 1987. These organizations include software products and services companies; computer hardware and semiconductor companies with large software businesses; financial services companies heavily dependent on software technology; and telecommunications equipment and services companies. I am also fortunate to have served on approximately a dozen boards of directors and advisers for software companies and venture capital firms in New England, Silicon Valley, and London. What I have written in this book, consequently, is colored not only by my experiences with the Japanese and Microsoft, but also from studying and working with a wide variety of software producers around the world.

SOME INTERNATIONAL GENERALIZATIONS

My international experiences (including residing in Japan for about seven years) have often led me to compare people and organizations in different parts of the world. Here I would like to offer some generalizations about how the software business might differ in three regions I know reasonably well: Europe, Japan, and the United States. Like all generalizations, there are exceptions. I also think these generalizations were more applicable a decade or two ago than they are today. But I believe that they still contain more than a grain of truth. They also reflect a key motivation for me to write this book: the conviction that software is too important to be treated simply as a technology, or as part of the field of computer science. *Software has the power to change the world, especially when treated as a business by managers, programmers, and entrepreneurs who also want to change the world.*

The Europeans

The Europeans, along with the Americans, pioneered a lot of the inventions in computer design. But too many European companies I have encountered tend to treat software as a *science*. The reason is not hard to understand. The Europeans have excellent university-level education in computer science, especially programming languages and principles of design. And so, from Europe, we get things such as formal methods (a way of specifying requirements for software systems in mathematical terms that can be verified and validated mathematically) and object-oriented analysis and design (a clever way of breaking up software programming instructions and data into small, reusable objects, based on certain abstraction principles and design hierarchies).

We also get from Europe enormously rich but complex applications remarkable in their detail and structure, like those the German company SAP has produced. In addition, we can find elegant but simple applications that enable nonprogrammers to query databases and generate useful reports, such as those the French company Business Objects created a decade ago around object-oriented technology. Europe has also produced stunning innovations such as the World Wide Web, invented by Tim Berners-Lee, an Englishman, while he was working at the CERN physics research lab in Switzerland. But I have often found that many European software producers place more attention on achieving elegance in software design than on shipping products for mass markets and making the most money they can from their excellent technical skills.

The Japanese

The Japanese, for much of their history, have followed IBM and a few other American companies in designing and building mainframe computer systems. Japan's computer manufacturers and software firms have shown significant skill in writing programs for all sorts of applications, ranging from real-time banking systems, to fault-free bullet train control and reservation systems, to video game software. But most of these systems are custom-built for specific customers in Japan and contain relatively few innovative features, by design. The largest Japanese producers of software mainly write code to sell hardware and services, as IBM has done for decades. The country has also underinvested in basic research and higher education. Not surprisingly, Japan has had relatively weak university training in computers and information systems. Japan has also lacked the broad diffusion of computers, knowledge of English typing, and programming expertise among young people that has led to a strong "hacker" tradition in the United States and, to a lesser extent, in Europe.

Accordingly, the major Japanese producers of software—Fujitsu, Hitachi, NEC, Toshiba, and NTT—have had to train most of their own people on the job and have ended up treating software development mainly as a problem in production. With some exceptions, such as game software and some more creative consumer electronics applications, the big Japanese companies I know well have tackled large-scale systems development with heuristics (engineering rules of thumb), process discipline, some capital (e.g., computer-aided tools), and manpower. Hence, we have *software factories*. The factories were and remain good at cranking out multiple versions of custom or semicustom applications that follow standardized design patterns and evolve little from their original parameters. Software built in this way is useful in selling hardware and performing basic tasks or making construction of third and fourth versions of similar custom systems a bit easier and cheaper. But it doesn't change the world or make anybody a billionaire.

The Americans

And then we have the Americans. People in the United States are unmatched in treating software as a *business*. That is, they see software technology as a vehicle for creating dedicated software companies that produce at least "good-enough" products and try to set industry standards as well as make lots of money in the process. And so, in the United States, we have companies like Microsoft and Netscape, both of which tried to and succeeded in changing the world. Bill Gates, who cofounded Microsoft with Paul Allen in 1975, wanted to see a personal computer on every desktop and was determined that those PCs run Microsoft software. Today more than 90 percent do. Gates also had the great insight in 1975 to conclude that the future value of computing would be in software, not hardware.[7] Marc Andreessen, who cofounded Netscape with Jim Clark in 1994, felt that an easy-to-use browser that ran on Windows as well as other software platforms would make usage of the Internet ubiquitous, for both individuals and organizations. It now is. Microsoft and Netscape went on to introduce products that were no more than "good enough" from a technical point of view: MS-DOS, Windows, and Netscape Navigator.

Of course, software programming can still be science for Americans. Like the Europeans, we have great universities and computer scientists. It most certainly can resemble disciplined engineering practice, especially in the U.S. defense industry and mainframe software worlds, but also in the commercial operations of companies such as IBM, Sun Microsystems, Hewlett-Packard, and, yes, even Microsoft, when it comes to building products such as Windows NT/2000. But many American companies, and the occasional European company that operates like an American company, at least in marketing (witness Business Objects and SAP), have found ways of generating oodles of revenues and profits, and tremendous excitement for their employees and investors, by *treating software as a business*. This book is about how to do that, whichever country you are from and whichever part of the software industry you are in.

BASICS OF THE BUSINESS: TWO CASE STUDIES

There are many issues of strategy and technology management that managers, programmers, and entrepreneurs in the software business need to understand in order to have successful companies in both good times and bad. To illustrate some of the key issues here, I introduce the stories of two companies I have worked for over the past several years: Business Objects and i2 Technologies. Both are public software companies. Business Objects (NASDAQ stock symbol: BOBJ) is based in Paris with a second headquarters in Silicon Valley, and i2 (stock symbol: ITWO) has its headquarters in Dallas and much of its development organization in India.

Business Objects is a clear-cut success story of a business intelligence company selling horizontal software to enterprises and institutions. From the beginning, it demonstrated a very focused strategy as a complement to Oracle and then other database products. It has benefited from superb leadership by the founder, disciplined operations, clever product development, and fast and profitable but not unwieldy growth. The company passed $450 million in revenues in 2002.

i2 Technologies, on the other hand, had a meteoric rise in the market for factory planning and supply chain management software. It went from $2 million in sales in 1992 to almost $900 million in 2001, but also lost nearly $8 billion that year, although most of these losses were write-offs of devalued acquisitions. Though it has made dramatic improvements in the past few months, i2 remains an example of a company that grew too fast during the height of the Internet bubble. The company nearly lost its focus and ability to serve customers. It has a founder and new senior management team with great determination to change, however, and that may be enough to turn the company around.

Business Objects

I was sitting in my office at MIT one day in April 1996. The phone rang, and it was Bernard Liautaud, the CEO and cofounder of Business Objects. He had read *Microsoft Secrets* and asked me if I could help him make his rapidly growing company work as well as Microsoft. I agreed to try. This led to a weeklong visit in May, a series of reports and recommendations over the next five years, and laudable efforts by Liautaud and many other people in the company to make Business Objects into what became one of the fastest-growing and most consistently profitable software companies in the world. In 2002, the company was the market leader in revenues for business intelligence software, a segment that the International Data Corporation estimated to be about $8 billion in 2001 and expected to double in size by 2005.[8]

Liautaud and a partner, Denis Payre, had founded Business Objects in August 1990. Both men were French nationals who had worked at Oracle France in sales or marketing. The original idea for the company's main product came from another Frenchman, Jean-Michel Cambot, an independent engineer and consultant who worked with Oracle database products. Cambot had approached Liautaud in the late 1980s with a concept for a new decision-support tool based on the latest object-oriented design technology—software as science leading to a commercial innovation. His product (actually, a short program or set of computer instructions) made it possible to generate SQL (Structured Query Language) statements from a simple user interface, without the user having to know SQL or any other database programming language. Cambot wanted Oracle to make his prototype into a product and distribute it for him. Oracle management declined, even though the response from a sample of Oracle customers to the product idea was very positive. Liautaud and Payre decided to create a company around the product. They secured some funding and bought the software from Cambot in exchange for royalties. After three years of successful sales, Business Objects went public in 1996.

In an interview for this book, Liautaud recalled that, from the beginning, Business Objects went after a big "horizontal niche" rather than a "vertical" market. It attempted to "cross the chasm" separating early adopters from mainstream users by riding on the backs of Oracle customers (more on horizontal versus vertical niches as well as chasm crossing and its alternatives in Chapter 2). Liautaud noted that the company was not trying to create a new platform to work with all database technologies, but rather was positioning itself as a "complement" to Oracle:

We viewed our market as Oracle customers, period. We said we were not going to go after Sybase, Informix, or Microsoft customers. We were going to stay pure Oracle at the beginning. And the main reason was that by doing this we would be able to work with the salespeople at Oracle. We would not be a danger to the Oracle sales force . . . We were a complement. It would improve their product. They didn't have anything comparable. It would make them win deals more. And, by the way, the very first deal we won with an Oracle France sales guy was a deal where he had lost against Sybase. We came back, and we managed to get a last-minute meeting with the decision maker in the company. We showed our product on top of Oracle, and the guy said, "I'm switching my database, because if that product doesn't work on Sybase, then I want Oracle because that's exactly what I want. I want that product and I will pick the database that works with that product." I can tell you we advertised that to all the Oracle France sales force, and they went crazy. . . . Our crossing the chasm was not a vertical strategy, like going retail. Our strategy was Oracle customers. . . . It was a big niche.[9]

The innovative technology alone was sufficient for leading-edge customers. The product was also attractive because it worked on DOS computers (the most popular business PCs at the time) with an extremely small memory requirement, about three hundred kilobytes. Windows was not yet available widely. As for pricing, the company ended up going with a high-end strategy—$15,000 for eight users as the minimum contract. It used as a pricing benchmark what Oracle was charging for its own query tools. Two years later, in 1992, Liautaud and Payre decided to extend the product to work on other databases.[10]

The two entrepreneurs grew the business from nothing in 1990 to more than $60 million in revenues by 1995, with impressive profits—surpassing $10 million in 1995 alone. (For financial data on Business Objects, see Appendix Tables 1 and 2.) This is the beauty of software product sales, usually called "software license fees." Software is a digital good, so making one copy or a million copies costs about the same. There is, as a result, tremendous potential in the software products business for economies of scale and rapid, profitable growth. Product sales accounted for more than 80 percent of the company's revenues during 1993–1995, with minimal costs compared to services such as product customization, maintenance, and technical support. In recognition of their performance, *Business Week* named Liautaud and Payre among the "best entrepreneurs of the year" for 1995.[11]

Business Objects did not do it all alone. The company reached an agreement in 1994 for IBM to resell its core product bundled with IBM's data-warehousing package as well as some industry-targeted vertical solutions. IBM quickly became the company's biggest reseller, a position it still had in 2002. Most of the company's revenues have been through direct sales channels, rather than resellers, although Liautaud commented on the benefits of the ties with IBM: "The [IBM] sales were not huge. It was probably five percent of our revenue per year, not much more. But it gave us the credibility. The marketing leverage was very important. It still is."

The company also had to overcome the usual problems of a rapidly growing start-up. For example, Business Objects' 1997 Form 10-K report to the U.S. Securities and Exchange Commission, with surprising candidness, detailed the difficult state of product development during the spring of 1996. The comedown from the banner year of 1995 was dramatic. The new 4.0 release was a year late—it had planned to ship the update in June 1995. Moreover, the company admitted that the product code was still riddled with bugs.[12] When I first visited the company, I learned that engineers and managers severely doubted they would ever get the defect level low enough to ship the new version of the core product. In the meantime, sales were dropping as customers waited for the new release. The problem was not easy to solve. Business Objects had redesigned the core product to run on Microsoft's new 32-bit operating system, Windows 95. But this new version (BusinessObjects 4.0) did not run well on the older 16-bit Windows, version 3.1, which was still the most common PC operating system used in corporate settings. Most customers had switched from DOS but had not yet upgraded to Windows 95 or Windows NT (which was also a 32-bit operating system with interfaces similar to those of Windows 95). Managing software design and development better and dealing with platform issues were only some of the hurdles facing the young company, though they were central to survival.

Business Objects did tail off in growth during 1997 ("only" 34 percent over the prior year) due to the delay of the new release, before returning to a more familiar pace (46 percent) in 1998. The company then grew about 45 percent annually, even as license fees (new product sales) declined as a percentage of revenues to about 60 percent in 2001. The company was not immune to the bad times that hit the entire software industry after the bursting of the Internet bubble. Nonetheless, in 2002, Business Objects topped $454 million in sales with operating profits of more than $47 million—excellent numbers in a bad year for most software companies. As of mid-2003, it had millions of users at more than 17,000 customer sites in eighty countries. More than half the company's sales were from North America, Business Objects' fastest-growing market, and about 40 percent from Europe.

Liautaud has presided over the growth of the company alone since 1996. Payre, who initially had taken the title of president and headed sales, left the company at the end of 1996 to become a venture capitalist in Brussels. It is also significant that Liautaud moved to the United States in July 1997 to give more priority to the U.S. operations. Increasing sales in the biggest software market was critical to making Business Objects a worldwide brand. In recognition of the company's success as well as his leadership, many awards have continued to come to Liautaud personally and to his firm. Of particular note, in 2002 *Business Week* called Liautaud "France's most successful software entrepreneur"[13] and *Time* magazine listed him as one of the twenty-five most influential business leaders in Europe.[14]

Business Objects had a clear strategy in the mid-1990s, but the company faced many hurdles in building more capabilities into the product, making the technology rock-solid for the mainstream enterprise market, and upgrading internal processes for software design, development, and testing. At the same time, the young French company had to figure out how to manage highly talented but temperamental French computer scientists, and transform a start-up French organization into a global corporation that could operate equally well in the United States and Europe. It was apparent in the first e-mail Liautaud sent me in 1996 how well prepared he was to tackle hard problems—the software development process, organization structure, task and project management, viability of the executive team, recruiting, employee morale—*before* the company and its challenges got any bigger:

Subject: Re: Consulting
Date: Tue, 16 Apr 96 10:06:30 WET
From: "Bernard LIAUTAUD"
To: "Michael Cusumano" <cusumano@MIT.EDU>

Yes, I am confirming. I would like to agree on the process and the deliverables for that week.

The way I see it is the following:

1) Short audit of our current software development process
2) Build a set of recommendations, with an emphasis on
   • organization (product teams, roles and responsibilities of managers, . . .)
   • reporting methodology and tools (to follow up progress of tasks and projects at the different levels of the org)
   • specific assessment of the potential of one or two current managers to fulfill senior positions in future organization
3) Discuss and refine the recommendations at two levels, first with me and one other manager, then to a larger group.
4) Plan future action items and progress review checkpoints.

. . .

In general, my goal for this quarter is to rebuild the software development process, get a clear picture of what the organization should be, start recruiting high level position (SVP Products?) if there is a need for it, and boost morale of the organization. I would also like to get recommendations from you on recruiting.

. . .

Thanks in advance
Bernard

I will have more to say on Business Objects in the next chapter, when I compare the strategies and financial statements of several software companies. Some of the material I present later on software design and development also draws on my experience in working with Business Objects, as well as with Microsoft, Netscape, the Japanese software factories, and many other companies. But let's now look at an even more striking case of a software business, with higher highs and lower lows.

i2 Technologies

Sanjiv Sidhu and Ken Sharma founded i2 Technologies in 1988. The firm quickly became known worldwide for leading-edge software products that analyzed and solved problems in factory planning, logistics, and supply-chain management. Sidhu had been working in the artificial intelligence lab at Texas Instruments when he came up the idea of creating a planning and optimization tool that incorporated realistic constraints by relying on a selected, limited number of variables. Sidhu was joined by Sharma, and the two entrepreneurs created their first product in a two-bedroom Dallas apartment. Similar to Business Objects, they positioned i2's product not as a stand-alone offering but primarily as "a complement . . . to existing MRP [materials requirements planning] and ERP [enterprise resource planning] solutions" used by large manufacturing companies.[15]

Sidhu and Sharma started selling a few software licenses and providing a lot of consulting—services accounted for 89 percent of revenues in 1992. (For financial data on i2 Technologies, see Appendix Tables 3 and 4.) But by 1994, i2 had grown to more than $11 million in revenues by becoming much more of a *products* company; software licenses accounted for 75 percent of sales in that year. i2 was growing extremely rapidly, averaging about *160 percent a year* over a five-year period (1993–1997). But it was still a small company.

Then the market explosion happened. The Internet suddenly provided a means to link suppliers to producers over easy Web connections, making supply-chain analysis and optimization tools even hotter items for manufacturing and retail companies. Dot coms started to buy billions of dollars worth of software and hardware to create online marketplaces for purchasing and selling components for all sorts of industries. Because the year 2000 was also approaching, companies allocated additional "Y2K" budgets to buy new software to streamline planning and procurement or improve management of factories and suppliers.

i2's growth rates slowed as the company became bigger. But in this new market environment it continued to grow very fast, mostly through internal growth but also through acquisitions. To fill in gaps, the company bought a variety of firms that helped it meet all the supply-chain needs of high-tech and other manufacturing firms. The long-term goal of management was to combine i2's factory planning and analytical software with new transaction software that would serve as a platform for linking thousands of buyers and suppliers in an enormous value chain. Initially reported revenues topped $1.1 billion in 2000 (later restated as $672 million) as the company became one of Wall Street's new high-tech darlings. Sidhu became a billionaire many times over.

And then the bubble burst. i2's stock price had gone from $20 in 1996, when the company first went public, to $111 in 2000, and then to *41 cents* in October 2002. The company also failed to submit its 2002 10-K report on time and was delisted from the NASDAQ market and investigated by the Securities and Exchange Commission (SEC). Writing off the value of acquisitions that never lived up to their promises caused i2 to lose nearly $8 billion in 2001, which included some hefty operating losses (about $278 million). Apart from Ken Sharma, who had died in 1999, much of the management team (below a few senior executives) when the company had a billion-plus dollars in revenues remained the same as when it had been a start-up.

I first visited the company as a consultant in April 2001, on the recommendation of a former MIT student of mine, Charles DeWitt. He was working at i2 in strategy and was trying to get the company back on track. We discussed my experiences at various companies, including Business Objects. I recall thinking at the time how different i2 was from the French company. Business Objects had grown quickly, too, but at nowhere near the pace that i2 had experienced. Liautaud had had much more time to think about and anticipate critical issues *before* the company and its problems became too large.

By contrast, Sidhu and key executives such as Greg Brady, a former sales executive at Oracle who rose to the CEO post during 2001–2002, focused on riding the Internet and Y2K boom in technology spending. They grew i2 at a torrid pace by selling bundles of software licenses almost as fast as they could write contracts. In sales, truly, the i2 team did a *remarkable* job. But companies facing once-in-a-century opportunities like the Internet and Y2K rarely have the time to confront the basic organizational, process, personnel, and product problems that inevitably emerge as a company passes beyond the start-up stage. Not surprisingly, by the year 2000, i2 had run into problems as enormous as its near billion-dollar revenues, and it took some strong action by Sidhu and other people to bring the sales process and software development operations back under control.[16]

In retrospect and as reflected in a restatement of 1998–2000 revenues in the 2002 annual report, the numbers show that i2 never really had a billion-dollar *business*. Like other companies that rode the Internet wave, its revenues reflected aggressive sales made possible by the short-lived bubble economy. Moreover, at its peak, the company's revenues quickly became far from profitable. In 2001, according to the restated financial information, it cost i2 about $1.32 for every dollar in revenues, *excluding* the cost of amortization and writing off the value of acquisitions, canceled software projects, and restructuring charges.[17] Including all operating charges and expenses, in 2001 it cost i2 $9 for every dollar of sales. In 2001–2002 the company also sold more servicelike items (maintenance, including special product enhancements and upgrades, as well as customized contract software, consulting for system implementation, and technical support) than new-product licenses. In fact, the major change in i2's restated financial results was to reclassify about $950 million in software license fees as "contract revenues" between 1999 and 2002. This new category reflects that the delivered software requires the company "to perform services that are essential to the functionality of our product."[18]

Most of i2's products, like those of competitors such as SAP and Oracle, were actually complex hybrid solutions that required time and expertise to install, tailor, and integrate into customers' information systems. The software was very difficult to sell in high volumes "off-the-shelf," unlike Microsoft Office or even Business Objects' products, without extensive customization and support. i2 consultants, who took charge of implementing systems, often underestimated just how difficult it would be to get systems up and running at customer sites, and i2 often had to bear the extra costs itself.[19] On the other hand, customers that successfully installed the software to run their manufacturing and supply-chain operations, such as Dell Computer, claimed to realize major cost savings and large returns on investment.[20]

It will be interesting to see which of these two companies ends up with the larger revenues over the next few years. Business Objects was continuing to grow consistently and generate steady profits, even in the bad times of 2001–2002. i2 Technologies, by contrast, had its last net profit in 1998, and software license fees were declining rapidly. In 2002–2003, i2's management was working hard to simplify product offerings, reduce head count, and return to profitability. As chief financial officer Bill Beecher noted in a November 2002 interview with

The Wall Street Journal, "i2 grew up being a profitable company. This has just been going on too long. You need ultimately to get your business to run on a positive margin."[21]

i2 had one advantage over U.S. competitors in that a large part of its technical organization was located in India, where costs are much lower. Sidhu, who reclaimed the CEO position in June 2002 after relinquishing it to Brady for a year, was leading the effort to restructure the company. Even in the 2001 annual report (prior to the restated results), he felt it necessary to offer this sobering message:

> 2001 was the most challenging year in the history of i2. Economic, geopolitical and market events combined to rapidly change not only the general climate of growth, but also to reverse i2's momentum. For the first time in our history, revenues fell and profits turned to losses. After growing by 97 percent in 2000, total revenues fell 12 percent in 2001 to $986 million, and in the second quarter, i2 reported its first quarterly pro forma loss. It would be easy to lay the blame for a disappointing year solely on outside forces, but we also feel our performance should have been better, and we accept that responsibility. Yet in every challenge lies an opportunity. We are seizing this opportunity to strengthen i2 and create a more operationally efficient and effective company. We are leveraging our industry-leading solutions, exceptionally talented and committed people, and a strong customer base to position i2 for a return to profitability and growth. As customers slowed spending, we reduced our quarterly cost structure by more than $100 million from the first to the fourth quarters. We reorganized our operations, reduced our workforce, refocused sales forces, consolidated offices, reduced discretionary expenditures and began transitioning more research and development to India, where we have a 3:1 cost advantage over development in the U.S.[22]

I will say a bit more about i2 in the next chapter, as well as relate other company stories that I find useful to understand basic issues of strategy and management. But the cases of i2 and Business Objects should be enough to suggest that there are many complex strategic, technical, and organizational challenges that managers, programmers, and entrepreneurs in the software business need to confront. Software companies must have a strategy and specific organizational capabilities to support that strategy and carry them through both good times and bad times. When times are good, it is easy for software products companies to grow revenues—perhaps to a billion dollars or more within a few short years. But when times are bad, revenues can collapse like a stone falling to earth because *customers can simply stop buying new products*. The companies most likely to survive the down times are those with a solid base of loyal, satisfied customers who pay "recurring" fees over long-term contracts for product updates, bug fixes, customization, and other services. I must add that these service and maintenance fees are also directly tied to new-product sales in most cases and also will drop soon enough if product sales do not recover or if companies do not replace these revenues with service offerings.

How to think more strategically about products and services, as well as customers, business models, and other issues essential to creating and managing a software business, is the subject of the next chapter.

2

Strategy for Software Companies:

What to Think About

When I think about strategy for software companies, I don't reach first for the usual tool kit in the strategy community. I am referring to powerful concepts such as Michael Porter's "five forces" (power of buyers, power of suppliers, intensity of rivalries, substitutes, and entry barriers) and the "value chain," Richard Foster's "S-curves," or Clayton Christensen's notion of "disruptive technologies" coming from the low end of a market that incumbent firms often overlook.[1] These are extremely useful ideas, and they do in fact provide a background for my view of strategy, historical evolution of firms and industries, and competition in the software business. But to give a more immediate sense of the problems that every software start-up and ongoing company must face, I think first about a few basic questions that deal with the fundamentals of products, markets, and strategic positioning:

- Do you want to be mainly a *products company* or a *services company?*
- Do you want to sell to *individuals* or *enterprises,* or to *mass* or *niche* markets?
- How *horizontal* (broad) or *vertical* (specialized) is your product or service?

- Can you generate a *recurring revenue stream* to endure in good times and bad?
- Will you target mainstream customers, or do you have a plan to avoid *"the chasm"*?
- Do you hope to be a *leader, follower,* or *complementor?*
- What kind of *character* do you want your company to have?

PRODUCTS VERSUS SERVICES

I will begin with the debate I hear most often among software entrepreneurs and managers, and even many programmers. The issue is whether it is better in the software business to be mainly a *products company* or a *services company.*[2] A common underlying assumption is that a company cannot be both at the same time and be equally good at both. It follows that products companies are usually better at creating products for general users than servicing individual customers. And services companies seem to fail most of the time when they try to generalize what they know and create products for the mass market.[3] I believe that products and services companies are fundamentally different, but the issue is not so black and white.

The past decade has been a good to great time for technology companies, at least before 2001. During these years, I believed—and I think most venture capitalists, managers, and entrepreneurs also believed—that it was much better to be mainly a products company. I no longer think this is true. But whatever your position on this question, the difference and interrelationship between products and services are the first things that people who want to understand the software business need to grasp.

To be mainly a *products company* means that the majority of a firm's revenues come in through sales of "shrink-wrapped" software packages, named for the plastic wrapping that is used to cover boxes containing the floppy disks or CD-ROMs (Figure 2-1). Companies such as Microsoft and Adobe (the leading vendor of print and digital imaging software) are the best examples I know of for this business model. There are potentially large marketing, support, and maintenance costs associated with a large user base. But in general, if it costs you roughly the same to make one copy or one million copies of a product, you would be a fool not to want to make and sell a million copies of every product you create.

Figure 2-1: Three Business and Life-Cycle Models for Software Companies

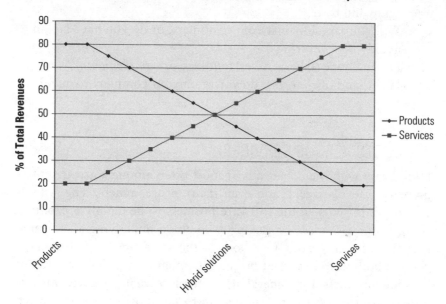

Software companies should want to make and sell a lot of copies of whatever products they make *as is*—that is, without adding changes such as one-of-a-kind features for individual customers. But some software companies get heavily into customizing their products for each customer and providing services such as strategy advice, training, and integration work with other software systems, as well as selling large amounts of maintenance (special product enhancements as well as regular product upgrades sold under long-term contracts) and technical support. If they go in this direction, then the more people they need, the more unique projects or labor-intensive work they undertake, and the more they lean toward becoming what I will call, for short, a *services company.*

Companies such as PricewaterhouseCoopers, EDS, Accenture, and Cap Gemini Ernst & Young are probably the best-known examples of traditional IT services firms. All of their revenues come from services and custom-built systems, although they rely heavily on reusing partial products for different types of applications. Some other software vendors that we often think of as products companies, though, are awfully close to the services firm model. For example, PeopleSoft, SAP, and i2 Technologies now have the vast majority of their revenues coming from services and maintenance contracts (including what i2 now calls "contract revenues"). They are not "pure" services firms in the sense of a PricewaterhouseCoopers or an Accenture, but neither are they "pure" products companies in the sense of a Microsoft or Adobe.

In bad times, customers (individuals or enterprises) may decide not to buy new versions of the software products they are using. What I now realize, all too painfully, is that this potential failure to buy puts the revenues of software products companies at considerable risk. At least, this seems true in the short term (say, three to five years), compared to other kinds of software companies that have lots of long-term contracts generating their revenues. It is possible for enterprise customers to renegotiate long-term contracts for reductions in the prices of services or product upgrades as the retail prices of the software they are using decline. This happened during 2001–2002. But in general, many software product sales are subject to fluctuation because they are *discretionary* in nature.

Because software product sales are subject to buyers just "saying no," it is now apparent that most healthy software companies need to have a balance of product and service revenues to survive in bad times and to grow rapidly and profitably in good times. Even at Business Objects and i2 Technologies, when product sales were growing rapidly in the 1990s, revenues from services and maintenance were growing even faster—from as early as 1994! (See Appendix Tables 1 to 4.)

We will also see later in this chapter that a software products company can greatly increase—*as much as double or triple*—its revenues over time through accumulation of contracts for services and custom software, including maintenance, even if new software product sales lag behind in growth rates. This is because software companies selling to large enterprise customers can generally expect to receive up to a dollar in service revenues for every new dollar in software license fees for the first year or so of the contract. They can also expect to receive between 15 and 20 cents in annual maintenance fees for every dollar of license fees—for the period that the customer uses the software.[4] Many enterprise software companies offer perpetual licenses to their customers as well—that is, the customer, as long as it pays the agreed-upon annual maintenance fee, has the right to upgrade to new versions of the software, with an occasional special charge, for example, to accommodate hardware platform changes or expansion of usage

Table 2-1: Example of Revenue Breakdown for an Enterprise Software Product

	Product License Fees	Service Fees	Maintenance Fees	Cumulative Total
Year 1	$1.00	$1.00	$0.00	$2.00
Year 2		$0.30	$0.15	$0.45
Year 3		$0.25	$0.15	$0.40
Year 4			$0.15	$0.15
Year 5			$0.15	$0.15
Total	$1.00	$1.55	$0.60	$3.15
Approximate Percentage	30%	50%	20%	100%

rights.[5] Therefore, over the lifetime of many enterprise software products, 70 percent or more of the total cost to a customer may come from service and maintenance fees and only 30 percent from the original product sale[6] (Table 2-1). The percentage from maintenance can become especially high for products in use for a decade or more. If a software company sells a lot of products early on but then fails to keep up a high rate of new sales to new customers, it will inevitably see the majority of its revenues shifting toward services and maintenance coming from the installed base.

Of equal importance, in bad times it may turn out that the *only* revenues a software company can really bank on are from services and maintenance charges derived from long-term contracts, even if customers renegotiate their costs on the margin. This is why some people refer to the business model of services- and maintenance-oriented software companies as being somewhat like that of a bank. Their installed base of users, along with long-term contracts for services and maintenance to be rendered in the future, are akin to a bank with assets on deposit generating a steady stream of interest. In contrast, the business model of software products companies, because they can replicate copy after copy with minimal marginal costs, is more like that of a printing press.

I noted in Chapter 1 that there is a *hybrid solutions* model—software companies that evolve to a point where they sell a mixture of products and services, including maintenance upgrades and maintenance of special product enhancements. One reason why software companies, even those with products to sell, may have high services revenues is that their technologies are often too complex to package as "off-the-shelf" products. As a result, they sell "solutions" that require customization (say, 20 to 50 percent of the total amount of code) or special integration and installation work. It is usually very difficult for enterprise customers to switch from this type of software, which often runs critical functions in the firm. Consequently, there is usually a technical "lock-in" effect that keeps customers tied to particular software vendors for long periods of time. PeopleSoft and SAP are in the category of hybrid solutions providers, though we should probably add Oracle, Siebel, i2, and many other software companies that used to have high products revenues but no longer do. Hybrid solutions firms as well as software services firms that sell custom or semicustom systems for enterprise applications both resemble the "bank" business model with assets on deposit, in contrast to the "printing-press" model for software products companies.[7]

A Healthy Tension

Software companies, especially young ones, often seem to struggle unnecessarily with the products-versus-services debate. The reason is that having a hit software package is like having a best-selling book. Publishers, like software products companies, can make enormous profits from just one best-selling product. In practice, though, it is probably just as hard to write a best-selling software product as it is to write a best-selling book. It seems even harder to follow that one hit product with a continuous stream of new products (the sequel business) that sell in both bad and good economies. Every successful software company that I know of has had to deal with the challenge of saturated markets, in which customers already have enough or "good-enough" products. Hence the tension that inevitably emerges in enterprise software companies with a strong products business: *They know they must eventually move toward selling more labor-intensive and less profitable services.*

And the struggle is more complicated than this. Software products companies that want more revenues from services generally get those revenues from service contracts to support their new product sales. They can sell services to old customers, to be sure. But the pipeline of potential service revenues will rise or fall in proportion to the rise or fall in new product sales, albeit with a lag of a couple of years, unless the company can decouple services from product sales (which a few firms, such as IBM and SAP, have managed to do). Therefore, most software companies with a strong services business must think more about selling products, despite their more sporadic and nonrecurring levels.

It is also possible for software products companies to gravitate too much toward services and ruin the potential of their products business. When they are first starting out, or in bad economic times, companies have to scramble to get customers. Customers usually want specific features that meet their particular needs. We saw in Chapter 1 that i2, in its first few years, was primarily a custom software shop before it learned how to package technology into more standardized products. But over time a software company that prefers to sell a standardized product might saturate this market and start offering customers special enhancements. This strategy leads to selling customized versions of the products, one at a time. The service portion of a company's revenues, and the cost of these revenues, start to rise dramatically. Maintenance releases also become more complicated because the upgrades have to include the special enhancements done for individual customers.

We can see all these trends in the financial data reported by leading enterprise software companies. Appendix Figure 1, for example, tracks eight firms between 1992 and 2002, including Business Objects and i2. SAP is the world's leading vendor of enterprise resource planning software, and competes with PeopleSoft. Siebel is the leading vendor of customer relationship management (CRM) software, with a market share of more than 70 percent, though it was under severe pressure from numerous competitors.[8] Compuware is a major vendor of IT services and software products for mainframes and some Windows computers. (Full disclosure: I was a member of the board of directors of NuMega Technologies when Compuware acquired the company in 1997 for approximately $150 million.) The IBM data reflect software products and services sales, and exclude hardware sales.

What we see is that service revenues have been growing in both absolute terms and relative to product sales and in some cases have exceeded product sales (Siebel in 2001, PeopleSoft in 1998, i2 in 2000, IBM before 1992, SAP in 1997, Oracle in 1998, and Compuware in

1993 or before). Appendix Figure 2 breaks down the revenues of these same companies during the technology boom-and-bust years of 1999 to 2002, using 1999 revenues as an index of 100. This analysis shows even more clearly how important rising or at least more stable service revenues have been to these companies.

The bottom line is that the distinction between a products company and a services company in the software business is not always clear or desirable. In many ways, hybrid solutions companies may have the best business model—they can leverage some core technologies like products companies but also generate recurring revenues like services companies. And over a few years, they can double or triple what their revenues would have been with little or no services.

Furthermore, if a company can decouple service contracts from product contracts, it has the potential to grow even faster than a more conventional enterprise software company that only sells service and maintenance with its own new products. As we will see later, IBM is one such company that has sent services growth on a new upward trajectory. SAP and PeopleSoft have also succeeded in this decoupling, at least during the early 2000s. Software companies with services businesses that grow (or decline) independently of their products may represent a new business model for software companies.[9] It is also possible to describe them as a special variation of the hybrid-solutions business model or simply companies that have services business (like IBM's e-business consulting and systems integration work based on open software, discussed in Chapter 3) that have minimal or no relationship to their product businesses.

You Still Need to Choose

Though a hybrid-solutions model can be effective at generating a steady stream of revenues and profits, managers of these kinds of software companies still need to choose a primary strategic orientation *and* understand the potential consequences of their decisions. The reason is that selling mainly software products to new customers requires very different strategies, organizational capabilities, and financial investments compared to selling mainly software services and product upgrades to an existing customer base.

The software products business is mainly about *volume* sales— selling or licensing the most copies of a standardized product as you can. The basic growth strategies here are scaling or duplicating what you have done in similar markets. Microsoft has set the model for firms of this type: it became the market leader through volume sales and set de facto technical standards that have "locked in" customers because their software applications and databases work only on a particular operating system or hardware platform. The development organization needs to focus on creating a stream of new products and upgrades that appear at regular intervals with standardized features that are "good enough" for the largest possible set of users. Mass marketing and distribution skills are critical. Part of the strategy for a products company might also include trying to become a platform leader (more on this later), though most software companies create *complements*—products that work with and add value to a particular platform, such as a Windows PC or UNIX workstation, or a hand-held device powered by the Palm or Symbian operating system.

The software services business—*including the services side of the business in a products company*—is mainly about people and building specific (not general) customer relationships. It is about getting enough profitable accounts to keep your consultants and developers busy close to 100 percent of the time. Companies such as IBM, PricewaterhouseCoopers, Accenture (formerly Andersen Consulting), and Cap Gemini Ernst & Young have set the standards here. A number of Indian companies (Infosys, Tata, Wipro, Satym, and Patni) have also come on strong as global competitors bidding for custom IT jobs. Hitachi, Fujitsu, and IBM Japan are leaders in this field in the Japanese market. These types of services are not scale businesses, not software licensing à la Microsoft. But services companies can be strategic as well as efficient. It is usually important to mix senior people with junior to maximize profits for any given client project, although the challenge is for a services firm to do this without damaging the relationship by having inadequately skilled people on the job.

For software products companies, again, the lure is potentially enormous *economies of scale* that come from selling multiple copies of the same piece of software. For software service companies, *economies of scope* are the holy grail to strive for, and these are more elusive. They can come from structuring knowledge such as how to do requirements, manage projects, customize applications, conduct user acceptance testing, or reuse design frameworks and even pieces of code across different projects and customers. Economies of scope can also come from clever account management—forming relationships with particular customers who buy a lot of your software and services over time.

Some Basic Financial Metrics

Software products companies are usually much more attractive to stock market investors and venture capitalists because of their potential for growth and profits. Industry analysts in particular usually place a high value on the percentage of a software company's revenues that come straight from licensing fees and the growth rate of this percentage over time. This metric is hardly an absolute measure of financial health or growth potential. As we saw in Appendix Figures 1 and 2, some software companies have steady service (including maintenance) revenues and depend on these to generate consistent growth or stable sales. In contrast, software products companies may see their license fees fall faster than services revenues, especially in bad times. i2 Technologies, for example, saw its license fees collapse from 63 percent of revenues in 1998 to as little as 10 percent in 2002, requiring an initially unplanned but eventually dramatic downsizing of the company, from 6,000 employees in 2000 to less than 3,000 by the end of 2002 (see Appendix Table 4). Nevertheless, software industry analysts use this measure to get some idea of how labor-intensive a particular company's software business is and how easily it might scale up revenues and profits in the future.

Another measure of health for a software company is sales productivity, or revenues per employee. Many software executives believe these revenues should average at least $200,000 per year for a products company to have a profitable business. It is a crude rule of thumb, and companies can have high sales productivity and still lose lots of money by overspending in R and D, sales and marketing, or general administration. But it is usually a sufficiently large sum to allow a company to hire enough people to staff critical functions adequately. In general, though, software companies should keep their expenses within certain boundaries. For sales and marketing, this should be about 25 to 30 percent of total revenues; research and development about 10 to 15 percent; and general administration about 5 percent. A fair profit target is 20 to 30 percent of revenues as operating income. Products and hybrid companies working at the edge of innovation or with very broad product lines may spend more in each category, especially R and D and marketing.

Again, high revenues and profits per employee—and low costs relative to revenues—are much easier to achieve if you have a best-selling shrink-wrapped software product that you can make copies of for pennies and sell in units of hundreds or thousands (as Business Objects has done) or millions (as Microsoft has done). It is harder to do if your revenues come from costly, labor-intensive maintenance and other services, or custom work with sales of a much smaller number of units. Firms that rely heavily on services cannot charge too much because many companies (including a large number of technically excellent low-cost firms in India) can do custom software development and enhancements or perform other IT-related services at lower cost. Customers with large IT departments, such as commercial banks and financial services firms, can also do a lot of the customization work themselves.

Obviously, the ability to charge high licensing fees can dramatically affect a software company's scalability of revenues and sales productivity. Some companies can charge thousands of dollars per copy, or "seat," for each customer. Most companies have a sliding scale that gives steep discounts to customers that want to use many copies of a particular software product. High-price strategies can work for years, even for companies not in a monopoly position, until products become more like commodities and low-priced—or even free—versions of the same software come into the marketplace.

Software vendors that do mainly custom development or service work can also make lots of money, but only as long as they hire lots of people. According to *Software Magazine,* which ranked companies by sales, IBM led all software and software services firms in 2002 revenues, followed by Microsoft, EDS, Accenture, and Oracle (see Appendix Table 5). Two of the top five (EDS and Accenture) and seven of the top ten (add Computer Sciences Corporation, Compaq, PricewaterhouseCoopers, Cap Gemini Ernst & Young, and NTT Data) were IT consulting companies. Note that nearly all of the top fifty companies sold primarily to enterprises, except for a few firms such as Microsoft, Apple Computer, and Intuit. (Fujitsu, with its consolidated subsidiaries, also sold billions of dollars worth of software products and services and should be on this list.[10])

We can see all of these forces at work in Table 2–2, which compares 2002 data from Business Objects and i2 with a small sample of other leading software companies. I have selected companies that are not primarily IT consulting firms or a mixture of hardware and software: Microsoft, Oracle, SAP, Siebel, PeopleSoft, Compuware, and Adobe. Of these firms, only Business Objects, Microsoft, and Adobe are clear-cut cases of software products companies. Oracle, Siebel,

Table 2-2: Comparison of Software Company Income Statements, Fiscal 2002–2003

(Percentage of total revenues, unless denoted by $)

Company and Fiscal Year	Bobj Dec. 2002	i2 Dec. 2002	Msft June 2002	Orcl May 2003	SAP* Dec. 2002	Siebel Dec. 2002	Psft Dec. 2002	Cpwr March 2003	Adbe Nov. 2002
Revenues ($ million)	$455	$908	$25,296	$9,475	$6,880	$1,635	$1,949	$1,729	$1,165
Revenues Breakdown:									
% New License Fees	54	10	NA	35	31	43	27	24	99
% Services & Maintenance†	46	90	NA	65	69	57	73	76	1
Gross Margins‡									
Software Licenses	99	97	NA	NA	NA	97	92	91	92
Services & Maintenance†	61	65	NA	62	NA	42	53	30	36
Costs (as % of Revenues)									
Software Licenses	<1	<1	NA	<1	NA	1	2	2	8
Services & Maintenance†	15	32	NA	25	NA	33	34	53	1
Sales and Marketing	49	22	19	22	28	29	26	23	33
Research & Development	17	19	15	12	15	22	17	6	21
General & Administrative	6	7	5	4	7	7	6	4	9
Operating Profit Rate	*11*	*(—)*	*42*	*36*	*23*	*(—)*	*13*	*(—)*	*25*
Average Employees	2,196	3,880	49,050	41,328	28,604	6,656	8,365	11,692	3,181
Sales/Employee ($1,000)	$207	$234	$578	$229	$240	$246	$233	$149	$366

Key: Bobj (Business Objects), Orcl (Oracle), i2 (i2 Technologies), Msft (Microsoft), Cpwr (Compuware), Siebel (Siebel Systems), Psft (PeopleSoft), Adbe (Adobe)

* SAP revenues are based on euro exchange rate €.93 = $1.00

† Includes contract revenue for i2.

‡ Gross margins calculated as percentage of respective license and service/maintenance revenues.

Source: Calculated from company reports. 2002 employee and sales/employee data are estimates for i2.

and i2 used to be products companies a few years ago but are now much more oriented toward providing services and maintenance upgrades to an installed base of users rather than selling new products to new customers; they have become like SAP, PeopleSoft, and Compuware. My definition is simple: *A products company should have well over half its revenues (around 60 percent) coming from new sales of software products* (software license fees, excluding product update fees included as maintenance or product support).

Unfortunately, publicly available data are limited, so we can make only crude comparisons. For example, SAP treats maintenance revenues as product revenues and lumps together all product-related costs, so we can separate out maintenance revenues but not maintenance costs.[11] Oracle does not break out software license fee costs and bundles upgrade costs with product support services in its external reports.[12] Adobe began breaking out services from products only in 2002. Microsoft does not break out services at all.

I do not think it is a coincidence that the companies with the highest sales productivity and profit rates—Microsoft and Adobe—sell mainly products rather than services. Equally important, their products are unique and serve more as platforms for other companies to build products and services around or tools to offer content. For example, many companies build applications on top of Microsoft Windows and Office; and many companies provide information through Adobe Acrobat. More data on more software companies would be useful to see how well these points about products and platforms hold. My basic argument, however, is mainly about potential: *In an ideal world, companies with higher percentages of new software license fees (product sales) have more growth and profit potential, especially in good economic times.* It is much easier and cheaper to expand revenues and profits by selling copies of a standardized digital product than by selling labor-intensive services or even discounted product upgrade licenses.

Products Companies Become Services (or Hybrid) Companies

I noted earlier that companies selling standardized software packages can also lose lots of money or see their profits and sales decline dramatically. Sometimes this occurs when software products become commodities and competitors emerge that drive down prices. This situation leaves firms that offer high-end custom or semicustom systems in a better position than the products companies that cannot differentiate themselves. Another problem occurs when the market becomes saturated or the economy turns bad: customers stop buying new products or postpone purchasing decisions. Some companies, such as i2 and Siebel, seem to get caught in the middle of a transition. Their financial reports suggest that both companies geared up for high-volume product sales during the late 1990s, with lots of people hired in R and D, sales, and marketing. Then they encountered low-priced competition and the economic slump. New sales to new customers required steep price cuts or complex deals of multiple products that proved expensive and difficult to install.

When times are bad for new product sales, software companies are left with services-oriented revenues or maintenance. If times are sufficiently bad, or if their markets are sufficiently saturated with products, the products companies may become services companies. We can see this in Figure 2-2, which presents the percentage of revenues coming from services and maintenance (that is, all sources except for

Figure 2-2: Services and Maintenance as Percentage of Total Revenues (2002)

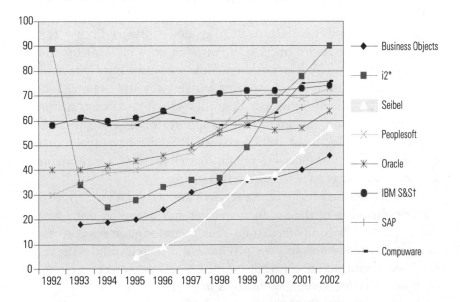

* i2 numbers include contract revenues or the restated basis.
† IBM numbers reflect services as a percentage of combined services and software revenues.
Source: *Company Form 10-K reports, annual.*

new-software license fees) at the eight companies cited earlier, usually from their first public data in the United States filed with the Securities and Exchange Commission. Between 1993 and 2002, Business Objects went from 18 percent services and maintenance to 46 percent; i2 (including contract revenues) went from 34 to 90 percent during this same period. Siebel went from 5 to 57 percent during 1995–2002. Between 1992 and 2002, PeopleSoft went from 30 to 73 percent and Oracle from 40 to 64 percent. Even firms that had a strong services orientation before the 1990s saw a shift to services: IBM went from 58 to 74 percent (excluding hardware revenues) and Compuware from 62 to 76 percent. SAP, during 1997–2002, saw its services and maintenance revenues go from 50 to 69 percent.

Figure 2-3 shows what this shift in revenues from products to services looks like in percentage terms. The two trend lines are, by definition, mirror images of each other; the data exclude revenues that are not software products or services and maintenance. What we see, though, is a crisscross pattern for firms whose services revenues eventually pass product revenues (Siebel, i2, PeopleSoft, Oracle, SAP). Business Objects seems headed in the same direction. IBM and Compuware already crossed this threshold sometime in the past before 1992.

The reason for this shift away from new-software license fees is straightforward: As products companies capture most of the "low-hanging fruit" in a market, new customers become harder to find. It then becomes easier and cheaper to sell services and maintenance—including incremental product upgrades—to the existing customer base. (Product updates and technical support, for example, totaled 41 percent of Oracle's fiscal 2003 revenues.[13]) Services and maintenance are relatively easy revenues to obtain. Better yet, they are *recurring*— a topic I will come back to later in this chapter.

Another reason for the rise in services and maintenance, though, is commoditization of the products market and dropping price points, forcing products companies to go back to tailoring at least 20 to 30 percent of the features in their products and therefore booking more services revenues. This is what happed to i2. As we saw earlier, its new-license sales have fallen from as much as 75 percent of revenues in 1994 to 10 percent of revenues in 2002. i2 also has turned to tailoring its products more to give it an edge over competitors such as Manugistics, which sells low-priced products with similar, though more basic, functionality. (Manugistics has also lost money for the past five years.)

Siebel is one of the newest hybrid companies, and it got there much too fast: product license revenues fell from 95 percent of total sales as recently as 1995 (when the company was just two years old) to 52 percent in 2001 and 43 percent in 2002. Needless to say, the company's growth and profit rates have sunk, and Siebel, with a net loss in 2002 of nearly $36 million, is facing difficult times.[14] Part of the problem here, again, was competition. Many firms jumped into the CRM market during the late 1990s and early 2000s, driving down prices and making CRM products into commodities. Salesforce.com, for example, offers products that compete with Siebel's at a fraction of the price. Customers also rent the software from Salesforce.com, paying small monthly fees and accessing the products through a browser.[15] One way to protect against this commoditization is to tailor product offerings or offer consulting and other services. This tailoring and special services work is at least part of the reason why Siebel's services revenues have been rising. Other ways to fend off commoditization are to release new, more advanced products, emphasize quality, or market heavily with a strong emphasis on the brand.

ERP companies understand the need to tailor products to individual customers, and they usually learn how to charge adequately for their services—or they go out of business. As a result, ERP companies are generally more oriented toward services and hybrid solutions than products, even in their early days. We can see this at PeopleSoft, founded in 1987 by Dave Duffield and Ken Morris. These entrepreneurs introduced a low-priced human resource management product that ran on personal computers rather than bigger machines. Over time, the company has moved to a broader ERP product line, added more industry-specific features to a growing product set, and, not surprisingly, placed even more emphasis on services.

Some people have suggested to me that SAP is an exception to the rule that products companies are better poised for rapid growth than are services-oriented companies. It sells high-end ERP applications that require extensive consulting, training, and maintenance contracts. It has generated a lot of new business from services, which have grown faster than license fees. SAP's revenues rose about 2.5 times between 1997 and 2002 (about $2.7 billion to $6.9 billion). However, the average head count at the company also rose about 2.5

Figure 2-3: Products and Services/Maintenance Percentage Comparisons

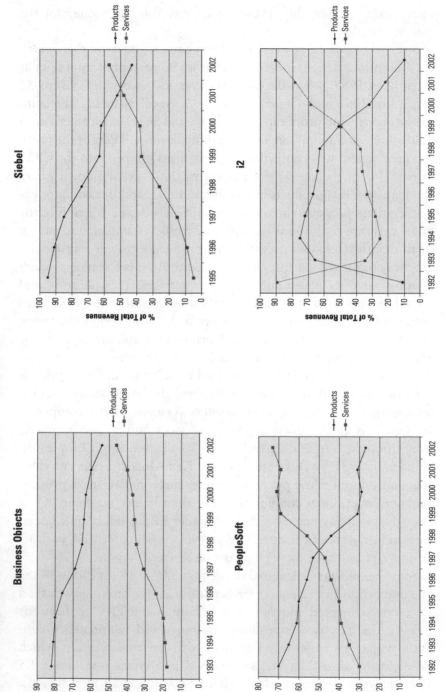

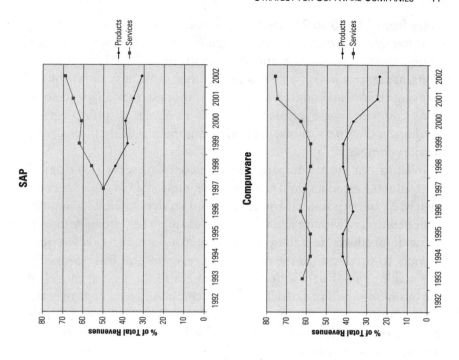

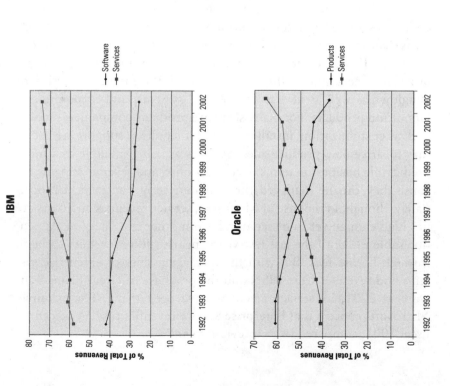

times from 11,558 to 28,604.[16] So the company is not an exception: *SAP has grown rapidly by hiring rapidly—a trend that cannot continue forever.* Compuware and PeopleSoft, as well as IT consulting firms, are largely in the same position: if they grow, it is mainly by increasing their head count. I will also say, though, that a hybrid solutions company has a greater chance of ramping up product sales (perhaps with a new release) and growing more quickly than a pure services company.

In short, for most enterprise software companies, the two sides of the business—products and services—are impossible to separate completely. Most corporate customers demand services (including maintenance contracts with a regular schedule of upgrades) along with new software products. In addition, it does not seem easy to evolve from services to products (as the majority of revenues), at least not without making major acquisitions and changes in the mental model of the business and in personnel. Software companies usually evolve the other way around, as Business Objects, PeopleSoft, Siebel, and Oracle have—from selling mostly products to selling increasing amounts of services and maintenance.

Even Microsoft—the premier mass-market packaged-software company—discovered the value of services when it wanted to increase sales of Windows NT and what it used to call its "BackOffice" products. It decided to create an in-house solutions group to help large customers and third-party firms install the enterprise version of Windows as well as new servers, e-mail systems, and corporate collaboration products. For many software products companies, services such as customization, installation, and integration support are necessary to drive new-product sales. Services are also valuable as a more predictable business in terms of costs, profits, and revenue streams because they can be managed through long-term contracts. Unfortunately, though, in the case of Microsoft, service revenues and costs are not high enough yet to be separated from other revenues (see Appendix Table 6). Until the last few years, nearly all its revenues came in through license fees. But with the increasing sales of enterprise systems and revenues from MSN and the purchase of Great Plains Software in 2001, its service revenues have been rising. For example, Microsoft reported that Enterprise Service revenues rose 34 percent in fiscal 2001, compared to the previous year.[17]

Dramatically Different Profit Margins

But what is most striking about selling software licenses compared to services is the *relative gross profit margins*. For example, at Business Objects (see Appendix Table 1 and Table 2-2), selling $244 million in license fees in 2002 consumed only about $3 million in directly attributable costs—a gross profit margin of nearly 99 percent! The cost of software license fees consists mainly of materials such as compact discs and printed manuals, packaging, freight, inventory, third-party royalties, and amortization expense related to capitalized software development costs. (Generally accepted accounting principles allow software companies to write off certain costs over a period of time corresponding to the estimated useful life of the product, such as eighteen months or three years, and deduct these capitalized expenses from current R-and-D costs on their income statements.) In contrast, Business Objects' service revenues of $211 million in 2002 consumed more than $71 million in costs (expenses related to technical support, consulting, training, and other services), for a gross profit margin of about 61 percent.

Gross margins are of limited value as a metric. Business Objects, for example, in addition to direct costs for its license fees in 2002, also had current R-and-D costs of about $75 million, or 16.5 percent of sales. Most of this expense went to product development, which would generate new licenses in the future, and some went into engineering and testing work. In addition, related more to current expenses, Business Objects in 2002 had sales and marketing expenses that equaled *nearly half of total revenues* (49 percent, or about $222 million). These expenses went toward selling both products and services. It is a big percentage compared to other software companies discussed in this chapter, except for i2, which had a comparably high level of sales and marketing expenses relative to revenues during 1999–2001. Both companies have had such high sales and marketing costs because of high head count, to be sure. But the head count is relatively high because their revenues are relatively low—an economies-of-scale problem. By contrast, in 2001–2002, Microsoft's sales and marketing expenses were a mere 19 percent of revenues. The other companies listed in Table 2-2 (Oracle, SAP, Siebel, PeopleSoft, Compuware, Adobe) had sales and marketing expenses ranging from 22 to 33 percent.

Even though we need to look at total costs for selling products or services, the gross profit margin numbers illustrate how much more profitable product sales are than services. The numbers Business Objects achieved are not unusual. Siebel had a gross profit margin of 97 percent on license sales in 2002. Oracle seems to be at 100 percent and does not even report license costs separately. PeopleSoft and Compuware were more than 90 percent. i2 went from 86 percent in 2001 to 97 percent in 2002. High license costs generally come from amortizing development expenses, or absorbing costs when fixing bugs in the field or reconfiguring customers' systems, without being able to charge for this extra work.

We can also see economies of scale as well as potential diseconomies of scale at work: As Business Objects' product revenues have grown, its gross profit margins have reached 99 percent, rising from 92 percent in 1993. Its gross margins on service and maintenance revenues, however, have been dropping slightly over time, from 72 to 61 percent over the same decade (Figure 2-4).

The disparity between products and services (including maintenance) is more striking when we look at how much lower service margins are at some companies—in 2002, 30 percent at Compuware, 36 percent at Adobe, 42 percent at Siebel, and 53 percent at People-Soft. At the same time, Compuware had high profit margins on its software license sales, comparable to software products companies. The management of this company should want to sell more products. But this has not happened. Compuware even showed a loss for 2002 and had trouble keeping its employees busy in the economic downturn. It had a relatively low sales productivity rate of merely $149,000. This number was good compared to pure IT consulting companies, however, which generally trail software products companies in employee productivity by considerable margins. According to 1999–2000 sales data, for example, PricewaterhouseCoopers averaged about $108,000 per employee, Andersen Consulting about $137,000, and Ernst & Young about $118,000.[18]

Compuware is a former services firm that has been trying to become more of a products company. Peter Karmanos, Thomas Thewes, and Allen Cutting founded the company in 1973 specifically to sell technical services and IT outsourcing. They later acquired software products by buying companies to help them diversify beyond mainframe software and services. One such acquisition was NuMega Technologies, the maker of PC support tools such as SoftICE, BoundsChecker, and DevPartner Studio. In both 2000 and 2001,

Figure 2-4: Business Objects' Gross Profit Margins, 1993–2002

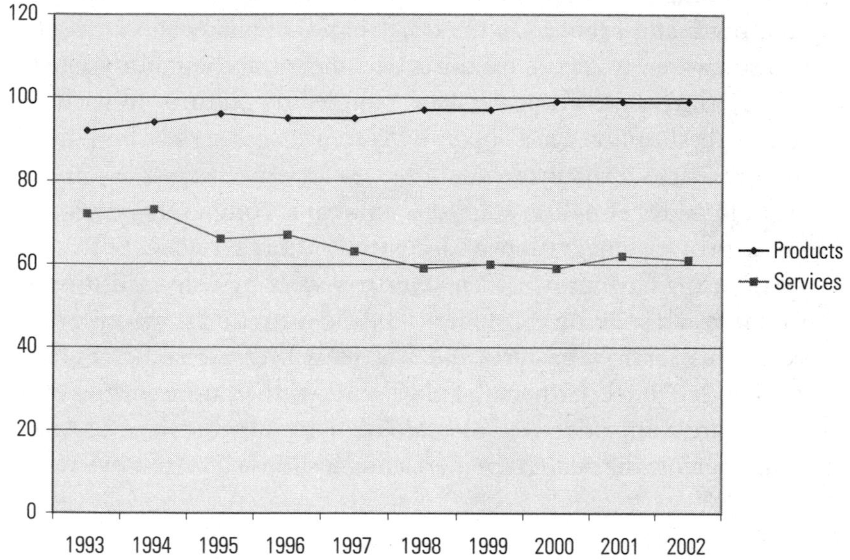

Source: *Company Form 10-K reports, annual (see Appendix Tables 1 and 2).*

Compuware's revenues topped $2 billion because it had some 12,000 employees. In 2002, its revenues fell to $1.7 billion. Only 24 percent of those sales came from software licenses, primarily of software tools (special programs) for development support and testing. Most employees worked in professional services (custom software development, IT outsourcing, and system maintenance, mostly for older mainframe systems).

In summary, we can say that software products (license fees) are generally *much* more profitable than services and maintenance revenues, and easier to grow without adding head count. This is why software companies should want to sell standardized products that generate license fees without the baggage of too much customization services and unique technical support and labor-intensive training or integration services. Software products companies in rapidly growing markets generally should try to minimize their service offerings, even though service offerings are often necessary to make a sale to enterprise customers. Companies in the custom software or IT services business may also want to try to "product-ize" or package their offerings to increase profit margins and growth potential. Investors such as venture capitalists generally have a strong preference for software products companies because they have a much greater potential for rapid growth and profits. On the other hand, in bad economic times, or as a software company's products become more commodity-like or "mature" (i.e., there are fewer new compelling features in each release), the best option for a company is to grow its service and maintenance revenues, broadly defined.

I should add that hybrid solutions companies often rely on outside firms to provide integration and customization services. Both SAP and Microsoft have grown their overseas sales by using third-party consultants and solutions providers. Hybrid firms that try to take over more of this services business themselves will create some conflicts with their "channel partners." This is part of the business, however, and software companies need to evaluate how valuable these partnerships are against the benefits of increasing in-house services revenues.

WHO DO YOU WANT TO SELL TO?

Whether a software company focuses more on products or services, another set of decisions concerns which of the many potential mass markets and niches to explore. The global software industry in 2001, according to Standard & Poor's data, generated approximately $600 billion in revenues—one third from packaged software products and the other two thirds from software services.[19] The services figure includes revenues from organizations such as IBM Global Services and EDS, which focus on information technology consulting, systems integration, network design, and IT training and education.[20] According to a Digital Planet 2000 study, North America accounted for about 50 percent of world revenues, followed by Europe (31 percent) and Asia (15 percent).[21] In general, we can think of the United States as the largest single information technology market, followed by Japan. Precise data on the number of firms in the software and information services industries around the world are difficult to obtain because of lags in data collection and variations in definitions. One estimate from the late 1990s counted about 35,000 companies worldwide with at least five employees each.[22] Including software firms with two to four people might double or triple this number.

The software business, however you measure it, is *big* as well as *global.* Nor do these revenues include the value of software produced by firms for in-house use or for use in a myriad of consumer and industrial products. The commercial side of the business has its ups and downs, to be sure. Software companies suffered particularly in 2001–2002, with the collapse of dot coms and telecommunications companies, a dramatic decline in the value of high-tech stocks, and a severe drop in technology spending by corporate customers in nearly all sectors around the world. It is also probably true that there are now *too many* software companies in the world by a factor of three or more, and far too many of them are public and have received venture capital funding. In 2002–2003, we seemed to be entering a major consolidation phase, with a variety of firms buying or attempting to buy their competitors (witness PeopleSoft's decision to buy J. D. Edwards and Oracle's attempt to buy PeopleSoft). But the sheer number of companies selling software products or services, even if a surfeit remains, reflects the many different opportunities that continue to exist around the world, in good times and bad.

In preparation for the good times that will return someday, managers, programmers, and entrepreneurs in software companies first need to decide which customers they want to target. For starters, software companies must decide whether to sell mainly to other companies (enterprises) or to individuals (consumers). Among enterprises, there are also small, medium-sized, and large firms. Small firms often resemble individual consumers in that they will buy off-the-shelf packaged software and make do with minimal services. In general, though, selling to medium-sized and large enterprises requires very different business models and organizational capabilities compared to selling to individuals. Another choice: Should you tackle the mass market, where the payoffs can be enormous but the competition may be stiff, or select particular niches where you have a greater chance of establishing a distinct advantage?

Selecting a Niche or Mass Market

Because software is not one but many technologies, driven by the nature of the application, the software business contains many niches and a few mass markets. If we take *Software Magazine*'s top 100 companies ranked by revenues and group them into some basic categories, we can see more clearly what the global industry looks like in terms of mass markets and niches. By my count, 29 of the top 100 firms were in systems and infrastructure software products (see Appendix Table 7). These consisted mainly of vendors of tools for infrastructure and systems management, programming, and storage, as well as a few producers of operating systems and servers. Another 28 of the top 100 were in services—including the single largest grouping for software companies, IT services and consulting (23). Enterprise application products accounted for 23 of the top 100. Most of the top 100 companies also sold software and services to other organizations rather than to individuals.

As in other industries, the average profitability levels in these different segments vary. Clearly, some segments have less competition than others and companies can charge higher prices or more easily benefit from economies of scale to lower their costs per unit sold. Some segments, such as services, can be very labor-intensive. Some mass markets, such as those for operating systems, database products, and shrink-wrapped applications, can achieve tremendous economies of scale since replicating the products costs so little.

The barriers to entry are also much lower in some segments. For example, it is relatively easy to enter the IT services and consulting segment but very hard for a single firm to compete in operating systems, especially for personal computers. One or two people can create an IT services company. But to build an operating system to compete with Microsoft's Windows 2000, or even Linux and Sun Microsystems' popular SunSoft version of UNIX, would require at least several hundred software designers, programmers, and testers working full-time for several years. Depending on its functionality, building a new operating system could cost $100 to $200 million or more. If a company built such a product and priced it comparably to Windows at about $200 (to use a round number), it would have to sell one or two million copies just to break even on development costs. The company would have to sell three or four million copies to break even if it tried to match Microsoft in advertising and marketing expenditures just for the Windows operating system. Worst of all, there would be no guarantee that such a large number of customers would buy a new operating system, no matter how many hundreds of millions of dollars a company spent on advertising and promotions. The product would have to be a lot better than Windows or other available products such as Linux or the Mac OS. It would have to work properly with the tens of thousands of existing software applications and the potentially millions of combinations of hardware, peripheral devices, and applications.

Fortunately for software entrepreneurs, there is usually no need to go head-to-head with Microsoft in operating systems. There are many other product and service opportunities in the software business, including niches within niches, usually defined by the underlying hardware and operating system platforms, and degrees of specialization in the application domain. There are also other development alternatives. The open-source movement has produced Linux, for example. In addition, producers of cell phones, led by Nokia, Ericsson, and Motorola, have banded together to create the 700-person Symbian joint venture to make an operating system for their products, especially Web-enabled phones. These companies have chosen not to go the way of PC manufacturers and cede control of their software platform to Microsoft and end up as commodity producers of hardware.[23]

Differences Between Enterprises and Consumers

The choice to sell to enterprises or individual consumers may seem easy to make, but the implications quickly get complicated. Enterprise software companies usually have to offer what Geoffrey Moore (discussed later in this chapter) has called the "whole product solution" in order to cross successfully into the mainstream market. This means that the software product must be rock-solid in terms of reliability and include easy-to-use features for late adopters, good documentation, thorough technical support, and a full array of complementary products and services. The whole product solution is really an IBM strategy that the company has followed since before World War II. I will talk more about this idea and its importance for enterprise software customers in this and the next chapter. The point to remember here is that potential revenues *and* costs can vary enormously depending on what customer set you target.

Software companies that sell to enterprises generally offer a combination of standardized products sold through software license fees and services with maintenance sold through separate multiyear contracts. Software companies that target individual consumers or small enterprises for the most part sell standardized products. The latter sell either directly to individuals or to intermediaries such as PC manufacturers or software resellers. Video game software companies are prime examples of firms with large standardized product sales. So is Microsoft, founded in 1975. In its early days, Microsoft primarily sold programming language products and then its DOS operating system and later Windows, as well as its basic Word and Excel applications, to individuals or intermediaries selling to individuals. Its percentage of sales to enterprises increased dramatically in the 1990s with products like Office, Windows 2000, and an array of servers.

Consumer and enterprise customers each have distinct advantages and disadvantages. Enterprises may produce very high revenues per sale (high "average selling prices"), but these revenues can be costly. The high revenues per sale are because software companies can generally charge medium-sized and large corporations more for their products than they can charge individuals. In addition, as noted earlier, corporate customers expect that the up-front software license fee will account for only about 30 percent of the total cost of the software over its lifetime, with the other 70 percent going to service and maintenance costs.[24] Enterprise customers are usually willing to pay for detailed product documentation, expert technical support, training, and specialized integration work to link one product with other products or databases. There is some sign that corporations have begun to rebel against the high postsale costs of software as well as high software license fees, but more time will be required to see how strong these trends are.

The downside of enterprise sales for a software company is that they can be more costly than consumer sales and generate little or no profit margin if the vendor is not careful. Medium-sized and large enterprise customers, for example, usually require a software vendor to have a large direct-sales force and support staff. This is changing with the Web, but not completely. Large enterprise customers often demand some customized features or at least changes in the development plans for the next release of a product—which managers often agree to if a customer is sufficiently important. Product development has to proceed more or less on schedule, even with the distraction of custom work (unless you have a monopoly); otherwise customers may switch vendors (if technically possible). The software vendor might also have to give a large discount to close a sale (this normally happens at the end of a quarter, and especially at the end of the fiscal year).

But there is a very positive side to enterprise sales, especially in "bad" markets for technology companies, such as during 2001–2002.

Despite the potentially high cost of sales, *when a software company targets enterprises, it has more ways of succeeding, even if it fails to develop a best-seller product.* A software company can tailor its products to meet the needs of a particular customer or type of customer (a "vertical" market) and charge for custom features, then help that customer integrate its product with other products the customer already has or wants to buy. The software company can offer training and consulting to help that customer use both its product and other products more effectively. Managers can be clever about designing maintenance and upgrade schedules for their customized products so that they generate a continuing revenue stream. It is common for enterprises to enter into contracts where, for an additional 15 to 25 percent of the initial cost of the software product, they can get upgrades for several years, like subscribing to a magazine. Many enterprise software companies also sell "perpetual licenses," granting customers the right to receive upgrades as long as they pay an annual maintenance fee (usually about 15 percent of the initial license).

Again, the great attraction of and frustration with trying to sell standardized software products to consumers—or enterprises—is that it is very much like publishing books and selling sequels. On the one hand, there are enormous profit margins if you have a hit and a demand for many copies. On the other hand, sequels or "product upgrades" get harder to sell because of diminishing returns to customers and the discretionary nature of this type of sale—if the earlier version of the product is still "good enough." Book publishers also can have great variation in their sales and profits from year to year and company to company. One best-selling book can make all the difference. But a software company that does not have a best-selling standardized product—a "killer app"—can easily rack up enormous losses simply due to the cost of R and D, sales, marketing, and distribution, whether the target customer is an individual consumer or an enterprise. In addition, even companies with popular products can get buried in support costs. WordPerfect (now part of Corel) found this out years ago when a very large percentage of its employees were manning telephones to answer customer queries on a toll-free unlimited-access number.[25]

Differences Between Mass and Niche Markets

Within the software business, as in other businesses, there are mass-market companies as well as niche-oriented companies. Let's take the database segment, which generated nearly $9 billion in sales in 2001, as an illustration. Oracle, founded by Larry Ellison in 1977, was the market leader in this segment for many years and claims that more than half of the top 100 companies worldwide use its database products. It turns out that Oracle has been slipping as competitors have attacked it both from the side and from below, with comparable or cheaper technology. In 2001, according to the Gartner Group, IBM for the first time edged out Oracle in database revenues, with 35 percent of the market ($3.06 billion) compared to 32 percent for Oracle ($2.83 billion) and 16 percent ($1.4 billion) for Microsoft.[26] Both Oracle and IBM (which also acquired Informix, a high-end database company, in 2001) target the enterprise mass market with sophisticated products. Microsoft has a cheaper product offering (SQL Server) targeted at more cost-conscious and less functionally demanding enterprise customers. It also has a low-end database product (Access) bundled with Office and targeted at individual consumers and small business users. Several other companies such as Sybase offer a variety of high-end and midtier database products.

In operating systems as well, there is a clear hierarchy of segments. Microsoft is again targeting both the enterprise and individual consumer mass markets with the Windows 2000 and XP Professional editions (upgrades to Windows NT) and other versions of Windows. Sun Microsystems, as well as IBM and Hewlett-Packard, are targeting the enterprise mass market with higher-end UNIX operating systems. IBM has proprietary operating systems that target mainstream as well as niche mainframe and minicomputer customers. Apple targets niche users who prefer especially easy-to-use computers or who do a lot of graphics work. Several companies offer versions of the open-source Linux operating system. The list goes on.

It may seem logical for a company to target the largest possible market, whether it be an enterprise mass market (like Oracle with databases and SAP with ERP applications) or a consumer mass market (like Microsoft with Windows and Office). Most software companies, though, appear to be niche players: they usually compete in a small part of the software business rather than in all segments or even the largest segment. Only the largest software companies have offerings in many segments, and they are usually market leaders in either mass-market enterprise or consumer segments.

As in other industries, selling effectively to different types of customers usually requires very different strategies and organizational capabilities. Of course, some segments have less competition and are more profitable than others. But some software segments, such as operating systems, also lend themselves to having one dominant player or platform leader and can be very profitable for this reason alone—as in the Microsoft case. Microsoft is also unusual in that it has strong platform and applications positions in both enterprise and individual consumer markets.

PRODUCT LINES AND MARKET SEGMENTATION

Another common choice in product strategy for software companies, particularly those who sell products, is *breadth:* Do you want to target a broad set of customers with a "horizontal" offering or focus on specific industries or applications—what we can call "vertical" market segments? There is a way to combine horizontal and vertical market perspectives by developing general-purpose products specialized for or tailored to particular industries or types of users. Companies also must decide if they want to sell individual products or product suites, bundling applications together as in Microsoft Office or an ERP suite, such as from SAP, Oracle, and a myriad of competitors.

Segment Markets Horizontally or Vertically or Both

Microsoft covers probably the largest number of segments in the PC software market and targets individual consumers as well as enterprises. Its products are also in horizontal rather than vertical markets. By *horizontal,* I mean a potential market that covers most or all PC users, regardless of their industry or functional specialization. By *vertical,* I mean a market that lies in a specific domain. The domain may consist of an *industry* (e.g., software for the health care industry, which is likely to be a suite of otherwise horizontal database, procurement, accounting, scheduling, and other programs tailored to the requirements of hospitals or doctors' office managers), a *technical specialty* (e.g., computer-aided design programs), a *technical specialty for a particular industry* (e.g., computer-aided design programs for semiconductor design engineers, apparel designers, or automobile designers), or a *platform-specific market* (e.g., an application that runs only on a particular operating system and computer hardware combination). It follows that horizontal segments are more likely to be mass markets and have much greater potential sales than vertical markets.

Segmenting markets both horizontally and vertically can provide software companies (and other companies) with a blueprint for diversification and expansion while still remaining close to their core of expertise. For example, companies can grow by moving laterally into more horizontal market segments, blurring the distinctions, as Microsoft has liked to do, across operating systems, applications, and networking or communications products.[27] Companies also can move vertically into more industry-specific segments, though this requires industry- or domain-specific knowledge, usually combined with some type of horizontal application.

A good example of a firm that combines horizontal and vertical market segmentation is SAP, Europe's largest software company and one of the top software companies in the world in terms of revenues. This German firm was founded in 1972 by five former IBM systems engineers. SAP (the name in German roughly means Systems, Applications, and Products) initially developed about a dozen back-office software packages designed to meet different "horizontal" enterprise functions. Because companies in each industry tend to have slightly different ways of treating these functions, most enterprise software companies have to offer extensive customization services or rely on partners to do the tailoring. SAP, however, decided to preempt some of this customization by creating nearly two dozen specialized versions of its horizontal products tailored to various vertical industry segments (see Appendix Table 8).

SAP still has enormous service revenues, but many of these come from training, installation, and integration work rather than customizing code for individual users. For the most part, SAP encourages users to *adopt* the procedures and data definitions built into its products, rather than *adapt* the software to user procedures and data. The extent of SAP's services even allows the company to grow its services revenues faster than one would normally expect from looking at its growth in product sales. This seems especially true in Europe, where SAP provides most services and maintenance itself, rather than through third parties, which handle a lot of work overseas. SAP's expansion formula has been an outstanding success: The company, which went public in Germany in 1988, had 2002 revenues of approximately $6.88 billion (7.4 billion euros). It employed more than

28,000 people and operated in fifty countries. The R/3 product line, introduced in 1992, and the MySAP Web version, introduced in 1996, are the basis of SAP's current product lineup.[28]

Beware the Lure of the Horizontal

Horizontal software markets (for individual consumers or enterprises) have great appeal in that the number of potential customers is roughly equal to the number of individuals or organizations with computers. Every individual PC has an operating system and probably some basic applications, such as a browser; every Web site needs to run on a server; and so on. But managers, programmers, and entrepreneurs need to beware of what I will here call the "lure of the horizontal."

First, it is easy to imagine new types of products that a company would like to sell to every user or corporate customer. But there are many variations among operating systems and hardware platforms, as well as many different types of users. It is too easy to overestimate the potential of horizontal markets and end up with products that have too few customers or that are too weak to combat the competition. When this occurs in a firm with multiple products, it will have to subsidize weak offerings (costs for design, engineering, testing, documentation, maintenance, and support on the technical side, as well as costs for sales and marketing) from the revenues from its stronger products. This variance occurs in most organizations; few firms with broad poduct lines have offerings that are equally strong. But when it occurs in software companies, it suggests unfulfilled dreams or uncontrolled portfolio management.

Microsoft in 2002 had more than fifty separate software products (though some are sold only in bundles) in four major categories (desktop applications, desktop platforms, enterprise software, and consumer software, including mobility and embedded systems) (Appendix Table 9). These are all potentially large horizontal software markets. Microsoft targets horizontal markets and is always on the lookout for new ones. But not all are equally profitable or large in terms of users. Based on new financial reporting data for fiscal 2003, it appears that only three product lines—the Windows clients, the Windows servers, and Office—account for more than 80 percent of the company's revenues and all of its profits (the other product areas were losing money in 2003).[29] Microsoft would be about 50 percent more profitable if it concentrated only on these three product areas, although some of its other offerings will undoubtedly become larger sources of revenues and profits in the future.

A more serious dilemma is that *horizontal markets can require enormous investment and skill to master.* Yet the lure is so great that they tend to attract software companies that shouldn't be playing the horizontal game, at least not while they lack the resources. I have had several experiences here, but one in particular comes to mind.

Beginning in the spring of 1999, I became an adviser to a now-defunct start-up called SkyFire Technologies (formerly Marbles, Inc.). I first became involved when the company consisted of three people and was looking to get some strategy advice and corporate introductions. It eventually grew to about twenty-five people and attracted $4 million in "angel" and venture capital funding. The company founders, Chris Knapp and Michael Arner, were superb engineers. They developed a unique client-server technology that made it possible to take data-intensive or graphically rich applications and make them run in near-real-time mode even over slow, low-bandwidth wireless connections.

It turned out that the SkyFire platform was excellent for porting PC applications or developing them anew for wireless handheld devices such as PDAs and Web-enabled cell phones. Because of its potential, the company always tried to go after the horizontal market—to get Microsoft, Palm, Nokia, or other platform vendors to embed the SkyFire technology in their operating systems or server software as a general solution to building wireless applications that ran lean and fast. The following excerpt from SkyFire's 2001 "Executive Summary" illustrates the horizontal nature of the company's basic technology and architecture strategy:

II. THE SKYFIRE SOLUTION
Imagine that you could securely and wirelessly connect from your PDA, laptop, or home PC to all of the applications and data that reside in your office. And imagine that you could begin to deploy solutions that do it ALL in only a matter of days.

SkyFire Technology & Architecture
At the core of SkyFire's intellectual property is a terminal-to-server architecture designed so that no data or applications ever reside on the

device. Our technology includes unique compression, encryption and transmission techniques, and device software that automatically enable any wireless device to perform like a computer terminal connected to the network. By enabling the device to function as a wireless "dumb terminal," user interaction with an enterprise application remains consistent, regardless of the type of device used to control and access it. SkyFire enables the enterprise to:

- Deliver an "always-on" remote connection to corporate applications that is device agnostic (our terminal runs on any Palm OS, Windows CE/Pocket PC, Win32, EPOC, and RIM OS device)
- Operate on any wireless network including CDMA, CDPD, TDMA, GSM, and pager networks, enabling enterprises to select the best network(s) to support their mobile workers
- Deliver exceptional performance over low bandwidth connections because all that moves across the network are keystrokes (sent from the device) and presentation logic (sent from the server)
- Rapidly deploy applications using standard tools with write-once-run-anywhere capability[30]

The horizontal market could have been a bonanza for the company, but it proved impossible to crack. There were a dozen other ways of doing the same thing with alternative technologies that were "good enough." It required several years of development to get the SkyFire platform to work on any type of computing device and with nearly any operating system and hardware combination—a true "horizontal" solution in search of a problem. The platform also required a particular programming environment (such as special application programming interfaces, or APIs). Perhaps most important, the market for wireless applications was very slow to develop and is still in its infancy.

From the very earliest days, it was clear that SkyFire needed to target the half-dozen or so *vertical* application areas and specific customers that really needed this solution—that *must have* a data-rich or graphically rich application run in real-time mode over low-bandwidth wireless devices. It would have been great to become a major horizontal player, but first the company should have created a few compelling pilot applications as a proof of concept for the technology, before approaching horizontal vendors such as Microsoft and Palm. Company advisers did make this suggestion, and early on the management team did identify some compelling vertical applications, such as for the navy (ship-to-shore inventory management), food distribution (warehouse to truck to customer delivery management), and personal finance (real-time stock quotes and trading). But the lure of the horizontal was so great that the company spent most of its time and resources in this formative period making the technology suitable as a general-purpose solution. When SkyFire built some industry-specific pilot applications in 2000, they were too few and slow in coming, and not complete enough functionally to lock in real paying customers. The management team also debated whether or not to host applications and offer an ASP (application service provider) service, and spent some time developing this alternative. Eventually, caught in between vertical and horizontal market opportunities and having bet more on the horizontal, SkyFire ran out of time and money and closed shop in the fall of 2001.

What should we learn from this example? *Vertical markets that are exactly right for your solution must be easier to conquer than horizontal markets that require general-purpose solutions that anybody can use.* If you can master a vertical market, then perhaps you can master another one, and another one (as SAP has done). By growing in increments, a company might eventually turn a vertical solution into a horizontal solution. But a new software venture needs to start somewhere and prove itself before tackling the world, and a narrow but attractive vertical market seems like a good place to start.

Beware the Lure of Product Bundling

Software companies also have a choice of selling their products one at a time or bundling them into multiproduct "suites" or "solutions." The idea is that a bundle of products at a discount may capture a broader or more horizontal spectrum of customers—more of a mass market. Suites have something for almost everyone and allow a company to lower prices because they can more easily achieve economies of scale and recover their sales, marketing, and distribution costs.

The suite strategy worked brilliantly for Office, which Microsoft began selling in 1990 when it packaged the popular Word and Excel products with the not-so-popular PowerPoint presentation package. Microsoft cut the price of what these products would cost as standalones by three quarters, and wiped out much of the competition (WordPerfect, WordStar, Lotus 1-2-3, Borland QuattroPro, Harvard Graphics, and so on). Microsoft had the Windows platform as well as the marketing and distribution connections and the resources to do this. It invested huge amounts of engineering time into making those mediocre offerings into very good products that shared about half of their code and worked extremely well together.[31]

The danger is that a software company may bundle weak products with strong ones and not improve them. The resulting "suite" then does little more than subsidize weak engineering or sales and marketing groups and raise costs while lowering or eliminating profits. It is a common problem in the industry; few companies are equally strong in all their products.

For example: Oracle built its business on leading-edge database technology but has branched out into applications, such as its E-Business Suite (Appendix Table 10). The collection actually comprises 13 suites covering everything from marketing to corporate learning, with approximately 100 separate products, including some used in more than one suite. Not surprisingly, the products vary greatly in quality and sophistication. The offerings acquired a poor reputation for quality when they first appeared. In particular, Oracle released the Iii version in the fall of 2001 before debugging the products properly and had to ship as many as seven thousand software "patches" to fix problems reported by customers. PeopleSoft, SAP, and other vendors had stronger product offerings in the same space, but Oracle was able to subsidize its E-Business product group through its database sales.[32]

Another company with a wide variety of products of varying quality, many of them bundled together in suites, is i2 Technologies. As I noted earlier, in 2001–2003, company executives were downsizing and rationalizing product lines in order to reduce R-and-D and administrative expenses (about twice as high as industry norms—see Table 2–2) and return to profitability.[33]

Some bottom lines here: Every software company should periodically reevaluate its products to determine if it is getting the breadth of offerings right. Some products seem as though they could be horizontal blockbusters, but they may need a vertical foothold to start. Managers also need to make sure that suites—a brilliant marketing idea that can also be very convenient for attracting a broader set of customers, *if* the products in the suite are integrated and interoperable—do not subsidize weak products that cannot stand alone.

Beware the Lure of Too Much Growth and Diversification

I have long pondered why companies in so many industries become obsessed with growth. I have come to the following conclusion: *Stagnate, and you die a boring death!* I believe this holds true for individuals as well as organizations. Various data from different industries support the observation that rapidly growing companies have much better chances of survival.[34] Not surprisingly, managers in software companies, like other companies, want to grow. They also usually reach a point where they feel they have saturated their markets, or they see a new opportunity on the horizon that offers much more promise.

In a recent article, Georg von Krogh and I outlined three basic strategies for rapid growth: scaling, duplicating, and what we called "granulating."[35] *Scaling* is simply doing more of what you are already doing, such as launching a bigger marketing and sales campaign to sell more of your software to similar customers. i2 did this initially with factory-planning software. Business Objects did it with database query, analysis, and reporting tools. A more famous case I know well—Netscape—did this with Internet browsers and servers. Netscape pushed sales of the same products from a few thousand sophisticated users to millions of more mainstream users. *Duplicating* is primarily extending your same strategy to other geographical markets (e.g., going overseas) or very similar product markets, such as selling accounting software originally specialized for automakers to boat builders. *Granulating* is diversifying product offerings and the organization structure by creating new, small business units to target new-product opportunities.

Johnson & Johnson is a great example of the granulating strategy. It started in the late nineteenth century by making medical supplies for hospitals and doctors, then diversified into health care products and pharmaceuticals. The company in 2003 consisted of some two hundred semi-independent subsidiaries, most of which consisted of just a few thousand people. In the software business, von Krogh and I wrote about the example of SAP. This company pushed scaling and duplicating its sales of ERP applications to the limit and then, from 1996, began creating new business units to take advantage of Internet technologies and markets. Another good example is Microsoft, which forms relatively small product units (these used to be capped in size at about 450 people) for each new business area.[36]

Diversification into related product lines and technologies is usually a good way to grow, compared to unrelated diversification. The closer new products are to the core expertise of the company, the more likely the diversification will succeed.[37] In software, companies can diversify by broadening their product lines or by moving into different types of services, as we have seen in the examples of Microsoft, Oracle, and SAP, as well as i2. They can also diversify by broadening the number of technology platforms (hardware and operating systems) their products run on. For example, a company that sold development tools for mainframe software could potentially double or triple its potential market by selling similar tools for developing PC and Internet software. This is what Compuware has been trying to do, though it had to acquire PC software tools companies to make the transition.

An example of a company that followed a near-disastrous growth strategy is Infinium Software. (Full disclosure: I joined the board of directors of Infinium in January 2000, primarily in an effort to help the company refocus on and build up its core applications.) Founded in 1981 by Robert Pemberton and two colleagues, the company produced ERP applications that ran on the IBM AS/400 and the successor eServer iSeries hardware. Infinium was moderately successful and grew to a peak of more than 650 employees and $120 million in annual sales in 1999 (see Appendix Table 11). It concentrated on a "niche within a niche"—a relatively uncommon hardware platform as well as a few horizontal applications tailored to particular types of customers. It specialized in human resource management (HRM), financial management, and process management for a few segments, especially gaming and hospitality (casino hotels), health care, and process manufacturers—combining a specific platform with vertical specialties. Infinium's applications offered near-mainframe functionality and performance at a lower total cost (including software license fees and service contract charges), using the power of IBM's midrange hardware.[38]

The problem with this company was the future. The AS/400 hardware market was not growing much—only about 10 to 15 percent a year in the late 1990s, and this was expected to drop considerably in the 2000s. Declining hardware sales meant declining demand for software applications. In contrast, from 1995 or so, demand began to grow rapidly for ERP applications running on much cheaper PCs using the Windows NT operating system. PeopleSoft and a few other companies capitalized heavily on this new market. To move the company into a growth area, Infinium brought in a Harvard MBA named Fred Lizza as CEO in 1997. Lizza directed the acquisition of a series of companies that produced applications roughly similar to what Infinium offered but ran on the Windows NT platform. (For technical reasons, it was very difficult to convert or "port" the code in the AS/400-based applications to other platforms.) The company strategy was in reality to exit, gradually, from the AS/400 market. The result was that Infinium stopped investment in its core applications and spent tens of millions of dollars on "NT acquisitions."

Buying companies that made NT applications helped Infinium double its annual revenues between 1996 and 1999. This was no small achievement, albeit there was a market boom for software in general during the late 1990s, spurred on by Y2K sales and Internet infrastructure investments. Most important, on the surface at least, Infinium became a new player in a hotter market. But movement into the NT space also put Infinium into direct competition with dozens of bigger companies that had better applications on the NT platform than Infinium now offered. Or at least these competitors were better positioned to market their applications to customers that did not know Infinium's reputation, which had been limited to a particular platform segment. More seriously, trying to sell relatively weak products from the NT acquisitions distracted Infinium's management from the alternative strategy of evolving its core AS/400 products and developing true Web-based applications. This neglect endangered Infinium's profitable and recurring revenue stream. Not even long-standing customers seemingly locked into your software will remain loyal if they believe that the vendor has stopped investing in the products and is not willing to help them incorporate new technologies, such as interoperability with the Web.

After operations started to decline and the board began to question the strategy of neglecting the existing base of customers, Lizza stepped down as CEO in July 1999.[39] Pemberton took back the top job himself on an interim basis until bringing in a new CEO, Jim McGowan, in February 2001.[40] McGowan was a twenty-year sales veteran from IBM who had left that company and then served as a CEO of Xerox Imaging Systems, Palladian Software, and other ventures. He led the divestiture of the NT units as well as a money-losing ASP facility. Infinium went back to focusing on its historical niche—AS/400 and iSeries applications—while continuing an incremental adaptation to the Web as a new platform (which Pemberton had strongly advocated). After three years of successive losses, the company finally returned to profitability. It earned about $13 million in net profits in fiscal 2002, compared to only $101,000 in 1998 and a net loss of $2.3 million in 1999, when sales peaked, and a net loss exceeding $27 million in 2000, when we began to restructure and redirect the company.[41]

There was lasting damage to Infinium from this failed attempt at more rapid growth through platform diversification. In 2002, the company was about half its peak size in terms of revenues and employees. Prospects for growth, and the technical capabilities to build new products in-house or offer new services, were not so easy to find. Lizza was right about the state of the IBM midrange market (though IBM in January 2003 announced a new two-year, $500 million marketing effort and price reductions to boost iSeries sales).[42] He was wrong about how easy it would be to diversify by acquiring companies building applications for the NT platform. Two thirds of all acquisitions fail, historically.[43] Infinium's acquisitions record was not even this good. Nonetheless, the "mother ship" returned to health and generated enough recurring revenues to become an acquisition target. SSA Global Technologies, a larger but private AS/400-iSeries applications company based in Chicago, bought the company for approximately $105 million in October 2002.[44]

THE IMPORTANCE OF RECURRING REVENUES

Infinium survived as a company and recovered nicely in 2002, despite badly neglecting its core products and wasting millions of dollars on acquisitions and an ASP facility. The reason? It had a large recurring revenue stream from relatively conservative AS/400 applications customers. These companies were pretty much locked into Infinium's back-office solutions because they had their data and their business procedures embedded in these products. (As someone once said about software customers, "Get their data, and their hearts and minds will follow.") It is hard for enterprise customers to switch when their data and procedures are deeply embedded into a particular vendor's software, usually through custom code or special configurations of the applications (such as writing macros to "customize" an Excel spreadsheet).

Services and Maintenance Generate Recurring Revenues

Services and maintenance agreements for product upgrades and enhancements are important because *the goal of every software company should be to establish large and growing revenues that are recurring*—that is, that can be predicted and counted on because they derive from long-term contracts or very predictable (i.e., "locked-in") purchasing behaviors. The best way is long-term contracts for maintenance (such as product upgrades, tailored enhancements, and regular bug fixes) and a variety of services (such as IT consulting, system integration, training, and technical support). The willingness and ability of enterprise customers to pay money in the present for products or services they will receive in the future is a major reason why enterprise sales contracts resemble assets on deposit. These kinds of revenues are attractive to software companies despite their lower profit margins compared to software license fees for packaged products. But, as I noted earlier, service and maintenance fees tied to new software licenses will dwindle over time in direct proportion to the drop in product sales. For most enterprise software companies— except those with decoupled services operations, such as IBM— product sales are the engine that drives that recurring stream of service and maintenance revenues.

For an example, let's look again at Infinium. This company experienced a drastic decline in software license fees to what may seem to have been a dangerously low level—about 14 percent in fiscal 2001, down from around 35 percent in 1997–1998 (see Appendix Table 11). Nonetheless, Infinium was able to rally around some $60 million in annual recurring service and maintenance revenues. These were steady revenues, whereas between 1997 and 2002, software license fees vacillated wildly. The ratio of the lowest annual license fees (2001) to the highest (1998) was 1 to 4. *It is hard to predict a variation of 400 percent.* In contrast, when we look at service and maintenance revenues during this time period, the lowest (2002) was about

60 percent of the highest (1999)—a variance of only about 40 percent. Under the new owners, Infinium's business should remain profitable for some time to come even if annual revenues for this product line never again reach $100 million.

Products Companies Can Generate Predictable Revenues, Too

Even software companies that do not have long-term contracts to generate future income can achieve predictable revenue streams. Automobile companies try to do this by making model changes on a regular basis and conducting marketing programs that persuade customers to "upgrade" to new models. Automobile companies also build some obsolescence into their products; most cars don't last beyond 100,000 miles. A better example is the laser printer industry, represented by companies such as Hewlett-Packard and Canon. They sell the platform product—printers—at or below cost. But each printer they sell generates a highly profitable and predictable recurring revenue stream from the sales of an essential (and costly) complement—toner cartridges.

Microsoft has achieved something similar to recurring revenues from both platform products and complements. It also works closely with its hardware complementors, such as Intel, and PC manufacturers, such as Dell and Compaq. Customers of Microsoft's operating systems and applications upgrade to new versions on a somewhat predictable basis because the older products become harder to use over time. Individuals generally trade in their personal computers every three to four years, and, when they do this, they usually buy a new operating system *bundled* with the hardware. They often buy updated applications as well. As computers have become more powerful and applications richer, customers have been upgrading at a slower rate. But they still upgrade eventually.

In some cases, software companies can practically force consumers and enterprises to upgrade their software—again, on a regular, predictable basis—as they build in incompatibilities with older file formats or at least make old software programs difficult to use with new versions of the same programs. Microsoft did this brilliantly some years ago, when it introduced Windows 3.0 in 1990 and then a series of updates to Windows during the 1990s and early 2000s. Applications such as Word and Quicken that Microsoft and Intuit rewrote to work in the new graphical Windows environment did not run on Microsoft's old DOS operating system. Customers *had* to upgrade if they wanted to use the new applications. In 1997, if someone sent you a document in Word 97 (probably purchased with Microsoft's applications suite, Office 97) and you were using an older version of Word (such as from Office 95), you could not read the file without going to the Microsoft Web site and downloading a special program to convert the new file to an older format. Most people, rather than go through this trouble, upgraded to Office 97. Office 97 could read documents produced using Office 95 or earlier software, but not vice versa. Microsoft has continued to build in some incompatibilities with newer products. It generally guarantees some measure of *backward compatibility* (i.e., you can read old files with new programs) but not *forward compatibility* (i.e., new with old). Lack of compatibility forces upgrades that companies can often predict.

There are also trends under way that blur the distinctions between products and services. One is the idea of renting software rather than buying it, which is connected with the application service provider (ASP) mode of software delivery as well as some uses of Web services. We have long seen a blurring between product and service sales when companies sell long-term maintenance or technical support contracts that include the right to receive future product upgrades.

Even Microsoft has moved aggressively into this regular upgrade business for its enterprise customers. It now offers licensing contracts or "subscriptions" under a new program called Software Assurance that gives customers access to new versions of Windows and Office for a multiyear period for an up-front payment of about 30 percent of the product cost. The new subscription program is meant to counter a trend that all software products companies are likely to face as their products mature: enterprise customers used to upgrade their software products every two or three years, but that pace has slowed to three years or more. According to some analysts, Microsoft customers will end up paying 20 to 30 percent more for software compared to the old system, unless they already upgrade every two years or less. Some customers were considering switching to other vendors, and Microsoft was likely to revise its pricing policies going forward.[45]

The subscription model for product sales complicates accounting (and creates some opportunities for abuse) in that companies must accumulate what are called "deferred revenues" and can recognize these revenues only as they deliver the software upgrades in the future.

Nonetheless, selling new products on a subscription basis will be a good business model for Microsoft and other software products companies. The accounts can generate large recurring revenues that look like a services stream but are actually based on lower-cost product sales—exactly the same as selling maintenance upgrades that require no special installation or integration work.

WHOLE-PRODUCT SOLUTIONS AND "THE CHASM"

Another issue that many new companies encounter is how to sell to conservative mainstream customers rather than leading-edge users. A classic book on strategy and high-tech marketing that discusses this topic is *Crossing the Chasm* by Geoffrey Moore, first published in 1991.[46] This book provides a useful model for thinking about how technologies get adopted in the marketplace and how a company can manage the process of R and D and product introductions to increase the likelihood that it will become a mainstream player and perhaps the dominant player. A key contribution is to challenge traditional thinking about high-tech strategy and marketing, which assumes that sales can grow continuously across the different market segments (Innovators, Early Adopters, Early Majority, Late Majority, Laggards) and that the previous group can serve as a reference for the next group. Moore cautions us mostly about the "chasm" between the Early Adopters and Early Majority. The customer lists look the same: Fortune 500 companies. But he argues that Early Adopters are buying *change agents,* trying to get a jump on the competition. They are prepared to deal with radical changes, discontinuities, and bugs. By contrast, the Early Majority want *productivity improvement tools* for existing operations. They don't want to debug somebody else's new product. As a result, the Early Adopters do not make good references for the Early Majority. But the Early Majority will not buy without good references—a classic "catch-22."

But all is not lost. Moore advises companies to cross the chasm by focusing on one or two market niches where they can afford to develop "whole product solutions" that provide the service and support mainstream market customers (conservatives) want. He thinks it important to focus on niche segments because new companies generally cannot afford to develop complete solutions and service a wide product range. But the trick is to find a compelling niche application or marketing theme that can propel a company across the chasm. To get to the mainstream, companies must also cultivate reference customers (that can be written up in one-page marketing cases) and relationships with these customers.

Once a company has crossed the chasm into the Early Majority with at least a niche product, it can be used as a base to expand into other segments. The niche should be a strategic "target market" in the sense that it can lead to a larger set of customers. Also, Moore argued that, once in the mainstream, companies no longer have to be state of the art, but just "good enough," although they need to stay close to the technology leaders—as Microsoft and Oracle have done. Furthermore, to develop the mainstream market, companies must shift their marketing from "product-centric" (fastest product, easiest of use, most elegant architecture, cheapest price, unique functionality) to "market-centric" (largest installed base, most third-party supporters, de facto standard, lowest cost of ownership, best quality support).

The biggest message to me from Moore's book is that a lot of new companies misread their early market successes. I have seen this many times. As sales to the Early Adopters rise rapidly with a hot high-tech product, a company invests more heavily in the sales force and distribution network, thinking that sales will continue to grow rapidly. Then, as the Early Adopter market is saturated, sales stagnate because the product is not quite easy enough to use or not quite stable enough or scalable enough for more mainstream customers. R and D gets bogged down dealing with mainstream customer problems or special projects, rather than continuing product innovation. The company's sales seem to fall off a cliff. Moore provides wonderful advice for this dilemma. But I have three particular caveats for the crossing-the-chasm model.

Products Companies Need to Understand Standards Dynamics

First, it is important for managers, programmers, and entrepreneurs in software products companies to understand how standards emerge in their industries to help them cross the chasm and succeed in the mainstream market—if that is where they want to go. For example, Moore argued that Apple crossed the chasm with the Macintosh, focusing on the desktop publishing niche. Apple then became a modest success, but most people would agree that its record of sales has been disappointing. Personal computers running the Windows operating system and using Intel or Intel-compatible microprocessors have become by far the mass-market standard (about 95 percent of PCs). This case suggests to me that competing in niche markets is very different from competing in mass markets, and managers may not learn from niche marketing what they need to know to become a truly successful mass-market player.

In particular, managers need to know how to become the standard or the platform leader in their industry. I suspect that Apple's managers (Steve Jobs, followed by John Scully) failed to expand the Mac's base into the mainstream market for reasons other than the chasm-crossing problem. Apple kept prices high, didn't license early, didn't get enough machines into the marketplace to attract as many complements (software) as the competition, and didn't keep innovating in the software, which allowed Microsoft to catch up. Another example Moore talks about is Novell, which he says crossed the chasm with its IBM-compatible LAN product. However, Microsoft successfully challenged Novell with Windows NT and Windows 95/98. Bill Gates and company came up with a better solution: build the networking software into the industry-standard operating system.

My key point here is that the managers at Apple and Novell did not understand the dynamics of mass-market standards and how to become platforms for other companies and customers. Microsoft and Intel, in contrast, have demonstrated a very deep understanding of the standards and platform business, even though Microsoft at times has abused it. We must emphasize (and Moore acknowledges this) that *simply crossing the chasm is no guarantee of long-term success.* It is not the same as *establishing* the standard and then *maintaining* it, as Microsoft and Intel have done with their products.

For advice on how to play the standards game, we need to go to other authors, such as Carl Shapiro and Hal Varian, authors of *Information Rules.*[47] They talk about the need to control seven critical assets: an installed base, intellectual property rights, ability to innovate, first-mover advantage, manufacturing abilities, complementary producers, and brand/reputation. They also offer lessons: (1) Assemble allies. (2) Preempt competition, such as through rapid design cycles, contracts, and penetration pricing. (3) Manage consumer expectations with aggressive marketing, public road maps, and early product announcements. (4) Don't become complacent—continue to improve your product and even cannibalize your earlier product versions. And (5), if you are not the standard, avoid "survival pricing" and instead try to compete on other dimensions (price/performance, quality, service), and try to "interconnect" to the standard.

You Can Still Be Successful as a Niche Player

Second, it is important to recognize that Moore is primarily concerned with mainstream or mass markets. But a lot of companies can be successful—and highly profitable—starting and remaining as niche players and never tackling mainstream customers or trying to be the one standard. Niche players should also use some aspects of the whole-product approach because it is a good way to do business and expand your customer base, however limited that may be. This seems especially true in software, where there are many market segments. Most segments also have a "high end," although companies in this space continually have to worry about competition from below if the technology standardizes.

A related issue is the difficulty of making the transition from a niche player to a mainstream player. How do you know if your niche application has expansion potential? More important, how do you cultivate the internal organizational capabilities to *change the way you compete and operate,* to be able to meet the needs of mass-market customers on a continual basis? Microsoft has made the transition. So did Business Objects. i2 Technologies is still working on it. Another company I have written about, Netscape, also struggled to become a professional enterprise software company after starting out as a hacker-type Internet software company.[48]

You Can "Leap the Chasm" and Accelerate the Crossing

Third, there are at least a couple of ways to accelerate the process of getting into a mainstream market from a niche beginning or a zero start. Some companies can transfer credibility they have built up with customers in one market to help them enter new markets without having to go through all the steps Moore talks about. For example, IBM was able to introduce the personal computer immediately into the mainstream market because of its credibility and also "free riding" on pioneering work done by other firms. Microsoft "leaped" into the markets for corporate operating systems and applications with Windows NT, Office, SQL Server, and several other products because of the credibility it already had with individual customers based on other products.

Another possibility—and Moore does point this out—is that a company can be "handed" the mass-market standard and use it to leapfrog the chasm. He says this happened to Microsoft when IBM gave it the DOS contract in 1980. This is true, and probably Microsoft could be less thorough in offering a whole product solution because its customers had relatively few good alternatives. But this leapfrogging works only when there are technical standards and complementary assets (such as software programs) that "lock in" customers quickly. Microsoft was also adept at copying or buying mass-market products developed by other firms (spreadsheet, word processor, presentation software, games, etc.). Then it used its marketing clout, understanding of Windows technology, and commitment to this new platform to push its applications products into positions of market leadership.

LEADER, FOLLOWER, OR COMPLEMENTOR?

Discussions of technology strategy usually include a long analysis of the benefits and disadvantages of being a first mover with a new technology.[49] But timing is only one small part of strategy for a software company. In many high-tech markets, the key issue is not how advanced your technology is and whether you are first to market or not, but whether you are in a position to become the *market leader*. In other words, is your product likely to become the most commonly used product? You might also have a core technology that other companies can build complementary products and services around, which presents the opportunity of becoming a *platform leader* as well as the market leader. Intel Chairman Andy Grove, in his 1996 book, *Only the Paranoid Survive,* highlighted this concept when he wrote about the importance of platforms and complementors.[50] In fact, he viewed the power of complementors as a sixth industry force, adding one to Michael Porter's well-known set of five forces that determine levels of industry structure and profitability. Complementary products (such as PC hardware peripherals or software applications) are often essential to make software and hardware platforms (such as the Intel-Windows PC) successful.

Platform leaders are also in an enviable position in down markets, as customers may continue to buy new-platform products while cutting other discretionary spending. Complementor companies (such as Dell in the PC hardware business) will often work hard to sell their complements (new PCs), which can drive more sales of the platform products (such as Microsoft Windows and Office, and Intel microprocessors).

Other authors have also talked about complementors, including myself and Annabelle Gawer.[51] Here, I want merely to point out the basic options: a software company needs to decide if it wants to be a technology leader or a platform leader (the two are not necessarily the same). Most companies, however, will probably choose to be followers or end up as such, making them complementors of somebody else's platform.

Technology Leaders Are Not Necessarily Market Leaders

The high-tech world is full of stories where technology leaders did not capitalize on their inventions or succumbed to the challenges of latecomers. One case that comes immediately to my mind is that of the home videocassette recorder (VCR). Ampex in the United States invented the basic product during the mid-1950s for broadcast use. In the mid-1970s, the company stood by while Japanese firms, led by Japan Victor Corporation and Matsushita, as well as Sony, captured most of the value from this innovation by mass producing VCRs for the home market.[52] Another well-known example is Xerox. Its predecessor company invented the plain-paper copier in the 1950s and had a monopoly for more than a decade but lost its lead to Canon and other Japanese companies in the 1980s when they invented around its patents and introduced highly reliable low-end products.[53]

In the computer hardware and software businesses, there are many examples of technology leaders that failed to take full advantage of their R and D or innovations or that succumbed to competition from below. Xerox comes to mind again, in a bigger way. It also invented or did very early development work on the personal computer, the mouse, the graphic user interface, the electronic spreadsheet, local area networking (Ethernet), and many other product ideas. But Xerox was a copier company and sat by while Apple and then Microsoft exploited its inventions and innovations.[54] But this is only perhaps the most prominent case. There are other examples. MicroPro introduced the first PC word processing program, called WordStar, but later gave way to WordPerfect and then to Microsoft Word. Visi-Calc was the first commercial spreadsheet for the PC, but this gave way to Lotus 1-2-3 and then to Microsoft Excel. Netscape introduced the first graphical Internet browser for the mass market and then watched Microsoft take the lead and never look back, except when forced to in a court of antitrust law.

It should be obvious that technology pioneers are like other pioneers in the old American West: they often make strategic or technical mistakes and get the business equivalent of arrows in the back. Being first with an invention or the commercialization of a new technology is no guarantee of long-term financial success. Microsoft has succeeded by copying the ideas of others, improving products incrementally and relentlessly, and then overwhelming the market with volume and low prices. Microsoft's products usually come close enough by version three to the market leaders in features and quality to compete effectively with them. Microsoft also usually cuts prices, sometimes by large amounts. Then the game is often over for the competition, though not always.

Intuit, the maker of Quicken, had over $1.6 billion dollars (70 percent product sales) in revenues in the fiscal year ending July 2003, with a net profit of $343 million and 6,700 employees. It withstood many challenges from Microsoft Money. Founded in 1983, Intuit succeeded because it was a very early mover with a very good product that it kept improving. Quicken acquired a loyal following of millions of customers who never found a good reason to switch. Microsoft tried to facilitate switching by building a porting tool into Microsoft Money (as it had done with Word and Excel, which enabled these programs to convert WordPerfect and Lotus 1-2-3 files). Gates would also have bought Intuit had it not been for antitrust opposition from the U.S. government, which led to the first consent agreement with Microsoft in 1995. But Intuit has survived on its own and added other mass-market products to its portfolio, such as a best-selling tax program, TurboTax, which accounts for more than a third of revenues, and popular products for small-business accounting, such as QuickBooks. The revenues from the tax products are about as close to recurring revenues as you can get from a packaged software product: people have to do their taxes every year. Since the laws and forms change annually, users of tax software are regular customers. Through some acquisitions, Intuit has also cleverly expanded into related financial services, such as offering bill payment services through Quicken, as well as payroll services and retirement solutions to small businesses and online loans. Its Web site, Quicken.com, generates advertising and transaction fee revenues from financial institutions that use the popular site.[55]

Business Objects and its main competitor, Cognos (a Canadian company that dates back to 1969), established their positions as leading vendors of business intelligence products by being early and sophisticated in this market. Siebel generated more than $2 billion in 2001 sales ($1.13 billion from products and $1.05 billion from services and maintenance) as an early market leader in CRM software. Netscape, for a short period, was the premier Internet software company in browsers and servers, and rode this position to a market value of more than $10 billion when AOL acquired the company in 1999. Even pioneering companies and market leaders saw their finances deteriorate with the market downturn in 2001–2002, but there is still a clear value in being a technology leader or pioneer. Software companies that are in a new market early have a good chance for their products to become standards or platforms, which can eventually make it difficult for customers to switch from one vendor to another.

It's Great to be a Platform Leader

The term "platform" can refer to a foundation product that has the most value when it works as the core of a system of components made by one or more firms. Intel considers the personal computer running Intel microprocessors and the Windows operating system to be the target platform for its microprocessors and chip sets as well as a myriad of other complementary hardware and software products, ranging from digital cameras to personal finance applications. Microsoft, taking a somewhat narrower view, considers Windows to be a platform technology for applications producers and makers of other kinds of complements. There are many platforms in high-tech markets that dominate the competition in market share: Matsushita's VHS-standard machines over Sony's Betamax for video recording; personal digital assistants running the Palm OS versus Microsoft's Pocket PC software; Web application servers running WebLogic from BEA Systems or WebSphere from IBM as opposed to specific Microsoft servers bundled as Windows products.

Not all industries have platforms that become dominant. But many high-tech mass markets and niche markets do gravitate toward a standard because they depend on core products and complementary products that are compatible. A company also does not have to be first to market or have the best technology to become the platform leader and achieve the dominant market share in its industry. This is clear especially from the case of Microsoft's DOS and Windows, which in the past overcame competition from potentially superior operating systems such as Apple's Macintosh OS in the mid-1980s and IBM's OS/2 in the late 1980s and early 1990s.

Platform leaders need to drive innovation around their particular platforms at the broad industry level because the value of the platform usually increases when there are more complements available (such as more VHS tapes or more Windows applications). The economics and strategy literatures have discussed this dynamic for years, using terms such as "network externalities" and "bandwagon" or "positive feedback" effects. The more people who use these kinds of platform products, the more incentives there are for complement producers to introduce more complementary products, which then stimulate more people to buy or use the platform, stimulating more complementary innovation, ad infinitum. It is therefore in the interest of a platform leader to make sure there is a lot of innovation going on around complementary products. Most platform leaders do not have the capabilities or resources to create all complements or complete product systems themselves in-house. As a result, they usually need to work closely with other firms.

The combined efforts of platform leaders and complementary innovators, together, can increase the potential size of the pie for everyone. The formula works especially well in good economic times, when individuals and enterprises have plenty of money to spend. But it also provides benefits in bad economic times. Customers do allocate spending for technology even when budgets are tight, especially if the spending can save them money. New platforms and complementary products and services can often offer customers new levels of efficiency.

In *Platform Leadership*, Gawer and I identified four "levers" or mechanisms that platform leaders can use to exert their influence over producers of complements. The first lever is the *scope of the firm*. By "scope," we mean what complements the platform producer makes itself versus what it encourages or allows other firms to make. It is similar to the old "make-versus-buy" debate in vertical integration, but rather than buying complements, platform leaders generally try to influence other firms to decide on their own to produce complements that make the platform more valuable. In any case, platform leaders need to determine if they should develop an in-house capability to create their own complements or let the market produce complements, or if they should take some intermediate approach, such as cultivating a small in-house capability. For example, Microsoft encouraged many third parties to develop applications (i.e., programs for the DOS and then the Windows operating systems). But since the early 1980s it has had the resources to make many of its own complements. Microsoft thus can pretty much ensure that new generations of its platform (such as Windows 2000 and Windows XP, as well as Windows.NET) will be at least moderately successful commercially. Other software platform companies, such as Palm, Symbian, IBM, BEA Systems, and Linux vendors, have to rely more heavily on third parties to provide complementary products.

The second lever is *product technology* (architecture, interfaces, and intellectual property). Platform leaders need to decide on the degree of modularity for their product architectures and the degree of openness of the interfaces to the platform. They also need to decide how much information about the platform and its interfaces to disclose to potential complementors, who may use this information to become competitors. For the PC, Intel relied mainly on interfaces that numerous companies, including Intel, IBM, and Microsoft, helped to establish and evolve. In contrast, Microsoft had a more dominating position with its Windows software and was able to establish interfaces that were mainly proprietary.

The third lever is *relationships with external complementors*. Platform leaders need to determine how collaborative or competitive they want the relationship between themselves and their complementors to be. Platform leaders also need to worry about creating consensus among their complementors. In addition, they may have to resolve conflicts of interest, such as when they decide to enter complementary markets directly and turn former partners into competitors. Microsoft generally limited the scope of its business but always maintained that it would compete with complementors if a business seemed sufficiently promising and appropriate. Its strategy for applications was to enter any horizontal business of large market potential, and its strategy for Windows was to ward off potential competition by enhancing the operating system with numerous built-in features that complementors often sold as separate products.

The fourth lever is *internal organization.* More specifically, platform leaders can reorganize to deal with both external and internal conflicts of interest. They may decide to keep groups with similar goals under one executive or to separate groups into distinct departments if they have potentially conflicting goals or outside constituencies. For example, Intel tried to establish a "Chinese wall" to separate internal product or R-and-D groups that might have conflicting interests among themselves or with third-party complementors that relied on Intel microprocessors and the PC platform. In contrast, Microsoft long maintained that it did not have such a wall between its operating systems groups and applications groups. Microsoft also insisted that "integration" of different applications, systems, and networking technologies (such as embedding an Internet browser in Windows or embedding its own instant messaging and media player technology into Windows XP) was central to its strategy and good for customers. Microsoft had the market power to push its choices forward, although antitrust litigation in the United States and Europe forced it to make some adjustments to its behavior and strategic plans.

Most Firms Are Platform Complementors

The reality is that *most software companies are not platform leaders; they are complementors of somebody else's platform.* This means that software companies have to make a more risky platform decision: Should they write applications for the Macintosh, for Microsoft Windows, or for both? Or for Linux or one of the dozen or so flavors of UNIX? Should they write applications for the Java environment or the Microsoft equivalent, .NET? What Web applications servers (WebLogic, WebSphere, Apache, Windows 2000) should they use as the environment for their applications? These are long-term, strategic decisions that can go very right or very wrong. Software applications companies that have specialized in the Macintosh and chosen not to develop products for Windows have faced an enormous market handicap, given that today there may be 400 million users of Windows computers versus 20 million to 30 million users of Mac computers. Platform choices, therefore, are closely related to other strategic product choices: mass markets (Windows, Palm OS) versus niches (Macintosh, Linux) and consumer markets (Windows, Macintosh) versus enterprise markets (Unix, Windows NT/2000, Web application servers).

Complementors always run the risk that they may fail to keep up with changes in their target platform. Or the platform leader may decide to absorb their products into the platform and make the complementary products itself. Microsoft has done this continuously with Windows as well as continuously expanding its applications groups, sometimes with acquisitions (most recently of Great Plains Software, a leading company in accounting software for medium and small-sized businesses) but usually by making internal investments.

Challenging platform leaders can also be dangerous for complementors. For example, Netscape's Navigator browser was a wonderful complement to Windows. Then Netscape (egged on by Sun Microsystems and Oracle) began promoting it as an *alternative platform* to Windows in that users could launch Web applications from the browser rather than relying on Windows or any other specific operating system.[56] Microsoft then responded by bundling its competing product—Internet Explorer—with new versions of Windows, nominally for "free" (although users had to pay for Windows). Microsoft won the browser war, but this was not unusual. It was used to beating competitors' products—it had done so with WordPerfect, Lotus 1-2-3, Novell's Netware and DR DOS, and even IBM's OS/2.

COMPANY CHARACTER

The subject of platform leadership (which often comes with a monopoly position, defined as 70 percent or more of a market), in addition to crushing the competition, brings me to a final topic for this chapter: *Strategy should also involve determining what kind of an organization you want to be.* It is fine to be aggressive in going after sales, profits, or market share. But at what point does aggressiveness cross the line into unethical behavior that will get a company into trouble not only with the antitrust authorities and the Securities and Exchange Commission but also with customers, employees, industry analysts, investors, and business partners?

Enterprise software companies are in a position that requires uncompromising ethics in how they treat customers as well as competitors, partners, and other stakeholders. Individual customers, billion-dollar corporations, and trillion-dollar governments put their trust in computer systems. If and when these systems fail, the consequences can be devastating. Airplanes may fall from the sky, the U.S. eastern seaboard may lose its telephone communications (this once happened due to a software glitch at AT&T), power plants might explode, billions of dollars in savings accounts or brokerage accounts might disappear. Software companies and IT departments in many other kinds of companies are in particular positions of trust because what they produce—computer code—is hard to see and harder to test. So managers, programmers, and entrepreneurs need to think hard about what kind of organization they want to create.

Be Careful with Revenue Recognition

Too many software companies and other high-tech firms, at one time or another, find themselves guilty or almost guilty of recognizing revenues they should not. In the Enron debacle, which unfolded during 2001–2002, the world witnessed how aggressive and destructive accounting procedures can become. The Financial Accounting Standards Board (FASB), the American Institute of Certified Public Accountants (AICPA), and the Securities and Exchange Commission (SEC) all have rules that contribute to what are called generally accepted accounting principles (GAAP). These rules supposedly govern how software companies and other firms may treat revenues, expenses, and other accounting data.[57] The following quotation from Infinium's 2001 Form 10-K is a typical example of how a public software company treats the subject of revenue recognition:

> The Company recognizes software license fee revenues in accordance with the provisions of AICPA Statement of Position 97-2, *Software Revenue Recognition,* and its related pronouncements. Revenue from software license fees is recognized when there is evidence of an arrangement, the product has been delivered, fees are fixed or determinable, and collection of the related receivable is deemed probable. Revenues from sales through distributors are recorded net of commissions. Revenues from sales of third-party products are recorded net of royalties. Maintenance revenues, including those bundled with the initial license fee, are deferred and recognized ratably over the service period. Consulting and training service revenues are recognized as the services are performed.[58]

One problem, even among companies that do not intentionally try to break the rules, is that the rules are subject to interpretation—aggressive *or* conservative interpretation and everything in between. Different financial specialists may interpret "evidence of an arrangement," "the product has been delivered," and "collection of the related receivable is deemed probable" differently. And there are other areas where companies may get into trouble. But let's start with some simple cases.

First, U.S. accounting rules are supposed to prevent companies from declaring preproduction or beta software "finished." But some companies still shortcut the development and testing periods and claim a product has been delivered when it still needs a lot of work to complete features or fix defects (called "debugging" and "stabilization"). The companies recognize the revenues anyway and then have large postship costs to finish the product. In the meantime, customers are dismayed that the "finished product" is not really finished. Some demand refunds or sue the vendors in court.

Then there are companies that try to accelerate the revenues from maintenance and upgrade contracts. They are supposed to recognize these revenues as they deliver the products or services over time, which is usually measured in years. Other companies hold back from recognizing some revenues from sold products and services in one quarter or fiscal year and then declare them in the next fiscal period. This seemingly benign accounting maneuver can mislead people by making revenues look more even and recurring—which analysts and investors like.

Perhaps the most serious type of revenue recognition problem is the one that drove the former high-flying ERP software company Baan (founded in the Netherlands in 1978) into bankruptcy and then a takeover by Invensys PLC in September 2000. Invensys then sold the Baan assets to SSA Global Technologies in July 2003. (Full disclosure: I did some consulting with Baan on software development methods in 1998.) A key problem here was declaring revenues upon the "sale" of software to distributors or resellers. The company initially got into trouble by making a string of bad acquisitions that drained cash and management attention. To bolster sales, top management began playing a virtual shell game with "sales" to distributors that were really subsidiaries it owned. When analysts and customers discovered that Baan had been wildly inflating its revenues, both its stock price and its pipeline of new customer orders collapsed. The company lost money for nearly two years before it restated its earnings and declared bankruptcy.[59]

Another case that resulted in bankruptcy came to light in 2002. This involved Peregrine Systems, a software company founded in 1981 that provided technology infrastructure management software. This company, owned by John Moores, the owner of the San Diego Padres baseball team, overstated its revenues by $250 million between 1999 and 2001. The financial misstatements led to an SEC investigation, massive layoffs and resignations, and a virtual end to new sales deals.[60]

A more complex example of recent note is that of Computer Associates (CA), which adopted a new method for recognizing revenues that does away with lump-sum up-front licenses and records revenues over the period of the contract. The SEC subsequently investigated the company for possibly backdating and forward-dating contracts to move revenues between quarters; bundling software products with maintenance contracts to justify more upfront revenue recognition than is normally permitted under accounting rules; and changing accounting procedures in a way that made it possible to recognize the same revenues twice and inflate sales.[61] CA executives maintain that they are merely trying to recognize revenues more precisely and eliminate practices such as customers waiting until the last minute at the end of the fiscal year to buy products. The company has also launched a major effort to improve its corporate governance, including measures such as adding several new independent directors to its board.[62] In any case, the result of the new accounting practices is that analysts and investors now find it difficult to compare CA's current financial results with past years' or to compare CA with other software companies.

There is no permanent escape for companies that commit illegal or unethical accounting maneuvers. Some managers pursue them with supposedly honorable intentions in that they simply want to smooth out quarter-to-quarter revenues or get through what they believe is a temporary down period. But laws are laws, and illegal behavior is illegal. Moreover, dealing with a loss of customer confidence can be much worse than dealing with the law.

Lose Your Credibility, and You Lose Your Customers
Losing customer confidence can start by losing credibility. *Like its close cousin, integrity, credibility is something that most firms, or in-*

dividuals, can lose only once. Loss of credibility can be fatal for enterprise software companies because they, especially, need to maintain a position of trust with their customers and stakeholders. Problems rarely require the kinds of maneuvers that Enron, WorldCom, or Tyco International employed in the early 2000s; they are usually more straightforward and subtle.

For example, do you deliver products and services to customers based on what you said you would do and more or less on the schedule you promised? Well-managed companies try their best to make good on their promises, even if they lose money in the process. Poorly managed companies try to "get the business" at almost any cost and cut corners on what they deliver or deliver late because they know they overpromised to make the deal. This behavior forces their sales, engineering, and support organizations to pick up the pieces (that is, try to mollify unhappy customers and finish incomplete products in the field). Of course, the vast majority of software projects are routinely late, and all software contains bugs. But this means only that a software company or IT department needs to build discipline into its sales agreements and product specifications, as well as add buffer time to schedules and protect its debugging and testing time, so that it does not overpromise and underdeliver.

Industry Leadership Comes with Industry Responsibilities

Platform products such as Microsoft Windows tend to become what some people have called a "natural monopoly." Users don't want too much variety in the foundation program they need to run applications. Companies that become platform leaders then have to decide how they want to treat customers who are "locked in" to their products and how they want to treat complementors or partners who are potential competitors. It is useful to remember that there is nothing illegal about having a monopoly. On the other hand, it is illegal to *abuse* a monopoly by tying sales of products in one market to those in another, deliberately overcharging customers, or thwarting competitors' legitimate efforts.

Microsoft in the 1970s and 1980s was not very sophisticated in how it treated its customers. Its products were buggy, and its managers invested little in testing or providing professional technical support. All this changed with the introduction of Windows 3.0 in 1990. Microsoft began to treat consumers better—much better. In particular, Bill Gates pushed for quality improvements because he feared that an enormous number of customer calls would come in after Windows started to sell in the tens of millions. Microsoft also lowered its prices on products such as its desktop applications—all to the benefit of consumers.

But how Microsoft treated its competitors, as well as complementors that became competitors—such as Netscape—was another matter. In June 2000, Microsoft was found guilty of violating a number of antitrust provisions. A year later, the U.S. Court of Appeals decided not to break up the company. Then, in November 2002, a federal judge rebuffed the challenge from nine states and upheld a settlement between Microsoft and the U.S. Department of Justice that required Microsoft to disclose various technical data, avoid exclusionary deals, and curb its pricing and business practices. Microsoft clearly had ventured into both unethical and illegal behavior. But its unethical and illegal actions were also, in my opinion, very unnecessary. One of the sadder parts of the Microsoft antitrust case is that Netscape, on its own, blundered in product development, marketing, pricing, partnerships, and other areas.[63] There was no need for Microsoft to bludgeon Netscape by offering Internet Explorer for free and threatening PC companies that preferred to continue bundling Netscape Navigator.[64]

It is fine to be aggressively competitive, but there are limits to what is acceptable behavior for a firm in a position of industry leadership. Microsoft executives, board members, and employees have been in a process of learning those limits. They have learned how to compete extraordinarily well, and I suspect that under new (since 2002) CEO Steve Ballmer and a more reflective Bill Gates, who remains chairman of the board and chief software architect, Microsoft will figure out how to be a responsible industry leader as well.

WRAP-UP COMMENTS

There is a lot more I might say about strategy for software companies, but this chapter is already long enough. I believe the overview provides many things for managers, programmers, and entrepreneurs to think about. The most critical choice still seems to be whether to become mostly a *products* company or a *services* company. We have seen that the strategy models and potential profit margins are very different: Products companies should try to be more like printing presses with best-selling books because they can have extremely low sales costs. Services and hybrid solutions companies should try to be more like banks with a large asset base (an installed user base, combined with long-term service and maintenance contracts) from which they can derive a steady stream of revenues, even if these revenues are more labor-intensive and costly than selling packaged software products.

Although the business models are different and require different organizational capabilities, enterprise software companies usually need to produce both products and services, especially to survive bad economic times. On the one hand, new-product releases are the source of many service revenues and maintenance upgrades. On the other hand, when sales of new products or upgrades are slow, as occurred after the Internet bubble burst in 2001–2002, services and maintenance provide a base for much-needed revenues and can mean the difference between success and failure as a company. Also, since products tend to become commodities over time and markets can become saturated with similar products, until there is some major change in technology, products companies usually find that their sales growth slows after a while.

It may actually be a "law" of the software business that software products companies inevitably become services companies or hybrid solution providers. Their strategy and management practices, as well as their internal capabilities, must adapt to this transition. At the same time, *because selling products is different from selling services, even hybrid solutions companies should have a primary strategic orientation of either services or products.* For most hybrid companies, the primary orientation will probably be products because that is usually the business model they began with and it should always offer some economies of scale and operating-margin advantages.

We also saw that software companies can segment markets both horizontally and vertically and use that segmentation as a blueprint for expansion and diversification. It is also possible to combine horizontal and vertical market concepts to create powerful applications tailored to particular users, as SAP has done so successfully. Strategies and the capabilities required for success differ considerably by market segment and business model, such as whether you want to sell to individuals or enterprises, or to mass or niche markets. Horizontal markets and product bundles have great appeal because they can potentially generate very large sales, but they also have strong downsides, as they are difficult and expensive to develop. Like too much diversification, broad product lines and bundles can end up subsidizing weak products and result in profitless growth or losses.

Mainstream enterprise customers generally require highly refined products complete with a full set of complementary products and services—what Geoffrey Moore has called the "whole product solution." They are generally less interested in leading-edge technology. It is useful to remember, though, that companies do not have to become mainstream players to be successful; in the software business there are plenty of vertical and horizontal niches to exploit. In addition, it is possible for a firm that has established market credibility in one segment to leapfrog the chasm when entering another segment.

Setting the standard in a mainstream or niche market generally involves becoming a platform leader, which differs from being a technology leader. Platform leaders can generate new-product sales even in bad markets because so many customers and complementors depend on the platforms for their businesses. But most software firms are complementors. They are better off recognizing what they are early on and adopting an appropriate strategy for managing both themselves and their relations with the platform leader.

Finally, I argued that a company's character should be an important part of its strategy, especially for a firm selling to enterprise customers. Customers need to be able to trust their vendors. It is also hard to judge the quality of a software product without using it. Software companies can demonstrate their character in concrete ways—such as how management treats practices of revenue recognition, promises to deliver new products and services, commitments to quality, and relationships with their customers, complementators, and competitors.

In the next chapter, I look back at history to explore how software became a business. Once again, we see that the unavoidable tension between services and products had a great influence on the shape of the industry today and the fate of the most successful computer company in history, IBM.

3

Services, Products, and More Services:
How Software Became a Business

Studying the past should help managers, programmers, and entrepreneurs understand a lot about themselves as well as the evolution of their businesses. First, a study of history often suggests patterns of technology and market evolution, which can tell us a lot about competition and disruption. The past may not be an absolute guide to the future, but it can often point the way. Second, history can help identify likely sources of new business opportunities. For example, I used to wonder how the software business came about: Who were the first entrepreneurs? What were they selling? How much of their business was services and how much products? What were the first products? Third, constructing sketches and deeper case studies of how particular companies have succeeded or failed is a useful exercise.

When I looked into the history of how software became a business, I asked these and other questions. I came up with several observations, around which I have organized this chapter:

- Systems software and services launched the software business in the 1950s, though systems products were bundled and used primarily to sell hardware.
- An independent software products business emerged in the 1960s, mostly around common user needs and application niches that the hardware manufacturers (led by IBM) ignored.

- IBM failed to treat software as a separate business until the 1990s; nonetheless, it built total solutions (made up of hardware, software, and services) that survived the transition from electromechanical tabulators to mainframe computers and PCs and generated new growth opportunities, mainly for services, in the age of e-business and open-source software.
- A new platform that appeared in the 1970s—the personal computer—created a whole new generation of programmers and entrepreneurs who had very different programming and marketing skills than their mainframe predecessors.
- The next new platform—the World Wide Web—provided opportunities for both new entrepreneurs and established companies such as IBM to link different kinds of computing systems.
- Open-source and "free" software present both opportunities and challenges for companies in the business of *selling* software, though the opportunities they create for entrepreneurs have been few.

The question to ask next is, what does history suggest about where new opportunities in software products or services might arise in the future? I will come back to this subject in subsequent chapters on entrepreneurship and the conclusion to this book.

SYSTEMS AND SERVICES LAUNCHED THE BUSINESS

It was a long road to selling software as a separate, standardized product capable of generating the kinds of scale economies that we now see a Microsoft or Adobe enjoy. Before the products market emerged, though, the technical limitations of early computer systems provided unique opportunities for software entrepreneurs to offer what we would today call systems products and custom programming services.

There are several reasons why the software business began in systems software, followed by custom programming. First, computers needed basic control or monitoring programs to operate. Second, the small market and lack of experience with programmable computers did not create enough demand for standardized applications products until the 1960s. A third factor was also important: IBM did not unbundle its systems software from its hardware sales until 1970.

The First Software Entrepreneurs in the 1950s

The first electronic computers, used mostly for military applications during the latter stages of World War II, had no software as we know it today. These machines required hardwired instructions and data that programmers inputted by setting switches representing machine language (zeros and ones). In 1944, while visiting the ENIAC (Electronic Numerical Integrator and Computer) team at the University of Pennsylvania, the Princeton mathematician John von Neumann came up with the idea of storing programming instructions as well as data within the computer's memory, rather than having to enter and reenter instructions manually every time a user wanted the computer to perform a particular operation. We can consider this development of the "stored-program" concept—first implemented in the EDSAC (Electronic Delay Storage Automatic Calculator) computer in 1949 at Cambridge University in England—as the enabling technical innovation that led to the creation of the software business. During the 1950s, the program instructions were commonly called "routines" (hence the common term "subroutine" when referring to a small program). The term "software" came into general use around 1958–1960.[1]

For the first software entrepreneurs, the introduction of programmable computers and the need for custom programs was like a slowly opening gold mine. Several independent software companies appeared at this time, especially in the United States for defense contracts. U.S. government procurement during the 1950s and early 1960s helped build the foundations for a remarkable software industry in the United States, on top of the hardware industry, and does much to explain why U.S. companies still dominate the business worldwide.

The largest early U.S. government project was the SAGE air defense system, developed between 1949 and 1962. The total expenditures were some $8 billion for a system that used at least 1 million lines of code. According to one estimate, of the 1,200 programmers in the United States in the late 1950s, 700 of them worked on the SAGE project.[2] Out of this project also came the first "software factory," established at the System Development Corporation (SDC) in Santa Monica, California. SDC was originally part of the Rand Corporation and later a division of Burroughs and then Unisys.[3]

Another important effort was Whirlwind, which developed flight simulators and led to the development of real-time computing and magnetic core memory storage technology. This project also stimulated creation of the minicomputer hardware and software industry in Massachusetts, pioneered by Digital Equipment Corporation, established by Ken Olsen in 1957. After working as a researcher on the project, Olsen came up with the idea of making powerful, small computers for engineers and scientists. These users could write their own software and did not need the expensive solutions that IBM and a few other big companies provided.[4]

But not all the high-profile applications were for government use; the commercial sector also had its software entrepreneurs. A smaller but important project was the SABRE airline reservation system. IBM and numerous subcontractors built this system for American Airlines between 1954 and 1964. The project involved about 200 software engineers and cost some $30 million.

Stimulus from Technology Innovation in the 1960s

As computers evolved during the 1960s, it became possible to create more elaborate software programs. On the hardware side, new processors, CRT displays, magnetic core memory for data storage, real-time software designs, and new communications technology (including the predecessor of the Internet) came from government-sponsored or government-funded projects. IBM and other U.S. computer companies quickly put these technologies to civilian use.[5] Most software innovations came from companies and universities, although a few came from government-sponsored projects. Government funding was especially important for development of the software industry when one considers the spillovers from defense projects to commercial applications and money provided to universities to buy computers and sponsor research.[6]

Beginning in the 1950s, computer manufacturers also started to lease their machines at relatively low prices in increasing numbers. More organizations began to install computers and require programming services and tailored systems. By the later 1960s, it became clear that the demand for computers was outstripping the ability of many in-house IT departments as well as IBM and other hardware manufacturers to provide all the needed custom software. The increasing sophistication of the machines and the programming requirements made it too difficult for novice users to build their own applications.

In the late 1960s, industry observers took note of this growing shortage of programming expertise by decrying an emerging "software crisis." The market opportunity for custom programming since the late 1950s had prompted many employees from IBM and other companies to establish their own software firms, and this trend accelerated in the 1960s. Some examples: Computer Usage Company, said to be the world's first independent software company, was started in 1955 by former IBM employees to provide custom software to companies in the oil exploration business and then to insurance companies and retail vendors. It went public in 1960 and by 1967 had 700 employees. It went bankrupt in 1985, presumably because it failed to manage both the products and services aspects of its business properly.[7] Computer Sciences Corporation, which had more than $11.4 billion in revenues and 68,000 employees in 2002, dates back to 1959. EDS, which had revenues of $21.5 billion and 140,000 employees in 2002, dates back to 1962.

By one account, the United States had between forty and fifty major software vendors by the mid-1960s and nearly three thousand smaller software companies, including two-to-three-person operations.[8] Although there were fewer software companies overseas, the United Kingdom, continental Europe, and Japan also saw a growing number of software firms appear during this same period. These companies built custom systems for IBM mainframes, IBM-compatible or -comparable mainframes (built by companies such as GE and RCA in the United States and Fujitsu and Hitachi in Japan), and other proprietary computers built by companies such as Honeywell (with Bull in France and NEC in Japan as its eventual partners).

THE FIRST SOFTWARE PRODUCTS BUSINESS

The early computer hardware companies did not pay much attention to building a separate software products business. There was not much programming expertise available, and large computer users were likely to have as much or more applications programming skill as computer vendors. Not until the late 1950s and early 1960s did entrepreneurs see an opportunity for what we would today call a software products business, and most of the products developed then served specific horizontal and vertical application niches. The new applications market was also very much a reaction to the services business, particularly the inefficiencies inherent in custom programming.[9]

The software products business emerged only when entrepreneurs were able to identify standard user features for particular applications and package them for multiple customers. The idea of selling products as opposed to custom programming services made powerful economic sense to vendors and customers alike. Even IBM understood the possibilities for standard applications, even though software products were not the focus of its business. For example, in the early 1960s, IBM introduced a program containing common features for insurance companies called Consolidated Functions Ordinary, or CFO. Following the conventions of the day, however, it bundled this product with its hardware and did not sell it separately.[10]

Applied Data Research, founded in 1959 as a custom software producer, appears to have been the first company to sell a software product independently of hardware. The impetus here came from a computer vendor. RCA asked ADR to develop a flowcharting program to help software developers map out the functions in their code. The product was later called Autoflow. ADR (which Computer Associates eventually acquired) wrote it for the RCA machines and then rewrote it for IBM platforms, which had a slightly different architecture. This program also became the first patented software product, though it had limited sales. The first software product to exceed $100 million in cumulative sales was what we would today call a horizontal application that fit the needs of many users and builders of custom systems. The product, Mark IV, was a simple database or file management package made by a company called Informatics, founded in 1962. Mark IV first went on sale in 1967 for the then-astounding price of $30,000 and reached the $100 million sales mark in 1983.[11]

Another inspiration for the products business came after 1964, when IBM began introducing the System/360 family of compatible mainframe computers. Each computer had a different level of processing and memory capability for customers with different needs. The new computers inspired IBM and other firms to write a lot of new systems and applications software, the most famous of which is probably the operating system OS/360. IBM bundled this massive program with the hardware—seemingly giving it away "for free."

IBM's Unbundling Strategy

The software products business did not really take off until after IBM, which had about an eighty percent share of the mainframe industry overall, unbundled its hardware sales from its software and services sales, at least to some extent. The company first made the announcement in December 1968 that it would begin pricing and selling some software separately beginning in 1970. The fact that IBM took this step reflects that software throughout the 1960s had not been a separate business even for the leading computer company; it was a technology and a service that IBM, like other computer companies, provided to sell hardware. After the unbundling, many new firms appeared around the world that made "IBM-compatible" software, especially applications programs, as well as "IBM-clone" hardware products (computers and peripherals). The unbundling decision also seemed to contradict IBM's approach of offering a complete solution of hardware, software, and services (more on this later). So what motivated IBM executives to change their strategy?

According to Watts Humphrey, who headed the OS/360 programming effort, IBM management decided to unbundle because of concerns that the U.S. Department of Justice would find bundling to be anticompetitive. At the time, RCA was planning to introduce compatible computers that would be able to run IBM software, and the Justice Department wanted to make sure that makers of compatible machines had a chance in the marketplace. In fact, as Humphrey explained, bundling gave IBM a tremendous advantage: "Because the separate parts of IBM's offering were not separately priced, competitors had to offer a similarly comprehensive bundle. Bundling, therefore, made it more difficult for small firms to compete with IBM in almost any part of the rapidly growing computer business."[12]

But another result was that unbundling enabled IBM to charge for its software! Management worried that customers would switch to cheaper compatible machines and continue to use the IBM software for free. Humphrey's team had already concluded in 1964 that RCA could produce computers that would run software for the OS/360 family (even though RCA engineers eventually made small architectural "improvements" that made their computers not quite 100 percent compatible with IBM machines).

To understand why RCA was able to clone a proprietary technology, we need to go back to IBM's 1956 consent decree with the Department of Justice. At this time, IBM agreed to offer its computers for sale rather than for leasing only and to price hardware maintenance and spare parts separately. The government also required IBM to make certain technical information publicly available so that other companies could service IBM machines. The availability of maintenance information would later make it possible for RCA as well as Amdahl and Fujitsu to build compatible machines. Hitachi, which partnered with RCA during the 1960s, also went on to build IBM-compatible mainframes.[13]

The task force IBM formed in 1966 to study how to unbundle its software and systems engineering services also formulated a strategy for protecting IBM's intellectual property—again setting a standard for how to do this in the software business. The task force members, headed by IBM director Howard Figueroa, decided that patenting would be too difficult because of the volume of software being produced and the many versions of each product. Instead, the company chose to rely on copyrights and licenses, with IBM retaining ownership of its code. Customers signed a licensing agreement that permitted them to use IBM software and even copy it under certain restrictions, such as for multiple computers on a particular site (called a "site license"). The IBM task force also recognized that application programs were a separate business from computer hardware and systems software and decided not to unbundle "system control programs" (the operating system and primary system management facilities). Much information on these systems was already in the public domain, and it was difficult to separate the hardware platform from the operating system software.[14] After the unbundling, it became the practice for IBM and other software products companies to charge an up-front fee for delivery and installation of their software products. Then they charged separate fees, paid over time, for maintenance and upgrades, as discussed in Chapter 2.[15]

More Impetus for Entrepreneurs: IBM-Compatible Software

More software entrepreneurs would have entered the business anyway during the 1970s, even without IBM's decision to unbundle, because the use of computers had already outstripped the ability of existing companies to provide software. IBM's successor to System/360, the System/370 family of computers, introduced in 1970, inspired another round of demand for more powerful programs.

Nonetheless, IBM's unbundling, as much as new hardware, created incentives for another generation of software entrepreneurs: those interested in producing software for IBM-compatible mainframes. As many as eighty-one new software companies appeared by 1972 in the United States alone.[16]

It is not hard to understand why unbundling encouraged entrepreneurship. Before the unbundling, IBM was the main source of systems programming expertise for its machines. It had a lot of applications expertise as well and worked on many projects for large firms and governments. Because IBM did not charge separately for much of its software, it made sense for customers simply to rely on IBM for their software needs. Many customers continued to go to IBM even after the unbundling because IBM lowered its hardware prices by only about 3 percent.[17] It was really manufacturers of cheaper IBM-compatible hardware, such as Amdahl (backed by Fujitsu), that most capitalized on IBM's unbundling. They targeted customers that did not like IBM's prices and finally had an alternative supplier.[18]

IBM's unbundling applied mostly to *applications* software, and this is where most new opportunities arose for software entrepreneurs. It is very difficult to sell a computer (or a cell phone!) that doesn't "boot up" when you turn it on. To boot up a computer, you need some kind of systems software already loaded at the factory or included on a tape drive or diskette. So, not surprisingly, IBM and most other computer hardware manufacturers continued to bundle their own or licensed operating systems and some other basic software with their machines. This practice continues today, though most PC makers license Microsoft Windows. Manufacturers of large computers (such as IBM, Sun Microsystems, Hewlett-Packard, Hitachi, and Fujitsu) as well as small computing devices (such as Palm and Nokia) continue to make at least some operating systems, either in-house or through joint ventures such as Symbian, based in the United Kingdom.

The mainframe business was actually very different from the less vertically integrated PC business. In the 1950s and 1960s, vendors of large-scale computers generally made their own processors and systems software to make sure they could optimize the two technologies and keep their products distinctive. Companies such as DEC, which developed minicomputers and workstations for enterprise and government customers, followed the same strategy. In the PC world, however, following IBM's decision in 1980 to outsource the operating system to Microsoft and the microprocessor to Intel, specialist producers dominated a vertically fragmented industry.

Opportunities in Application Niches

When we look back at history, we also see that another source of opportunities for software entrepreneurs has been *market segments where the dominant companies of the generation did not have much to offer or into which they chose not to enter.* These niches made it possible for software start-ups to gain a business foothold and avoid becoming "roadkill," run over by the likes of IBM or, in later years, Microsoft.

For example, by the late 1960s, it had become clear that there was an important gap in the mainframe software market: good database products. IBM did not have any strong offerings. This oversight led to a niche—and eventually an enormous horizontal market—for independent software vendors. Cullinane Software, founded in 1968 and later acquired by Computer Associates (founded in 1976), became the early leader in database software. The German company Software AG, founded in 1969, saw an opportunity as well and began marketing its database products in the United States in 1972. Some other early database companies, such as Oracle (founded in 1977), Sybase (1984), and Informix (which sold its database business to IBM for a billion dollars in 2001 and then reorganized as Ascential Software), all went on to become major players.

Some companies used database products as a foundation for selling related enterprise products. Computer Associates in particular became a highly diversified software company by aggressively acquiring database companies and other niche players. In 2000, it peaked at $6.7 billion in revenues with some five hundred separate software products, before sales declined by about a third in 2001 and the company changed its accounting procedures. As discussed in Chapter 2, Oracle also expanded into a variety of enterprise applications beyond databases, though database products remained by far the largest source of revenues and profits for the company.

A second horizontal mass market became enterprise resource planning (ERP) applications—programs to manage personnel administrative details, finance and accounting, internal communications, supplier contacts, and other essential operations. Individual companies generally have different procedures and unique ways of treating data and key operations. This is why custom-built software and hybrid solutions have been so popular among large firms and organizations. Most enterprise applications packages need some work to install them and tailor them to particular customers. But many functions are common among firms in the same lines of business, as IBM discovered with the CFO insurance package in the late 1950s. This similarity creates an opportunity for software firms to sell standardized products that they or third parties can modify for individual customers.

I noted in Chapter 2 that SAP has been one of the most successful hybrid solution vendors. Founded in 1972, the German-based company has mastered both the products and services sides of the business as well as combined horizontal and vertical market strategies. SAP sells enterprise products specialized for a wide array of industry-specific markets and, with many partners around the world, offers extensive consulting and technical support services as well as long-term maintenance contracts for enhancements. SAP software initially ran on IBM mainframes but now runs on every major hardware and operating system platform. Software licenses (not including maintenance-related licenses) accounted for only 31 percent of revenues in 2002 (see Table 2-2).[19]

But the relatively inflexible nature and high installation costs of SAP's offerings (in particular the pre-Web versions of its products) created opportunities for smaller competitors in the United States, Europe, and Japan to offer their own back-office applications. These alternatives are usually cheaper, easier to install and customize, or more specialized—but not necessarily "better" in terms of functional richness or reliability. A highly regarded U.S. competitor, for example, is PeopleSoft, founded in 1987 as a vendor of PC-based enterprise applications for human resource management. It later diversified into vertically tailored versions of its applications but has had most of its success in the health care and financial service sectors. Another competitor mentioned in previous chapters is Baan, founded in Belgium in 1978. Baan had more modularized and less expensive products that supposedly did the same things SAP products did. But Baan's offerings did not scale up as easily to the needs of large organizations such as Boeing and had other problems that helped push Baan toward bankruptcy before Invensys PLC and then SSA Global Technologies acquired the company.

Many accounting firms also moved into the custom software business by developing applications and providing customization services such as for financial management and other back-office functions. As we saw in Chapter 2, Accenture (formerly Andersen Consulting), KPMG, PricewaterhouseCoopers, Cap Gemini Ernst & Young, and others fall into this category. Although they are primarily vendors of custom software, many of these firms have in-house packages for different applications, and they use these packages as a base for providing what are in essence "semicustom" solutions, referred to in this book as "hybrid" solutions. The Japanese computer manufacturers Hitachi, Fujitsu, NEC, and Toshiba also built large custom software practices around this same idea of providing semicustom solutions for back-office or industrial applications.

It is also worth noting that enterprise software is subject to increasing commoditization and packaging, especially for small and medium-sized firms. Smaller firms have relatively similar needs and generally cannot afford custom systems or multimillion-dollar installations, like SAP's. These types of enterprise customers constitute their own horizontal market and bought some $19 billion worth of software in 2002. It is not surprising that Microsoft has decided to move into this market. To pursue this area, it acquired two ERP vendors that target midsized firms: Great Plains Software, purchased in April 2001 for $1.1 billion, and Navision, a Danish company, purchased in May 2002 for $1.3 billion.[20]

IBM: ONE HUNDRED YEARS OF CUSTOMER SOLUTIONS

IBM is so important in the history of the computer industry that it merits a separate discussion of its strategy and success formula, as well as its limitations. Perhaps most important, no company better illustrates how to sell complete solutions as well as survive potentially disruptive changes in technology and markets.

The history of this remarkable firm dates back to the Tabulating Machine Company, founded in 1896. In that era, various companies introduced electric tabulating machines for sorting census data and then for handling similar data processing applications, such as for the insurance industry.[21] By the 1930s, IBM became the leader in the tabulating field. Success in those days depended on applications, sales, and service, as well as continual and incremental upgrades in system performance. Success also required a vision of the mass market, not simply a strategy of providing machines for specialized applications, such as the census. It is striking how similar IBM's formula for success was in tabulating machines compared to mainframes and office computers after World War II.[22]

The "Whole-Product Solution"

Long before Geoffrey Moore published *Crossing the Chasm* in 1991, IBM had discovered the value of offering a whole-product solution. It drove sales by understanding customer needs and mastering the skills of marketing and service, rather than by providing leading-edge technology. Moreover, unlike Microsoft, no one can accuse IBM of being "lucky." It became the dominant player in the computer industry because of its great strategic and organizational flexibility, as well as its superior capabilities and resources, compared to those of its competitors. Both before and after World War II, IBM demonstrated remarkable strengths:

- A deep understanding of business applications that required data processing
- Large and effective sales and support organizations
- A continuous revenue stream from rentals, starting with older tabulating machines and then new electronic computers, which made it possible to invest consistently in new products and services
- A wide array of complementary products, such as punch cards and printers, that attracted customers as well as generated large revenues and profits
- R and D targeted not at offering technology for technology's sake but at helping customers perform their work better
- A growing set of services—systems engineering, hardware support, software support, applications development, and eventually IT strategy—that attracted and kept customers as well as generated additional revenues and profits, adding to IBM's recurring revenue streams
- Increasingly modular computer systems, especially those designed after 1960, which allowed and even encouraged users to move up to more powerful machines

In the years immediately following World War II, it became apparent in the office equipment industry that the new electronic computer would make electromechanical tabulating machines obsolete. In response to this threat, IBM began R and D on computers and entered the industry with its first computerlike product in 1949, the Card-Programmed Calculator. It then followed with machines such as the 701 (initially called the Defense Calculator) in 1952 and the 650 in 1953, which turned out to be a great commercial success.[23] Most significant is that IBM made its entrance into the computer industry merely by incorporating electronics into its existing solutions, which solved existing business problems for organizations that had to do a large number of calculations and keep track of a great quantity of data, such as the insurance industry. IBM quickly became the market leader in mainframe computers.

For the record, we must note that IBM had plenty of competition in the mainframe market when it started. In the early 1950s, some forty companies were competing in the new computer business. They fell into three categories: control equipment manufacturers (mainly RCA, GE, and Honeywell), business machine manufacturers (Remington Rand, Burroughs, and NCR), and start-ups at the leading edge of the technology (UNIVAC, taken over by Remington Rand in 1950, and Control Data Corporation). The UNIVAC, introduced in 1951, was the first commercial computer to use magnetic tape. Its designers, John Eckert and John Mauchly, had previously built the ENIAC vacuum tube computer at the University of Pennsylvania and then, in 1946, founded their own company, which Remington Rand absorbed in 1950. The UNIVAC also had the first business (data processing) applications and started the mainframe era as we know it.

By 1960, the industry had delivered approximately five thousand computers in the United States and perhaps as many as two thousand in the rest of the world. IBM was now a $2 billion company with more than 100,000 employees. In 1962, sales of IBM computers finally surpassed those of its traditional punch-card tabulating machines. Helping IBM achieve this level of sales was a breakthrough product called the 1401, introduced in fall 1959. This was a fully transistorized computer with an advanced magnetic drum for memory storage and a high-speed printer. The 1401 was clearly a total computing solution that set the tone for future IBM products. Martin Campbell-Kelly and William Aspray, two historians of the computer industry, described

the characteristics of this product and how it demonstrated strengths
that enabled IBM to dominate the mainframe era:

> The technocrats at IBM . . . were overridden by the marketing man-
> agers, who recognized that customers were more interested in the solu-
> tion to business problems than in the technical merits of competing
> computer designs. As a result, IBM engineers were forced into taking a
> total-system view of computers—that is, a holistic approach that re-
> quired them to 'take into account programming, customer transition,
> field service, training, spare parts, logistics, etc.' This was the philoso-
> phy that brought success to the IBM 650 in the 1950s and would soon
> bring it to the model 1401. It is, in fact, what most differentiated IBM
> from its major competitors.[24]

Students of strategy and business history will note that IBM could
have gone a very different route and not become such a powerful firm
in the computer business. In the 1950s, IBM managers and engineers
might have become enamored with the new computer technology and
lost sight of what their customers actually needed to do with advanced calculating machines. They did not. In the 1960s, IBM managers might have maximized the company's short-term profits by
selling incompatible product lines and ignoring the difficulty of offering customers compatible products that used the same software assets. Again, they did not.

During the early 1960s, IBM made seven incompatible computers
of different sizes and purposes (business versus scientific). Providing
software that met evolving customer needs for all these different machines was technically difficult and expensive. This prompted IBM to
design the System/360 family of computers. These machines involved
many technical compromises but optimized software compatibility.
They eliminated the need to rewrite software when customers upgraded to more powerful computers, which they inevitably did. The
family concept of compatible machines was so valuable to so many
customers that it allowed IBM to overcome its mediocre circuit
technology (there were no integrated circuits in the first System/360
machines) and mediocre software technology (no time-sharing; expensive and buggy operating system and applications).[25]

The Limits of IBM's Software Capabilities

One can learn a great deal about the history of software engineering as well as what to do and what not to do from studying IBM's software projects. Not only did the company serve as a prime contractor for SAGE and other government or military systems in the 1950s, but OS/360 was the biggest programming effort ever attempted to that time. It took some five thousand person-years (one thousand–plus people) between 1963 and 1966, required more than 1 million lines of code, and cost half a billion dollars—four times the original budget.[26] The software was a year late and very buggy, and inspired one of the managers, Frederick Brooks, to publish, in 1975, a classic treatise on software development entitled *The Mythical Man-Month*. As I noted in Chapter 1, one of the key observations Brooks made was that, for a large programming effort, numbers of people and months of labor are not interchangeable. He found that adding people to a project that was late usually made it later because of the geometrically increasing communication and coordination problems that developed as a team expanded in size.[27]

IBM's difficulties led to a broader recognition that writing software and managing large projects required special efforts. Programmers and managers at IBM as well as at other companies and universities created a new field called "software engineering" in the late 1960s and early 1970s. The goal was to bring industrial discipline, methods, and tools to software development. These efforts resulted in process innovations such as structured programming techniques (top-down hierarchical design, progressively hiding lower-level details from higher levels), formal methods (a math-based approach to defining and testing system requirements or specifications), and the life-cycle model for project and product management (incremental releases and maintenance enhancements).[28] Other process innovations at a more detailed level included design and code reviews (sometimes called "inspections") and collection of statistical data on projects to improve schedule estimates and quality analysis. These and other approaches would later become more refined in Japanese software factories and in a set of recommendations from the Software Engineering Institute (SEI), funded by the U.S. Department of Defense and based at Carnegie Mellon University.

But despite its long record of achievements in software development, in the 1980s and much of the 1990s IBM was unable to translate its mainframe programming skills to the new world of personal computers. Its near absence in the PC software market created an enormous gap, especially given the fact that, unlike in the mainframe business, there were minimal entry barriers for PC software entrepreneurs. Start-ups such as Digital Research (headed by Gary Kildall, the inventor of the CP/M operating system, who declined to do business with IBM), Microsoft (headed by a college dropout named Bill Gates), and Seattle Computer Products (which hired Tim Patterson, inventor of the original DOS program, based on CP/M) needed just a handful of programmers. The platform standards, defined by the IBM PC in 1981, based on Intel and Microsoft products, constituted a relatively "open" technology. IBM foolishly did not retain rights to the Intel microprocessor architecture or to the operating system, DOS, which it had asked Microsoft to develop. The millions of IBM and IBM-compatible PCs flooding the market by the mid-1980s prompted hundreds of new entrepreneurs to establish their own software companies and enter the PC applications business. IBM, meanwhile, went into decline, until revived by Lou Gerstner in the 1990s.

Services, Services, Services!

Even though IBM after 1980 is partially a story of lost opportunities, it is still impressive how the company managed to hold its own through revolutionary technological and market transitions. Previously, IBM had dominated tabulating machines as well as mainframe computers—two very different technologies. But the customer set and the applications remained similar in both eras, and this similarity made it possible for IBM to continue dominating the computing business through the 1970s and into the 1980s. It was the PC era that brought the greatest challenges to the dominant computer vendor because of the much wider range of customers and applications that appeared. Eventually, however, IBM again found a way to compete successfully by exploiting its broad technical and marketing skills as well as its deep knowledge of enterprise customers and their computing needs.

It is well known how far IBM's fortunes fell during the 1990s as clusters of powerful PCs and workstations took on many of the programming tasks once reserved for mainframe and midrange computers. IBM had faced threats before, such as from smaller computers (usually called minicomputers) produced by Digital Equipment Corporation (now a unit of Hewlett-Packard). DEC's PDP-8, introduced for the commercial market in 1965, sold for a mere $18,000, compared to half a million dollars or more for a small IBM mainframe. By 1970, DEC had become the third largest computer manufacturer and was challenging IBM directly, at least in the smaller mainframe business.[29] IBM managers eventually recognized the challenges that DEC posed and introduced their own midrange machines. When it came to the personal computer, IBM executives allowed a new business unit to enter the market; however, overall, they underestimated how much this new product would affect the company's primary business.

In 1993, IBM recorded one of the largest annual losses in corporate history, $8.9 billion. This seems to pale in comparison with today's corporate losses attributed to write-downs in the value of acquisitions made during the Internet boom. AOL Time Warner, for example, posted a loss of *$100 billion* for 2002, mostly due to the drop in value of the AOL property. In terms of real money rather than inflated stock prices, however, IBM's loss was and remains a staggering sum. In part it was due to management's decision to lay off more than eighty thousand people from all areas of the company before launching a new hiring wave, mostly in services, in the later 1990s.

Then, in 1993, in came Louis Gerstner as CEO, the ex-McKinsey consultant who had served as an executive at American Express as well as CEO of RJR Nabisco, before joining IBM. Under Gerstner's leadership, IBM underwent a remarkable recovery. It is no longer the dominant provider of hardware and software solutions, and, despite a revival, still has much less influence than Microsoft. But IBM has once again become an influential and highly profitable "total solutions" vendor of computer hardware, software, and services. Gerstner, in many ways, merely went back to what IBM had always done well: focusing on customer needs and applications, rather than technologies. But what he did is important to understand because other dominant players in the business, including Microsoft, may have to undergo similar transformations in the future.

Rather than breaking IBM up into thirteen smaller separate companies in an attempt to become more nimble, which his predecessor, John Akers, had planned to do, Gerstner decided to keep IBM together. His strategy was to leverage IBM's R-and-D breadth and its ability to be a "one-stop shop" for different kinds of hardware and software products and services. He dealt with the issue of nimbleness by eliminating bureaucratic organizational structures and procedures and reducing unneeded head count. More significantly, as chronicled by Steve Lohr in a *New York Times* profile, Gerstner made three specific changes.[30]

First, he set up a new services unit—called IBM Global Services—to sell bundles of hardware, software, consulting, and maintenance services. IBM had been building up its services business for years, of course. What was different about the new unit was its mission to sell and service not only IBM products, as in the past, but also the products of major industry vendors, including those of rivals such as Microsoft, Oracle, and Sun Microsystems. In other words, *Gerstner decided to make services in a neutral sense as important as or perhaps more important than the company's proprietary hardware and software products.*

Second, Gerstner decided to embrace "open systems"—that is, he would make IBM adopt standard protocols so that IBM software could run on different types of hardware, including competitors' machines, and IBM hardware could run different types of software. As part of this strategy, IBM became a champion of the Linux operating system, the multiplatform Java programming language, and the open-source Apache Web server for low-end Web hosting and applications. It also produced development tools to help programmers use these open-source technologies and Java to create new applications and custom systems for IBM customers. IBM engineers had already learned to deal with the Windows and UNIX platforms because these were important to IBM customers, so this move to adopt open systems fit into the company's pattern of offering whole product solutions.

Third, in 1995, Gerstner decided to embrace the Internet and meld it into a vision of "networked computing." This approach suited IBM especially well, as it could easily adapt the company's mainframes and midrange computers to become data servers on the Internet. IBM's software groups also built products such as WebSphere, one of the industry-leading Web application servers and a popular "middleware" program for linking different applications and processing transactions. In addition, the consulting arm of the company quickly learned how to help clients conduct "e-business." And the open-source interface standards and use of Java helped IBM connect its systems to the diverse computers and software programs being used on the Internet.[31]

I should add that in the mid-1990s Gerstner finally made a decision *to treat software as a business* and not as some incidental activity that

IBM undertook simply to sell hardware. When Gerstner became CEO, IBM had greater revenues from software than Microsoft did, but it had no specific strategy or organization for the business. In Gerstner's own words, this was a legacy of the past that he decided to change:

> Software, to IBM, was simply one part of a hardware-based offering. Since every computer needs an operating system, and most need databases and transaction processing capability, IBM built many of these software assets but never viewed them as a unique business. Rather, they were buried inside IBM hardware or sold as an add-on feature. And critically, none of this software worked with computers made by manufacturers other than IBM. . . . IBM had 4,000 software products, all of which were branded with separate names. . . . They were made in more than thirty different laboratories around the world. There was no management system, no model for how a software company should run, and no skills in selling software as a separate product.[32]

Gerstner began to fix this enormous problem late in 1994 by appointing John Thompson, who had been running the server group, to be the executive in charge of IBM's entire software business. Over the next two years, Thompson centralized the management system and consolidated IBM's sixty software brands into six, reduced the thirty development labs to eight, and hired five thousand new software sales specialists and then another five thousand by the year 2000. Meanwhile, Gerstner refocused IBM's software strategy by ending the development of OS/2 and the losing battle with Microsoft over the PC platform, and authorizing Thompson to put nearly all of IBM's software resources into Internet middleware and open systems. It was also Thompson who convinced Gerstner in 1995 to acquire Lotus for $3.2 billion in order to increase IBM's presence in collaboration software and Internet servers—a move that helped change IBM's culture from one of a staid mainframe company into one of a more dynamic software and services company that also sold hardware.[33]

The Gerstner Legacy and Beyond

Between 1992, the year before Gerstner arrived, and 2001, his last full year as CEO, IBM's annual revenues in its core hardware business were stagnant, at roughly $33 billion. IBM showed modest increases in software product revenues, from $11.1 billion to $13 billion. But company revenues grew from $64.5 billion in 1992 to $85.9 billion largely on the basis of an increase in service revenues—from $15 billion (23 percent of total sales) to $35 billion (41 percent). In 2001, for the first time, IBM's service revenues passed its hardware revenues. Hardware revenues then saw a major decline in 2002, when IBM sold its data storage business to Hitachi. Services and hardware were both relatively labor-intensive and had much lower gross margins than software. Nonetheless, services have been essential to maintain the growth of the company and invaluable as a recurring source of revenues and profits (see Figure 3-1 and Appendix Table 12).

Perhaps more important, as I noted in Chapter 2, IBM has been able to decouple many of its service revenues from software product sales *in a good way.* Its management consulting and e-business practices, as well as its open-source systems consulting and integration work, have enabled IBM to grow its services revenues much faster than just selling IBM's software product revenues would have done.[34]

What Gerstner did also seems rather bold strategically. It is hard to imagine the other industry giant, Microsoft, so eagerly embracing the

Figure 3-1: IBM Revenue Comparison, 1992 and 2001–2002

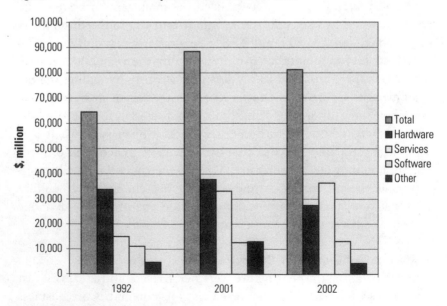

Source: *Company annual reports.*

technologies of rival firms such as IBM, Oracle, Netscape, and Sun Microsystems, or pushing Linux and Apache in favor of its own products (which IBM was doing). Indeed, a judge had to order Microsoft in December 2002 and again in January 2003 to install Java software, made by Sun Microsystems, in the latest version of Windows.[35] Making customer solutions so central to its strategy also differed from the approach of other industry giants, such as SAP. The German company sold comprehensive solutions, heavily laden with its own or third-party services, but its solutions often required customers to adapt to the SAP software, rather than the other way around—a very different model for doing business.

One can be more cynical about IBM's transformation. As another journalist argued, to some extent IBM's strategy under Gerstner merely changed from locking in customers with proprietary technology to locking in customers with "irreplaceable IT services."[36] And the old strategy of selling IBM solutions may not be dead anyway. I have heard from IBM sales and marketing people that, though they do sell products from different vendors, they continue to try to steer customers toward IBM hardware and software whenever possible. One would expect IBM people to do this, even though they may not admit it for the record.

It is also true that IBM's financial picture may not have been quite as rosy as Gerstner wanted investors and analysts to believe. For most of Gerstner's reign as CEO, his financial staff made sure that profits rose even though sales did not, even if it required manipulating IBM's pension fund, buying back IBM shares ($44 billion worth between 1995 and 2001[37]), or selling off pieces of the company to make the quarterly targets. Revenues and profits also fell in 2002 compared to the previous year's.

On the other hand, in late July 2002, IBM management was sufficiently positive about the services side of the business to buy PricewaterhouseCoopers Consulting for some $3.5 billion. This was the same business that Hewlett-Packard had been negotiating to buy for $18 billion in the fall of 2000. PWC Consulting had annual revenues of nearly $5 billion as well as some thirty thousand employees, and focused heavily on strategic as well as information technology consulting. IBM planned to lay off some of these people, and it expected to lose some PWC business that was going to its competitors in the computer industry. Nonetheless, the acquisition was a good fit for IBM and should increase its ability to grow services faster than software product revenues.[38]

More manpower for the services business was also important for IBM's next big push, which new CEO Sam Palmisano called "on-demand computing." This idea was similar to the concept of "Web services" talked about at Microsoft, Oracle, and Hewlett-Packard. IBM's strategy was to make software products available over servers so that, instead of buying software products, customers would pay for software usage as they would for a utility such as electricity or telephones. IBM was in an especially good position to push this model of computing because of its extensive offerings in server hardware, Web software such as WebSphere, and an army of consultants and technical support personnel to help clients install the new systems.[39] To extend its offerings, IBM also announced in December 2002 that it would purchase the leading software development tools vendor, Rational Software, which had one thousand professionals offering various services to support software development and project management.[40]

Gerstner has often liked to present himself as a nontechnical person and "merely" a Harvard MBA. In truth, though, he studied engineering as an undergraduate at Dartmouth, and he spent a lot of time thinking about information systems as a user at American Express and other companies. But Gerstner continued the tradition among IBM executives of not letting technology dominate the business, but of putting customer needs and business strategy first. The changes he made worked brilliantly and provide another illustration of how companies in the computer industry can effectively mix products with services.

NEW ENTREPRENEURS FOR A NEW PLATFORM

IBM survived the personal computer and the Internet and has reemerged as a strong player in corporate computing and services. But the introduction of the PC began a new era of mass-market software, coupled with cheap hardware that required a new generation of entrepreneurs to master. In the early 2000s, there were some 400 million users of personal computers. There were an even larger number of cell phone users, with devices that were increasingly taking on

PC-like characteristics (witness the Nokia Communicator). In order to understand the software business today and where it is likely to go in the future, it is worth reviewing why the PC business departed from the pattern of mainframes.[41]

The Emergence of PC Hardware and Software

First, we must give credit where credit is due. The microprocessor, as developed primarily at Intel during 1969–1971 but also at companies such as Texas Instruments and Motorola, was the "enabling technology" that allowed the PC industry to emerge. Individuals and companies that built personal computers and mastered how to program microprocessors made the PC software business possible. The software technology was challenging in the 1970s and early 1980s, even though many people saw the first PCs as hobbyist toys. Programming PCs in the early years was very much like programming mainframe computers in the 1950s in machine and then assembly languages.

In the first couple years of the PC software business, the most prominent companies identified new horizontal markets—systems software and programming tools—so that buyers of PC kits could make the machines do something useful.[42] In the mainframe era, computer vendors such as IBM produced hardware, systems software, and programming tools. In the PC era, these areas constituted enormous horizontal market opportunities for new companies specializing in different types of software. There was, for instance, the now-infamous Digital Research, established by Gary Kildall. He designed the eight-bit CP/M operating system, which ran on many machines of that era and eventually sold as many as 200 million copies.[43] Then Microsoft appeared with a version of BASIC and then other languages. Both companies sold their software to hardware manufacturers, which bundled the systems software products with their machines. The market perhaps totaled a couple of million dollars by 1976–1977, but no more than that.

As in the mainframe era, technical improvements in PC hardware and new enabling software technologies led to new hardware products and then new software applications. For the new PCs, however, the user base initially consisted of sophisticated individuals, not enterprises. In the later 1970s, PCs appeared that were specifically designed for consumers, such as the Apple II, the Commodore PET, and the Tandy TRS-80. They stimulated new horizontal and vertical markets, beginning with games such as Space and Star Trek. PC hobbyists and technology enthusiasts were the main customers. Next came a wave of educational programs, especially for the Apple II, such as for learning math, music, languages, and science. Schools and colleges, as well as a few enlightened parents, became the new customers. Then, in the late 1970s and early 1980s, the horizontal segments for packaged business applications began to grow, particularly for spreadsheets and word processors—a small market movement that would soon become an avalanche. The first year for which we have PC software statistics sales is 1981, when the total was $140 million. Microsoft was still a minor player, with sales of merely $16 million and 130 employees. By 1984, the market was $1.6 billion, though Microsoft still had only a tiny portion of this market, with sales of $97 million.[44]

Start-up entrepreneurs who had the vision to foresee new uses and markets for the PC were important in all these cases. The story is well known how, in 1979, a Harvard MBA student, Dan Bricklin, teamed up with a programmer friend, Bob Frankston, to create VisiCalc, based on his vision of an electronic spreadsheet. It was a remarkable tool for anyone who wanted to do a series of calculations without having to recalculate each row or column of numbers. The program ran on the Apple II and found a new audience: businessmen and accountants. Lotus 1-2-3, introduced in 1983 by Mitch Kapor's company, Lotus, for the IBM PC, would later make spreadsheets a household word. Word processing took a bit more sophistication when PC hardware and printers began to be able to represent on-screen type accurately on printed pages, but this application began to take off after 1979–1980 as well. The key entrepreneur in this case was Seymour Rubinstein, who founded a company called MicroPro in 1978. The following year, the company introduced WordStar, which quickly gained two-thirds of the small market. Within five years, MicroPro was a $100-million-a-year business, before being eclipsed by WordPerfect and Microsoft Word.

Then, of course, IBM entered the PC market in 1981, making this new niche technology more legitimate for the business mass market. Because IBM had weak PC programming skills in-house, it followed the outsourcing strategy that had worked for PC hardware: it contracted with Microsoft and several other firms for the systems and applications software to be bundled with the IBM PC. During the next few years, most other major PC manufacturers (except Apple) switched to making IBM-compatible PCs running Microsoft DOS. The clone makers gave further momentum to the new mass market of PC software, which has become increasingly segmented and sophisticated as each year has passed.

PC Software as a New Mass Market

Two points about the new PC software business deserve special note. One is that PC software resembled many new mass markets, ranging from automobiles in the early 1900s to mainframes in the 1950s. There was a quick expansion in the number of firms in the first few years, until a standard platform or dominant design emerged. In the PC era, Microsoft defined the key systems software standards while Intel defined the key hardware platform standards. IBM, at least initially, acted as the system architect, until being replaced in this leadership role by Intel, Microsoft, and a combination of other firms during the late 1980s.

Another point is that the new software business was developed by new entrepreneurs with new programming and marketing skills. Firms that had made software products for mainframes and minicomputers were largely nonplayers in PC software. Similarly, with the exception of IBM, the most important PC hardware manufacturers were also new firms that were much more oriented toward selling to mass markets, including both individuals and enterprises. It is true that IBM sold millions of PCs and later tried to make an impact on PC software. But PCs were largely a peripheral business for IBM, and its main systems software effort for PCs (OS/2) was a market failure. PC software and hardware were, at least for the mass market, a new commodity game of products more than services or hybrid solutions.

With all its faults, Microsoft has defined the best model for how to run a mass-market software products business. Bill Gates and Paul Allen were not simply the lucky beneficiaries of IBM's mistakes or weaknesses. They were truly among the pioneers of PC software as a *business* as well as a *technology*. They developed the first programming language (a version of BASIC) for a PC before there was even a market. Their innovation made it possible for thousands of individuals to write applications and other kinds of software that were necessary to fuel the PC revolution.

Moreover, Gates made it clear to the world that PC software was a business and the source of his livelihood and that of many other people. Shortly after he cofounded Microsoft in 1975, Gates began speaking at conferences and published an open letter to hobbyists in a leading computer magazine. He railed against the custom of pirating software, copying it freely, and giving it away. Pirating is a practice that has existed since the 1950s in the computing community and that has recently reached enormous proportions in developing countries. Gates insisted that programmers like himself were in the business of writing code and deserved to be paid for their labor.[45] Many people did not like Gates's insistence on charging money for software but eventually enough people agreed to make for-profit PC software companies economically feasible.

The PC software business, in other words, faced an initial hurdle similar in some ways to that which the mainframe software business had to overcome. In the 1950s, hardware customers considered programming a service that they should receive for free. They expected hardware manufacturers to give software away, often at enormous expense. In the PC era, and continuing through the Internet era, many users viewed software as a public good that they were entitled to use for free. A number of PC software entrepreneurs disagreed and created the business that I am now writing about. I will return to this subject later when I talk about open-source and free software.

The Fragility of Mass-Market Success

Another important characteristic of the PC software business was the low entry barriers for firms wishing to enter. Microsoft started out with two people borrowing computer time (illegally, as it turned out) at Harvard University, where Gates was enrolled during 1973–1975. Users in the first few years after the introduction of the Altair computer were mostly sophisticated hobbyists. They did not need zero-defect software, elaborate programming manuals, or much in the way of technical support. In other words, they did not need the "whole-product solution" that late adopters required. As a result, thousands of individuals started software products companies in the late 1970s and 1980s, all chasing the enormous pot of gold promised by writing a "killer app" that might sell in the tens of thousands or millions. Few companies achieved this level of success, of course, but many people shared the dream.

But as I look at the business today, it seems that success for PC software companies may also be more elusive than it was for players in the mainframe software business. PC software companies have the ability to grow at enormous rates by tapping a global mass market for packaged products. But they need hit products to achieve such growth. Moreover, once packaged software producers saturate their market or inspire low-priced similar products, they either have to design another hit—which is hard to do—or learn how to manage a maturing business, like IBM and other mainframe software vendors before them. I mentioned in Chapter 2 how a maturing software business requires services and regular upgrades that can generate recurring revenues. Upgrades need only one or two new features that are sufficiently compelling to persuade existing customers to buy new versions of what are essentially the same products. But coming up with compelling new features that consistently attract new users is hard to do.

PC software companies also have to worry about creating new products and upgrades in step with a continuously and sometimes rapidly evolving technology. Compared to the mainframe business, where software written in the 1960s and 1970s continues to run in many organizations, the PC business has already seen two major shifts, and a third one (Web services) is already on the horizon. One shift was from character-based DOS technology as the user interface during most of the 1980s, except for the relatively small Macintosh market, to graphical computing in the Windows format. Windows, like the Macintosh, required a very different style of design and programming. Many firms that dominated in the previous era, like Word-Perfect and Lotus, failed to retain their dominance in the Windows era. Of course, Microsoft had special advantages as the developer of Windows as well as of applications programs. Bill Gates also made sure that Microsoft acquired experience in graphical applications; he hired people from Xerox PARC and Apple, and Microsoft became the most important provider of Macintosh applications after Apple introduced the machine in 1984 (a fact that critics of Gates and Microsoft tend to forget).

The other major transition PC software providers and users are still adapting to is the Internet. This new technology provided an opportunity for a wave of new software firms to emerge and dominate new segments, at least for a time (such as Netscape in browsers and

BEA Systems in Web application servers). Microsoft managed this second transition well despite its usual late start, even though it was more revolutionary and disruptive than the transition to graphical computing. Learning from the past, IBM's software groups also adapted to the Internet much better than they had to the personal computer, perhaps because the Internet is really a form of massively distributed client-server computing. But not all firms are able to make these transitions.

The final point to note is that despite the enormity of their market opportunities, even successful PC or Internet software firms may be no more than one-hit or temporary wonders. The PC and Internet software businesses have not been as stable as that of mainframe software, where some firms have forty or even fifty-year track records, due largely to "locking in" enterprise customers and selling them long-term contracts for product upgrades and services. If history is any guide, PC software companies will also have to grow the services side of their business if they are to survive the ups and downs of the software products market.

THE INTERNET "GOLD RUSH"

Most readers of this book probably experienced firsthand how the software business went through a rocketlike surge upward after 1994 with the appearance of the World Wide Web as a graphical user interface for the Internet. The Web did not begin as a commercial venture touching everyone's lives. In 1989, Tim Berners-Lee, an expert in UNIX programming who worked at the CERN physics lab in Switzerland, designed a browser and set of communications protocols that used servers and hyperlinks on the Internet.[46] These software technologies made it possible to jump from one site to another with the ease of simply clicking a computer mouse. His purpose was to make it easier for scientific researchers to share information and data by using the Internet, which had been in place for twenty years or so but was hard to use and tolerated mainly by academic and government researchers.

In 1993, Marc Andreessen and a handful of other college students working at the National Center for Supercomputer Applications (NCSA), based at the University of Illinois, developed the graphical

Mosaic browser, which ran on Windows PCs and Macintosh computers as well as UNIX workstations. They opened up the Internet—through what became known as the World Wide Web—to millions of additional, though still sophisticated, users. Netscape appeared in 1994 with the Navigator browser, a refined version of Mosaic. Then Microsoft bundled its Internet Explorer browser "free" with Windows 95. The Internet, through the World Wide Web, quickly became a tool for e-commerce and then for mass consumption of content and services, accessible not only through personal computers or workstations but also through handheld devices and Web-enabled cellular phones.

Opportunities for New Software Products

The new technology generated demand for new types of software products—a variety of systems and server software, middleware products, applications, and content management tools. For example, Netscape, Microsoft, and IBM, soon joined by newcomers such as BEA Systems and too many other firms to list here, developed a variety of servers and tools to create Web sites and distribute content, e-mail, and applications over the Internet. Sun Microsystems developed Java, a programming language especially well suited to building applications based on servers and accessed through Internet browsers. Various companies and open-source groups produced scripting languages that evolved beyond the original text coding language of the Web, HTML (Hypertext Markup Language), to include JavaScript (developed at Netscape) and XML (Extensible Markup Language), developed between 1996 and 1998, which make it easier to build and link Web pages and databases distributed over the Internet. Companies introduced new versions of operating systems, servers, and applications that accommodated new technical standards, driven by companies such as Cisco Systems and Microsoft and standards bodies such as the World Wide Web Consortium (W3C) and the Internet Engineering Task Force (IETF), to make sure that different networking systems and modes of communication were able to operate together. New middleware software products emerged (they are so pervasive I think they should be called "every-ware") to do things such as link Web "front ends" (sites) with traditional mainframe computer systems and guarantee the security of online transactions.

The World Wide Web especially created a demand for new types of applications. By the end of the 1990s, trying to do business over the Internet—dubbed "e-business" or "e-commerce"—had became the equivalent of a modern-day gold rush. A new generation of "dot-com" entrepreneurs demanded software that would enable their new firms to do everything that was being done in the "old economy" on the Internet. They hoped to take advantage of global economies of scale and seemingly miniscule costs. Both the computer hardware and telecommunications industries benefited because most of the dot-com firms purchased large quantities of computer software, hardware, and telecommunications technology to create their Web sites and trans-action capabilities—even though the millions of paying customers they expected were slow to materialize. During 2001–2002, most of the dot coms faded or failed due to the absence of sufficient customers and staggering infrastructure costs. But developing systems to enable firms to do business over the Internet became standard practice for "old-economy" firms as well as newer firms.

Opportunities for New Software Services

In the 1990s, client-server computing and connecting back-office databases and applications to PCs and Internet "front ends" became more important. As this happened, the different worlds of large machines (mainframes and minicomputers), intermediate machines (workstations, mostly running UNIX but increasingly running Windows NT/2000/XP), and personal computers, aided again by the increasing power of the smaller machines, tended to converge. The need for integration or communication has brought the software producers for large machines (IBM, Compuware, Computer Associates, EDS, et al.) closer to the PC software world and prompted them to set up PC and e-business divisions that work across the technologies. In the Internet era, it also became very common for software and IT consulting firms, ranging from IBM to start-ups such as Razorfish and Sapient, to offer a new set of "e-business" services that combined consulting with systems design and software development. I like to break down the evolution of demand for these services into three overlapping stages.

The first stage is simply when customers want to *use the Internet to enhance their existing business models and operations,* whether back-office functions, supply-chain management, or direct-sales operations. For example, most ERP companies had to create browser-based versions of their applications, such as SAP and its MySAP applications suite. Business Objects created a Web version of its product that allows users to access and manipulate databases through a browser interface. Most of the company's sales now come from the Web version of the product, called WebIntelligence. Usually, the new Web software from companies such as SAP and Business Objects included improvements that made it easier for customers to use the programs or make changes themselves and customize menus. This first stage has generated enormous work for programmers and some new revenues as customers upgrade to Web-based versions of their products. Customers have not upgraded as quickly as many software companies had hoped, however, so many users are still in this first stage.

A second stage of e-business is when customers want to *use the Internet to create new products or services in traditional businesses.* Amazon.com and eBay are good examples here. Bookselling is an old business dating back to the Middle Ages, but Amazon has used unique software to create a virtual bookstore with millions of titles. It also connects buyers with publishers, although it has built its own warehouses, too. More interestingly, Amazon's databases and software agents track what customers buy and might like to buy, sending out e-mail recommendations or making suggestions while a customer is actually on its Web site. Auctions are an ancient business, dating back at least to Roman and Greek times. eBay has developed software to enable auctions to take place electronically among thousands of people located around the globe. Again, there are really no new business models here, but the power of the Internet makes it possible for entrepreneurs to offer new kinds of products and services.

The third stage of e-business is when customers want to *use the Internet to create totally new businesses.* This is much tougher to do. At a relatively simple level, Yahoo!, MSN, Netscape, AOL, and other Internet "portals" fall into this category. They serve as windows into a variety of information, products, and services available over the Internet and generate revenues through advertising and transaction fees, as well as some pay-for-service fees. We could not really have portal businesses without online networks such as the Internet. And the Internet is far more pervasive than proprietary networks such as AOL's. The third stage also has generated more interesting examples, again using the computing and communications capabilities of the Internet. We should note, though, that making money from these new business models has been difficult.

For example, Napster, founded by a college student named Shawn Fanning, was potentially a new type of business enabled by the technology and scale of the Internet—peer-to-peer trading of files, in this case, music. Fanning took advantage of MP3, an audio compression format that allows users to send music files over the Internet. At its peak in 2001, some 80 million people had downloaded the company's software. A very large percentage of these individuals were exchanging personal music files "for free." The recording industry started suing promoters of MP3 in 1999 and then, in mid-2000, targeted Napster. One problem for Napster was how to respect intellectual property rights and pay the artists or companies that owned the rights to the music. Another problem was how to make money from the technology and a service that the company gave away for free. With 80 million "eyeballs" coming to the site and many more potential users, I don't think the second problem was the most serious hurdle the company faced, but the management team never did find a solution. After lengthy court battles, Napster declared bankruptcy in May 2002. A few months later, Roxio, Inc., a digital media publisher, bought the rights to the Napster brand name for $5 million. It planned to introduce a for-pay online music service by the end of 2003, although it was not clear whether or not the new Napster would succeed under different ownership. In 2003, other types of pay services for music, using similar peer-to-peer technology, as well as various open-source programs, were becoming popular.[47]

Priceline.com, founded in 1998, is another case of an Internet-only kind of business. It provides a transaction service that resembles a "reverse auction," though it is somewhat different. Customers come into the Web site and bid on different items, primarily airline tickets and hotel rooms, but also loans and automobiles. Priceline.com then goes out and tries to find a vendor that will sell the goods or services at the desired price. We have never had customers bidding on items they want to buy on this kind of scale before. It is so new an idea that I place it into the third category. Despite the novelty, Priceline.com lost more than $1 billion in 1999 on sales of $482 million. It pared these losses down to only $19 million on sales of just over $1 billion in 2002 but was still losing money in 2003 due to decreased demand in the travel business.[48]

Affiliate marketing over the Web is another Internet-only kind of business. Be Free, for example, was a start-up founded in 1996. It created technology to track "click-through" sales of a vendor's products to customers who came into a Web site from other sites, including Internet portals. The companies or individuals that own the affiliated Web sites and that transfer traffic get a percentage of the sales. The site owners who get the click-through sales have to pay the affiliates from their revenues. Be Free got Barnesandnoble.com as its first customer in 1997 after Amazon.com developed its own affiliated marketing program and click-through technology. It seemed to be on a fast track for growth, but the affiliate sales, and Web sales in general, never reached the proportions that Internet pundits once predicted. Be Free's business model also required a lot of investment in technology as well as a large number of people in sales, marketing, and services. The company helped clients find and contract with affiliated Web sites, as well as set up the click-through system. Like Priceline.com, Be Free lost tens of millions of dollars in its first few years of operation. But unlike Priceline.com, it had dim prospects of ever making a profit and merged with ValueClick in mid-2002. ValueClick, founded only in 1998, provides "cost-per-click" Web advertising solutions. Its prospects are not very bright, either; the company had sales of about $62 million in 2002 but losses of more than $10 million.[49]

We now know that thousands of entrepreneurs around the world believed the Internet would create magical economies of scale as millions of users flocked to their Web sites. They didn't anticipate the millions of Web sites that companies and individuals would create and the great cost of getting customers to come to one particular site. So most dot coms died as a result of high customer acquisition costs as well as the large investments they made in software and hardware to support a large business that never materialized. Many of these dot coms fell into the second stage of e-business, although others are in stage three. We are currently in the midst of a consolidation phase, much as the PC software industry experienced in the later 1980s and early 1990s. A small number of software companies that have solid businesses and solid technology will survive in the lasting niches and mass markets created by the Internet, though some are being challenged by software that is free.

OPEN-SOURCE AND "FREE" SOFTWARE

I cannot conclude a chapter on the history of commercial software without saying something about a somewhat peculiar slice of the business: open-source and other "free" software. The jury is not yet in about the implications for software as a business for entrepreneurs, but many users clearly have benefited from the availability of source code and free programs. Some commercial companies have suffered from the competition as well.

Some Background

The term "open source" refers to software programs whose source code is freely available, such as through Internet sites, and generally not owned and sold by any one person or organization, though there are some exceptions. The Open Source Initiative (OSI) was founded in 1998 by Chris Peterson, Eric Raymond, and a few other colleagues to promote the development and use of open-source programs.[50] The basic premise, from the Open Source Initiative Web site, states the case: "When programmers can read, redistribute, and modify the source code for a piece of software, the software evolves. People improve it, people adapt it, people fix bugs. And this can happen at a speed that, if one is used to the slow pace of conventional software development, seems astonishing."[51]

The availability of free software, as well as the idea of distributing a piece of software (at the level of source code) and hoping that other programmers will take it and improve upon it, is much older than the OSI group. It dates back to the 1950s, when user groups emerged to promote the free sharing of programs—SHARE for users of IBM computers and USE for users of UNIVAC computers.[52] Projects at MIT and other universities in the 1960s funded by the U.S. Department of Defense's Advanced Research Projects Agency (ARPA), including efforts such as Project MAC, Multics, and the establishment of the Internet (once called ARPANET) itself included free software. In addition, since the development of the UNIX operating system at AT&T in the late 1960s, individual developers, government laboratories, and companies have created a wealth of software—not all have been refined enough for me to use the word "product," though many were—available for people to use, revise, expand, and circulate.

The best-known programs whose source code is openly available and free, for the most part, are the Linux operating system (patterned after UNIX and used in 2002 by somewhere between 4 and 27 million people[53]), the Apache Web server (the most popular Web server in the world but limited in functionality), and the Mozilla Internet browser (the open-source version of Netscape Navigator). There are many other open-source programs available through Internet sites, including basic applications such as the StarOffice suite, which Sun Microsystems used to distribute for free but now sells for $75.95.[54] Commercial companies such as Oracle, Corel, and IBM also made some of their products to run on Linux or to work with Apache and other open-source software.

Microsoft is still watching Linux and the open-source movement carefully, to see what kind of demand it might create for applications as well as what threat it poses to its own proprietary solutions. Nonetheless, even Bill Gates has been forced to accommodate the open-source movement. To compete with Linux, for example, Microsoft announced in January 2003 that it would provide copies of most of its Windows source code (Windows XP, 2000, and CE) for free to government customers, primarily so that they could evaluate for themselves how reliable and secure Microsoft software is. Governments would also be able to add their own security software to the Windows code. Although Microsoft had already indicated in 2002 that it might do something of this sort and had provided its code to NATO and the Russian government, it is a remarkable change in the historical strategy of the company, which has been to protect the proprietary Windows platform at almost all costs.[55]

Positive Implications for the Software Business

There are clearly some positive implications of open-source and free software for people interested in software's commercial aspects. First, and perhaps most important, open-source types of activities have promoted behavioral norms that enable many programmers around the world—numbering in the hundreds and perhaps thousands for Linux—to participate in a widely distributed and loosely coordinated innovation process. Users can contribute more than ideas: they can take the source code for a software product and make it do something better than it did before or make it do something entirely new. Malleable technologies such as software make it relatively easy for a distributed network of users to have an impact on the design of products they want to use and contribute inventions that users can then take and improve upon. For researchers who have long believed that users are important innovators, open-source software provides important evidence of how right they may be.[56]

Second, the open-source phenomenon has increased the availability of important software products or technologies—for free. Some of these have made major contributions to society as well as to the evolution of software and information technology. The Internet and the World Wide Web are the best examples. The original browser and server technology, developed by Tim Berners-Lee at CERN in the late 1980s and early 1990s, as well as the Mosaic browser, developed at NCSA, were all made available for free, at least initially. (NCSA later licensed Mosaic code to Microsoft and other firms through a corporate spin-off called Spry.) In addition to Apache as a Web server, the Sendmail program for using the Internet to send and receive e-mail is another widely used and important technology that comes from the open-source community.

Third, there have been some new business opportunities. A number of commercial ("for profit") firms have attempted to exploit the open-source movement and the interest in programs such as Linux, although the record here is not good. The most prominent examples in the Linux market are Red Hat (founded in 1994), VA Software (formerly VA Linux, founded in 1993), the SCO Group (a merger of Caldera Systems, founded in 1994, and SCO, founded in 1979), and Turbo Linux (a private company founded in 1992). These companies all sold special versions of Linux that packaged the free software with a bundle of utilities (such as special installation programs or development tools) and applications as well as service and support. Through 2002, however, none had managed to turn a profit. Some had large public stock offerings in the latter 1990s, though share prices came quickly down to earth even before the crash of the NASDAQ stock market. Some of the losses were staggering, albeit the figures are improving. For example: VA Software had revenues of only about $150 million over the two-year period 2001–2002, along with net losses of $525 million in 2001 and $91 million in 2002. In the first nine months of fiscal 2003 (through April), it had pared its losses down to only $11 million, but its revenues were a meager $17.7 million.[57] Caldera, which produced several products, had net losses of more than $131 million in 2001 and nearly $25 million in 2002, with 2002 revenues of about $64 million.[58]

There were also several cases of software products or solutions companies that explored different ways to take advantage of the open-source movement to enhance their platforms or generate complementary products. Netscape, for example, released the source code for the Navigator browser in 1999. It has benefitted from some improvements from the open-source community, though they have been slow to appear and not enough to reverse the decline in market share relative to Microsoft's Internet Explorer.[59]

IBM presents perhaps the most commercially successful example of mixing open-source, free software, and for-profit business. In June 1998, it announced that it would ship the high-end WebSphere application server with Apache, the open-source software that was the world's leading Web server product in terms of market share.[60] Although IBM had a basic Web server product of its own, it had a miniscule market share. The company decided to drop the in-house product and adopt as well as enhance Apache, adding any new code from IBM programmers to the open-source pool. The purpose, of course, was to sell more servers and treat Apache as a complement to IBM hardware. The ploy worked, at least after IBM committed to offering technical support for Apache. IBM next adapted Linux to work on its servers as well—another move that made the IBM server hardware more popular.[61]

The fact that a major commercial producer of hardware and software embraced Apache truly stood out as a landmark move. This product was an important complement to Linux. In many ways, Apache was the "killer app" that made Linux a serious alternative platform to UNIX and Windows NT/2000. In addition, IBM gave tremendous credibility to the open-source movement as a source of complements for a platform product.

Negatives and Question Marks

The open-source phenomenon also contains some negatives and open questions for the software business. Most frustrating for managers, programmers, and entrepreneurs is when their company is selling a certain software product and then an open-source product appears that is as good or better—and *free*. For example, Linux probably has hurt sales of UNIX and UNIX-based workstations more than it has those of Windows and PCs. Companies that have tried to sell Linux bundled with special installation utilities, applications, and support services, such as Red Hat, have also struggled.

SCO, for example, has depended on UNIX licenses for revenues and, despite distributing Linux, now sees another opportunity to earn money: it has argued that IBM included proprietary UNIX code, which SCO acquired from Novell in 1995, in its open-source Linux code.[62] The company terminated IBM's right to use the software and is suing for $3 billion as well as indicating that it may demand payments from vendors and users of Linux—not what Linus Torvalds and other Linux advocates had in mind when they developed the operating system.

The positive spin to all this, of course, is that for-profit companies that make products that compete with open-source programs or "free but not free" software products—such as software that Microsoft bundles with Windows (you have to pay for Windows, even if you don't pay separately for the component products) or that IBM bundles with its hardware (you have to pay for the hardware system, even if you don't pay separately for WebSphere)—must make their own products so much better that people will pay for them. So even though it can be a painful stimulus for managers and entrepreneurs, who have to rethink their business or go out of business, we can say that open-source and free software provides an important stimulus for continuing innovation in the software business.

Time will tell if for-profit software companies can make a business out of selling services and products that complement free software. So far, the results have not been promising. This has been the case, for example, with Red Hat, the premier open-source company trying to sell services and products to accompany Linux.

Red Hat had revenues of more than $90 million and about six hundred employees in the fiscal year ending February 2003, with a net loss of $6.5 million. This was a significant improvement over previous years; Red Hat had lost more than $86 million in 2001 and $140 million in 2002 (see Appendix Table 13). It had a mix of 53 percent products revenues and the rest services revenues, and revenues per employee that were comparable to those of other hybrid-solutions companies. One useful service Red Hat sold helped companies convert their software from running on pricey UNIX system software to running on cheap or free versions of Linux.

As with other software companies, Red Hat had higher margins on its software license fees, which it referred to as "subscriptions." The company's financial problem has been mainly on the cost side. Compared to other software companies (see Table 2-2), even putting aside temporary amortization and restructuring charges related to acquisitions, Red Hat has had extremely high general and administrative costs and high R-and-D costs. The latter in particular should be low given that Linux is an open-source product, but this has not been the case. In addition, Red Hat has spent a lot on sales and marketing to get customers. It is very hard to make much money with this kind of cost structure, especially when the company's main product—Linux—is free and its sophisticated users do not need a lot of services. As the company's revenues have increased, though, these heavy expenditures have been dropping as a percentage of sales, and its net losses have been dropping sharply as well. The challenge now is to reach breakeven on continuing operations (which Red Hat has yet to do) and then make a net profit.

WRAP-UP COMMENTS

This chapter has merely scratched the surface of a short but complex history. To wrap up this discussion, I would like to highlight several points that should provide some "lessons of the past" for today's managers, programmers, and entrepreneurs.

First is the observation that the software business for large and medium-sized enterprise customers will probably always have a large services component. The growth of the software products market has not diminished the demand for software-related services. The needs of enterprise customers are rarely fully met by packaged software, which creates an enormous and continuing global market for customized software and integration services. As I argued in Chapter 2, for start-ups and established firms in the enterprise software field, *the key choice is not simply whether to be a services company or a products company, but how much emphasis to place on one type of business over the other.*

Second, history suggests that *which part of the business to emphasize more than the other should change at different times in the evolution of a software company's customer base and product lines.*

Business models may need to change with the economic times as well. The more "mature" the company and its products, the more likely it is to emphasize services as a source of recurring revenues. When times are bad for technology spending, or when old products are not selling so well (as in the case of IBM during the 1990s), services can again emerge as a steady source of revenues.

A third point is that *changes in platform technologies generate new demand*—both for new products and for new services to help customers reuse their existing software assets. We have seen this with the transition from mainframes to minicomputers and from mainframes to PCs and client-server computing, and with the Internet, Web services, and wireless devices. In the past, systems software products for new platforms, particularly operating systems, represented enormous horizontal markets and invaluable recurring revenue streams for the firms that dominated these segments. The possibilities for new entrepreneurs have been greatly limited, however. Hardware companies (such as IBM in mainframes or Sun Microsystems in UNIX-based servers) and a very small number of software companies (like Microsoft in desktop PCs) usually establish the platform standard and are extremely difficult to dislodge. Nonetheless, hardware companies that offer total solutions, including hardware, software, and services (such as IBM, DEC, and Sun), are rarely able to cover all horizontal and vertical software segments, and sometimes they do not have the skills to build systems software for a new platform. They also may not be good at treating software as a stand-alone business. These characteristics leave hardware-based solutions companies vulnerable to niche competition from more dedicated software producers.

Fourth, the history of the business suggests that *niche applications and new platforms are the best places to look for new software product and service opportunities*. In the late 1990s and early 2000s, rather than systems products for standardized hardware, vertical and horizontal application niches (databases, ERP, etc.) and new computing platforms (PCs, Web-enabled cell phones, handheld devices) have been a great source of new business opportunities for software entrepreneurs. This trend will likely continue in the future, with increasing use of non-PC platforms such as Web-enabled cell phones and handheld computers, as well as Web services.

I also spent a lot of time on IBM in this chapter. The company's formula for success should be instructive to every enterprise software company, particularly those that offer hybrid solutions. IBM, under antitrust pressure, gave a great push to the software products market—applications in particular—when it unbundled its software from its hardware in 1968–1970. Perhaps most interesting about IBM, though, is how it survived so many technological transitions during the past century by focusing on solutions rather than technology and how it reemerged as a strong player in Internet technology and services during the late 1990s and early 2000s.

Finally, I noted that the open-source movement has great potential for getting users more involved in software development and innovation. It also has some potential for creating new services businesses to help users deploy the free software. Commercial companies, however, have had trouble both exploiting open-source developers and selling services to the relatively sophisticated users of open-source software. As a result, it is not yet clear what implications the open-source movement will have for the software business.

One constant theme throughout the history of the computer industry has been the difficulty of writing and testing new software systems, particularly for new platforms and applications. How to create a process for software development that balances the needs of the business, such as to accommodate rapid change in technology or uncertain customer demands, is the subject of the next chapter.

4

Best Practices in
Software Development:

Beyond the Software Factory

Software development is the core technical activity for all companies in the software products and services business. It is also a critical activity for organizations that create software or tailor purchased software to run their operations—ranging from financial services firms to telecommunications companies to "click-and-mortar" as well as Internet retailers. If firms cannot build, customize, or install top-notch software products and systems, they probably will not be able to compete effectively over time. A software company or in-house IT department may get lucky and have a hit product or deliver well on a particular project, but it takes more than luck to be able to repeat a successful performance time after time. Yet, as many firms have discovered, including IBM in the 1960s with OS/360 and Microsoft in the 1980s and 1990s with Windows and new graphical applications, software development can be extraordinarily difficult to manage well on a consistent basis. Problems in software development can hurt a company's short-term profits and long-term credibility with customers. This is especially true as software products and custom systems have increased in size, complexity, and importance, and as platform technologies and user preferences have changed quickly and sometimes unpredictably.

This chapter is about best practices in software development, a topic I have been studying since 1985. Despite the persistence of similar problems decade after decade, I believe we now understand a lot about how to manage software development in particular settings. We also know something about practices that are good for most software projects regardless of their objectives. For example, Microsoft and other PC software products firms in the United States have done a great job in devising a development process that meets the needs of a printing-press type of business model. The style of development that Richard Selby and I have referred to as "synch-and-stabilize" is particularly useful for creating new products for mass-market users, adapting easily to change during a project at the features level, and producing incremental releases relatively quickly. I argue in this chapter that this approach is inherently superior for most types of software, at least compared to the overly structured "factory-like" or "waterfall" approaches that were popular in years past.

As noted in Chapter 3, the field of software engineering has been around since the late 1960s. There is now an enormous literature on the subject.[1] In this chapter, I provide only a brief overview. Again, I have organized my observations into topics that reflect my personal experiences as a researcher and consultant:

- A review of common problems in software development and solutions that include the Japanese factory approach and recommendations from the Software Engineering Institute
- Excerpts from a recent software assessment I did that reflect the common problems of relatively new software firms building complex products for fast-paced markets
- Basic concepts and techniques associated with the synch-and-stabilize approach, which I believe represents best practice for combining structure and flexibility in software development
- A more detailed discussion of how to implement synch-and-stabilize concepts and techniques in different phases of software projects and in different business contexts
- Preliminary data from an international survey on the popularity of different approaches in the United States, Japan, India, and Europe, as well as regional differences in programming performance
- Some words of caution on outsourcing, even to elite firms in India, as a potential solution to problems in software development

COMMON PROBLEMS AND SOLUTIONS

I have often found myself thinking that the major problem in software development is that good programmers are *too* creative and individualistic—"too many chiefs and not enough Indians," as one manager at Bell Labs complained to me during the 1980s. At that time, we were discussing the benefits of a Japanese *factory-like* process for software development. I had defined this as including a specific product domain focus, standardized development methods suitable for particular types of projects, common training for new recruits, systematic rather than ad hoc reuse of designs and code, investment in computer-aided tools and process R and D, rigorous quality assurance techniques, and project management through statistical data.[2]

I have since come to realize that, in product development generally and in software development more specifically, the trick for managers and programmers is to create enough structure to keep projects under control but not so much that "the process" stifles creativity and flexibility. An organization needs to be able to invent, innovate, and adapt to changes in the technology and customer needs. The factory-like approach had its moments and still has some value, but there are better ways of developing software for most applications.

Problems That Keep Recurring

Whether a software company primarily makes packaged products or offers services such as custom programming, to be successful in both good times and bad times, it has to learn to manage process without becoming a slave to it. By process in this context I mean everything from defining product requirements and system architectures to final testing and technical support, including the feedback mechanisms during the different phases and the functions involved in completing a product. The kinds of problems that software researchers and practitioners identified in the 1960s when tackling large-scale projects such as OS/360 became a hot topic of debate. But while the field has made progress, the same problems that were common in the 1960s have reappeared with disturbing regularity in the 1980s, 1990s, and 2000s. In fact, one of my favorite lists of typical problems in software development comes from a report compiled at a 1968 NATO conference on software engineering, which highlights

Table 4-1: NATO Report on Software Engineering Problems (1968)

- Lack of understanding in system requirements on the part of customers and designers.
- Large gaps between estimates of costs and time with actual expenditures due to poor estimating techniques, failure to allow time for changes in requirements, and division of programming tasks into blocks before the divisions of the system are understood well enough to do so properly.
- Large variations, as much as 26:1 in one study, in programmers' productivity levels.
- Difficulty of dividing labor between design and production (coding), since design-type decisions must still be made during coding.
- Difficulty in monitoring progress in a software project, since "program construction is not always a simple progression in which each act of assembly represents a distinct forward step."
- Rapid growth in size of software systems.
- Poor communication among groups working on the same project, exacerbated by too much uncoordinated or unnecessary information and a lack of automation to handle necessary information.
- Large expense of developing online production control tools.
- Difficulty of measuring key aspects of programmer and system performance.
- A tradition among software developers of not writing systems "for practical use" but trying to write new and better systems, so that they are always combining research, development, and production in a single project, which then makes it difficult to predict and manage.
- Rapid growth in the need for programmers and insufficient numbers of adequately trained and skilled programmers.
- Difficulty of achieving sufficient reliability (reduced errors and error tolerance) in large software systems.
- Dependence of software on hardware, which makes standardization of software difficult across different machines.
- Lack of inventories of reusable software components to aid in the building of new programs.
- Software maintenance costs often exceeding the cost of the original system development.

Source: *Compiled from Peter Naur and Brian Randell (eds.)*, Software Engineering: Report on a Conference Sponsored by the NATO Science Committee *(Brussels: Scientific Affairs Division, NATO, January 1969), published in Michael A. Cusumano,* Japan's Software Factories *(New York: Oxford University Press, 1991), p. 67.*

common issues ranging from requirements and estimation to reuse and maintenance (Table 4-1).

The persistence of similar problems over decades, as well as observations that as many as 75 to 80 percent of software projects are typically late and over budget, suggests that the field of software development has *not* made enough progress. I believe the issue is more complicated. Again, software producers have made progress. We know a lot more today than we did two or three decades ago about how to manage software projects to achieve desired results. There are far better programming languages and support tools available today than there were in the 1960s. The capabilities and sophistication of programs developed for a growing variety of computing devices are astounding. Throughout the world, there are billions of dollars of existing software assets that have become essential to running modern organizations.

That being said, we also now realize how difficult software development is and will probably always remain. Writing program algorithms is usually not a routine activity. It generally involves creativity and invention on some level, as well as problem solving and trial and error. In custom software projects, users often do not know what they want until they see part of the system in front of them. In the products market, users often want compelling features before they will make a purchase. Therefore, it is unreasonable to expect most software projects to have both successful outcomes and be easy to manage.

But exacerbating the difficulties is the fact that many software development organizations too often seem to want to reinvent the wheel when it comes to managing projects and thinking about process. One reason may be serious disagreements—which often become very emotional—among highly competent managers, programmers, and researchers about what approaches are most effective in different contexts. Of course, some projects require more invention and innovation than others, and invention and innovation are difficult to structure and predict. Some customers have mission-critical reliability requirements, others do not. But whatever the situation, my experience tells me that too many managers and programmers do not systematically apply best practices to software development. Too many individuals and organizations treat too many software projects as unique events and try to invent solutions from scratch each time. And so, not surprisingly, similar problems recur decade after decade.

The Software Factory Solution

To make software development more tractable, managers at companies ranging from General Electric and AT&T in the 1960s to System Development Corporation and the Japanese computer manufacturers in the 1970s and even Microsoft in the 1980s have dreamed of creating "software factories."[3] Other technologies (such as semiconductor design and production, and biotechnology product development and mass production) have succumbed to the structure of manufacturing and engineering discipline and scientific rigor. Why not software?

The answer, again, is not so straightforward. Most fundamentally, software development is not a manufacturing activity; it is more a form of product design, where the design is the product and replication is trivial. The design process, moreover, has some unique characteristics, requiring a combination of art, science, engineering, and management skills, especially in new applications and large projects. These characteristics make the design, construction, testing, and maintenance of software systems somewhat difficult to control. This is especially true for software systems that comprise millions of lines of code and require the invention of new algorithms, the basic instructions or mathematical recipes that make computer programs work.

Yet it is also true that some companies have created *factory-like* organizations and processes to develop certain kinds of software and to manage certain kinds of projects with particular kinds of people. Some factory organizations have tried to separate the requirements generation and high-level design process from the program construction (coding and debugging) and have outsourced programming and testing work to subsidiaries or overseas contractors (such as in India). Some factory-like organizations have done very well by certain measures, at least compared to their results before they became more factory-like. Other organizations have had less success or have failed for a variety of reasons, including the difficulty of managing iterations in development, understanding changing customer requirements, standardizing development methods for widely varying contexts, and reusing code systematically. Fast-paced markets with rapidly changing technologies and customer requirements, such as PC and Internet software in their early years, seem poorly suited to structured methods of software development. Talented, creative programmers also usually do not fit well into factory-like environments. But mainframe software development during the rather stable period of the 1970s and 1980s, especially in companies that were creating "me-too" versions of IBM operating systems and industrial applications, was more suitable for this approach.

Between 1969 and the mid-1970s, Hitachi, Fujitsu, NEC, and Toshiba created software factories in Japan that brought together thousands of programmers and systems engineers in single facilities. These organizations became highly adept at building large-scale industrial software systems that had a great deal of commonality from one project to another. The best Japanese projects also came close to achieving zero defects. The Japanese organized projects mostly by following a sequential "waterfall" process, moving in sequence from high-level design to detailed design, functional design, programming, and testing. Managers allowed some iterations back and forth but tried as hard as possible to get complete specifications before the programmers started to write code or hand off specifications to subcontractors. At the time, Japan did not have a large pool of people trained in computer science to draw on. Accordingly, standardized development methods, reuse libraries, computer-aided tools, and extensive in-house training served their needs relatively well. But the factory approach—still popular in Japan for mainframe software development—proved difficult to adapt to the fast-paced world of personal computers and new "client-server" architectures that combined networks of PCs or workstations with mainframes. For these kinds of systems, the Japanese and companies around the world had to devise a more flexible but still structured development process.

Software factories are historically significant as part of an industry-wide effort to figure out how to manage software development better and apply good practices more consistently. That effort continues. I can now say that software factory concepts still apply well to firms that need to make multiple versions of similar systems or build hybrid solutions based on well-understood requirements with many external constraints. Embedded software development for printers, machine tools, consumer electronics devices, and similar products often can use a factory-like waterfall approach effectively and even deploy computer-aided tools to generate a lot of the final code automatically. But as we have seen, software products and custom systems vary enormously in content, depending on the application and the platform. No one approach fits the needs of all companies engaged in the business of producing software.

The Software Engineering Institute

Nonetheless, reducing problems and improving quality and reuse in software development, particularly for defense and space applications, became a major area of concern in the United States by the mid-

1980s. At least some U.S. officials and company managers were responding to the progress that Japan had made with its software factories and other efforts to promote software research and applications, such as the Fifth-Generation Computer Project.[4] In 1984, to codify and disseminate best practices in software development, the U.S. Department of Defense founded the Software Engineering Institute (SEI) at Carnegie Mellon University in Pittsburgh. Because this organization has come to have an enormous influence in the field, it is important to understand its basic philosophy and modus operandi.

Most of the practices SEI has recommended derive from IBM's experiences in developing operating systems and complex industrial and government applications, particularly as related by former IBM manager Watts Humphrey.[5] Through detailed project audits, experts trained in the SEI process rank project organizations on a scale of 1 to 5 according to the Capabilities Maturity Model (CMM). The assumption is that organizations with more mature processes can better meet customer requirements within given cost and schedule constraints.

The lowest level—CMM Level 1, the *Initial Process*—is chaos. There is little or no formal project management, no quality assurance group, no defined process to handle changes in requirements or designs. Most software organizations in the world are at this level, or at least this is where they usually start. Level 2—the *Repeatable Process*—indicates a degree of control whereby an organization has devised formal project plans, scheduled reviews of actual versus budgeted costs and progress, and established orderly procedures for managing changes. Level 3—the *Defined Process*—is rarer. It requires organizations to have engineering teams dedicated to specifying and improving the development process. They also need to demonstrate an architecture that defines technical and management roles in development, as well as a very clear set of development methodologies and tools. At Level 4—the *Managed Process*—projects gather quantitative data by using designated databases and analyzing cost and quality measures for each product. Level 5—the *Optimizing Process*—is extremely rare. Organizations at this level of sophistication take the idea of quantitative measurement and feedback one step further: they automate most data gathering and are able to use statistical data to improve the actual development process continuously.[6]

There remains some controversy over these levels, such as whether it is really cost-effective for firms to try to reach Level 4 or 5. The top grade in particular entails considerable investment in software process engineering groups, quality control and testing procedures, detailed documentation, and metrics and databases. For example, I once supervised a series of case studies that included the Loral facility (formerly an IBM facility) making space shuttle software in Houston, Texas. This was ranked at Level 5, but it had very high development costs.[7] This study, as well as my recollections of debates within Motorola during the early 1990s, left me with the impression that moving to a high SEI level has a short-term cost that can prove daunting to small development teams. Most observers I have talked with consider Microsoft and the Japanese software factories to be around Level 3, though one of the Japanese factories scored at Level 5 in an audit done in the mid-1990s. Motorola facilities in the 1990s ranged from Levels 2 through 5, and many managers I know seemed quite happy to be in the middle of the rankings.

One problem with the SEI approach is that it cannot guarantee a specific return for investing heavily in process. It does not ask for or publish productivity and quality data associated with the SEI levels. Nonetheless, SEI does provide examples of impressive improvements achieved at representative organizations.[8] In the long run, I am now convinced that firms can gain significant savings by following the SEI recommendations. Reducing defects and improving the ability to trace bugs back to their sources can save enormous time and effort when it comes to software debugging and stabilization. Companies with more mature process capabilities should be better at managing schedules, cost overruns, and change requests, as well as overall quality.

On the other hand, I came to the conclusion after consulting with Motorola during the early 1990s, as well as studying Microsoft, Netscape, and other firms, that the SEI approach seemed to apply best to large firms building complex enterprise software for relatively stable markets. It did not provide a philosophy for how a firm can improve its time to market or its ability to get innovative features into a product as quickly as possible without overly compromising quality. In particular, as seen in the software assessment example summarized in the next section, relatively new or entrepreneurial software companies have special problems. They usually dislike bureaucracy and have to compete with lean budgets in fast-paced markets, as well as continually making changes to their products *during the development process.*

Excerpts from a Recent Software Assessment

The following excerpts date from the late 1990s and early 2000s and illustrate a variety of managerial, technical, and strategic problems common to most young software companies and to many established firms with evolving development practices. The firm described here is a typical midsized enterprise software company. It has one major product, a horizontal application, that it sells with several derivative products (special applications and tools for IT managers) as well as variations for different operating system platforms. The CEO wants to remain anonymous, and I did not receive permission to go into detail on my recommendations and follow-up work because some of the problems are ongoing.

Project Management

When I wrote up the initial assessment, I began by noting three high-level problem areas related to how the company was trying to manage the overall development process: scheduling and project control; planning and resource allocation (of both time and people); and risk management measures.

First, the executive staff set engineering schedules *by decree,* rather than having engineering managers and programmers evaluate technical hurdles and specific programming tasks. What was worse, the development managers had no easy way of adjusting dates and project scope to have any hope of meeting their target dates. There were a lot of small schedules for components, but no one was really in charge of coordinating work and monitoring a master schedule. It was hard for managers and programmers to tell how much work had progressed.

The schedule in place also shortchanged the up-front phase (planning to determine what to do and how to do it) as well as the back-end phase (testing and "stabilization" or debugging of the code). Under the pressured schedule, misallocation of people became more serious. There were too many unplanned changes in designs, too much haphazard response to changes, and, as a result, too much rework on an understaffed project. Everyone was rushing and not paying enough attention to quality. The number of bugs in the product code and documentation were increasing at an alarming rate.

Part of the problem was the absence of a limit on project scope and deadlines. People just kept making changes in response to demands from the sales force, marketing personnel, technical support, large customers, and executives. Products that shared key components did not have synchronized schedules or independent components, so that one team was continually waiting for another. The idle time reflected a lack of advance planning and coordination among the component groups. Developers' time allocations were also inaccurate because many of them were pulled off the current project to fix bugs in older product versions still in the field.

The lack of risk management measures was a problem in that the company had no buffer time in the schedule and no "Plan B" in case the project ran into trouble, which it did (and that is when I became involved). An alternative plan might have been to build new features based on the code of the previous version as an incremental release. The company also did no exploration of technical feasibility for what they wanted to do in the project—and they ended up taking on a challenge akin to "rocket science" (in my view) without knowing it beforehand. The hedge that the development team came up with was to create separate code branches for the different versions of the product that were to run on different operating systems. This would later enable the company to ship at least one version supporting a major operating system, but it encouraged duplication of work in design, coding, testing, and documentation.

Software Design and Development

The best way to convey the problems I saw in this area is simply to reproduce my list and then provide some examples from the report. I identified nine issues:

- Lack of a comprehensive and effective development strategy and process
- Product design difficult to stabilize, modify, evolve, and migrate
- Chaotic product concept and architectural design process
- Undisciplined functional design and specification process
- Nonstandardized build process that could be faster
- Little parallel work or automation in development, integration, and testing
- Weak formal and informal reviews of designs, code, and documentation
- Poor change control system
- Inadequate customer feedback and design input mechanisms

Most striking—but very common among young software companies and a particular target of the SEI approach—was the lack of any defined, repeatable approach to software development that everyone understood. Nor did this firm have any mechanism for making technical and strategic trade-offs that would support the overall competitive strategy and product strategy. As examples, I suggested that one strategy might be to offer across-the-board Windows compatibility; this would mean de-emphasizing UNIX. Or the company might target a lower end of the market with a narrower product line. But the company was going for broke: the executive team wanted a full set of products that would run on all major versions of all major operating systems and that would be state of the art in functionality as well as priced for the Windows market. Here are some specific problems people talked about, which I have also found common in many other software firms:

- The main modules in the product suite are technically very tightly coupled and not really separate products.
- The lack of an interface layer to isolate the product code from target operating system platforms makes the product difficult to migrate to different platforms and difficult to evolve as vendors such as Microsoft modify their APIs. The multiplatform objectives are, therefore, technically correct. Senior managers, consequently, must make a *strategic* decision whether or not to continue pursuing the multiplatform objectives or focus on Windows.
- The product architecture does not adequately identify common or kernel components (i.e., those shared by multiple groups) and minimize the interdependencies among them, which makes it difficult to build stable common components.
- The common components at present need to be too large to contain the shared functionality, making them especially difficult to design, stabilize, evolve, and migrate.

Even companies with the capabilities of Netscape and Microsoft get into such situations, especially when the development teams are relatively inexperienced. It is usually because they attempt too much in a project without having a good process for generating the product concept and the architectural design. This particular start-up had no process or team assigned to handle these kinds of challenges. It had no document describing how the product should work. Yet it had several product teams that had to share key components. There was no time allocated to exploration, but the developers were trying to design code that would work on multiple operating system platforms. This was a recipe for what I called "the multiplatform debacle and memory leaks," which is what the company created.

The product's functional specifications were not detailed enough to give developers adequate direction to focus their work and make technical decisions and trade-offs. For example, there was no list of most important versus least important features. The product designers also continued to add features and request hasty changes throughout the development phase. Changes that improve the product are fine, but I noted that "late design changes without a good process for handling the changes can cause too much rework in development as well as in all other affected areas (integration, QA testing, documentation, marketing and sales preparations)."

Testing and Quality Assurance

The "build" process (the activity of putting pieces of code together to create a working version of the evolving product) was haphazard and slow, leading to many frustrations among the development team. These were some of the more serious problems, which are also common among inexperienced teams trying to be fast and flexible without appropriate discipline and infrastructure:

- Code file check-in and check-out procedures are not standardized, so developers often waste time figuring out what to do and when, or work with outdated files.
- The process from file check-in to acceptance and global compilation takes one to two days; there is not enough computing power to speed this up.
- The global compile of the product itself takes three hours. This is a problem because developers need to recompile the entire product to validate changes made in any one module, often wasting three hours or so each day they do this. The result is less frequent builds by the developers.
- There is no set time on a given day for integration builds, resulting in developers' not getting their most recent work into

the build and having to work with outdated files from other developers—creating rework for everyone.
- The builds prior to alpha test are infrequent, although relatively frequent after the alpha phase (builds have averaged about one every three days for the past ten months).

The lack of parallel work and test automation created a number of important issues. Developers did not do much testing before they tried to check into the builds. The integration team only compiled and linked files and ran a very simple usage test; it did no real validation or regression testing that could find serious problems early. *The company's approach to testing largely resembled a waterfall style, even though it was building frequently.*

There were other issues: QA had a Minimal Acceptance Test (MAT) but could not run it in parallel with development because the developers made too many design changes and left no document trail that the QA team could use to update the tests. One way around this would have been to pair testers with developers, as Microsoft does, but the company organized people into functional teams that sat in different locations. QA might have given developers a copy of the latest MAT, but the test required a typical user's PC; developers (and some testers) had machines that were too powerful. The QA team also had little time to prepare automated tests that developers might have run themselves. Only 3 percent of the tests were automated.

It is difficult to allocate time to reviewing designs and code if the code is changing all the time. On the other hand, reviews and more formal inspections—which IBM made famous in the 1970s'—can help prevent unnecessary changes or changes due to errors found later in the process. In any case, this company had no formal process for reviewing *any* software artifacts—design documents, code, or customer manuals. QA did some review of specifications, but this was a team of test engineers, not developers; they could not really detect architectural or coding errors. Developers did not review one another's designs or code, even when they were sharing components.

Customer feedback is critical to a software products company that wants to target mainstream users. But this firm was so new that marketing and development had yet to figure out a way to incorporate what customers were telling them about the product in the field and about what features they wanted in the next version. The developers rarely talked directly to the customers. And since the developers wrote features and ran their code on PCs that were far more powerful than the average user's, this increased the distance between them and the customer. Nor was there a standard tool for handling design and code changes or version control and configuration management of the evolving product. There was no process for setting priorities on what to change or fix—a critical task because the company was planning a release in six months' time.

Knowledge and People Management

At the end of my report I talked about the "softer" issues: knowledge and people management. Often these are the hardest problems for software companies to handle. You can suggest to a programmer how to design a better regression test or why a different architecture might decouple product modules better. But telling someone how to manage *knowledge* better or how to treat *people* better quickly gets into awkward territory. Of course, the key assets of a software company are entirely intellectual; *they are all about knowledge and people.* This particular firm had many things to work on, as the list compiled from my interviews suggests:

- Architectural and design knowledge vague and not widely shared
- Available product and project information difficult to locate
- Poor communication, feedback, and learning across groups
- Serious overwork and low morale
- Confusing recruitment and assignments
- No training or skills development
- No career path or personnel management system

The complexity of the product architecture and component technologies, as well as how poorly even the senior developers understood how everything worked, raised a serious flag of concern for me. The problem was likely to get worse, rather than better, as the product became more complex and as senior people left the organization in the usual turnover rhythm. The company had information on the product that could be useful in overcoming some of these "knowledge bottlenecks," such as written specifications, existing code, and software development kits (SDKs) created by some of the teams. But there was no central depository of these artifacts or a formal sharing mechanism.

Another issue was political: some developers did not want to share what they knew and were "simply guarding their small 'turf.' " In addition, small groups were responsible for small pieces of the product and nothing more. They "have no way to give feedback or critique parts of the product that don't work well."

Not surprisingly, the company was beginning to experience serious problems with morale. The growing pressure to ship—the current project had been supposed to finish the product in eighteen months but was already a year late—was frustrating everyone. The senior managers were pressuring the heads of the technical teams. Everyone contributed to letting a negative climate emerge, as the following observations, summarizing a large number of interview comments, illustrate:

- Unrealistic schedules and lack of communication and recognition have created high levels of stress and overwork, as well as low morale.
- Developers feel that managers and other people view them as "the bad guys" because they make bugs.
- People are afraid of talking openly about problems because they might get fired.
- New hires are excited by the financial and marketing success and international reputation of the company, but then quickly get demoralized when they see how poorly certain aspects of the company have been managed.
- People are frustrated because they feel that management incompetence has prevented "smart people" from producing a good product.
- Demoralized people cannot work up to their capabilities or focus on producing a high-quality product.
- Developers feel as though managers have treated them as "children," and they are not used to making decisions and feel they have to consult their managers on too many small issues.

Recommendations and Outcomes

Working together with the head of the products group as well as the CEO, we tackled each of the areas listed in this assessment. We prioritized the problems to work on immediately, over the next couple of months, and over the next year. We introduced a Microsoft-style development organization, creating smaller teams around the basic product and identifying functional roles for program managers, product managers, developers, testers, and documenters. We eliminated the previous structure of large functional groups. We also introduced several synch-and-stabilize development techniques, focusing on daily builds with integration testing and well-defined milestones with realistic schedules for completing specific product features.

The development organization responded immediately. Over the next several months, the team made gradual but significant improvements in both the product and the development process. They completed the features under development, fixed the major quality problems, and shipped the product within six months. The product also turned out to be a big hit in the marketplace, generating hundreds of millions of dollars in new sales. This success was the culmination of years of design work, not the recent process changes we introduced, but the process improvements made it possible for the company to succeed as a business. It now had large product revenues, a base for recurring service and maintenance revenues, and a repeatable development process that would enable it to create new versions and other products in the future, including a Web version and various applications.

THE ESSENCE OF SYNCH-AND-STABILIZE

"Synch-and-stabilize," as applied at Microsoft, Netscape, and many other PC software firms, including the company described above, is both a philosophy of product development as well as a set of specific concepts and techniques. Richard Selby, my coauthor on *Microsoft Secrets,* and I coined the phrase after observing Microsoft's best projects (mainly Excel, Word, and Windows NT) during the mid-1990s. The underlying philosophy and the specific techniques have been around the PC industry for many years and are not specific to Microsoft, though this company did an exceptionally good job of defining how to do software development this way. The core idea is to encourage programmers to innovate and experiment but frequently *synchronize* their designs with other team members by creating "builds" (working versions) of the product as often as possible, and then periodically *stabilize* (debug and integrate) their code before proceeding to the next set of development tasks.[10]

This style of development has limitations, like any approach. It does not solve major architectural problems or strategic blunders, for example. Projects can also implement the concepts poorly or design weak features that fail in the marketplace. Nonetheless, synch-and-stabilize techniques recognize that the waterfall approach such as used at IBM or Japanese software factories is too inflexible and slow to meet the needs of fast-paced markets. To a large degree, it was Microsoft's mastery of synch-and-stabilize techniques, along with its programming talent, that enabled it to build a version of Windows that worked in 1990 as well as products such as Excel and Word that made it the dominant producer of Windows applications in the 1990s. Microsoft also relied heavily on its development skills and resources to overcome a late entry into Internet software and come up with new products such as Internet Explorer and new versions of Office quickly after 1995. How well Microsoft fares in the future will continue to depend heavily on its skills in product development. In early 2003, the company was again engaged in a massive redesigning and rewriting of its products to accommodate the concept of .NET and Web services—more usage of distributed architectures over the Internet and program components that communicated through new technologies such as XML.

Basic Philosophy

It is important to realize that the synch-and-stabilize techniques as first introduced at Microsoft in the late 1980s reflected the company's unique business situation. It was no longer building small-scale programs based on the DOS platform. The new operating systems and applications were graphical, following the lead of Apple with the Macintosh. IBM was also building a heavy-duty operating system for the PC named OS/2, which would set new standards for reliability. So Microsoft had to respond quickly to these and other changes in the marketplace and PC technology. It had to encourage its teams not only to evolve designs in an iterative, incremental fashion but to get new, more complex products out quickly, with much higher quality levels.

The goal that Microsoft managers set was to provide developers with just enough structure to work effectively as a large team. They needed more people to create relatively large products that were running into hundreds of thousands and even millions of lines of code. The structure would come from a few simple but rigid rules that still allowed considerable flexibility in implementation. To illustrate the idea of structure in this context, I like to quote Dave Maritz, a former tank commander in the Israeli Army who headed Microsoft's Windows 95 testing group:

> In the military, when I was in tank warfare and I was actually fighting in tanks, there was nothing more soothing than people constantly hearing their commander's voice come across the airwaves. Somebody's in charge, even though all shit is breaking loose. . . . When you don't hear [the commander's voice] for more than fifteen minutes to half an hour, what's happened? Has he been shot? Has he gone out of control? Does he know what's going on? You worry. And this is what Microsoft is. These little offices, hidden away with the doors closed. And unless you have this constant voice of authority going across the e-mail the whole time, it doesn't work. *Everything that I do here I learned in the military. . . . You can't do anything that's complex unless you have structure. . . . And what you have to do is make that structure as unseen as possible and build up this image for all these prima donnas to think that they can do what they like.* Who cares if a guy walks around without shoes all day? Who cares if the guy has got his teddy bear in his office? I don't care. I just want to know . . . [if] somebody hasn't checked in his code by five o'clock. Then that guy knows that I am going to get into his office [italics added].[11]

Maritz creates an analogy that reflects both Microsoft's development style and its company culture. The programmers could easily go off on their own and do whatever they pleased, whenever they pleased. One of the great fears of Microsoft managers, in fact, was that some developers would "go dark" on them and never emerge from their offices or communicate and share what they were doing. But the sync-and-stabilize techniques were enough to force even wayward programmers to come back into the fold and become part of the team, lest they write too much code that did not "sync up" with the work of other programmers. A few basic concepts, enforced by managers such as Dave Maritz, made this kind of synchronization possible.

We also have in this description *a picture that resembles that of an army:* divisions of Microsoft programmers working in individual offices that resemble individual tanks. Everyone is marching forward to attack the enemy, but the coordination comes from e-mail rather than the radio. The comment about five o'clock refers to the deadline the

Windows 95 group had for checking in code to the daily build, which nearly all Microsoft projects do religiously. The goal of the build process is to see what functions work or what problems exist, usually by completely recompiling the source code and executing automated "regression" tests that make sure the changes did not harm the existing basic functions. The daily build is one of those few rigid structure points that force everybody to come together and help the company build complex products such as Windows 95 and, most recently, Windows 2000 (which reached some 35 million lines of code and had perhaps as many as seven hundred developers and testers working on this single product). A company cannot build products of this size and scope without a structured project organization, clear development goals, and good teamwork, no matter how talented the individual developers and managers are.

Most Microsoft managers and programmers eschewed the kind of disciplined environment that one can see in traditional Japanese software factories or CMM Level 4 and 5 facilities. Rather, they generally tried to "scale up" a more informal small-team or "hacker" style of software development. The process called for several small teams (say, three to eight developers each, with parallel testing "buddies" in a one-to-one ratio) to work on separate "features" (chunks of functionality that a user would recognize) and work together as one relatively large team (see Figure 4-1). A very big product, such as Windows 2000, could have fifteen, twenty, or more of these small feature teams working in parallel. The advantages of this small-team, feature-oriented approach, with daily builds and constant regression testing, is that it becomes possible to build large products relatively quickly but still allow individual programmers and feature teams enough freedom to evolve their designs incrementally. Feature teams are free to innovate within certain parameters, though individual programmers and teams must synchronize their design and coding changes frequently or the process will break down because many features interact with one another or are interdependent in some way. From time to time, all feature work in Microsoft projects also stops so that developers and testers can "stabilize" (test, integrate, and debug) the code they have built to that point and make sure that the separate features or product components work together properly.

In a variety of industries, for the past decade or more, many companies have used prototyping as well as multiple cycles of concurrent design, build, and test activities to develop products through iterations

Figure 4-1: Microsoft Project and Feature Team Organization

Note: **Bold** type indicates project leaders.

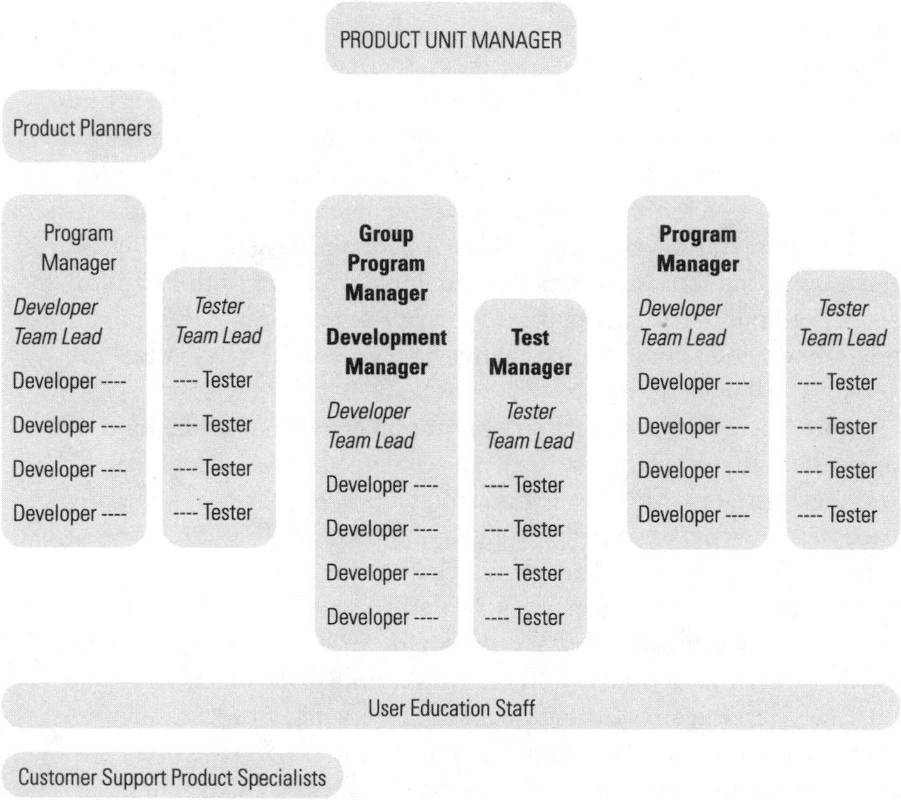

PRODUCT UNIT MANAGER

Product Planners

Program Manager		Group Program Manager		Program Manager	
Developer Team Lead	*Tester Team Lead*	**Development Manager**	**Test Manager**	*Developer Team Lead*	*Tester Team Lead*
Developer ----	---- Tester	*Developer Team Lead*	*Tester Team Lead*	Developer ----	---- Tester
Developer ----	---- Tester	Developer ----	---- Tester	Developer ----	---- Tester
Developer ----	---- Tester	Developer ----	---- Tester	Developer ----	---- Tester
Developer ----	---- Tester	Developer ----	---- Tester	Developer ----	---- Tester
		Developer ----	---- Tester		

User Education Staff

Customer Support Product Specialists

Source: *(Michael A. Cusumans and Richard W. Selby,* Microsoft Secrets: How the World's Most Powerful Software Company Creates Technology, Shapes Markets, and Manages People *(New York: Free Press/Simon & Schuster, 1995), p. 75.*

as well as to incorporate incremental design changes.[12] In the computer software community, since the mid-1970s, researchers and managers have talked about "iterative enhancement," a "spiral model" for sequencing the different project phases, and "concurrent development" of multiple phases and activities.[13] In more recent years, there has been a more radical form of incremental design and development in the Extreme Programming (XP) movement, which promotes, among other things, the idea of writing minimal specs before coding and evolving architectures, designs, code, and test cases concurrently as a project proceeds, with programmers working in pairs.[14]

There is a basic concept shared by these and similar approaches: Users' needs for many types of software are so difficult to understand, and changes in hardware and software technologies are so continuous and rapid, that it is unwise to attempt to design a software product or complex information system completely in advance. Moreover, making design changes during a project is not always bad, particularly if the changes represent successful efforts to incorporate late user feedback or respond to critical changes in the marketplace. Developers should continuously move among design, coding, and testing, as well as concurrently managing these activities in multiple subcycles while moving forward to completing and shipping an actual product.

As I pointed out earlier, this iterative, incremental, or concurrent engineering style contrasts to the more sequential or waterfall approach to product development that was common in the software factories I studied as well as in IBM mainframe groups during the 1980s. In the waterfall model, software teams attempt to "freeze" a product specification, create a design, build components, and then merge these components together—generally at the end of the project in one large integration and testing phase.[15] This approach to software development, while especially common from the 1960s to the 1980s, remains a basic model for project planning in many industries.[16] It can also be useful in some software projects.

Compared to their mainframe predecessors, Microsoft and other PC software companies adopted a different style of development because they had different business needs. They were all competing in fast-paced, rapidly changing markets, with developers who usually wanted to make improvements in their code *until the last possible minute*. More broadly, though, I believe this development style represents best practice for most software projects and many different types of product development. It is inherently good for engineers to *synchronize* continually what they are doing both as individuals and as members of product teams working in parallel on interdependent components. And it is inherently good to break up a large project into smaller subprojects working on chunks of functionality and periodically *stabilize* the features under development as team members add more functionality to the product. I also believe it is an outdated practice to wait until the end of the development cycle before trying to integrate components and test them to see if the different parts work together properly as a system.

Infinite Defect Loops

One potential consequence of *not* synchronizing and *not* frequently stabilizing a software product under development is that the project may fall into what Microsoft people used to call "infinite defect loops." There is, of course, a story behind the use of this term (which reflects a state that is common to programmers at many firms) and how it resulted in changes in Microsoft's development style. One key event was a May 1989 off-site meeting organized by former IBM executive Mike Maples. At this meeting, senior engineers reflected on why so many projects were so late and why they could not get the level of bugs—defects—down to an acceptable level. As a countermeasure, they decided to break projects up into smaller pieces (milestones) and create working versions of the evolving product (builds) every day, from as early as possible in the schedule.[17] But the impetus for these changes went back many years.

When Selby and I were writing about Microsoft, the director of development, Dave Moore, gave us all the postmortem reports and related memos in his files. These dated to 1986 and the first Word for Windows (WinWord) project. The WinWord effort started in 1983. The project manager at the time predicted that it would take one year to complete. It ended up taking *five* years. What is even more striking is that the development team reevaluated the schedule every year and always thought it would be shipping within a few months or at least by the end of the year. *The Word team was usually two or three hundred percent off in its estimations until a year before the product actually shipped.*[18]

This was a particularly bad scheduling job, even worse than the project I described earlier in my assessment report. But it was typical of Microsoft in the 1980s. As we read through the postmortem reports and memos, we realized that Microsoft people were truly afraid: The company seemed unable to ship Windows and Windows applications, which were an order of magnitude larger in size and far more complex than MS-DOS and DOS applications. They knew that they had to learn to develop more complicated software products quickly or Microsoft would cease to be a viable business. We noticed a particular concern with what the reports described as "infinite defect loops." I have illustrated this concept in Figure 4-2.

Too often, Microsoft projects would start with some loose definition of requirements and functional designs, as well as a schedule, and

Figure 4-2: Waterfall Model with Infinite Defect Loop

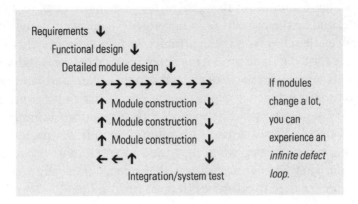

Requirements ↓
   Functional design ↓
     Detailed module design ↓
       → → → → → → → →
       ↑ Module construction ↓
       ↑ Module construction ↓
       ↑ Module construction ↓
       ← ← ↑   ↓
       Integration/system test

If modules change a lot, you can experience an *infinite defect loop.*

then get trapped in debugging and integration problems, with no end in sight. In the late 1980s, the product design for Word and the platform technology (what would become Windows 3.0) were changing too quickly—particularly because projects were going on for *years*. Individual programmers or feature teams might be able to build functional modules that worked on their own. But as dependencies built up with other modules and operating system functions and interfaces that were changing constantly and unpredictably, individuals and feature teams had trouble getting different pieces of the product to work together properly. For example, one team might write a printer driver and another would write a drawing module. As both teams made changes to create the best driver and the best drawing module possible, suddenly they couldn't print the graphics output. Printing technology was changing, font technology was changing, graphics technology was changing, and the underlying software that controlled the computer and the printer—Windows—was changing. Meanwhile, Intel was rolling out new microprocessors every eighteen months, encouraging everyone to make continual changes to update their code and take advantage of the latest hardware capabilities.

Over a five-year period, you can imagine how much change went on for the group building the first version of WinWord. At the time, Microsoft teams actually spent years designing and redesigning parts of the product without ever being able to put the whole thing together and test it properly. As a result, the Word group in particular, but also other Microsoft projects that followed a similar path, frequently fell into this infinite-defect-loop scenario. Any change developers made in one module would invariably generate one or more bugs in another module, and so the project could never get the number of bugs down to a low enough level to say the product was stable and ready to ship. The code for a database product that predated Access was so bad that Microsoft simply threw it out. That was a smart and courageous thing to do—much better than shipping junk. Microsoft's experiences were very similar to what happened with Navigator/Communicator in 1997–1998. Netscape had a 3-million-line pile of spaghetti that teams kept destabilizing when they tried to enhance it or convert to Java code. They had to retest the entire product completely every time a programmer tried to add a new feature or fix a bug.[19]

Proponents of the waterfall model might argue that the problem Microsoft and Netscape faced was obvious: they did not have a good set of initial requirements, they did not have a good architecture with stable interfaces defining how components should interact with each other, and even when they had these things, they did not have enough discipline to follow a plan. Project managers always let engineers make too many changes, and that of course always destabilized the product and created infinite defect loops. But Microsoft's postmortem reports suggest that managers knew they could resort to a waterfall process (which their partner in OS/2 development, IBM, was using religiously) and solve the infinite-defect-loop problem that way. Microsoft managers also believed that adopting the waterfall method would create more serious problems—*business* problems as well as technical problems.

Microsoft managers and senior engineers wanted an approach that would be responsive to unpredictable changes in the market and would allow developers to make frequent changes but still ship a product within a reasonable time frame and with better (but still "good enough") quality. Following an arbitrary schedule that some executive created or trying to eliminate bugs completely was not a viable business goal for a PC software company in the late 1980s and early 1990s. Speed to market with good-enough products (to get ahead of Lotus, WordPerfect, and Apple) and backward compatibility with DOS (to keep the installed base of customers) were more important to Microsoft.

The solution they came up with worked. Microsoft first used the milestone and daily build techniques together in 1989 for an Excel project that came in only eleven days late on a one-year schedule. This team, led by Chris Peters, set new standards within Microsoft for project management as well as architectural elegance. Projects that followed these principles would never again get into the situation of programmers' doing years of coding and feature development before trying to integrate the modules and see if the whole product actually worked. They were also able to make major changes in midstream more easily, rather than blindly following an original spec and perhaps delivering a bug-free product "on time" that few people, however, would want to buy.

Here are two examples with enormous importance for the business: The original Windows 95 specification, done around 1993, did not include a Web browser, which by 1994–1995 became an important new technology. And the original specification for Windows NT, done in the late 1980s, did not include a graphical user interface.[20] Microsoft made major changes to both product designs in midstream, and ended up with very successful products. Microsoft won the browser war with Internet Explorer (albeit with some unfair play). And Windows NT opened up an entire new opportunity for Microsoft to sell enterprise operating systems to corporations and other large organizations, as well as replacing the aging Windows 3.1/95/98 code base.

Key Concepts and Techniques

At Microsoft, the first step in the synch-and-stabilize process is for projects to begin with a "vision statement."[21] This document defines the goals and market for a new product and describes as well as prioritizes the user activities that need to be supported by individual product features. Product managers (often MBAs who are marketing specialists) usually take charge of writing up this document, which they do while consulting program managers as well as other members of the product unit. Program managers are more technically oriented employees who specialize in writing up functional specifications of the product and coordinating project work. They are not actually the "managers" of the programmers, however. The developers report to their team leaders and a development manager. In addition, the program managers are supposed to consult with developers when they write up a functional specification, and senior developers generally have veto power over feature suggestions because, after all, the developers have to write the code.

The functional spec should outline the product features that the team has agreed to do in sufficient depth for project managers to organize feature teams, estimate schedules, and allocate staff. Microsoft's specification documents generally do not try to decide all the details of each feature or lock the project into the original set of features. During product development, the program managers and developers revise the feature set and feature details as they learn more about what should be in the product. Our interviews at Microsoft indicated that the feature set in a typical specification document may change by 30 percent or more by the end of a project. Again, this kind of change is usually *good,* not bad.

Microsoft projects are usually led by a committee consisting of the product unit manager, the development manager, the test manager, and the head or "group" program manager. Together, with input from other team members, they decide on the initial feature set. Then they can divide the product and the project into parts (features and small feature teams) and divide the project into three or four milestone subprojects (see Figure 4-3). The milestones represent completion points for major portions of the product, usually represented by clusters of prioritized features. All the feature teams go through a complete cycle of design, development, feature integration, usability testing, integration testing, debugging, and stabilization in each milestone subproject. Moreover, throughout the whole project, the feature teams synchronize their work by building the product, and by finding and fixing errors, on a daily and weekly basis. At the end of a milestone subproject, the developers are supposed to fix most of the bugs and all of the truly serious defects (those that will "crash" the system) before they move on to the next milestone or ship the product. This debugging or error correction work stabilizes the product and enables the team to understand which features are done and which need more work.

Focus Creativity

To define products and organize the development process, Selby and I described Microsoft's strategy as *focus creativity by evolving features and "fixing" resources.* We identified five specific principles or guidelines that product groups used to implement this strategy:

1. Divide large projects into multiple milestone cycles with buffer time (about 20 to 50 percent of total project time) and no separate product maintenance group.

Figure 4-3: Synch-and-Stabilize Process Model

Product vision

Architecture design and functional specification → → → → → → → →

Milestone 1	Milestone 2	Milestone 3
Design	Design	Design
Code	Code	Code
Usability test	Usability test	Usability test
Test	Test	Test
Daily builds	Daily builds	Daily builds
Test	Test	Test
Debug	Debug	Debug
Integrate	Integrate	Integrate
Stabilize	Stabilize	Stabilize
Buffer time	Buffer time	Buffer time
Alpha release	Beta release	Feature complete
		Beta release
		Visual freeze
		CODE COMPLETE
		Final test
		Final debug
		Stabilize
		Final release

Source: *Based on Michael A. Cusumano and David B. Yoffie,* Competing on Internet Time: Lessons from Netscape and Its Battle with Microsoft *(New York: Free Press/Simon & Schuster, 1998), p. 241.*

2. Use a vision statement and outline feature specifications to guide projects.
3. Base feature selection and prioritization on user activities and data.
4. Evolve a modular and horizontal design architecture, with the product structure mirrored in the project structure.
5. Control by individual commitments to small tasks and "fixed" project resources.

These principles bring discipline and structure to a project in several ways. The basic idea is that, while having creative people is important, it is often more important to direct their creativity. Managers can do this by getting engineers to think about features that customers will pay money for and by putting pressure on project personnel by limiting their resources, such as staffing and schedule. If managers fail to do these things, software projects run the risk of never shipping anything to market. This risk especially becomes a problem in fast-moving market segments, when individuals or teams have unfocused or highly volatile user requirements, frequently change interdependent components during a project, or do not synchronize their work adequately.

Microsoft got around these problems by organizing a project into sequential subprojects containing prioritized features. Managers also introduced buffer time between each subproject milestone and the final ship date to allow staff time to respond to unexpected difficulties or delays. Projects used vision statements and outlines rather than complete specifications and detailed designs before coding because managers and programmers realized they could not determine *in advance* everything that the team would need to do to build the right product for the market. The incremental evolution approach left the team room to innovate or adapt to change or unforeseen competitive opportunities and threats.

By the mid-1990s, most of Microsoft's products also had modular architectures. Modularity allowed teams to add or combine features incrementally in a prioritized fashion, somewhat like a horizontal list of most to least important features. Particularly for applications products, development teams also tried to come up with features that mapped directly to the activities typical customers performed. This mapping required continual observation and testing with users during development. In addition, many Microsoft managers allowed team members to set their own schedules, but only after the developers analyzed tasks in detail (half-day to three-day chunks, for example) and asked developers to commit personally to the schedules they set. Managers then "fixed" project resources by trying to limit the number of people they allocated to any one project and limiting the time they could spend on projects. These fixed limits were more enforcable in applications projects, where teams could more easily delete less important features if they fell too far behind schedule. (Cutting features to save schedule time is not always possible with operating systems projects and other systems software, however. In these projects, the reliability of the system is usually more important than its features, and many features are closely coupled and cannot be easily deleted individually.)

Most important, prioritizing features, fixing resources, and modularizing architectures simplified project management. Instead of creating a long wish list of features and then guessing how many people and how much time would be necessary to do the job, Microsoft project managers generally scheduled in a simpler way. For example, the senior team leading the Office product unit might say that they want a new release in twelve months and they have 100 developers and 100 testers. The problem then becomes how many new features can a team of 200 engineers build, debug, and stabilize in eleven months or so, with some time set aside as buffer? If they have done their prioritization and design work correctly, they can cut features if the project falls behind and include them in the next release or not at all.

Work in Parallel but Synchronize Continuously

To manage the process of developing and shipping products, Microsoft followed another strategy that Selby and I described as *do everything in parallel with frequent synchronizations*. We saw teams implement this strategy by following another set of principles:

1. Work in parallel teams but "synch up" and debug daily.
2. Always have a product you can ship, with versions for every major platform and market.
3. Speak a common language on a single development site.
4. Continuously test the product as you build it.
5. Use metric data to determine milestone completion and product release.

These principles impose discipline on projects but in a subtle, flexible way—without trying to control every moment of every developer's day. In this approach, managers allow many small teams and individuals enough freedom to work in parallel yet still function as one large team so they can build large-scale products relatively quickly and cheaply. But the feature teams and individual engineers must adhere to a few rigid rules that enforce a high degree of coordination and communication.

For example, one of the few rules developers must follow is that on whatever day they decide to check in their pieces of code, they must do so by a particular time, such as by 2:00 P.M. or 5:00 P.M. This allows the team to put the available components together, completely recompile the product source code, create a new build of the evolving product by the end of the day or the next morning, then start testing and debugging immediately. Another rule is that if developers check in code that "breaks" the build by preventing it from completing the recompilation, they must fix the defect immediately. (This resembles one aspect of Toyota's famous production system, where factory workers stop the manufacturing lines whenever they notice a defect in a car they are assembling.[22])

The Daily Build

The typical build process as used at Microsoft required several steps. First, in order to develop new features, developers checked out private copies of source code files from a centralized master version. They evolved their features by making changes to their private copies of the source code files. They then created private builds of the product that contained the new or more evolved features and tested the builds on their own. Once they got a build to work, they checked in the changes from their private copies into the master version of the source code. The check-in process included an automated regression test to help ensure that their changes to the source code files did not cause errors elsewhere in the product. Developers usually checked their code back in to the master copy at least twice a week, but they sometimes checked in daily or more frequently, especially toward the end of a project and during the final stabilization phase.

Regardless of how often individual developers checked in their changes to the source code, a designated developer or a dedicated person on the team, called the project build master, generated a complete build of the product on a daily basis using the master version of the source code. Generating a build for a product consisted of executing an automated sequence of commands called a "build script." This created a new internal release of the product and included many steps that compile source code. The build process automatically translated the source code for a product into one or more executable files and might also create various library files that would allow end users to customize the product. *The new internal release of the product built each day was the daily build.* Projects generated daily builds for each platform, such as Windows and Macintosh, and for each market, such as the U.S. and major international versions.

Product teams also tested features as they built them from multiple perspectives, including bringing in customers from "off the street" to try prototypes in a usability lab. In addition, nearly all Microsoft teams worked on a single physical site with common development languages (such as C and C++), common coding styles, and standardized development tools. A single site and common programming languages and support tools helped teams communicate, debate design ideas, and resolve problems face-to-face relatively easily. Project teams also used a small set of quantitative metrics to guide decisions, such as when to move forward in a project or when to ship a product to market. For example, managers rigorously tracked progress of the daily builds by monitoring how many bugs were newly opened, resolved (such as by eliminating duplicates or deferring fixes), fixed, and active. Developers and testers would test the builds until they reduced the number of bugs to a relatively low and stabilizing level before moving on to the next development milestone or shipping the product.

Process Modifications for Internet Software

For the most part, Microsoft's process for developing Internet products after 1994 followed this same style of synch-and-stabilize described above, with a few differences to speed up development or use the Web for communication and management purposes (such as sharing documents and project information).

During the late 1990s, Netscape also used a similar style of development, adapted for the Internet.[23] For example, Netscape projects usually began with an informal meeting or series of meetings among core team members from development and marketing. At some point, the product teams came together in an advance planning meeting (APM). Next, product management created a product requirements document (PRD) that resembled Microsoft's vision statements, laying out product themes and priorities for the next release or for a new product. Again, as at Microsoft, Netscape teams expected the product specification to evolve, and they had a specific process in place to manage this evolution. The teams set a rough schedule, organized around product features or subsystems. Managers then broke the schedule into milestones—target dates by which they expected to complete certain features or degrees of functionality and release beta or field test versions. Netscape teams generated daily builds of the evolving products and tested as they went along, though not as thoroughly as in Microsoft projects. In addition, Netscape projects incorporated feedback from users during development, from beta or field testing, as well as from some usability testing and other customer contacts.

There were significant differences between Netscape and Microsoft in both process implementation and functional roles. Netscape did not have formal program managers. Instead, Netscape developers generally wrote both the functional specification and the product code, though technically oriented product managers sometimes wrote parts of the specifications. The browser division also had a release manager to coordinate and drive each project to completion, rather than a committee of functional managers running each project. Netscape did not coordinate features, feature teams, and milestones as neatly as Microsoft did. Microsoft also made use of scheduled buffer time to keep to the project deadlines. Netscape, in contrast, did not add buffer time but set ship dates within three-month windows. More significantly, Netscape developers did not themselves conduct tests on each daily build in addition to testing done by a separate build team. Nor did Netscape assign testers to programmers in a one-to-one ratio but had about one tester for every three or so developers, and the testers worked separately in functional groups. Netscape also appeared to be less intensive and systematic in incorporating user feedback during development.

Of course, Microsoft had variations and lapses in its product teams, especially within the Internet groups. If managers of new projects wanted to move *really fast*—for example, on the early versions of Internet Explorer and NetMeeting—developers usually took the lead in proposing features and writing up specification outlines. In these cases, Microsoft program managers came on board later and worked mainly on managing project schedules, writing up test cases with testers in parallel with development, working with interface or Web page designers, and building relationships with outside partners and customers. In such projects program managers played less of a role and mainly worked with customers or prepared for the sales effort. The best-written representation of the spec, in such fast-moving projects, was also usually the set of test cases, rather than a more formal functional specification.[24]

IMPLEMENTATION STRATEGIES AND SUBTLETIES

In general, software companies need to adapt any philosophy or set of development techniques to the needs of specific projects and business models. Products companies try to understand general user needs and ship products quickly if there is competition. Services-oriented companies that are building custom systems or hybrid solutions have to work closely with a particular client, who influences the schedule and the content of the project. *In general, there is no one best way to develop all software for all kinds of customers.* It follows that there are many different strategies and subtle implementation issues that managers, programmers, and entrepreneurs need to understand when managing software development directly or overseeing software projects. In this section, I have collected a number of general guidelines that cover each aspect and phase of software development, from defining high-level process goals through testing and quality assurance.[25]

High-Level Process

There are three basic points to think about when establishing high-level principles to guide software development. One, as Dave Maritz put it so well, is that all projects involving more than a handful of people need some structure. That structure defines the underlying process and should be repeatable across different projects. Second is that the structure should fit the nature of the product. Third, the structure should fit the market and the business strategy. The conclusion one should draw is that *software development groups and projects within the same organization usually need to define different kinds of processes for different kinds of products, markets, and customer requirements.*

No "One Best Process"

Too many managers want to define "one best development process" for their entire organization in an attempt to improve quality and productivity by introducing an SEI-like or factory-like *repeatable process*. This is desirable only to a certain extent. Software products can differ greatly not only by the application and the market, but also by specific customer requirements. There is mission-critical software that controls nuclear power plants, the space shuttle, or real-time banking operations, which have to be rock solid. There are small applications such as Word or video games that are not mission-critical or running on networks of users, even though their quality is very important to the individuals who use the products. So it is wrong to think that all software projects should use the same approach to building so many different types of products and systems, even though they are all "software."

The market and business strategy issues introduce more complexity into process choices. There are fast-paced markets with lots of competition and slower-paced markets with minimal competition. In some cases, at some times, speed to market and innovation are far more important than product quality, such as reliability. If you wait to deploy the latest science or technology to create the "perfect" product, you may never deliver anything and the market will pass you by. On the other end, if you finally move to the mass market, whether it be made up of enterprises or consumers, quality in the sense of reliability, support, and maintenance generally becomes much more important than speed to market or innovation.

What to Emphasize Most

Depending on a company's business objectives, software managers need a varying high-level process strategy and varying development approaches. The process should vary in terms of how much emphasis is placed on things such as writing as complete a spec as possible before coding, or applying a software factory or SEI type of "full court press" in quality control. In mission-critical projects with extremely high reliability requirements, managers should insist on more specification and architecture work before coding (though still leaving room for feedback and evolution of the spec, such as in the user interface).

Managers should also insist on design and code reviews, continuous builds as well as unit and integration testing, and thorough documentation of the design as well as the code. They should make sure teams have debugged features as thoroughly as possible before moving on to the next milestone; otherwise problems build up. Managers should also collect product and process data during and after a project, and invest in a process group to study how to do things better with each project and to define at least some standards and common procedures. These are all good things to do in general, but they are essential for mission-critical software. For other kinds of projects, it is possible to cut some corners sometimes, although managers, programmers, and entrepreneurs should never forget that shipping products with bad quality, bad architectures, or bad documentation usually annoys customers and comes back to haunt the development and support organizations.

Innovation and Design Strategy

In PC and Internet software companies, there certainly are *many* projects where managers want to encourage creativity and invention, even late in a project and at the risk of producing more bugs and delaying the ship date. The danger is that loose projects will spin out of control—never shipping anything because of infinite defect loops or because they attempt the impossible (too much to invent in too short a time period with not enough people and forethought). Most important is that managers need a strategy to manage innovation and design, rather than leaving too much to chance and to the developers themselves.

The Level of Control

Netscape's philosophy was that being "slightly out of control"—less structured than Microsoft, for example—would stimulate innovative thinking and creativity, which it did. Microsoft, in an earlier era, had chosen to be less structured than IBM because it also wanted to be more innovative, faster to market, and more flexible in everything. The downside of the Netscape philosophy taken to the extreme is that too few controls can lead to chaos and attempting the impossible or improbable.

The U.S. and Russian governments remain pretty good at funding rocket science, building missile systems and rocket ships with public funds and without real competition. Sometimes attempting rocket science is the right thing to do even for a commercial company. In a sense, IBM tried this and succeeded with OS/360 in the 1960s. But this software project was enormously costly and required the resources of an IBM to pull off. Microsoft's .NET initiative has some characteristics of rocket science as well. It remains to be seen how well Microsoft will do with this effort, though the company is so accustomed to repackaging incremental innovations as new products that it will undoubtedly continue to deliver new products within a now watered-down .NET framework. But many times—perhaps most of the time—tackling enormous technical challenges in a single software project leads to disaster, especially for start-ups or firms that have no strategy for incremental development or procedures for evaluating and managing risk.

Risk Management

Synch-and-stabilize techniques are particularly useful for risk management in the sense that they provide a mechanism for assessing progress in a project and making adjustments continuously. Projects can use daily builds and milestone subprojects to proceed in iterations, conduct experiments as needed, and frequently reevaluate technical feasibility, feature sets, resources, quality, and ship dates.

Many people believe that Netscape lost the browser war to Microsoft because Microsoft bundled its browser with Windows and bullied or bribed companies such as AOL, Dell, Compaq, and Apple into supporting its technology. While these accusations were true, it is also the case that Netscape was its own worst enemy. The Internet start-up lost at least a year of browser development work because it lacked adequate controls in software design and development. As Netscape moved beyond the third and fourth versions of Navigator, the code base grew from a few tens of thousands of lines to several million. Meanwhile, Netscape teams attempted to build two new versions of the browser and Communicator suite (5.0, an incremental upgrade, and 6.0, a new Java-based design) at once. This lapse was perhaps the major factor that proved fatal in its battle with Microsoft. As Netscape cofounder Marc Andreessen recalled, "The people running the 6.0 project violated my cardinal rule of how you do product development, which is incrementally. They were trying to do way too much all at once. The project was unbounded in time, had no deliverables even defined. I just didn't kill it soon enough. . . . 6.0 turned into rocket science, and it was driving me nuts." [26]

Synch-and-stabilize techniques such as vision statements, evolving specs, work broken up into subcycles, daily builds, milestone stabilizations, early integration testing, and various customer feedback mechanisms during development represent an approach to risk management somewhere between a highly bureaucratic style of software development and a potentially chaotic style. The vision statement that kicks off a project is essentially a team contract that should indicate very clearly what the team hopes to do and what it is not going to do. I have seen Microsoft vision statements that were one paragraph long, one page long, and many pages long. Evolving the product spec from an outline and reevaluating it periodically during the project avoids spending time detailing specs for features that the team will never get to or reject.

Project teams should also have a "multiversion release" mentality, if possible. The idea here is that there is no need to try to create a "perfect" product that includes everybody's pet features and invents the next greatest technology. If the team is successful, it will probably build second and third versions. Even in custom projects, software companies usually have a chance to refine their work with maintenance releases. So there is rarely a need to attempt so much in any one project that the risk of failure is higher than the likelihood of success.

Late Changes Can Be Good

The other important idea here is that *late design changes can be good*. Managers should not treat them as "mistakes" or unwanted feedback from customers or the testing department. Some managers find this hard to understand, no doubt because of their education and experiences with delayed schedules and buggy code. I once thought the same way, before witnessing firsthand the faster-paced market for PC software.

I remember learning two precepts of traditional software engineering in the mid-1980s. One was that most problems occur because projects did not have a good requirements document and a complete specification before people started coding. A second precept was that late changes in the code or the design destabilized the product, created bugs, and made the project late, which then created a destructive dynamic. Too often a software team would feel forced to shortchange testing and ship a buggy product.

The Japanese software factories got around this problem by giving tremendous authority to their QA departments. QA managers had to approve any product ship decision, and they used historical data to determine how many bugs they should be finding in design documents or code at different stages of development and how much more testing would be necessary before they could consider a product to be of high quality.[27] But new products for new markets don't have this kind of historical data. Furthermore, fast-paced markets may require different standards and procedures, within certain limits. You never want to ship a *bad* product that, as in a recent Oracle case, requires you to ship five thousand to seven thousand patches.[28]

But my point is that managers should recognize that any initial specification will be incomplete. Encouraging evolutionary design allows a team to respond to unforeseen market changes, user feedback, and competitors' moves. As I will discuss in more detail later in this chapter, research indicates that late changes do produce more bugs and schedule delays. But proper countermeasures—such as frequent builds, design and code reviews, and integration testing with each change—can mitigate the level of bugs and lateness. *A process that expects and allows projects to accommodate lots of change with a minimal impact on quality and productivity is a great competitive advantage for many software firms.*

Economies of Scope

Another aspect of innovation and design strategy is how to increase not simply creativity or structure when one of these is necessary but also *economies of scope*—efficiency across building separate products—which is almost always important to an ongoing business. The idea is to leverage work and creativity across multiple projects, rather than treating each project as a unique undertaking done from scratch. Scope in software development comes from reusing artifacts and knowledge, including architectures, design frameworks or patterns, pieces of working code, support tools, test cases, and historical product and process data (such as how long particular kinds of projects usually take and how much testing they normally require). Taking code reuse as a simple example, Netscape undertook some economies of scope management by sharing components across its client and server groups. Microsoft pushed standardization and sharing even further in operating systems and desktop applications such as Office, whose Word, Excel, and PowerPoint products share half or more of their code. Japanese software factories have been especially adept at reusing large amounts of code in industrial applications, which they "semicustomize" for different clients.

Engineers I have worked with tell me that code reuse happens most often when companies package components in ways that are easy for developers in other groups to understand and redeploy, like black-box parts in the auto industry. If programmers have to change a lot of the design or code to use a part, reuse can become inefficient. Toshiba, before the days of object-oriented design, found that its engineers could change up to 20 percent of a module and the reuse effort would still be cost-effective. If they needed to change more than that, they were better off writing new code from scratch. Toshiba also kept track of reused modules and gave out awards to encourage programmers to think about reuse and writing popular modules—an interesting way to channel engineers' energies and creativity.[29]

Another way to achieve economies of scope—for both software producers and users—is to buy or license components that fit the needs of an organization or a particular product. It should go without saying that the fastest way to get a piece of software delivered is not to write it but to buy it. This is not always possible, and cheap standardized packages or libraries of components usually require some compromises in functionality. Nonetheless, determining what can be bought rather than built should be part of every organization's innovation and design strategy.

Architecture Strategy

Unfortunately, for some companies (and here I include Netscape's browser group), the style of development that comes with evolving specs, lots of feature changes during a project, and daily builds requires a particular approach to product architecture.

The Importance of Modular Designs

The most important point is that *synch-and-stabilize techniques work best with modular product architectures*. I have seen computer scientists argue for days about how to define a line of code. Defining a module leads to similarly lengthy debates. There is no one definition. Moreover, there is a sliding scale of modularity for almost any complex product, whether it is a software system or an automobile. For example, most automobiles have about fifteen thousand discrete components. However, most automakers design and build their cars using subsystems. At some companies, the number of subsystems is relatively low, such as 25 at Ford and 60 at Fiat. At others, it is relatively high, such as 290 at Toyota. The difference is the degree of modularity that the company designs into the architecture of its products.[30]

However you define it, a module in software should be some subset of functionality that is smaller than the whole product and that designers can isolate from other small chunks of functionality and, to some degree, test as a separate unit. Microsoft people like to think in terms of "features," which contain modules within some larger subsets of functionality understandable to a user, such as the cut-and-paste feature in Word or the spreadsheet recalculation feature in Excel. The opposite of a modular architecture is an integral architecture, where components are tightly coupled and interdependent. It is difficult to change and test pieces of a product with an integral architecture without creating bugs in dependent components.[31] Integral architectures do the equivalent of binding the legs of everybody in a project together, slowing down even fast developers. In some cases, though, this kind of product architecture can lead to superior performance, such as a custom-built racing car optimized for speed.

Some small software programs might have integral architectures that minimize their size or optimize their performance. But as code bases grow to thousands and often millions of lines of code, modular architecture becomes more important. The architecture needs to define what the subsystems of the product are, how the subsystems (collections of modules) relate to one another, perhaps what a module within a subsystem is, and, most important, what the interfaces are so that subsystems and individual modules can exchange data or instructions and work together. Interfaces should be stable for some period of time and not altered without changes being carefully communicated to a development team because developers need to know how to get modules to interact with one another.

Modularization also helps a project team prioritize features and build them in order of importance to the product or the business, like a sequential (or "horizontal") list that the team gets to one by one. With prioritization and modularization, a team usually has the option to cut lower-priority features if a project falls behind schedule. If the modules are too interdependent, a project might need a very large team to build all the desired features in parallel. Or a smaller team might build pieces of the product sequentially. With the sequential process, the project will usually have to follow a waterfall type of schedule and not test the pieces in an integrated fashion until the team is mostly done—when it may be too late to fix major problems or make important changes for the customer.

Incremental Architecture Evolution
It is also possible to evolve the architecture of a software product incrementally to make it more modular, even if it didn't start out that way because of time pressures or simply a lack of foresight and experience. Microsoft, for example, gradually rearchitected Office over

several years to make the applications within Office able to share features. The company used to sell Office as a collection of packaged "vertical" applications that were really separate products. Each product (Word, Excel, PowerPoint, and Access) had its own separate features for text processing, file management, table creation, cut-and-paste, printer drivers, and so on. A separate team figured out how to link the products "horizontally" and build popular features that could be shared across the applications.

Within a few years, Office itself became the product, with Word, Excel, and PowerPoint becoming subsystems that shared about half of their code. This sharing evolved to the point where, for Office 2000, fully 38 percent of the developers working on the product were creating common features shared by one or more of the applications.[32] Microsoft also did some similar incremental architecture redesign of its mass-market Windows product, which did not start out as a modularized product at all but rather was a graphical user interface cobbled together to sit on top of MS-DOS. Microsoft's now-flagship product has evolved nicely from Window 3.0/3.1 to Windows 95/98 and then to Windows 2000/XP/2003, finally shifting to the new code base developed in parallel from the original Windows NT project in the early 1990s.

The Pressure to Ship

Market pressures explain a lot of why Netscape allowed the Navigator code base to grow from 100,000 lines in 1994 to 3 million lines in 1996 with little thought to architecture and modularization. The development team also expanded during these years from 10 to 120 programmers, with another 80 engineers serving as testers on the last project. But, by 1996, it had become impossible to add new features without destabilizing the entire product and going through an elaborate testing and debugging exercise—slowing down Netscape in a race for survival with Microsoft. Bob Lisbonne, former manager of the browser division, described writing software for the Navigator/ Communicator product as analogous to running a three-legged race:

> When our teams grew beyond a certain point, they began to resemble a 200-person three-legged race where, even if you had really fast sprinters, to the extent all their legs were bound, you were guaranteed to have stumbles and slow down through no fault of any particular per-

son or group. . . . That's why the component-ization or the modularization of the product is so key, so that ultimately we can get back to
lots of small teams each doing their own thing—doing the right thing—
and not getting caught up in one another's efforts.[33]

By mid-1997, Lisbonne and other Netscape managers realized that
they would have to fix their architecture problem because it was
affecting their ability to compete. So they split the browser development team in half and assigned about a hundred people to rewriting
the code base into neater modules, and doing it in Java as well. The
other half of the team worked on new features for the next release.
But the architecture work proved to be too hard. Increasing numbers
of developers were pulled off feature development until Netscape
managers finally admitted failure and canceled the project. By then
the company had lost its lead to Microsoft in the browser war and
never recovered. Michael Toy, release manager for Navigator, made a
comment to David Yoffie and me regarding Navigator/Communica-
tor 4.0 that would later become part of Microsoft's opening defense
in the 1998 antitrust trial: "We wrote this code three years ago and its
major purpose in life was to get us in business as fast as possible. We
should have stopped shipping this code a year ago. It is dead. We are
paying the price for going fast. And when you got fast, you don't
architect and so you don't say, 'I want those three-years from now
benefits.' "[34]

Many new software companies have to ship products quickly, usually within a year or two. Otherwise, the window of opportunity for
their market may disappear. It is unreasonable to expect new companies to devote too much effort to figuring out how to design a product
architecture that will last for years. I am not sure what the right number of staff to allocate to architecture development is, especially for a
start-up. But to make zero investment in architecture for the future is
usually a mistake. And it also seems unwise to devote half of a development team to fixing the mistakes of the past rather than writing features to help the firm compete in the present.

My experience with different companies, including the firm described in the assessment excerpts (which also had serious architecture problems with its product), suggests that a firm should devote
about 20 percent of its engineering staff to architectural work for ongoing projects. It might allocate more for new strategic products or

best-selling products that desperately need rearchitecting, but not too much more. In any case, the best strategy is to encourage the team to think ahead and, from the beginning of a new product's cycle, devote at least some engineering effort to designing an architecture that will last a few years and accommodate functionality that will be needed in the future.

Team Management

Another piece of common wisdom in the software engineering field is that a small team of great people works much better than a large team of mediocre people and that talent is more important than experience.[35] I also believe these generalizations to be true. Every experienced software manager has encountered programmers who, as indicated in a NATO study in the late 1960s, could write ten or twenty times as much code or more than the worst programmer on the team, in the same amount of time. And the superprogrammers probably have fewer bugs, too. The rule of thumb given by Tom DeMarco and Timothy Lister, the authors of *Peopleware,* is that your best programmer will probably be about 10 times better than your worst programmer and about 2.5 times better than your average programmer.[36]

The Problem of Large Teams

But one problem with managing by this philosophy alone is that *superprogrammers are hard to find and harder to keep.* In Japan, they have been especially hard to find because of weak university programs in computer science (compared to those in the United States and Europe), relatively few computers in secondary schools until recently, and the lack of a U.S.-style hacker tradition. Not surprisingly, the Japanese evolved specific process techniques and organizations— the software factories—as a way of compensating for a lack of good people experienced in software development. But not even Microsoft, which recruits people from around the world, can find enough superprogrammers to develop all the software it would like to develop. So *the more common problem many software companies have is how to get relatively large groups of people with varying abilities and skills to work together like nimble and talented small teams.*

Much of what I have talked about under the synch-and-stabilize banner is designed to tackle this problem—how to make large teams work like small teams. Selby and I first stated these factors in *Microsoft Secrets:* project size and scope limits; modular architectures; project architectures mapped to the product so that everyone knows why they are building what they are building; projects divided into small relatively autonomous teams (say, three to eight developers per feature team); rigid rules to force coordination and synchronization; good communications and shared functional responsibilities; and product and process flexibility to handle unknowns.[37]

Effective Teamwork Principles

I have also found it important to have strong project leaders to make sure that even the superprogrammers (who tend to be "prima donnas") follow a few basic rules that improve teamwork. It is easy to overlook another aspect of Microsoft's approach: *overlapping functional responsibilities.* Product managers take charge of writing vision statements, but they are also responsible for consulting program managers. Program managers write functional specs, but they have to consult developers, who generally have a de facto veto power because they have to estimate the time and people required to write the code. Developers and testers are paired and are jointly responsible for testing code. Good communications and overlapping responsibilities help an organization avoid becoming too functionally oriented and too compartmentalized, with large, separate groups that simply hand off work to one another. My favorite quote to illustrate this kind of teamwork philosophy is from a videotaped presentation given by former Microsoft Vice President Chris Peters, who was the chief evangelist for Microsoft's development approach in the late 1980s through the mid-1990s: "Everybody in a business unit has exactly the same . . . job description, and that is to *ship products.* Your job is not to write code, your job is not to test, your job is not to write specs. Your job is to *ship products.* . . . You're trying *not* to write code. If we could make all this money by not writing code, we'd do it."[38]

Peter's philosophy also provides a way for companies to avoid getting bogged down in a bureaucratic organizational structure. Microsoft has become more bureaucratic as it has become larger, with more layers of senior executives, although CEO Steve Ballmer (who took this position over from Bill Gates in 2002) has been cutting the layers and working more with leadership teams. Gates, for example, now heads a small group that directs the development of advanced strategies and technologies and other teams that are in charge of Microsoft's "integrated product road map," the company's server and platform software strategies, and strategies for Windows PCs, MSN, and other company products and services.[39]

In general, along with frequent communication across groups, Microsoft continues to rely on separate units for each product and small feature teams for development within these product units. Managers can also scale this structure up easily by creating more feature teams and more product units. Within a product unit that has an effective leader, the right set of development techniques, and the right product architecture, it is possible to have a large team of several hundred people working together almost like one small team. Synch-and-stabilize techniques, consistently used, ensure that a large number of small teams will continually communicate, share responsibilities, and synchronize what they are doing.

Project Management

The most important thing to remember is that the traditional waterfall model for project management, though it may deliver software on time, matching requirements exactly and with few bugs, is not a good response to fast-paced markets driven by the need to adapt to continuous innovation, uncertainty in customer requirements, and competition. The waterfall model originally came about in complex but fairly stable development projects, such as rocket systems, where NASA needed to control requirements and schedules in great detail. To NASA, not making changes that might create bugs is far more important than being innovative or fast to market. Most software producers, however, whether they make mass-market products or custom systems, need a process that will let them evolve designs and incorporate customer feedback in real time, during a project. In such an environment, projects should do requirements specification, design, coding, and testing as concurrently as possible, with some planning and architecture design up front to give the project focus and the technical means to divide up tasks and module or feature development.

Divide and Conquer

This last thought brings me to the age-old principle of "divide and conquer." In software, this means you should break large projects into multiple subprojects (Hewlett-Packard uses the term "subcycles") or milestones of no more than a few weeks' or months' duration. It is much easier to manage several small groups that are doing a smaller amount of work and have a deadline that is only a few weeks or months away than to manage one large group creating a large number of features that it is supposed to deliver in a year or more. Too many things can go wrong or change when a project deadline is too far in the future, when a team is too large, or when the amount of feature design and integration work is too overwhelming.

When Selby and I were studying Microsoft, we heard a lot of horror stories about IBM's old style of development on OS/2 and mainframe software. IBM would define in an up-front specification document everything management wanted to accomplish in a project, then gather a huge number of people who would build all the different pieces in parallel. Then, sometime in the future, near the end of the project, in one "big bang," the team would try to integrate all the pieces. It is a classic waterfall model. One problem, though, was the difficulty IBM had integrating so many different components at once, especially if they were not carefully modularized. The synch-and-stabilize approach would be to break up the project and therefore reduce the integration problem and the overall project uncertainty. Microsoft managers even felt that a few small teams working on smaller chunks of functionality in separate subprojects, done sequentially, would actually finish faster than a larger team working on all of a project's components at once. The reason is that integration at the end becomes simpler and there are many more opportunities in midstream to get feedback from users, find and fix problems, and reallocate resources.

There were other horror stories about how inept the IBM programmers were (many were just hardware maintenance people who had been quickly retrained to write PC software) as they struggled to write code for OS/2. For example: IBM and Microsoft split the programming tasks for OS/2 roughly in half. Microsoft had a couple hundred or so top-notch programmers on the job, while IBM deployed a thousand or so people to do a roughly equivalent amount of work. Microsoft managers disparagingly referred to the IBM approach as "masses of asses programming."[40] Microsoft programmers would also spend time going over their code to reduce its length in order to make programs run faster and would sometimes allocate an entire month or so to this kind of optimization work. IBM managers, who measured productivity by counting lines of code per person, when they first observed this behavior, argued that Microsoft had "negative productivity" on the project and owed IBM money![41]

Individual Commitments and Project Discipline

It is essential to get people's commitment to work as a team and deliver on individual promises. Programmers and testers should schedule their own work, rather than managers dictating schedules (as at the software company I described in my assessment). But managers need to keep historical data on projects and individuals to judge the accuracy of the estimates and keep everyone honest. It is often not necessary to press programmers to shorten their estimates, however, at least at companies like Microsoft and Netscape, because they tend to be overly optimistic about what they can do anyway. As Chris Peters noted to Selby and me, *self-scheduling by the developers not only produces an aggressive schedule, which managers like, it also produces both the appearance and the reality of being a fair schedule because it comes from the bottom up.* Historical project data is also useful so that managers can schedule some buffer time into a project to accommodate unforeseen changes or problems that turn out to be more difficult than the engineers had anticipated.

Another issue is how rigid to make the project rules. The goal should always be to ship a great product, not simply follow rules or a process. At Microsoft, we had the impression that there were in fact very few rules but a "military-like discipline" about the few rules that projects did have. We did not see this level of discipline at Netscape, where everything was looser. However, if a programmer checked in code that broke the build, whether at Netscape or at Microsoft, it was impossible to hide.

Infrastructure Investments

Microsoft and Netscape invested in various tools and build teams to make checking in easier and faster for programmers and to automate a lot of the testing—as well as to catch people who wrote buggy code. A check-in could take a few minutes or an hour, depending on the amount of code the developer had written, but no more. If check-in times are too long, the daily build process becomes burdensome and programmers will avoid it. But the real beauty of a smoothly working build process is that, again, a few simple rules can be enough to enforce discipline and still be subtle. Programmers do not like to have to rewrite their code. What happened at both Microsoft and Netscape is that the rule requiring developers to fix their own code if they broke the build created a dynamic where people, on their own, decided to check in very frequently—a couple of times a week and once a day or more toward the end of a project. That way everybody stays in synch, and projects maintain the illusion of having lots of freedom and very few rules.

Testing and QA

Finally, we come to the topic of testing and quality assurance—a tedious topic for many senior managers but essential for a software company to become a successful business. The battle between Microsoft and Netscape over browsers in particular has forced me to think a lot about how to write high-quality code and do adequate testing in a fast-paced environment.

You Can Never Do Too Much Testing

Many people are surprised to learn how many people Microsoft allocates to testing—as many as it does to programming, with testers usually assigned as "buddies" to developers in a one-to-one ratio. Some people are also surprised that, given this enormous investment in testing, Microsoft's quality isn't higher. It is important to understand why.

First, Microsoft's quality has improved dramatically over the past decade and in multiple ways—from reduced numbers of bugs to products that are much easier to install and use compared to the old MS-DOS- and DOS-based applications. These results directly reflect the enormous investment in testing as well as, more broadly, in process and product improvement. But I don't like to spend time apologizing for Microsoft. It still has a lot of room to improve in terms of product stability and usability. Second, many of Microsoft's testers, especially in the applications groups, are more like an advance army of beta users. These testers try to use a new product or version under development as a user would and try to detect user types of problems early on. It is a good investment to make because Microsoft sells tens of millions of copies of many of its software products. A few bugs or products that are difficult to use can generate millions of customer inquiries and complaints.

The basic logic is that *there can never be too much testing*. This is especially true for a mass-market software products company. Not even Microsoft can afford to have millions of dissatisfied customers calling in to its help lines on a daily basis. Bill Gates came to this realization in 1990, when Windows 3.0 started selling in the tens of millions and too large a percentage of its users started calling in with problems. Microsoft had already spent millions of dollars on product recalls in the 1980s, on much smaller sales volumes. Gates also began to worry that Microsoft would become like WordPerfect, with half the company answering telephone calls.[42] It did not. From that time on, Microsoft has put enormous effort into usability testing by developers as well as into hiring testers and product engineers who analyze each customer complaint and channel this information into the development groups each week. The sole intention has been to improve reliability, usability, installability, and other aspects of product quality in order to avoid the costs of massive product support.

Building in Quality Through Continuous Testing

In automobiles and other industries, we learned from Japanese companies decades ago that it is ultimately cheaper to "build in" quality continuously rather than to test and fix it in at the end of a development or production cycle. This has been especially true in waterfall projects, where fixing a bug in the field at a customer site can cost a hundred times as much as finding and fixing it early in a project.[43] Software products with modular architectures and built with synch-and-stabilize techniques can accommodate design changes and bug fixes late in a project more easily and with much lower costs. But fixing problems in the field by sending out patches is still expensive and bad for a company's reputation. In any case, how should we interpret Microsoft's one-to-one tester-to-developer ratios and so much daily testing of builds? Is this testing in quality or building it in continuously as a product evolves?

Microsoft people, dating back to 1989, believe their techniques build in quality continuously. Testing in quality would be like having engineers at the end of a waterfall process to find and fix bugs. I must admit that the Japanese software factories did this to achieve their astounding quality levels, even with only about 10 percent of their project manpower devoted to testing.[44] The Japanese, though, asked developers to spend a lot of time doing their own testing as well as participating with QA staff in design and code reviews. In the synch-and-stabilize approach, which can easily incorporate conventional best practices such as design and code reviews, the use of tester buddies, daily builds, and milestone stabilization junctures provides opportunities to find and fix bugs throughout a project, not just at the end. This idea is very similar to Extreme Programming, where paired programmers continually write test cases and review each other's work as they write code.

Another point here is the importance not only of continuous feature testing—done manually by human testers or through automated tests—but of continuous *integration* and *system-level testing.* For example, creating a better drawing feature is fine. But if the object drawn cannot be printed or used with other features in the application, the new feature is not properly integrated and a bug exists. It is better to identify such problems earlier rather than later and avoid falling into those nasty infinite defect loops. Data from process surveys I have done have reinforced this point as well: the earlier a project team can begin integration testing and the more it does so, the higher the quality and the more likely the project will be close to the schedule and budget targets.

It is also important for projects to automate as much feature or unit testing as well as component integration and system-level testing as possible. Automation makes it possible to rerun tests frequently, such as with each code change, and find bugs generated by those changes. However, it is a myth that automation significantly reduces the need for people. Netscape found this out and had to double the number of people it had allocated to testing. The reason is that people are needed to update the tests as a project moves forward and incorporates more functionality or changes in user interface designs. Most automated tests run off the user interface and have to change as the user interface changes.

Continuous Process and Product Improvement

Over multiple projects, it is desirable to have a strategy to improve process and product quality on a continuous basis—the now-familiar Japanese notion of *kaizen.* One way is to conduct postmortem analyses, share the results with the team, and then act on the conclusions. The Microsoft reports that we looked at generally had three parts to them, compiled by the managers for each function on each project: product management, program management, development, testing, customer support, and user education (documentation). Each manager was supposed to interview his or her team members and come up with a summary of (1) what went well on the project, (2) what went poorly, and (3) what should they do differently the next time. Most of the Microsoft teams stayed together for a few years and had an opportunity to apply what they learned in subsequent projects. We concluded, though, that Microsoft teams could have done an even better job at following through on recommendations from the reports.[45]

Another great source of learning is data received from customers through the product support organization. With tools such as Scopus (now marketed by Siebel Systems), it is possible to create detailed lists of bugs and fixes. Good teams also develop heuristics about how to avoid and fix common bugs. Microsoft routinely created checklists for its testers and developers to help them avoid common errors. The Japanese tended to create short handbooks.

A phrase common at Microsoft and other companies—"eat your own dog food"—captures yet another useful practice: using the product internally as it is being built so that there is a firsthand, immediate experience of whether or not it is any good. For example, if you are building the next version of Windows, as soon as you get to a point where basic functionality in the build works, you should start using it to do basic things, such as saving your files and running your e-mail program. If the product is lousy and crashes, you have to eat the programming equivalent of dog food.

Beta releases also can provide important feedback from actual customers on the quality as well as the design of a product. Beta releases have been around for a while, but Microsoft first started using them in massive numbers with Windows NT. Then Netscape raised the order of magnitude of beta testers from tens of thousands, which were typical Microsoft numbers, to millions. It was the use of the Internet to distribute betas that made it possible for Netscape to achieve these numbers as well as get feedback automatically, without having to set up special online accounts for beta users or swap diskettes or CD-ROMs in the mail. Netscape released so many betas so early in its development cycles that users provided feedback on design, not only on quality. In contrast, Microsoft projects generally released betas after they had completed designs to get user feedback more on reliability and usage rather than on features and design issues. But betas that come too late in a development cycle do not allow a team enough time to make major design changes.

On the other hand, since the early 1990s, Microsoft has made extraordinarily good use of different measures to get customer feedback during development, far surpassing Netscape in this regard. One technique was the use of usability labs, where Microsoft would bring in people "off the street" to test features under development. Programmers watched from behind one-way mirrors to see what percentage of users had to struggle to understand a product's features. Developers were expected to continue revising their features until a large majority of users in the lab could understand a new feature the first time they tried to use it. Microsoft also did things such as sending developers and testers to staff customer support lines after a new product shipped so that, again, they could get firsthand feedback on customer reactions. Product teams complemented the usability lab data and customer support data (summaries of which teams received on a weekly basis) with customer satisfaction surveys, product usage surveys, and other feedback mechanisms.[46]

Last, a good practice to monitor and improve the operations of a software development organization is to have each project track a small number of quantifiable metrics covering product quality, the size and performance of the product, and the development process. And I emphasize "a small number." I remember visiting Hitachi in the mid-1990s to get an update on its software factories. One of its chief engineers proudly showed me a new project management tool that tracked 150 different product and process variables. While the tool was probably useful for doing intensive research on some projects, I thought it was overkill for project management. It may be that 150 or more variables affect the performance of a software development team and the quality of its output, but this is too many factors for a manager to keep track of and actually *manage*. I felt much more comfortable with a smaller number of metrics. In any case, it is important to understand what the major factors that drive the performance of your teams and customer responses to your products or the systems you deliver are. And projects need to be able to measure these factors quantitatively if the team is to manage them effectively. This idea of statistical analysis and feedback is also central to the SEI philosophy, especially for projects aiming to reach CMM Level 5.

INTERNATIONAL COMPARISONS

Most of the comments I have made about implementation strategies and subtleties come from observations at Microsoft, Netscape, the Japanese software factories, and several dozen other companies. But a couple of years ago, I became curious about how widespread synch-and-stabilize techniques were becoming around the world, in contrast to more waterfall-like approaches, and what, if any, measurable impact they were having on project output measures, such as quality, productivity, and scheduling.

To follow up on this idea, during 2001–2003, I initiated a survey of software development practices and performance with several colleagues: Alan MacCormack of the Harvard Business School, Chris Kemerer of the University of Pittsburgh, and Bill Crandall of Hewlett-Packard.[47] Appendix Table 14 is a preliminary list of summary data for 104 projects, excluding 14 projects with incomplete data and another 30 projects from Hewlett-Packard (including the Agilent spin-off) that we used for a pilot survey.[48] Companies participating in the global study included Motorola India Electronics, Infosys, Tata, and Patni from India; Hitachi, NEC, IBM Japan, NTT Data, SRA, Matsushita, Omron, Fuji Xerox, and Olympus from Japan; IBM, Hewlett-Packard, Agilent Technologies, Sun Microsystems, Microsoft, Siebel Systems, AT&T, Fidelity Investments, Merrill Lynch, Lockheed Martin, TRW, and Micron Technology from the United States; and Siemens, Business Objects, and Nokia from Europe.

Differences in Practices

First we asked about conventional best practices. For example, in how many projects did programmers write architectural and functional specifications as well as detailed designs before coding? How many used code-generation tools? How many implemented design and code reviews? Then we asked about the newer synch-and-stabilize techniques, with some XP techniques included as well: How many projects divided up into subcycles or milestones, used beta tests, paired programmers with each other and with testers, followed daily builds, and did regression tests on each build? We also divided the sample into regions: India, Japan, the United States, and Europe. We are currently still analyzing the data statistically and collecting some corrected numbers, but I can offer some general observations.[49]

In terms of practice, about 85 percent of the sample wrote functional specs, and nearly 70 percent wrote architectural and detailed design documents, rather than just writing code with minimal planning and documentation. These conventional good practices were especially popular in India, Japan, and Europe. The major difference was that few U.S. software developers wrote detailed designs. I observed a decade ago that Microsoft programmers in general did not write detailed designs but went straight from a functional specification to coding in order to save time and not waste effort writing specs for features that teams might later delete. This seems to be a common practice in the United States. Code generation (a technique that uses special software programs to generate code from design frameworks or design tools) was most popular in the Indian sample. Design and code reviews require particular process discipline, as promoted by the SEI recommendations. Not surprisingly, all the Indian and Japanese projects utilized design reviews, and all but one of the Indian projects utilized code reviews as well. Most projects in the other regions also followed these good practices, though not universally.

As for the newer techniques, these were popular around the world, with some variations. Most projects used subcycles, for example, though these were most common in our Indian and European samples, and least popular in Japan. Projects that did not use subcycles, in our definition, followed a conventional waterfall process. More than half the Japanese projects, therefore, seemed to follow a conventional waterfall schedule. Most projects also used beta releases, which, as I noted earlier, have become useful testing and feedback tools since the arrival of the Web. More than 40 percent of the projects surveyed paired testers with developers—a Microsoft-style practice especially popular in India. Thirty-five percent of the projects used the XP practice of pairing programmers, and again, this was especially popular in the Indian sample (58 percent). More than 80 percent of the sample used daily builds at some time during the project and about 46 percent used them at the beginning or middle, which is closer to the Microsoft style of development. More than 83 percent of the projects also ran regression tests on each build. Again, this good practice was most common in the Indian sample (nearly 92 percent).

Links Between Practice and Performance
Researchers on software engineering over the past two decades will not be surprised by two of our preliminary findings from analyzing

the Hewlett-Packard and Agilent sample.[50] We are still examining the global sample.

First, the HP and Agilent developers tended to be more productive in terms of code output when they had a more complete design before starting to write code. Second, more complete designs before coding correlated with lower levels of bugs. These results make sense and have led many software managers to insist on having complete specs before people start writing code—the old waterfall process. Programmers can be more productive in a technical sense if they have to make fewer changes during a project. They also have less chance of introducing errors if they make fewer design and code changes.

Yet, in a business sense, *locking a project early into a particular design may not produce the best product for the customer or a rapidly changing market.* We did, in fact, find some evidence that HP and Agilent managers thought their customers were more satisfied with designs that evolved during a project. We also found that use of early betas and prototypes—which created opportunities for customers to provide early feedback on the design—was associated with higher code productivity and fewer defects, probably because the HP and Agilent projects were able to be adjusted early on. In addition, running regression tests with each build, breaking projects into multiple subcycles, and conducting design reviews were associated with fewer bugs.

The most important preliminary conclusion we can draw from the pilot data is that, at least within a single development culture (HP and Agilent), *synch-and-stabilize techniques appear to form a coherent set of practices.* Software projects can be more flexible in the sense of accommodating design changes with minimal impact on quality and productivity when they use several of these techniques together, rather than just one or two. Our results suggest that there are trade-offs associated with using different techniques, especially with regard to allowing specifications to evolve after the start of coding. The use of particular techniques, however, helps projects overcome these potential trade-offs.

In short, when the HP and Agilent projects used beta releases to get early user feedback, conducted design reviews, and ran regression tests on each build of the code (that is, after each change or addition of new code), the correlation between having an incomplete design when coding starts and bugginess disappeared. Thus *software producers can have the best of both worlds.* With the right set of techniques, they can both write high-quality code in a productive manner and adapt quickly to customer feedback and changes in the market-place during rather than after a project.

Regional Differences in Performance

Project performance across firms is difficult to measure and even more difficult to compare regionally from such a small sample, but we used some crude measures and found some interesting differences. The numbers I report here are preliminary and are subject to further analysis and data collection, which we will report on in a future series of papers.

Based on the preliminary data in Appendix Table 14, the Japanese had the best quality levels (median of .020) in terms of defects reported per 1,000 lines of code in the twelve months after implementation at customer sites. The Indian projects (.263) and U.S. projects (.400) were more similar and very good by historical standards but still 13 to 20 times more "buggy" than the Japanese projects. Projects from Europe and other areas (.225) were similar to the Indian levels. In terms of lines of code written per programmer per month—a measure of programmer output but not really productivity—the Japanese ranked at the top. They had a median output level of about 469 lines of code per programmer-month, unadjusted for programming language or type of project. This was more than twice the level of the Indian projects and about 70 percent more than the U.S. projects, though only slightly higher than the European and other projects.

In a study I did with Kemerer in 1990 as part of my research on software factories, we also found higher levels of code output and fewer bugs from Japanese software projects compared to U.S. projects, so the Japanese results are not surprising.[51] U.S. programmers often have different objectives and development styles. They tend to emphasize shorter or more innovative programs and spend much more time thinking about what they are writing and optimizing code—which reduces lines-of-code productivity in a gross sense. The Indian companies have mainly U.S. clients and may have adopted a similar U.S.-type programming style, which tends to see shorter programs as better than longer programs. Nonetheless, we expected the bug levels in India to be similar to the Japanese levels, given the emphasis of the Indian companies on achieving high SEI rankings. The Indian projects did produce fewer bugs than the U.S. projects but they are still far behind the Japanese.

Overall, the data suggest some strengths in India and continued strengths in Japan. But, as is common in this type of research, due to the extreme variations in performance from project to project, it is hard to draw any definite conclusions. It is important to remember as well that no Indian or Japanese company has made any real global mark in software innovation, which has long been the province of U.S. and a few European software firms. Code productivity is by no means a good measure of business performance and is less valuable than quality numbers in judging a software development organization. Japanese companies still seemed preoccupied with producing close to zero-defect code, and one can only wonder how much this practice constrains their willingness to experiment and innovate in software development. The preliminary data also show that Indian companies are doing an admirable job of combining conventional best practices with flexible synch-and-stabilize techniques. The rising importance of the software business in this developing country, as well as the general issue of outsourcing software development, takes us into the last topic for this chapter.

OUTSOURCING TO INDIA AND ELSEWHERE

It does not surprise me that Indian software companies are on top of best practices and doing well in process for software development. For a decade or more, organizations in India have been studying Japanese factory approaches and aggressively adopting SEI concepts and some synch-and-stabilize techniques. The India story could be the subject of an entire book. My comments here relate mainly to the sources of India's process orientation and success in receiving outsourcing work.

The Rise of the Indian Software Business

It is difficult to overestimate the importance of the software business to India's economy, which has struggled in so many sectors. The country has excellent universities for training software engineers and computer scientists, and the quality of the people has attracted both domestic entrepreneurs and foreign investors. Most major software producers in the United States and Europe—including Microsoft, Oracle, Sun Microsystems, IBM, Hewlett-Packard, Lucent, and Cisco—now have subsidiaries in India. As a result, software and related services generated $8.26 billion in revenues for India during 2001, a growth of 55 percent over the previous year. Total revenues for 2002 were up about 12 percent. Indian software exports accounted for $6.2 billion and domestic sales for $2.06 billion in 2001. Exports rose about 30 percent in 2002 to around $8 billion. Offshore project revenues were also up 49 percent between 2001 and 2002. In addition, software and services accounted for nearly 2 percent of India's gross domestic product in 2001 and are expected to reach nearly 8 percent by 2008.[52]

When I first visited India in January 2000, of the top two dozen or so software development facilities rated at CMM Level 5, eleven were in India. One was in Japan, and most of the rest were in the United States. The eleven Indian firms included U.S.-owned subsidiaries such as Motorola India Electronics and IBM Global Services India, but also local companies such as Tata Consultancy Services, Tata Infotech, Satym Computer Services, Wipro, and Infosys.[53] More recent data from May 2002 indicate that forty-three of the sixty-six organizations listed at CMM Level 5 and that agreed to be identified were located in India.[54] This is truly an impressive statistic.

Motorola in India

My initial exposure to the Indian software business came indirectly, through an unsuccessful attempt to create a software factory within Motorola in the United States. In the late 1980s, Motorola managers concluded that some 80 percent of their engineering work and most of their project delays and quality problems were in software development. Part of the reason was that former hardware engineers were running the company and had no systematic metrics or processes in place for managing software development. All that changed in the 1990s as Motorola extended its in-house training programs as well as its Six Sigma quality control initiatives to software. As part of this process, from the late 1980s, Motorola managers began studying Japanese software quality control and reuse practices and engaged me during 1990–1992 to help in their analysis and planning.

Another consultant that Motorola hired, Victor Basili of the University of Maryland, complemented the Japanese factory concepts with his notion of creating an "experience factory." Basili's idea was for organizations to establish centralized development facilities to collect data and reusable artifacts from a series of projects and package these "experiences" for reuse in project management, design, programming, and testing activities on subsequent projects. Many of the experience factory concepts have been implemented successfully at NASA's Software Engineering Laboratory at the Goddard Space Flight Center in Maryland.[55] It seemed like a great idea to try them at Motorola as well.

Robert Yacobellis and George Smith from Motorola's new software process research group, plus a few senior executives, decided to combine best practices from the Japanese with Basili's experience factory to create their own Motorola software factory. The goal was to bring together many of Motorola's small, distributed groups of programmers, give them a set of methods and tools, collect data on their projects, and help them manage software development and quality assurance more systematically. With the small groups of programmers that existed in the company at the time, distributed across Illinois, New Mexico, and other locations, it was hard to get any real scale or scope economies in process research or develop learning curves from doing multiple projects with the same groups of people.

We overlooked the fact that Motorola managers and engineers were very independent and liked to work in small, integrated teams (which is generally a very good idea). The Americans in particular did not like the proposal to create a centralized "software factory." But instead of giving up on the idea entirely, the Motorola managers who were in charge of the new software initiative decided to try a "clean sheet" approach: *They would create a software factory in India.* In 1991, this became Motorola India Electronics, Ltd. (MIEL). MIEL went on to build software for wireless and fixed-line communication systems, network management, testing tools for communications systems, digital signal processing, system software for Motorola chips, and computer-aided design tools for semiconductor chip design.[56] During my January 2000 visit, MIEL had more than five hundred software engineers as well as an SEI Level 5 rating, acquired in 1993.

The reason for MIEL's gaining such a high rating so quickly was simple: the Motorola managers *designed* MIEL to be a Level 5 facility. They set up the organization from scratch and put in procedures that mapped to the Level 5 audit requirements. They seem to have maintained these high standards, although, again, one must assume that there is more variation in practices than managers are willing to admit publicly. Other Indian facilities listed at SEI Level 4 or 5 appear to have done the same thing: managers designed their procedures and groups to map to the CMM scale, so they scored high when audited. Nevertheless, these facilities adopted very good practices for software engineering, and their rising popularity and fame attest to that fact.

MIEL looked to me very much like a Japanese software factory with a strong SEI influence and some synch-and-stabilize techniques in place as well.[57] The emphasis was on tight project management, with carefully prescribed methods extending from project management to detailed performance metrics, quality plans, and reuse promotion. All projects were supposed to contain five key roles: project manager (heads the project), systems engineer (sets technical direction), test engineer (oversees independent testing), configuration manager (controls code and design changes), and quality engineer (oversees independent quality assurance activities). After determining the requirements of the product or system they would build, the Motorola projects divided people into smaller "threads" or subprojects of no more than seven to eight people (very similar to Microsoft's feature teams). Project controls revolved around the definition of small tasks and weekly reports, with multiple iterations around requirements rather than a simple waterfall. Project data indicated defect reductions of 77 percent, down to about 0.4 defects per 1,000 lines of C++ code, as well as major savings in programming staff effort from code generation and systematic reuse of components and design frameworks.[58]

It is particularly impressive that what Motorola did in India is not unique. Many local entrepreneurs and foreign firms took advantage of the excellent technical education in India and the English-language skills of their software engineers. There were some three thousand software companies in India in 2002, far too many to describe individually.[59] Many are truly world class in terms of process, and they compete aggressively for outsourcing work, mainly from the United States but increasingly from Europe and Japan. A brief account of one of the most impressive Indian firms with an international reputation—Infosys—provides another example of how India has become a global force in the software development outsourcing business.

The Infosys Story

Infosys (NASDAQ symbol: INFY) was established in 1981 as a consultancy by Narayana Murthy and several colleagues. It fits the business model of a software services company doing mainly custom development, although it has grown extraordinarily fast and is unusually profitable. In 2003, Infosys had more than 10,000 employees and generated about $754 million in revenues for the fiscal year ending in March 2003. About 70 percent of its revenues came from North American clients and 20 percent from Europe.[60] Also, for the year ending in March 2003, using U.S. GAAP, Infosys booked about $195 million in *net profits*, that is, after taxes, with total operating expenses of only $118 million.[61] This is a net margin of 26 *percent*, which is Microsoft territory!

Infosys began soliciting U.S. projects by establishing an American office in 1987. The company still grew relatively slowly until the late 1990s but then capitalized on the boom in technology spending and outsourcing. Infosys established a European office in 1996 as well as launched a series of different practices to get more clients. The practices included e-business (1996), engineering services (1997), enterprise solutions (1998), and consulting services (1999). Infosys reached $100 million in revenue in 1999, the same year it received SEI's CMM Level 5 certification, and then kept doubling its revenues every year or two.[62]

In mid-2003, Infosys listed some three hundred clients, many of them blue-chip companies. The practice areas covered engineering (Airbus, Boeing, Siemens), financial services (Fidelity Investments, Dresdner Bank, ABM AMRO, First USA, Royal Bank of Canada, Aetna), technology (Microsoft, i2 Technologies, Cisco Systems, JDS Uniphase, Lucent, Nortel), manufacturing (Apple, Dell, Reebok, Monsanto), retail (Adidas, The Gap, J. C. Penney, Nordstrom, Pier 1 Imports), and energy systems (Schlumberger). Infosys is also no longer a completely India-based company. To do consulting and design work at customer sites, since 2000 it has opened several development centers in the United States, Canada, and Japan, staffed primarily with Indian engineers. Infosys was also building a small software products business for the banking industry but remained primarily focused on building custom systems and doing contract programming based on specifications received from clients. The company's Web site describes Infosys's development approach:

Many companies choose a consulting firm that understands business strategies and is good at generating ideas, but lacks the technical expertise to turn those ideas into reality. Others enlist a technology company that is adept at designing and deploying information systems, but fails to comprehend the precise needs of the business. These firms leave you with snazzy new technologies that don't solve the problems at hand, or—worse still—create new problems altogether. We take the time to understand your requirements, and then tailor complete solutions that deliver tangible value to the enterprise. We listen to your ideas, delve into your concerns, and consider every aspect of the problem—from the underlying business processes to the importance of change management to the merits of various technologies. Then we craft unique information systems that move your business forward and yield a measurable return on investment.[63]

The company's development process—which Infosys claims was "proven for iterative and waterfall models"—followed CMM Level 5 guidelines. This means that the company had in place well-defined systems for project planning, change control, configuration management, quality assurance, technology standards, design reviews, code inspections, testing procedures, process research, statistical measurement, defect prevention, and automation, where possible. In addition, Infosys packaged these techniques into what it called a "Global Delivery Model." This is another way of saying that the company built software in *distributed teams,* relying on its base back in India, which itself spread to eight different cities. On the customer site, Infosys promises to do system analysis and planning, some prototyping, high-level design, and user interface design, as well as coordinating the project and then coming back for testing and implementation. In India, Infosys engineers take care of detailed design, additional prototyping, coding, unit testing, and documentation, as well as bug fixes and long-term maintenance support. Infosys also promises to send customers weekly status reports on their projects by e-mail. The company clearly has covered most of the issues that outsourcing customers would be concerned about and has a long list of testimonials indicating that the global development approach works, if done carefully.[64]

A Word of Caution on Outsourcing Software Development

The remarkable performance of Infosys, Motorola, and other Indian companies suggests that outsourcing may be the best solution for dealing with common problems (and high costs) in software development. Outsourcing development as well as management of information systems has become widespread in the United States, Japan, and Europe. However, there are many pluses and minuses that customers need to consider.

First, it must be recognized that outsourcing development can come in different forms, throughout a spectrum. One approach is for a customer's engineers to do all or some of the analysis and high-level design work (architectures and functional specifications) and then subcontract the programming tasks (detailed design, coding, and unit testing) to offshore subsidiaries (such as MIEL, in the case of Motorola) or other firms (such as Infosys). This kind of outsourcing has been common in the operations of Japanese software factories and other Japanese firms since the 1970s and has become increasingly common elsewhere around the world. At the opposite end of the outsourcing spectrum, a customer relies entirely on an outside organization to do everything, from high-level design through final testing and implementation. This approach appeals especially to IT services organizations such as Infosys in India but also to U.S. firms that compete with the Indians, such as IBM, PricewaterhouseCoopers, and Accenture, as well as Japanese and European software houses specializing in custom systems.

The problem with the first type of software outsourcing is that it requires a "factory-like" separation of design from product construction and usually results in a waterfall approach to project management. Division of labor between design and production is a fundamental practice in most mass production industries, but it often becomes a problem in software. It is most cumbersome when customers do not know what they want or when a development team needs to do a lot of experimentation to come up with the right design or a compelling new feature. Whether the target is a fully customized system or a mass-market product, software projects *always* need to iterate through many design, coding, and testing cycles to get the functionality right for a particular customer or for a particular market. Structuring these iterations and checking continuously for bugs is the essence of the synch-and-stabilize process. Breaking a development team apart geographically is possible with modern-day communications technologies, but it is usually not optimal from either the engineering or the business point of view. The waterfall approach, accordingly, is a popular management style for offshore or distributed development projects.

Again, we have seen in Japan as well as India that the separation—the outsourcing—of program design from development can work in well-defined situations and with particular procedures aimed at minimizing risks and problems. It can work well when designers have a lot of experience in writing down specifications that capture the functionality they need and when programmers have a lot of experience reading these specifications, building the application, and working with the design team as well as the customer. Being able to communicate in the same language (Japanese or English) helps enormously. Hitachi, for example, generally insists that subcontractors come to the software factory and work on the same site as the system designers. This is one way to solve the design-coding separation problem. Infosys and other elite Indian companies have also been taking on more of the design work themselves and moving key people to customer sites.

In many cases, outsourcing software development to low-cost custom shops in India, or to the many firms that are now appearing in China and elsewhere in Southeast Asia, is a good idea and can save money. But whether the company is Motorola or Microsoft, it needs to have a clear strategy for what to outsource and how to manage the divided process. Outsourcing program construction is not the best way to do innovative software development. It can force projects into a rigid waterfall model because it is easier to structure work sequentially and takes more effort to do frequent builds and incorporate customer feedback quickly if the development team is dispersed or separated from the customer. Outsourcing more of the whole development process makes more sense, and elite firms in India have demonstrated the ability to handle high-level design tasks for many applications. But, again, software producers and heavy users of software need to be selective in what they ask other firms to do for them, lest they give up too much sensitive knowledge or diminish their internal capability to create and use information technology effectively.

WRAP-UP COMMENTS

I began this chapter with a discussion of recurring problems in software development and attempts at structuring the technology through software factories and other efforts in the field of software engineering. The software factory in particular has been an important learning experience for me personally and for many organizations in the industry. Companies attempting to create software factories have learned what to do—and what not to do—in managing software projects and programmers. For some managers, programmers, and researchers, the software factory has represented misguided thinking. For others, it has represented a move beyond the craft stage of the 1960s and 1970s. The truth, no doubt, lies somewhere in between.

Most important, software factory efforts in the United States and Japan have been far from the last word on how best to manage software development. The SEI notion of creating a repeatable process around IBM-style practices and statistical control and the Microsoft philosophy of frequent synchronizations and periodic stabilizations have become more important. The combination of older and newer techniques in particular makes it possible to build increasingly complex software products and respond quickly to changes in technology and the marketplace. But the basic premise of factory proponents that not all software projects are completely different, and that not all need to start from scratch each time, remains true. In concluding my study on Japan a decade ago, I cited two references—one comment by the late Dr. Yukio Mizuno of NEC and another by Bruce Arden, author of *What Can Be Automated?* I still find their words helpful to explain the significance of Japan's software factories and all subsequent attempts to promote best practices in software development:

> To understand the true origin and character of these facilities, it is useful to recall the comment of NEC's Yukio Mizuno that the software factory was essentially a *concept*, not a thing; a philosophy that at least some software could be produced in a manner more akin to engineering and manufacturing than craft or cottage-industry practices. . . . The historical methods used to pursue this topic appeared unusual to some participants in the study. To this author, however, determining how firms have evolved seemed a logical starting point to consider future prospects—an approach eloquently sanctioned in a recent report on the state of computer technology: "People built bridges that stayed up and airplanes that flew, long before scientists discovered the underlying mathematical principles and structures. If we want to make further progress in software, we must go back to study what can be done and what has been done, until we find out how to do it well." [65]

• • •

The next two chapters attempt to apply much of what I have talked about in this book, particularly regarding strategy and business models as well as product development, to the challenges of creating a successful software start-up. We will first look at the elements I consider most important and then examine ten case studies of recent software ventures.

5

Software Entrepreneurship:
Essential Elements of a Successful Start-up

Much of what I have already discussed in this book should be useful for software entrepreneurs as well as managers in firms who want to create or grow new software businesses within their organizations. I include in this latter group former "hardware" companies such as Motorola and Nokia, as well as big systems companies such as IBM, Fujitsu, NEC, and Hitachi. Entrepreneurs and "intrapreneurs" need to think about how to position their new businesses strategically and decide whether to emphasize products or services or to combine the two in a hybrid solution. They need to think about lessons from companies that have gone before them and try not to repeat the mistakes of the past in either strategy or technology management. They need to figure out who should be on the management team, what the business model will be, what problems are likely to occur in bringing a product or service to market, and how to attract paying customers. These and other elements are necessary to make a viable business that earns more than it spends.

This chapter offers some guidelines for software entrepreneurs and new-business managers as well as venture capitalists who want to evaluate the viability of a software start-up and its business plan. My focus is on two topics:

- Interpreting the odds of failure versus success
- Some essential elements of a successful software startup

THE ODDS ARE AGAINST YOU

In mid-1999, before the burst of the Internet bubble, I can remember writing about a "sinking feeling" that the Internet was spawning not only tremendous entrepreneurial creativity but also tremendous entrepreneurial mediocrity.[1] Too many weak companies were raising millions of dollars but had little or nothing to offer investors and customers. But spotting companies based on bad ideas and bad business models was becoming easier because they were all around. When start-ups had to invest tens of millions of dollars to set up operations and then spend $400 to get a new customer who might spend only $300 per year (for example, Pets.com), obviously they were using a flawed business model.

Good Times and Bad Times

Two trends were much harder to see, at least in mid-1999. One was how much the stock market value of established businesses had departed from reality because of their enormous short-term increases in sales. Another was how bad the good times would soon become: how much trouble start-ups were going to have getting funding even if they had great technology, great people, and, in normal times, very good prospects of becoming viable businesses.

For venture capitalists smart enough to avoid fanciful e-commerce ventures, it seemed to make sense to invest in software, hardware, telecommunications, and e-business service companies that offered innovative infrastructure technology, had strong management teams, and could feed on the growth of the Internet. If mainstream companies such as Business Objects could come out with a Web version of its client-server product and go from $3 to $150 per share, why not invest in start-ups that might do the same or better? And many start-ups, including once-shining stars such as Akamai, an MIT spin-off founded in 1999 that had a unique technology for delivering Web content quickly around the globe, did generate billions of dollars for investors before crashing back to reality.[2] Its share price soared to more than $320 in January 2000 before falling to a low of 56 cents in 2002 and hovering around $5 in mid-2003.

Who knew that stock prices would rise so fast and fall so far? Who knew that the NASDAQ would lose 80 percent of its value within a couple of years? Who knew that the IPO and acquisition markets would dry up so quickly? Who knew that companies were overinvesting so much in technology that they would later impose a multiyear freeze on new spending? Most people did not see these trends and their implications for software entrepreneurs until the decline was already upon us, no matter how closely they were looking at the world around them.

As I reflect on these events, what happened seems clear. Between 1998 and early 2000, we experienced a once-in-a-century event, equivalent to and perhaps surpassing the introduction of the transcontinental railroad, commercial electricity, the telephone, the television, and the computer. The Internet and the World Wide Web are truly revolutionary technologies. People were right to get excited about them and try to capitalize on changes in markets and customer behavior. But the principles that determine why businesses succeed or fail over the long run remained in place, and investors as well as venture capitalists eventually had to face this fact.

During the boom and bust periods, the highs were so high and the lows so low that it became easy to let this unique period shape one's views of software entrepreneurship, on the positive or negative side. During 2001–2003, after the dot-com and Internet bust, obtaining venture capital, taking a software company public, or selling a software company to an established firm became unusually—and I think *unreasonably*—hard to do. This is not the usual case, just as the ease of getting funding, going public, or being acquired during 1997–2000 was not the normal state of affairs.

The Normal State of Affairs

So when considering what it takes to create a successful software start-up and a viable company over the long haul, we need to put aside outlandish expectations as well as unwarranted pessimism. We need to think about what is a potentially profitable software business in the normal state of affairs and not fall prey to booms and busts or jump too quickly onto the bandwagon of an interesting fad or a nifty technology. At the same time, part of the essence of entrepreneurship is to be able to take advantage of short-term "blips" in the market and see opportunities (including subtle but fundamental changes) that other people do not see.

During the Internet boom, it was relatively easy to get funding for a start-up and "cash out" successfully in one form or another. In normal times, however, the reality is that financially successful start-ups, in terms of either profits or cash events for investors, are rare events. Venture capitalists understand this, and this is why, in normal times, they are reluctant to commit money to a start-up. Too many VCs either forgot about the odds during the boom or decided to put cash in and then pull it back out as quickly as possible, to take advantage of the boom. This was their choice. Software entrepreneurs, though, are usually in a business for the longer haul, and they especially need to understand how difficult the odds of success actually are, in both good times and bad.

My colleague Ed Roberts at MIT, author of *Entrepreneurship in High Technology,* told me long ago that MIT data indicated that nine out of ten start-ups fail.[3] I have never forgotten this daunting statistic, but the numbers become far worse when you consider early-stage ideas that never even become companies. According to John Nesheim, author of *High Tech Startup,* only *six out of one million* ideas for a high-tech business actually turn into successful public companies. Here are some other daunting statistics from Nesheim's research, which relied mainly on records from Saratoga Venture Finance:

- VCs generally finance only 6 out of every 1,000 business plans they receive each year.
- Fewer than 20 percent, and more like one in 10, of funded start-ups go public.
- In "normal" times (i.e., excluding bubble periods), start-ups generally require about five years to go public.
- About 60 percent of high-tech companies that get VC funding go bankrupt, and another 30 percent end up in mergers or liquidations.
- VCs generally own about 60 percent of the equity in software start-ups by the time they go public.
- Founder-CEOs generally own less than 4 percent of their ventures after the initial public offering, an amount usually worth about $6.5 million.[4]

And things were getting tougher for entrepreneurs in the bad economic climate. After the burst of the Internet bubble, venture capital firms were imposing draconian terms on start-ups they funded. Companies that only a few years before had been valued at $15 million to $100 million were now being valued at $3 million to $10 million. VCs were limiting their investments to $2 million to $10 million per round, about a third of the typical amounts invested during the bubble. A lot of the new VC money was also contingent on start-ups' meeting certain goals, such as revenue targets—hard to meet when customers are reluctant to spend on technology, especially from a start-up that may disappear within a year or so. Furthermore, when selling a company in the past, VCs had tried to get their investment back in full, and then everyone else had divided up what remained. In the postbubble world, many VCs are insisting that they get *several times* their investment back before anyone else—including the founders—gets any money.[5]

Of course, not all software entrepreneurs need to go to venture capitalists for start-up funding. It remains very common for entrepreneurs to use their own money to "bootstrap" the operation, or to go to family and friends for additional funds. Entrepreneurs can look for individual wealthy investors ("angels"), as well as taking out loans from banks or getting credit from suppliers and landlords. For a time, some four hundred or so early-stage venture firms or "incubators" were also popular sources of money in the United States in particular, although most funded bad ideas that regular VCs wouldn't touch and consequently went bankrupt. Corporations such as Microsoft, Intel, and Cisco also remain valuable sources of funding as well as assistance for companies that have compelling technologies.

In general, though, convincing any one venture capital firm to fund a particular idea appears to be an extraordinarily difficult task—far more difficult than creating a successful company, which is difficult enough. It follows that budding entrepreneurs who want outside money need to approach many VCs as well as consider different paths to funding. They also need to take extraordinary care—especially in bad times but also in good times—in planning and presenting their business plans and forming a reputable management team before they ask for funding. Perhaps most important, budding entrepreneurs should not let the dismal funding and success statistics become too discouraging. *You can't succeed without trying.* Some start-ups will get the billions of dollars lying dormant in the coffers of venture capitalists, and one of them may very well be yours.

At the same time, accepting venture money when you don't need it, or accepting more than you need, can often become what I call "the kiss of death." Venture funding or even cash from a premature IPO is artificial wealth. Start-ups are too likely to spend the money they raise to hire too many employees, pay high salaries to executives, furnish lavish offices, buy too much equipment, or invest in rocket-science development projects. A common outcome is that they incur a level of overhead that prevents them from ever making a profit, and they never make enough money to pay the investors back. Small software products companies and IT services companies, in my experience, are particularly susceptible to the "kiss-of-death" phenomenon and are better off bootstrapping their operations.

WHAT TO LOOK FOR IN A SOFTWARE START-UP

In my MIT class going back to 1997, through student presentations, course papers, and class visitors, we have evaluated the business potential of dozens of new software technologies and business plans. Appendix Table 15 presents a sampling, eliminating some redundancies from year to year. The list pretty much mirrors technologies that were "hot" or becoming hot at the time, though most were still in the emerging stage. Our debates centered around what else the technologies needed to become widespread or successful commercially (including infrastructure needs, such as high-bandwidth availability, which are outside the control of any one company) and what types of specific business opportunities existed for firms that offered products or services based on these technologies.

For example, in fall 1997 we discussed how popular Internet telephony and videoconferencing might become, whether or not Java would become a dominant technology for enterprises, and what might be the commercial opportunities for firms building products that incorporated artificial intelligence or offered superior ways of doing audio and video streaming, electronic payments, and Internet-based groupware. A hot topic in 1998 was the emergence of MPEG (compressed music files) and companies such as Napster that were using peer-to-peer technology to allow individuals to trade music files. The future of voice recognition, intelligent agents, e-commerce services, and applications hosting were also topics we debated. In

1999, students identified Bluetooth as a promising new wireless technology for connecting computers and peripherals within a short radius, though we concluded that the business opportunities were there for device manufacturers. Web services was a topic we covered first in 2000, though it is still being debated heavily in 2003. Other topics we looked at in 2003 included mobile software for Web-enabled cell phones, grid computing, and new artificial intelligence applications.

We also try to evaluate software start-ups through this filter of separating out interesting technologies from commercial opportunities. One of my colleagues at the MIT Sloan School, Chris Dellarocas, often has lectured in my class, using a simple framework that I have found helpful for thinking about this problem (Figure 5-1). His argument is that there is a "system dynamics" effect between infrastructure and applications, as well as organizational changes, that influences what kind of demand appears for different technologies or products. One enables the other in a sort of continuous loop. For example, new PCs and cheap networking over the Internet have enabled organizations to adopt new processes, change quickly, and decentralize as well as become global much more easily than in the past. These new organizational changes enable demand for new software applications in the

Figure 5-1: Predicting Trends in Information Technology

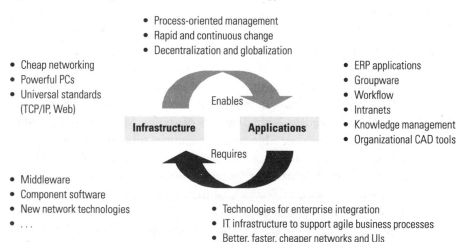

Source: *Chrysanthos Dellarocas, "A Framework for Thinking About Trends in Information Technology," presentation to the course "The Software Business," MIT Sloan School of Management, October 17, 2000, p. 10*

back office but also in groupware, workflows, intranets, knowledge management, and elsewhere. The new applications, in turn, inspire advances in particular technologies, such as for better enterprise integration and cheaper network connections. These new application demands then inspire or even require improvements in infrastructure, such as middleware, component software, and new networking technologies. With this framework, it becomes clearer why technologies are likely to fail if they lack an appropriate infrastructure to make them successful or if they do not inspire new applications.

Assuming that a start-up has a promising technology, the wannabe entrepreneurs then have to write up a business plan that will capture the attention of investors. There are many books and software packages that help write business plans and generate sales and cost projections. But entrepreneurs can easily get lost in the details of such plans and number crunching through their spreadsheets, and lose sight of what it takes to create a successful company. When I talk with potential entrepreneurs or read their business plans, I go through a mental checklist of several elements that are necessary for a software start-up to succeed as a business *and* raise venture capital. Some of my points overlap, and they all intersect, though there are important distinctions among them, as I will discuss below.

Point 1: A Strong Management Team

Many venture capitalists will tell you that they invest primarily in people and secondarily in ideas. In other words, if an entrepreneur comes to them with an idea that is modest but a founding team that has a strong track record of success in similar ventures, the company is a better bet than a start-up with a great idea but no one to carry it out. One sign of a strong management team is its level of experience. Another is its breadth. A small group of strong founders with a solid business idea should be able to get commitments from other experienced, talented managers to join the team and cover the basic functions needed to get started and land some customers.

The need for particular kinds of managers on the team also varies with the type of company and the stage it is at. A start-up with a complex product concept needs a strong technical team, but this must still be counterbalanced by a strong marketing and sales executive. The CEO is probably less important than the heads of development and marketing or sales. Teams dominated by their technologies will tend to spend most of their time refining the product and too little time getting the product ready for real customers and actually closing a deal. When the company has a prototype that it can show to customers, the nontechnology executives become more critical and there needs to be a CEO who can present an "adult" face for the company. I have also found that a chief financial officer (CFO) is important not only to keep track of cash, raise new funds, and communicate with investors but also to serve—I hope—as the "voice of reason" when the technologists want to spend too much or overpromise to customers and create problems of proper revenue recognition later on.

The issue usually arises of what to do with the founder, who often serves as the first CEO. Many VCs will not fund a start-up unless the founder is moved out of the CEO position in favor of an experienced executive. I like to see a founder stay on in some capacity (such as chairman of the board or chief technology officer) because I believe that succeeding in a new business is as much about passion as it is about anything else, and founders usually have passion. At the same time, there are cases of founder-entrepreneurs becoming successful CEOs, ranging from Bill Gates and Michael Dell to Bernard Liautaud, and many in between. But founders who want to become CEOs need to develop management skills, such as listening to others without being overly intimidating, accepting different points of view as objectively as possible, deciding how to allocate resources (people, time, and money), and avoiding what I call "panic management." The last item refers to the tendency of novice managers to respond to the latest crisis each day and lose track of the bigger picture. Customers often have this effect on new CEOs—the latest demand from an important customer tends to become the new-product "road map" or the new strategy, regardless of what other customers want or what commitments the company has already made.

Point 2: An Attractive Market

The potential market for a start-up's main product or service should be large enough, growing fast enough, or potentially profitable enough to get the attention of outside investors. The market can be horizontal or vertical. More important, it needs to be *structurally attractive* in a "Porterian" sense: there should be relatively high entry barriers to keep out competitors; not so many rivals that competition is likely to devolve into cutthroat price wars; limited power of buyers or suppliers to negotiate prices downward or the cost of inputs upward; and no good substitutes for the basic product or service.[6] In addition, if complementary products or infrastructure elements (what Andy Grove has called the "sixth" industry force, adding to Porter's five) are essential for the company to succeed, these need to be available or coming soon.[7]

In addition to industry structure, an attractive market has the potential for a company to grow its business rapidly and profitably. In software, the easiest products to scale up in this way are horizontal packages. But the easiest businesses to start are custom services in specialized vertical segments. If entrepreneurs can tell me a good story about how they plan to start in a vertical segment that does not have much competition and then gradually turn it into a horizontal business, I start to listen more carefully. As I noted in Chapter 2, however, I have learned during the past two years that the "lure of the horizontal" can lead to wasted investment with little or nothing to show for it.

One of the worst ways for entrepreneurs to explain potential market attractiveness is to describe some huge market or segment (such as how much U.S. financial institutions spent the previous year on information technology and content, or how much U.S. firms spent the previous year in software contracting) and then argue that, if they could get only 1 or 2 percent of that multibillion-dollar market, they would have a viable business. Size alone does not make a market or a business proposition attractive. There is no guarantee that a start-up will get *any* percentage of a market unless that start-up has some real advantage over its competitors, good access to customers, and some way of preventing imitation, among other things. Luck and timing can also be important. *In general, the most likely percentage of a market that a start-up will get is zero.*

A final point here relates to complements and infrastructure, such as in the system dynamics model I introduced earlier. In software businesses, complements often consist of hardware devices, software applications, and "middleware," or connecting programs that help one application communicate with another. Infrastructure includes such things as the availability of computers, Internet or wireless services, networking standards, and other hardware servers. If these elements are essential for a new company to succeed, they need to be available in the marketplace or coming soon.

Point 3: A Compelling New Product, Service, or Hybrid Solution

A start-up should offer something that is *compelling* to a specific type of customer. That something can be a product, such as a new software development tool that many programmers are likely to find useful. It can be a service, such as middleware design and programming skills needed to link new Web sites with legacy databases. Or it can be a combination, a hybrid solution, such as a new tool for information searches that requires tailoring to a specific customer's needs.

Some software entrepreneurs are more deliberate than others in how they go about finding that compelling product concept. They may have a deep familiarity with a particular technology and then spend some time analyzing the market space before they identify a customer need that remains unfilled or poorly met. Bill Gates and Paul Allen did this with Microsoft when they identified the need for programming languages for PCs. Jim Clark and Marc Andreessen did it with Netscape when they identified the need for commercial-grade Internet browsers and servers. Bernard Liautaud and Denis Payre did it with Business Objects when they identified the need for simple database analysis, query, and reporting tools that ran on personal computers and targeted nonexpert users. Sanjiv Sidhu and Ken Sharma did it with i2 Technologies when they identified the need for better factory and supply-chain planning systems and found a way to package their unique optimization algorithms.

To attract outside funding, entrepreneurs should plan to provide quantitative and qualitative data showing how their offering would provide superior benefits to customers over what competitors (or substitutes) already offer or are likely to offer in the future. How compelling the product actually is will be reflected in how much customers are willing to pay. The key question here is one of *value* to the customers—which is easy to overlook if you are focused on the technology or the challenges of managing a difficult software project. Value is affected directly by what other companies offer and what they charge for a similar product or service, as well as by what is freely available and what potential substitutes exist or are on the horizon.

When I evaluate a start-up, I often insist that the company do some objective benchmarking, or hire an outside consultant to do it. By this I mean commissioning reports or running experiments to compare their product with other products to see which is better, faster, or cheaper. The start-up's product usually has to be significantly better than competing offerings to get the attention of customers and investors. How much better is subjective, but 50 percent cheaper or faster is a good start for a product or service that has a large potential market.

For example, I recently evaluated a start-up idea for a multibillion-dollar chemical company. A researcher in its central laboratories had developed some novel algorithms for analyzing patterns in very-large-scale data sets. The company used the techniques internally for quality control in chemical manufacturing, but it saw a great potential in other areas—everything from detecting credit card fraud to identifying new protein-based drugs and predicting short-term movements in stock market averages. The originators of the technology and some managers in new-business development wanted to create a start-up company. They all had visions of revolutionizing data analysis and becoming multimillionaires in the process. However, they could not tell me how much better their approach was for doing the kinds of things they said the technology could do.

My approach was, first, to get the company to do benchmarks of their technology versus conventional tools. A consulting firm eventually did the testing. There was enough promise to proceed, but the new solution was not better in all scenarios and was a lot better in only a couple of applications. My next task for the start-up team was to identify comparable companies and evaluate their business prospects. Here the exercise became more sobering. They identified about sixty firms in the large-scale data analysis business, but only a handful of them were making any money—a bad sign. Most were very specialized and leading a fledgling existence. I advised the parent company to look for a partner to market the technology or put the idea on hold. It eventually found a partner and licensed the technology.

Point 4: Strong Evidence of Customer Interest

Entrepreneurs should present evidence to investors that *actual customers are willing to buy the offering.* One good piece of evidence is letters of intent to purchase the new company's products or services. Companies that agree to become beta users or partners are another sign of commercial interest, although these are low-cost commitments compared to letters of intent to purchase. It should go without saying that customers will be interested in a start-up's product only if it has a demonstrable advantage over offerings from competitors, if there are any, as well as potential substitute products or technologies.

In Chapter 2, I talked about SkyFire Technologies, which offered a software platform that enabled real-time applications to run on low-bandwidth devices, such as PalmPilots and other mobile computers. One reason the company had trouble finding customers and investors was that bandwidth and the computing power of handheld devices were increasing all the time. So even if SkyFire offered an advantage to potential users, it was likely that this advantage would become less important or disappear over time—and quickly. There were also many other ways (i.e., substitute technologies) to make applications run over wireless devices, such as by using simpler Web connections and "clipping" technology. Perhaps these other methods were slower and less elegant, but most required less effort and were "good enough."

It is usually difficult to get a potential customer to write a letter of intent to purchase without seeing a prototype or early product version. Creating a prototype helps everyone visualize how easy or difficult it will be for a new company to market, sell, distribute, and support its product. There is also some evidence that firms starting off without a product have trouble evolving and surviving.[8] Most software start-ups and even established companies vastly underestimate how difficult it will be to build and deliver an easy-to-use software product to customers.

Point 5: A Plan to Overcome the "Credibility Gap"

One of the most difficult problems a start-up—even a well-funded start-up—has to overcome is what I call the "credibility gap" with potential customers. This refers to the fear among customers that *the start-up—like 90 percent of all start-ups—will fail.* No one wants to be left "high and dry" with no source of technical support or future stream of product upgrades, and perhaps not even a completed product. No confident words from the start-up's CEO or other executives or salespeople are credible if the start-up has no customers and doesn't have enough cash (or commitments for cash infusions from the backers) to last for at least a couple of years. In other words, a sales pitch alone is not credible. A potential customer may well draft a letter of intent to purchase, if it has sufficient interest in the new product. But this is still different from closing a deal and sending a check. The easiest thing for fearful customers to do is not to make a deal with a start-up and instead go to an established vendor, even if the established vendor has an inferior or more expensive product.

This problem also leads to a catch-22: Often a start-up cannot raise more money to become more credible if it cannot line up some paying customers that can serve as references for other new customers. And even interested customers will not sign on the dotted line if the start-up doesn't have enough money to stay in business for some significant time period. Over the past several years, this credibility-gap problem has killed or at least severely hindered many good start-ups. I like to see entrepreneurs who have thought about this problem because my experience suggests that there are several ways to overcome or reduce the credibility gap:

- Do everything possible to get the first reference customer, even if it means giving the product or service away almost for free. This first customer can break the catch-22 cycle.
- Look for an established partner that can guarantee continued product support or services, even if the start-up itself goes bankrupt. This partnership can generate new business for the established company as well as help the start-up get established—a win-win scenario.
- Concentrate on lining up a network of small investors, advisers, and reference experts who can give potential customers some level of confidence that the start-up is a viable enterprise worthy of a deal.
- Focus, at least initially, on a niche business, perhaps a project-based customization or service, that does not require longevity. Then build up a list of customers and move on to selling a product or expanding service offerings.

Point 6: A Business Model Showing Early Growth and Profit Potential

Wannabe entrepreneurs and their business plans should be able to describe not simply an interesting idea, technology, or product concept, but a proposal for *a growing and profitable business* at an early stage of the company, such as within one or two years. That is, the entrepreneurs need to say exactly how they plan to generate revenues and profits relatively soon. Especially in bad economic times, profits are important for credibility with customers as well as investors. Of course, when or if a new firm will actually make money is difficult to predict. No one knows for sure how customers will behave, how competitors will react, or what new technologies might appear. But startups that claim to need tens of millions of dollars of investment capital and years of work before they will have any revenues or profits are too risky for me. I have also seen cases where, in addition to millions of dollars of investment, the entrepreneurs had no realistic idea of what they would be able to charge for their product or service—another bad sign.

The mistake that many entrepreneurs and venture capitalists made during the recent boom was to assume that the Internet would lead to dramatic increases in the amount of pet food, books, flowers, or other items and services that individuals and enterprises would buy. So spending $50 million or $100 million to set up a company infrastructure and market the brand was supposed to pay off, eventually. But many of these arguments did not make much sense based on historical analogies from other markets. Many of the arguments also failed to take into account the fact that Internet-based businesses that sold physical goods had to confront the same logistics and costs as other businesses: how to inventory and deliver products to customers.

It is also the case that most software businesses are two- and three-person consulting operations. They may be very profitable for the individuals involved. But if a consulting service depends entirely on the knowledge of the people in the consultancy and there is no way to "product-ize" what they are doing, there is not much potential for expansion—or for an IPO or acquisition. Some IT consulting firms have managed to scale up their businesses by creating reusable design templates, design-support tools, component libraries, training programs, and project management techniques that mix experienced and inexperienced people. Infosys in India, as I mentioned in the previous chapter, has packaged some of its expertise in banking applications for the Indian market and now sells a few products. i2 Technologies was once mainly a consulting and services (custom solutions) firm, and it is going back to those roots. So it is possible to structure or scale up even a service operation and gain some economies of scale and scope. But most individual IT consultants or contract programmers do not know how to do this. Or, as they grow, they become increasingly less profitable because they take venture money and acquire more overhead—such as expensive offices, executives, and staff—that they then have to support.

Point 7: Flexibility in Strategy and Product Offerings

Flexibility in both strategy and the product or service increases the chances that a start-up will find the right formula. In the strategy field and in business history in general, we have seen many cases where success emerges only over time, through trial and error; success stories are rarely planned exactly in advance.[9] We also have seen that most companies need to keep evolving their strategies, product lines, and business models as times and technologies change. Companies that do well over long periods are probably reinventing themselves multiple times. To make this point, I need only cite the examples of IBM (which moved from tabulating machines to computers to software and services) and Microsoft (which moved from programming languages to operating systems to applications to just about everything else related to software).

Software start-ups are no exception to this need for flexibility. They will most likely have to adapt their initial strategies, business models, and products or services to the realities of market opportunities and competitors as they encounter them. Very few entrepreneurs are smart enough or lucky enough to see the future with crystal clarity. In the case of software, one thing that can be done is to evaluate the potential of a start-up for flexibility.

One way of evaluating strategic flexibility is to talk to the founder and the management team and try to understand how they think about different options and how rigid their personalities are. You have to make guesses about people. The flexibility of the technology or product is often easier to evaluate objectively. For example, you might want to know how tightly the code is tied to a particular platform and programming interfaces or how generalizable the architecture or functionality is. Has the team thought about what else could be done with the technology it is building and the technical skills it is cultivating?

There are many great examples of strategic and technical flexibility in the software industry. Not even Bill Gates foresaw the product areas that Microsoft would enter. He and Paul Allen started with programming languages. Gates and Allen wanted to be the dominant provider of PC software, wherever that idea led them. Marc Andreessen and Jim Clark wanted to capitalize on the network effects of the Internet and use the browser as a window into that new, networked world. Netscape started with a browser and then deftly moved on to servers, applications, and content. In both cases, the visions of the founders were powerful and steady, but the technologies were flexible, making it possible to create different types of products as the markets evolved. A former Netscape executive, Roberta Katz, gave a particularly good description of how the Netscape vision remained steady but created the foundation for a highly flexible approach to strategy and product development:

> There's the "big vision," and then there is the more pragmatic imple-
> mentation of the vision, which changes. So to the extent we've had
> change, in '95, '96, '97, I put that in the second category. The big vision
> has not changed that much, and the big vision, the one that I noticed
> when I first came down here, has to do with the power of networks. . . .
> The first product [Navigator] was a clear reference to the ultimate
> scaleable network, the Internet, but then you start thinking, "Okay,
> how else can I use this? Where else can I take advantage of the efficien-
> cies and the strengths that come from a very scaleable network?"
> There's always kind of this overarching vision there, and then the ques-
> tion is, "Okay, in today's marketplace, since we have to make money,
> what's the best way to do it?" [10]

Point 8: The Potential for a Large Payoff to Investors

Finally, the business plan should include prospects for a significant "payoff" to outside investors and a reasonable return on investment (at least 25 percent), within a time frame that VCs are comfortable with based on the life span of their investment funds (typically, no more than seven years). Again, nobody knows in advance how much money, if any, a start-up will eventually make for investors. But the earlier points I have discussed all provide information that informs this issue. Perhaps most important, the market opportunity has to be large enough to suggest that a firm will become big enough to be valu-able to somebody. So market size immediately comes to mind. So does the potential of the business model—the potential for scaling up sales and generating real rather than imaginary (such as "pro forma") profits. *If the business of the company is not very scalable, it may never go public or be acquired for a large sum of money.* In this case, the venture will probably not attract many outside investors. Would-be entrepreneurs in this situation might decide to reinvest any profits and "bootstrap" the company on their own, and see how far they get.

Some VCs like to see a section in the business plan that deals with "exit strategies" for investors and possibly the founding team. Investors need some sort of "liquidity event" that can turn their investment into cash or marketable securities. The usual exit strategy is to sell out to a larger firm (for cash or stock) or go public (in which case the shares will trade on the open market). During the Internet boom years, both options were common and lucrative. In normal times, acquisitions of start-ups by larger firms are fairly common. Public offerings are rarer events. In bad times, such as 2001–2002, acquisitions became rare and IPOs almost nonexistent. Personally, I don't need to read what the founders think about their exit options. I know what they are, and what to do usually becomes clearer over time. *My preference is to grow a company and plan to take it public until it becomes clear that this is not the best option.* An IPO is the most exciting alternative and often the most lucrative, though we found out during the bad times of the 2000s that going public and seeing the stock price fall to pennies is always a possibility.

An indication of what the payoff might be for investors can be gained by researching specific examples of how similar start-up companies have fared. Such a list of reference companies—firms with comparable products that have made it from start-up to viable enterprise—is a good reality check. How many comparable companies are out there? How big are they? How many make a profit? How many have gone public or been acquired, and for how much? These are the kinds of questions that indicate what the value of a particular start-up might be.

WRAP-UP COMMENTS

Nearly twenty years ago, I attended a course in managing innovation at the Harvard Business School. The professor, Richard Rosenbloom, showed us the *New York Times* report from when researchers at Bell Labs had invented the transistor in 1947. It was a small one-paragraph article buried pages into the newspaper. There was no indication whatsoever that this invention would soon transform the world. Most people have also heard of the consulting firm Arthur D. Little's embarrassing errors in the late 1940s and 1950s—dismissing the future of the computer as well as the plain-paper copier machine.

These writers and consultants were not using their imagination or access to area experts to think about how the technologies might evolve and what applications or uses might result.

On the other hand, there are cases (e.g., Bill Gates, Steve Jobs, Marc Andreessen, the Xerox PARC researchers) where people have used their technical understanding and imagination to see the future pretty accurately and play a major role in making that future happen. I will cite another example from Netscape. John Doerr, one of Silicon Valley's premier venture capitalists and an early Netscape backer, gave this account to David Yoffie and me of his first meeting with Andreessen a few months after helping to form the company:

> I vividly remember Marc sitting in his chair [in the summer of 1994]. Twenty-three years old and he said, "This software is going to change the world." And there was an alignment of the planets, as far as I was concerned. . . . [My friend] Bill Joy once told me, "John, someday you guys are going to back an eighteen-year-old kid who'll write software that will change the world." And so here's Andreessen, just five years older than eighteen, and I'd seen Mosaic, the Unix version of it, running on a Sun Web Explorer in January of that year. Marc earned $3.65 an hour, or whatever the University of Illinois had paid him, and he posted this thing on the Web, and two million people were using it. You would have to be as dumb as a door post not to realize that there's a business opportunity here.[11]

My philosophy is that the more historical and contemporary examples you understand, the more open-minded you will become and the better your judgment should be—*if you don't end up being so cynical that nothing looks promising*. Netscape kinds of examples are rare, but they do happen. Entrepreneurs and investors also need to learn how to separate personal biases from more "objective" evaluations of what is promising and what is not.

When I reflect on how well my MIT students did in predicting which software technologies would make the best business opportunities in the near future (three to five years ahead or so), I was often struck by how much personal experiences dominated. Students who had worked in and around wireless applications saw this as the most promising bet for the future. If they had had exposure to artificial intelligence or natural-language programming, they saw these technologies as most promising. If they had worked in a video game company, graphics and multimedia seemed to have the most allure. Students who liked music and traded files on Napster were fascinated by the potential of peer-to-peer applications. Linux users seemed convinced that open-source software should provide at least service opportunities. I am not saying these evaluations were or will be wrong. But I am saying that we are often drawn to what we know and like. But the kind of momentum that John Doerr saw behind the Mosaic browser was not a personal bias; it was real, and the Internet browser has changed the world.

Some technologies may change the world but still be bad business opportunities. Linux, for example, is an important product technology, and many companies may save money by using it. But as we saw in Chapter 3, few software companies have been able to make money from Linux directly. Bluetooth is an important new software technology and may help device manufacturers sell more of their products, but it is not clear where the business opportunities are for software companies. Initially, Bluetooth required expert programmers to implement, so there was some consulting and tool development work. In any case, software entrepreneurs and potential investors need to think about how a new technology can translate into products, services, or hybrid solutions for which some significant set of customers will pay money—enough to cover operating and sunk costs and to make a profit or lead to a large liquidity event.

The next chapter examines the cases of ten software start-ups in each of the three categories of business models I talked about in Chapter 2. I also use the eight-point framework suggested in this chapter to evaluate each of these cases.

6

Start-up Case Studies:

Software Products, Services, and
Hybrid Solutions

In earlier chapters, I discussed several examples of relatively new software firms and start-ups (Business Objects, i2, Infinium, SkyFire) I have worked with personally. This chapter focuses on several other start-ups I have come to know as a director, adviser, or consultant. These companies represent a combination of successful, failed, and still-uncertain ventures. More important, they illustrate the three different business models for creating a software business that lie at the center of this book.

First, I discuss four *software products start-ups*. We have already seen that most software products are actually infrastructure systems (such as operating systems, servers, or networking middleware) or specialized applications and tools. The companies I review made tools for software debugging (NuMega Technologies), financial planning (Customer Dialogue Systems), multimedia content editing (Concentric Visions), and wireless as well as business intelligence applications (firstRain). The first company was very successful, the next two were not, and the fourth is ongoing with reasonably good prospects.

Second, I discuss three *software services start-ups*. They competed in the design and development of high-end middleware and e-business systems (NetNumina Solutions), low-cost contract design and programming (Oneworld Software), and networking and security (Cybergnostic). The first and last have been modest successes. The second was not, though it survived bankruptcy and part of the company still exists after merging with another firm.

Finally, I discuss three *hybrid solutions start-ups*. They offered a combination of software and services, neither of which had much value without the other. One start-up was in financial services content and transaction integration (Investhink), another in vendor-supplier transaction management for the marine industry (Marex), and the third in digital information search technology (H5 Technologies). Of these hybrid companies, the first two failed and the third is still afloat, with modest prospects.

At the end of each case discussion, I review the company in light of the eight-point framework introduced in Chapter 5 for evaluating software start-ups. This is a retrospective analysis and by no means "scientific," although I have tried to assess how the ventures appeared in their early stages. In addition, while reading these cases, it is useful to recall some of the basic strategy questions I posed in Chapter 2. For example: Regardless of what the business plan says, what *should* the company be selling—a standardized product or a hybrid solution? Is it clear who the customers will be? How broad (horizontal) or narrow (vertical) are the target markets? Will there be recurring revenues? Does the company have a chasm to cross or an alternative plan? Will it be a platform leader or a complementor? Will there be a character problem with the management team based on how it has operated so far?

SOFTWARE PRODUCTS START-UPS

NuMega Technologies: Great Products, Modest Market, Very Good Outcome

The founders of NuMega Technologies, Jim Moskun and Frank Grossman, started their careers as programmers at Wang during 1982–1983. Wang, located in Lowell, Massachusetts, was then a highly successful producer of dedicated word processors and was moving into minicomputers as well as dabbling in personal computers. It had leading-edge word processing products (hardware and software) and local-area networking (LAN) technology, but personal computers from IBM, Apple, and IBM-clone manufacturers would soon destroy the dedicated word processor business. Wang's costly diversification into minicomputers (another declining business) was also about to fail spectacularly and help force the company into bankruptcy.

To its credit, Wang management attempted to build personal computers and assigned Moskun and Grossman to work on the software.[1] According to Moskun, the Wang PC was technically excellent— "superior to the IBM PC/AT lines and had good market traction from the start." But it was not IBM-compatible and quickly ran into a market dead end. Wang executives did not let their engineers build IBM clones until it was too late. Moreover, they insisted that the company's PCs had to support the minicomputer business, which tied the hands of the PC team.

It was at this point that Moskun and Grossman decided to form a company that would serve the emerging PC software business. They did not want the kind of interference they had seen from Wang executives, so they avoided corporate money and venture capital. They realized that it would be possible to "bootstrap"—grow the firm incrementally from their own resources and revenues. In deciding what products to create, though, Moskun and Grosman took months and did some systematic thinking about the problem.

PC programmers at the time did not have the kinds of error detection and debugging tools that existed for mainframes, minicomputers, and UNIX workstations. The development of PC software debugging tools was a niche that was small enough for a couple of engineers to handle but growing quickly. They decided to focus on this idea, left Wang in 1987, and started operating NuMega Technologies as a partnership in Nashua, New Hampshire. Moskun and Grossman designed some tools that they found useful and started to sell them out of one of their homes. Their first product "froze" hardware, operating system, and application software data at the moment a PC crashed, making it easier to find the source of the problem. They named this tool "Soft-ICE." Another product (called "BoundsChecker") identified potential bugs due to overloading available memory. Moskun recalled how they came up with the product concepts:

We . . . limited our choice to products that could be built and sold by two engineers. We felt there were two strong market dynamics that we could ride and that we also had a high level of expertise in. The first was the emergence of Intel's 386 chip architecture. . . . The second dynamic was OS/2. . . . Our approach was to write one-page business plans around product ideas that would leverage one or both of these market dynamics, was protected from competition in some way, and that we could bootstrap. In the end, we ended up picking the idea with the smallest market potential (from our point of view), which was Soft-ICE. We chose this because, first, we had a technically innovative way of turning features that Intel had put into the chip for a protected mode, virtual memory O/S, into hardware-level debugging features for MS-DOS. This created a very big value proposition for a relatively small number of software engineers that accessed the hardware directly. Second, at Wang, we were ideal customers for this kind of product, so we had customer sensitivity. Third, we felt that the niche we were going after was too small for established companies in the tools space (Microsoft, for example) to be interested in.[2]

Moskun and Grossman operated NuMega by themselves for a couple of years, selling their products at about $300 each. When they got to about $1 million in annual revenues, they began bringing in a few top-notch engineers as well as some experienced managers to help them in engineering, marketing, sales, and operations. By 1995, there were about sixty employees in the company and they began thinking about going public. The founders hired an experienced manager to take over the CEO job: Tom Herring, a former sales and marketing executive at Sybase and PowerSoft who had earlier been recognized as the "High Technology Sales and Marketing Executive of the Year" by *Upside* magazine.

When I joined the board of directors in 1996, NuMega had about 95 employees, 100,000 users, and nearly $17 million in annual sales, mostly to sophisticated Windows programmers. The core customer list read like a "Who's Who" of technology companies (Microsoft, Oracle, Lotus, Sybase, Cisco, Motorola, Adobe, Xerox, Intel, IBM, Netscape, Informix, Hewlett-Packard, Apple, PictureTel). It also boasted dozens of large corporations that wrote sophisticated Windows programs for their own use (Reuters, AT&T, Bell Atlantic, Shell, FedEx, Ford Motor Company, Fidelity Investments, Pepsi-Cola, Fujitsu, Citicorp, Boeing, Wal-Mart, MCI, Lucent, Charles Schwab). NuMega began to accumulate a long list of awards and made products named among the "Best of 1990" by *PC Magazine* and others that received citations from *PC Magazine* in 1993 and 1996. Company products were also named to the *"Software Development Magazine* Hall of Fame" in 1997.

NuMega's business was growing around 50 percent annually in the mid-1990s and was profitable to boot. It was easy to manufacture the products—they were shrink-wrapped software packages. The sales process was low-cost, mostly by telephone but also through specialty programmer product catalogues, advertisements, and displays at programmer gatherings. Support was cheap because users were sophisticated. But growth was slowing down as the company saturated its market niche of high-end Windows programmers.

According to company data, in the mid-1990s there were about 5 million Windows developers worldwide, including about 700,000 users of C++, 400,000 of Java, and 3 million of Microsoft's Visual Basic. Only a small percentage of these programmers used sophisticated error detection and debugging tools of the type sold by NuMega as well as competitors such as Segue Software and Rational Software (which IBM purchased in December 2002 for $2.1 billion). But NuMega had reached a point where some 80 percent of the more sophisticated professional Windows programmers (those writing mainly in C and C++) were already using SoftICE and Bounds-Checker. These programmers bought the tools either as individual products or in a new discounted suite that NuMega introduced in 1997 on the model of Microsoft Office, called DevPartner Studio. There were millions of less sophisticated programmers who did not use NuMega products at major corporations, including banks and other firms. These companies were not in the software business but had thousands of programmers on their staffs. But to reach this much broader market would require a lot more investment in product refinements as well as mass marketing, sales, and support. NuMega would also have to learn how to sell directly to corporate managers of IT departments, rather than to individual programmers. Other tool vendors, such as Rational and even Microsoft, were after this customer base and had much larger resources.

After considerable discussion, the NuMega management team and the board concluded that expanding sales to less sophisticated programmers working at a variety of corporations would require considerable expansion of the company. The alternatives were to form a partnership with a much larger firm (such as Compuware, with which Herring was negotiating) or get outside funding. Herring was already

actively marketing the company to investment bankers and analysts
and setting high expectations for sales to IT departments as well as
for an IPO based on the promise of this larger market. Moskun and
Grossman also wanted some cash return for their decade of efforts,
and they did take in some outside investment in 1997.

Moskun and Herring concluded that they could get a higher valuation for the company from an acquisition. Another concern was that
going public would make it difficult for the founders and executives
to liquidate their holdings, should they want to do so. Ultimately, the
board agreed to sell the company to Compuware, which was not interested in a partnership but had made a strong offer to buy NuMega.
As I noted in Chapter 2, Compuware was a billion-dollar company
with a large national sales force, and it was looking for Windows development tools in order to diversify beyond mainframe software. It
was a good fit. NuMega closed the deal in December 1997 for what
later amounted to about $150 million in Compuware stock. The
value was nearly nine times NuMega's annual revenues for 1997.
Moskun described why the Compuware acquisition was the best alternative:

> Tom and the executive management team that he had built were over-
> whelmingly in favor of this deal. From the executive management
> team's perspective, it was an easy decision. First of all, they had only
> been at NuMega about a year, so they did not have a strong personal
> identification with the company. They were also under immense pres-
> sure to meet very aggressive expectations. On the other hand, they
> could "cash in" with accelerated vesting and potentially move on.
> From the perspective of Frank and me, our die was cast when we hired
> Tom. Tom was a strong manager and very good at his job. Within a
> year's time the culture had dramatically changed from a very strong
> corporate bootstrapping mentality, where technical excellence was key,
> to one where liquidity was the main goal. In a sense, our choice was as
> dipolar as that of the management team. We could cash out or have an
> extremely unhappy management team on top of the competitive busi-
> ness challenges.[3]

After the merger, Compuware continued to grow the NuMega
business successfully, more than doubling its revenues over the next
couple of years.[4] The senior management team stayed with the com-

pany for a year before moving on to other ventures. Moskun and Grossman, along with several other former NuMega people, joined to start a new software products company, Mindreef, which builds diagnostic tools for Web services developments.[5] Herring went on to work as a venture capitalist for Polaris Ventures and in 2002 also took on the post of chairman of Expressive Technologies, a speech recognition software company focused on the medical industry.[6]

I came away from my experience with NuMega thinking about two aspects of software entrepreneurship. One was that *it is possible to analyze a market very deliberately and then select a segment in which to play.* Moskun and Grossman were highly analytical when founding their company. They didn't stumble across PC software development tools as a business but thought carefully about different kinds of products to sell and where existing and evolving market needs were unmet. They concluded that they could make PC development tools into a business because the need was there, they had the technical knowledge and a product concept, and the products would be relatively easy to build and sell. They knew that the market opportunity would be small in the beginning but felt it had growth potential and little competition when they entered. In addition, they could tell early on that they had a viable business. Even primitive versions of the products did useful things that customers were willing to pay money for (an experience that i2 Technologies and Business Objects also had with their first products).

Another lesson I took away from NuMega—and this is very similar to my experience as a director at Infinium Software—is that *there is no point pushing a company to continue when the founders and critical members of the senior management team want to move on.* At NuMega, for one thing, expanding sales to less sophisticated users required more money, people, time, and effort than the founders and the new executive team seemed willing to put in, especially given the risk of going up against competitors that had far more resources. Moskun and Grossman had proved they were talented programmers and successful entrepreneurs, and Herring had proved he could sell software and run a company. But in 1997, NuMega's sales were not growing rapidly despite the rising popularity of Windows NT, Java, and Internet-based applications, and everyone there was beginning to worry about the future.

Nor did the NuMega management team feel confident it could beat its major competitors without some help. I remember board meetings where marketing executives insisted we had better products than Rational and other competitors but that this was not enough to win; we had to be able to sell our products more broadly. Rational was relatively small in 1996 (revenues of $188 million), but it was still more than ten times the size of NuMega.[7] Rational was also growing faster, and, indeed, it quickly became a dominant player in the software tools business. In fiscal 2002, prior to the acquisition announcement by IBM, Rational had 3,600 employees and annual revenues of nearly $690 million.

In sum, NuMega looked good to me in 1996 and as I look back the venture ranks high on my eight-point checklist. The management team was solid and the market was reasonably large, though not huge. The product offerings were compelling to sophisticated customers, and early sales demonstrated lots of interest. The start-up had very high credibility because of the reputation of the founders and the awards they were winning, as well as the background of the new CEO. The business model was fine—the products were packaged and scalable though becoming harder to sell to a broader set of customers that were across the chasm in the mainstream of software tools users. There was not much flexibility, however. The company was technology-driven and focused on tools for sophisticated programmers, but it was possible to go after new markets, such as Java programmers. The payoff potential for investors seemed reasonably good because this was a scalable software products company. A larger tools firm in particular could do a lot with the NuMega products. It should also have been possible to take this company public, though it would have required large amounts of venture capital to grow it aggressively enough or make significant acquisitions.

Customer Dialogue Systems: Good Small Business, Hard to Scale

Based in Leuven, Belgium, just outside Brussels, Customer Dialogue Systems (CDS) developed a well-regarded financial planning tool that it sold to banks and insurance companies. A local entrepreneur, Yannick Loop, founded the company in 1990. At the time, Loop was in charge of marketing and training at the Belgian Futures and Options Exchange. A major part of his job was to help banks that were members of the exchange sell new financial products, such as options. He noticed that banks had trouble educating their salespeople about the new products. So he started a firm that he worked with part-time to develop computer-based training courses to help banks in their sales and marketing efforts. Loop recalled how he had gotten the idea for his company:

> It took us several years to find out that there exists an important difference between "passive" and "active" knowledge, and that it would take more than training alone to change the behavior of the sales people in relationship to the customers. That's why I decided to join CDS in 1996 on a full-time basis, changed the name of the company (into Customer Dialogue Systems), and changed its mission. From then on, the mission of CDS was to develop software in order to enable financial institutions to switch from "product-pushing" to "customer-focus." The first blueprints of the product didn't mention "financial planning." The first versions of the product were called "Technology Enabled Buying/Selling" systems. It is only progressively—while making the system more and more sophisticated—that we got into "financial planning." [8]

The local market for financial planning tools was very small at the time. There was only one competitor in Belgium in 1996, and that firm had revenues of about $250,000. Loop managed to get some customers in the Netherlands and Germany. He received $4 million in venture funding during 1999 and then another $31 million during 2000–2001, from investors such as the Gilde IT Fund, Deutsche Venture Capital Gesellschaft, Robeco, Gerling, Brokat, and Advanced Technology Ventures. The cofounder of Business Objects, Denis Payre, also invested in CDS. [9]

In December 1999, when I first visited as a consultant (through Payre's recommendation), CDS needed help with everything from executive management to software development and product management. The firm had grown to about seventy-five employees but had few professional managers or formal procedures in place. CDS had about ten customers at the time, led by the Dutch bank ABN AMRO and Deutsche Bank of Germany. Revenues for 1999 were about $3 million, which the CEO expected to double or triple in 2000. The company was losing money.

Loop's strategy was to become a products company selling to banks, brokerages, and insurance companies. These firms had financial advisers and salespeople who used computer-based financial planning tools to analyze their clients' assets, portfolio mixes, and lifetime financial goals. They all had different types of financial products, ranging from home equity or educational loans to certificates of deposit, mutual funds, and life insurance. CDS's financial planning tool (called Customer Dialogue Manager) made it possible for each company to put in information on all their different products as well as their specific business rules and local tax regulations. Users could input some data on their own, but more complex business rules (such as how a bank wanted to treat particular customers or structure discounts for a bundle of products) and tax rules (which numbered up to fifteen thousand per country and changed every year) required changing the programming code in different layers and components of the product. Consequently, CDS had to develop a consulting and implementation practice along with a products business and find third-party solutions companies to help with the localization, configuration, and updating work. It was important for the credibility of the company that Andersen Consulting (the former Arthur Andersen, later renamed Accenture) signed on as a partner for large implementation projects.

In its first few years, CDS created new versions of CDM in conjunction with releases to particular customers. As it tried to get new customers, CDS struggled with how to create a more generic product that would meet the feature requirements of different users and their tailoring needs more easily. The potential competitive advantage of CDS was that its product was powerful in terms of functionality and could be customized for individual firms as well as countries. The customization and configuration features were important in Europe, since each country had different tax laws and each bank's financial products varied by country. The problem CDS faced, however, was that its product design had evolved somewhat haphazardly to meet the needs of different customers as they appeared; it was not neatly layered and modularized. The result was that skilled programmers had to configure the product for different customers and rewrite logic code to update business rules and tax laws. This work was not easy to outsource, even to a firm with the skills of Andersen. In short, *CDS was not really a products company; it had a complex hybrid solution and a business that was hard to scale up profitably.* Customers were balking at paying large sums for customization, considering that they had thought they were buying a product that would be easy to set up.

Table 6-1: Customer Dialogue Systems Financial Data, Actuals (1998–2000) and Forecasts (2001–2002)

(In thousands of dollars)

	Year Ended 31 December				
	1998A*	1999A*	2000A*	2001E*	2002E*
Statement of Operations					
Revenue:					
Software licenses	$ 1,138	$ 1,551	$ 5,478	$13,522	$34,500
Maintenance	71	768	886	827	2,600
Services	530	765	1,123	2,725	3,200
Total revenue	1,739	3,084	7,487	17,074	40,300
Operating income (loss)	(2,536)	(4,196)	(6,378)	(9,329)	6,155
Net income (loss)	$(2,650)	$(4,119)	$(6,329)	$(8,710)	$ 6,871
Balance Sheet Data:					
Cash and cash equivalents	323	3,099	9,225	20,931	26,659
Working capital	372	(2,878)	(3,432)	(1,109)	3,154
Total equity	$ 367	$ (636)	$21,834	$33,084	$39,954

A = actual; E = estimated forecast

Source: *Yannick Loop, e-mail correspondence, December 19, 2002.*

If we look at the revenues of CDS through 2001, it looks very much like a software products company (Table 6-1). Sales quadrupled between 1998 and 2000, rising from $1.7 million to nearly $7.5 million. Growth largely came on the strength of software license fees, which accounted for 65 percent of revenues in 1998 and 73 percent in 2000—easily fitting my definition of a software products company. But CDS also *lost* $13 million during 1998–2000 because of the high cost of developing a better product and catering to the needs of individual customers. CDS should have been charging customers much more for tailored solutions but was unable to do this because of competition and underestimates of how much it would have to spend on R and D, consulting, and implementation.

CDS also got caught up in the hype of the dot-com boom. The Internet provided a means of making the financial planning product more accessible to mobile investment advisors as well as easier to use and update. The initial product ran off a CD-ROM. Not surprisingly, CDS's executive team, investors, and board of directors all wanted to grow the company aggressively and tackle the Web. So throughout 2000, CDS engineers worked on redesigning the product to create more discernible layers and modules (similar to what Netscape attempted with Navigator/Communicator) and enable the product to work through a browser interface and off a Web application server. These were daunting tasks, especially given that "panic management"—hasty responses to last-minute requests from particular customers for this or that feature—continued to drive much of the work on new features.

By early 2001, CDS had made a lot of progress. It had hired several experienced managers and instituted better techniques for software development and product management. In addition, the company had bolstered its engineering resources and knowledge of Web technologies by spending $4 million in the fall of 2000 to acquire a small Boston company called Asset Sciences, which had been founded by a former Fidelity Investments executive. This firm had thirty employees as well as a Web-based financial planning tool called AssetPlanner. CDS merged the engineering teams and created a more mass-market oriented version of its product, renamed AssetPlanner.

But several strategic and financial problems remained that eventually doomed the venture. Asset Sciences had wanted to be a mass-market Web products company. It claimed to have a million users of its free product and had hoped to get major U.S. financial services firms to adopt AssetPlanner as their planning tool. The Boston start-up had competed fiercely with U.S. firms such as Financial Engines as well as in-house development groups at banks and brokerages.

CDS now planned to use its new Boston base to go after U.S. customers with the help of Andersen Consulting. Since the new version of its product was more easily configured and updated as well as Web-based, selling to U.S. customers was now technically feasible. But CDS had not yet established a profitable business in Europe. Its strength was that it knew the European market and had a configurable product, not a mass-market product tailored to American customers. For example, even the latest version of AssetPlanner had very limited features for 401(k) retirement planning, which was essential for the United States. Meanwhile, by 2001, the Internet boom had become a bust, and interest in financial planning tools had declined dramatically. Local European firms were getting most of the European business that existed. And CDS had burned a great deal of cash over the previous twelve months on design and engineering for the future—a future that, when it arrived, saw old customers suddenly dropping out and new ones becoming increasingly difficult to find. I described the strategic dilemma for the board of directors in a March 2001 memo, which updated my original report:

> *CDS is still in a strategic muddle.* It needs more clarity as to what its competitive advantage is and where to apply that advantage. For example, the US market is extremely attractive because it is so large and use of the Internet is so advanced. But I worry that the US could become CDS's Waterloo (a la Napoleon), or Vietnam (a la the US government). It may take all of CDS's resources simply to match the US competition in product functionality. This is separate from the resources required to sell aggressively to US financial institutions or Web portals. Moreover, CDS has designed its product with layers that facilitate configuration for different countries and different clients—customization and localization that the European market requires. This layered product architecture may slow down adding functionality to the product—a "feature-war" type of competition that often occurs in the United States. . . . In my opinion, for the next two years or so, CDS should focus the development and sales organizations on delivering and selling a product tailored for the European market. Do not get too distracted with versions that may not have a large market at the moment, such as US customized versions or a "white label" version for US Web portals. Do not get distracted with another major redesign of the product architecture. I would explore US customers or portal customers, but *selectively*—look for customers that can use the core product with minimal customization and localization for the US. Focus on "winning Europe." And then use Europe as a base for expanding in the United States and other markets, such as Asia.[10]

CDS's financial plans had predicted $17 million in revenues for 2001 and $40 million in 2002, with a net profit in 2002 of nearly $7 million. The company never came close to these numbers. It generated less than $5 million in revenues during 2001 while losing another $8 million. It managed to secure an additional funding round of about $8 million in November 2001 and eventually decided to focus on its few remaining European customers. But as the firm ran low on cash in 2002, its ability to present a credible image to potential customers suffered. Finally, in August 2002, the board decided to dissolve the company. What had once been a potentially exciting small business—valued in May 2000 (during the third funding round) at $200 million (after the $8 million infusion)—was, little more than two years later, headed for bankruptcy. The board managed to sell the company's product assets and remaining business to Accenture for a few hundred thousand dollars, but this was a paltry sum compared to the $35 million that investors, including the founder, Yannick Loop, had put into the company.

The main lesson I took away from the experience of this company is *how easy it is to ruin a good small business if you get the business model wrong*. CDS underestimated what it would take to create a profitable large business and signed on customers that cost too much to service. It was best positioned as a hybrid solutions company that bootstrapped revenues, much as NuMega Technologies did. Instead, the CEO and the board went for bigger game and lost everything.

Not surprisingly, Customer Dialogue Systems fares much less well on my eight-point scale than NuMega. The management team initially lacked experience, but this was not a major problem. The market was reasonably attractive, and there appeared to be enough customer interest to promise a reasonably large payoff to investors. CDS also solved the credibility gap, at least initially, by getting significant venture funding as well as landing a global partner, Andersen. The fatal flaw was that the product was difficult and costly to tailor for different customers as well as to localize and update yearly. Hence, the product's business model turned out not to be viable, although a hybrid solutions business putting much more emphasis on charging fully for services rendered could have worked had the company been able to switch to this. The decline in the stock markets worldwide, as well as competition from other firms, made it too difficult to start charging fully for customization services or raising software license fees. In retrospect, VC funding turned out to be equivalent to the "kiss of death" because it allowed the company to hire too many people and invest too heavily in R and D. CDS should have continued to bootstrap the business and grow only with profitable revenues—or not at all. In fairness, though, it was not so obvious in the late 1990s how costly the business would become when scaled.

Concentric Visions: Expensive Product in an
Exciting But Weak Market

A more puzzling software products start-up was Concentric Visions, founded in 2000. This company developed a highly touted application for creating and editing "rich" multimedia content (i.e., containing audio, video, and other images). The target customers were in-house creators of Web sites and corporate presentations, such as are used in marketing and training programs. Concentric reached a peak of fifty-five employees and generated revenues of about $2 million over a two-year period from customers such as Nikon, Cingular Wireless, and the U.S. Department of Defense. But then—and here is the puzzle—in July 2002 the board voted to dissolve the company. Concentric had received modest funding, totaling some $10 million, from well-known venture capital firms during 2000–2001, including Sigma Partners and GrandBanks Capital. The main early investor in the company, I-Group Hotbank (which also closed down in 2001 after exhausting its funds), was a start-up incubator funded jointly by a wealthy Boston family (led by Ellen and Stephen Roy) and Softbank of Japan. (Full disclosure: I was a member of the I-Group Hotbank advisory board and received stock in Concentric in return for introducing the founder to the investment fund.)

Concentric's product solved a real and growing problem for users of sophisticated multimedia presentations and Web sites: how to compose, edit, and update multimedia content easily and quickly without having to resort to programmers or outside design shops. A June 2002 article in *EContentMag.com* described the company and its origins in glowing terms:

Concentric Visions got its start in early 2000, when a group of special effects developers headed by Sundar Subramaniam pondered a question: how could they make the Internet as eye-catching and engrossing as television and radio? At the time, these developers—who would become the brains behind the company—realized, along with the rest of the world, that streaming video wasn't the answer. There weren't enough people with broadband connections and those with dial-up wouldn't sit and wait for video to download. They would, however, wait the few seconds for Flash animation. . . . Banking on the fact that Flash would take off—and it has in spades—the special effects developers went looking for funding and management so they could build rich media management tools for Web publishers and designers. It didn't take long. Subramaniam, who has launched eight companies including I-Cube [later sold to Razorfish] and Cambridge Technology Partners [later sold to Novell], secured $1.75 million from venture capital firm I-Group and the company he founded, Internet Business Capital Corp., a business incubator.[11]

Flash was a novel Web animation technology introduced by a software company called Macromedia. The technology was a vast improvement over multimedia content created using HTML or even Java, but it required skilled programmers who understood animation coding. In addition, once created, multimedia Flash presentations required programmers to return to the code level in order to edit and change the content. The whole development and editing process, therefore, made Web site design or multimedia presentations too slow and costly for most companies to create themselves. Concentric's solution made it possible for nonprogrammers to create and edit multimedia content. The output was not as sophisticated as a professional design house might produce.[12] But the business idea was similar to what Business Objects did—use a novel set of algorithms to simplify a complex task for nonexpert users.

Unlike Business Objects, however, Concentric did not start out with a clear product concept. The team first thought of offering a content management service, such as for Internet-based news broadcasting, and an ASP service. By 2001, however, under pressure from investors, Concentric had settled on becoming a products company. It came to market with an application suite called Dynamic Media Manager (DMM), with a basic price of $50,000 for an enterprise license.[13] The tool broke down Flash animations into layers and objects, allowing users to label and then change objects in one or more layers through a simple table-driven menu. The software also handled other video formats as well as audio, text, and static images in a similar manner. Concentric engineers wrote the product in multiplatform Java. It ran on PCs with Windows NT/2000, but also required a BEA Systems application server and an enterprise-quality database such as Microsoft's SQL Server or Oracle to store the multimedia files. According to former CEO Garth Rose, there was no direct competitor for DMM, given "what we did with Flash."[14] Moreover, the market was potentially vast. Concentric's customer testimonials were particularly powerful and written up in a variety of publications.

So why did Concentric fail as a company? At one level, it simply started running low on cash and didn't have enough sales in the pipeline to cover its costs, which consisted mainly of rent and salaries. A deeper analysis suggests that Concentric encountered what turned out to be a weak market for a relatively expensive product, given the functionality it offered. Web sites relying on rich multimedia content never lived up to their promises for boosting marketing and sales, even though marketing through Web sites and using multimedia presentations on Web sites are surely important trends for the future. Simple Web sites proved to be effective enough and did not require a firm to purchase a $50,000 tool. Using Concentric's product suite was cheaper and faster than going to a design house for the job, but it was not a trivial purchase. Moreover, Dynamic Media Manager required specialized training to use it properly, and the output was good—professional quality—but not great. Despite the end of the Internet boom, the company's revenues were $2 million in 2001, up from $100,000 in 2000. The company was on track to generate another $2 million in 2002, but the number of customers willing to buy the application was falling fast. Rose recalled the company's situation:

At $2,000 a day and taking weeks to edit/update some Flash files, we thought businesses would need us more and more in the future. What we learned as the economic climate got worse was that rich media was usually a "nice to have" and rarely a "got to have." The pool of prospects ended up shrinking in 2002. Prospects who were willing to spend $50,000 and more for the DMM moved very slowly to a decision, being cautious to make sure that all the value of the system would pay off in a strong enough ROI. The long sales cycle ended up killing many opportunities as the economy got worse and budgets got put on hold. We explored selling at lower prices and closed some small sales but felt caught because our investors wanted to see a scalable enterprise software business model and prices below $50,000 were not attractive for their future investment.[15]

Another problem was that Concentric had natural partners for its product in companies such as Razorfish, the e-business consulting and custom software firm. Developing these "channel partners" was starting to work for Concentric, but their business was suffering as well.
Ultimately, the investors decided not to put in more money. The

board then sold the remaining assets (including about $1.5 million in cash) to another company that belonged to one of the major investors. This other firm, which built Web-based training and learning tools, also took on several of Concentric's top software engineers.

Ron Schreiber, who represented one of the VCs that had invested in Concentric, felt the company should have developed a larger consulting practice in content management to help fund development of its product set and keep the business going.[16] This idea fits with the hybrid solutions strategy, in which a firm does not package its technology too completely (which avoids commoditization and copying). In fact, according to Rose, this is what Concentric had started to do before it ran out of time and money. In 2001, $1.6 million of the $2 million of revenues (80 percent) came from the services side of the business:

> By doing the services we got close to the customer, learned what they wanted, built it, and incorporated it into the DMM. However, our new investors wanted us to be an enterprise software company with an approximate mix of 50 percent services to 50 percent product license revenue. Further, they were investing in a technology company and felt that we needed to significantly beef up the engineering part of the business. The services group was paying the bills and getting us into customers, so they stayed, but then we hired 15 engineers (with their added payroll costs) to build an enterprise-class, scalable DMM. When Sept 11th happened and all the VCs' portfolio companies trimmed their headcounts, it was strongly suggested that we also cut back. We couldn't cut engineering because they were what the VCs had invested in, so we had to cut marketing and services.[17]

Viewed through the eight-point lens, Concentric looks to be an average start-up. If the market for multimedia content management tools had turned out to be large, it might have done reasonably well. There were customers, but not enough. But there was nothing outstanding about the product itself. This view fits with the impression of my colleague Ed Roberts, who also sat on the advisory board of I-Group Hotbank and reviewed the company in the early stages. He recalls complaining that Concentric "had no proprietary skills, no clear vision, just a bag of media tricks—and no market focus."[18] My view is that more of a hybrid solutions model might have worked better, and by far most of the company's revenues came from services. But the investors wanted to see a products company, and they ended up with nothing.

I learned two things from this start-up. One is that *if a hybrid solutions or services model is working, this is the way to go,* despite the allure of being a products company, especially in a horizontal market. Trying to turn a hybrid solution into a high-volume product is tempting but too likely to fail. Another lesson is *how easily a board can dissolve a company and leave the holders of common shares and options—including the founding team—with nothing.*

firstRain: Building on Buzz, Believers, and Flexibility

firstRain (named for the start of the Indian monsoon season) was initially organized in March 2000 to build wireless infrastructure technology and content management and search tools for the Internet. The inventors of the core technology were two computer scientists from Princeton University (Jaswinder Pal Singh and Randolf Wang). They were soon joined by a Yale computer scientist (Arvind Krishnamurthy) and two young industry veterans, Navaid Farooqi and Gaurav Rewari, among others. Rewari, who took the CEO job, had three degrees in engineering from MIT and had formerly been a vice president at MicroStrategy, the business intelligence firm, where he had helped grow the company during 1994–2000. Farooqi, who headed business development at firstRain, was the "common thread" who brought the founding team (which totaled eight people) together.[19] A veteran of Oracle and Merrill Lynch, Farooqi had an MBA from the MIT Sloan School and had gotten to know Singh as well as Rewari while at MIT. The company did most of its software development in India but had its headquarters in low-cost leased space near Pennsylvania Station in Manhattan—a good midway point between Princeton and Yale, where several of the founders maintained their teaching positions. In mid-2003 the number of employees totaled about eighty-five, including forty-five in India.

I agreed to join the firstRain advisory board in March 2001 after hearing about the company from Farooqi, a former student of mine who wanted some introductions to venture capitalists and potential customers such as NTT DoCoMo. I was most attracted by the technology its computer scientists had developed for creating "snippets" of content from Web sites or running applications, primarily for use on the small screens of handheld mobile devices such as cell phones and PDAs. I had been advising another wireless infrastructure start-up, SkyFire Technologies, so I knew a little about the market. I thought firstRain had a simpler and more elegant approach to creating content for handheld wireless devices. With Web sites and Web-based applications, firstRain's snippet screens change as the original Web sites change, but users can view the content or interact with the applications through their small screens. In addition to this tool, the company was building servers and a host of other content management and search tools.[20]

Perhaps the most remarkable feature of the company was the "buzz" it generated. After formally incorporating in July 2000, first-Rain raised $2.2 million in angel funding within a month from a variety of industry and academic luminaries connected personally with the founders. These early backers included Greg Papadapoulos (CTO of Sun Microsystems), Rajat Gupta (head of McKinsey), and John Hennessey (provost of Stanford University and the founder of MIPS).[21] firstRain then sought $8 million in VC funding but actually raised $11 million in a series A round closed in October 2001, led by Allegra Partners and Diamondhead Ventures. At the same time, Steve Walske, the former CEO of Parametric Technology Corporation, joined as chairman of the board to add deeper software business experience.[22] A. Michael Spence—the former dean of Stanford Business School, a Siebel director, and a Nobel laureate in economics—also joined the board of directors in March 2002.[23]

Unlike many other Internet start-ups, firstRain had some real (albeit modest) revenues during 2002, its first year with an actual product offering. The company earned about $2 million and expected to double this number in 2003. firstRain also listed numerous blue-chip customers in an impressive range of industries, suggesting various avenues for business development: Anglo-Eastern Group, PSA, and Tanker Pacific (shipping); Intel, Sun Microsystems, Schlumberger, and NP Test (high-tech manufacturing); J.P. Morgan Chase, Mellon Financial, and Moneyline Telerate (financial services); Pharmacia (pharmaceuticals); and Scientific Games (lottery tickets).[24] The common theme in these domains was the use of firstRain products to provide real-time alerts or notifications. The high-tech press was also quick to praise firstRain for its technology and applications, with write-ups in *Info World, The Venture Reporter,* and others.[25]

In truth, firstRain had a *novel technology in search of applications and customers.* For this reason, I became intrigued with how the company continued to reposition itself strategically and technologically as it explored various opportunities and experienced the boom and bust of the early 2000s. When the wireless market did not evolve as fast as expected, the company switched gears to emphasize how its products facilitated applications accessed through servers and used as Web services. When Web services did not take off as quickly as expected, the company began to emphasize another specialty familiar to Rewari: business intelligence.[26] This latest idea takes advantage of firstRain's technology to enable organizations to track and analyze transactions and other information on their customers as well as their competitors and direct this information (sometimes in the form of real-time alerts and notifications) within and outside the organization and to mobile devices, if necessary.[27] The management team and advisers also had enough expertise in diverse areas to help firstRain refine and change the way it marketed various "solutions."

It is significant that the original technology was flexible enough to use in different ways, even though the vision of wireless infrastructure and Web services software still drives the company. According to Jaswinder Singh, the company CTO, to market their products in the business intelligence space, firstRain engineers had to create a new product called eventServer as well as extend an existing product, viewServer, to handle finely tagged XML data. The two products then enabled a customer to do things such as track price changes in competitors' products, rather than just route unstructured pieces of HTML content. eventServer evolved into a content-based routing engine that treats "events" as structured XML documents and "subscriptions" as requests for particular pieces of data or notifications.[28]

In 2002, about 70 percent of firstRain's revenues came from software license fees (product sales). The other revenues came from services, an area where firstRain relied on a crack team of ten engineers and three other full-time employees, mostly based in New York. The company's products required some installation and configuration work, although it generally did not bill this time as services unless customers requested specific enhancements or training. The biggest deal landed by the company so far was for $400,000, twice the average for a production order (as opposed to a pilot deal). firstRain was also able to stretch its financial resources more than most start-ups because of its India base, opened in October 2000 near the Indian Institute of Technology campus in Delhi.

Looking at firstRain through my eight-point lens, the company looks promising, though a bit less so than in 2000. Its strengths are an experienced management team with a great deal of technical talent, high credibility with customers and investors, and extraordinarily flexible technology, which has made it easier to adapt the firm's strategy as market opportunities have appeared and disappeared. I find their solution for creating applications for handheld wireless devices compelling, but this market remains minuscule at present. So there is the big issue of what to do with some interesting technology. It's not yet clear what the real market will be—business monitoring is probably better than wireless applications development tools, but next year the market could be different. Since it is hard to say what the most promising opportunity will be, one cannot say much about the potential for payoff to investors, even though the company is selling products and should do relatively well in 2003–2004.

My take-away lesson from this company is that *there is no guarantee that a start-up, even with unique technology, money, and broad-based support from industry luminaries, will succeed.* The technology has to be made into products with clear applications and a certain number of customers. To continue operating throughout 2003–2004, firstRain raised another $8 million dollars in mid-2003. The company also faced major strategic questions, such as which were the best and biggest markets to target. firstRain has dabbled in various areas, with mixed success. The company's technology complements more traditional business intelligence as well as CRM applications, but it has yet to find a good way to describe what its products do. "Real-time business activity monitoring" is firstRain's latest attempt to characterize the range of business intelligence, transportation, manufacturing, financial, and other applications of its products.[29] This characterization seems reasonably accurate, though firstRain is likely to have to shift gears again if alerts and notifications do not turn out to be a big enough business.

SOFTWARE SERVICES START-UPS

NetNumina Solutions: Viable Niche, Modest Business, No IPO

NetNumina Solutions is a high-end custom-systems design and integration company with headquarters in Cambridge, Massachusetts.

Table 6-2: NetNumina Revenues and Employees, 1997–2001*

Year	Revenues	Year-End Employees	Average Employees	Revenues/Average Employee
1997	$ 1.2 million	15	13	$ 92,300
1998	$ 2.4 million	20	18	$133,000
1999	$ 3.8 million	40	30	$127,000
2000	$14.4 million	175	108	$133,000
2001	$19.5 million	115	145	$134,000

* All numbers are estimates.
Source: *www.netnumina.com/company/history/index.html* and author's
interview with Chairman of the Board Imran Sayeed, November 24, 2002.

It specializes in e-business systems, particularly in financial services and, more recently, in pharmaceuticals. (Full disclosure: I became an adviser to the company in May 1999.) It was founded in April 1997 with 10 employees and peaked at about 115 employees and nearly $20 million in revenues in 2001 (Table 6-2), before scaling back. The head count and revenues for 2002–2003 remain confidential.

The origins of the company date back to Open Environment Corporation (OEC), a start-up founded in 1992 by John Donovan (a former MIT Sloan professor) and Sundar Subramanian (the entrepreneur who started Concentric Visions, among other firms). Other founders were Imran Sayeed, Anish Dhande, and Greg Sabatino, who would form the core of NetNumina's initial executive team. OEC went public in 1995 with an IPO worth about $200 million and at its peak had revenues of some $30 million a year and 250 employees. Its main product was a "middleware" solution, including some proprietary and open software, and a "DCOM" product that supported the Microsoft components standard and linked various types of enterprise systems.

Borland, a major software tools and desktop products company, purchased OEC in 1996. But the Borland executives who had pursued the merger left shortly after the acquisition in a management shake-up. According to NetNumina's chairman, Imran Sayeed, the new Borland executives preferred to emphasize desktop products rather than enterprise software. OEC customers also expressed concern about how much support they would get from Borland in the future.[30] To deal with potential customer liability problems, Borland allowed the OEC team to create another start-up to serve its existing customers and gave it $1.5 million in guaranteed revenue, with no claims on the equity of the new company. As part of the deal, the spin-off—named NetNumina Solutions—worked with Borland to continue servicing the existing OEC customers and help develop a new version of the OEC product suite, Entera. In addition, the OEC spin-off team was anxious to take advantage of the Web. OEC had specialized in custom "mission-critical" solutions for enterprises, and the founding team felt that NetNumina would be well positioned to compete in this niche on the Web—creating heavy-duty systems linking back-office databases and enterprise applications with new Web front-ends.

Sayeed recalled that the NetNumina founders debated intensely whether to be a services company or a products company, like OEC and Borland. Ultimately, they decided to focus on services. They felt there were already a lot of middleware and enterprise architecture products available or forthcoming from companies such as Web Logic, Sun Microsystems, BEA Systems, Microsoft, and IBM, among others.

The business idea was a good one. NetNumina was soon designing and building e-business systems for blue-chip customers such as Citigroup (an OEC customer) and Wellington Management. For Citigroup, NetNumina built an award-winning Web-based currency-trading system, the first time a company had used the Web for such an application.[31] These customers, and the experienced management team and their connection to Borland and OEC, gave the start-up immediate credibility. Other early projects brought awards and helped increase the new company's credibility. A particularly notable prize-winning project was for the Massachusetts Port Authority (Massport) in Boston. NetNumina built the middleware piping that enabled Massport to put a variety of real-time information on the Web, ranging from flight data for Logan Airport to project bidding information.[32] Like NuMega, this company accumulated a long list of awards. In 2002, it was named to *Software Magazine*'s top 500 software and IT services companies, as well as to the "*Inc. Magazine* 500" list of the fastest-growing private companies in the United States (as number 182).[33]

Revenues started growing dramatically as e-business applications came into wide demand. From $1.2 million in sales in their company's first year, 1997, revenues tripled to $3.8 million and then more than tripled again to $14.4 million in 2000, by which time the head count had risen to 175 people. The client list included financial services powerhouses such as Fidelity Investments, State Street Global Advisors, Merrill Lynch, Prudential, Morgan Stanley Dean Witter, Liberty Mutual, Standard & Poor's, Credit Suisse First Boston, Citigroup, Banknorth, and MFS. Other clients included Johnson & Johnson, Pfizer, Biogen, and Philips Medical (formerly Agilent). NetNumina's management deliberately tried to limit the company's exposure to dot coms that might not be able to pay their bills. Nonetheless, demand for its services peaked with the Internet boom and fell after the crash.

Ironically—and I find this to be a common story—NetNumina was profitable or at least at breakeven before it got venture funding in May 2000 but lost money thereafter. Two premier venture capital firms—Greylock and TA Associates—each put in $10 million. Other investors included BancBoston Ventures, BEA Systems, and Allaire/Macromedia. The outside funding made it possible to expand head count as well as lease expensive new offices in Cambridge and New York (first opened in February 2001). The biggest drain, other than head count, was rent, but the company managed to renegotiate its leases. With the reduction in force, NetNumina came close to breakeven by the end of 2002 and should be profitable again in 2003.

What made NetNumina an attractive start-up for me—besides the market opportunity in the late 1990s—was the technical expertise of the management team and their thoughtful approach to middleware systems development. The company had a core of experienced computer scientists who deeply understood middleware and component architectures as well as enterprise applications, from before the Web era. Their approach was also very much driven by a combination of system architecture, user requirements, software design options, and business needs, with a special emphasis on creating solutions that used open standards and off-the-shelf technologies as much as possible. Management was committed to remaining small enough to be very selective in hiring. Around 2000, the company also decided to focus on clients' needs in a particular vertical market, financial services, where I was able to help, given my experience as a consultant. Many of these customers, led by Fidelity Investments, spent heavily during the Internet boom and continued to spend afterward as well to keep their systems up to date and get an edge over their competitors. By 2002, NetNumina had also completed some 175 projects, giving it extensive experience in a range of systems.

In 2002, approximately 70 percent of NetNumina's business came from financial services clients. Existing customers provided about three fourths of revenues. The largest clients were Fidelity, Johnson & Johnson, and State Street. The dollar amount of the average project deal was also rising, from approximately $100,000 in 1998 to about $400,000 in 2002, with nearly half a dozen contracts at $2 million or more. Annual revenues per employee were comparable to those at other high-end IT consulting firms, around $130,000. The company averaged about $160 per hour per person when it billed clients, though large customers were able to negotiate better prices than this—a source of frustration since the top five clients accounted for 85 percent of revenues.

As another way of growing, NetNumina started moving beyond its focus on software development and more into IT strategy. Sayeed claims that the low-cost companies in India and elsewhere that provide custom development services have pushed them into this change in strategy. In 2002, about 30 percent of revenues came from IT strategy work and the rest from traditional development projects.

In an interview for this book, I asked Sayeed why NetNumina has survived when so many other Web consulting and custom software firms have folded.[34] He gave me three reasons. First, when services companies were expanding so fast, NetNumina focused on projects it could handle and didn't grow as fast as it might have. Second, NetNumina differentiated itself by focusing on specific verticals that were promising in terms of size and growth rates—financial services in particular. This specialty helped the company weather the downturn in IT spending. Third, NetNumina emphasized efficiency in operations—especially in sales and project management, with incentives tied to delivery on time and on budget. Of particular help in this area were Al Lucchese, who joined as president and CEO in April 2001, and Steve Richards, a former Sybase executive who joined as CFO in September 2000 and took on the role of vice president of operations in February 2002.

Sayeed and his cofounders did not do everything right. They had a chance to sell NetNumina to BEA Systems in 2000 for more than $50 million. But after having experienced a $200 million IPO with OEC, they chose instead to get venture funding in the hope of going public. *Bad decision.* Once the Internet boom died, the chances for relatively small software services companies to go public evaporated. Firms under $500 million in revenues, in Sayeed's view, are just not large enough to sustain both good and bad times and provide sufficient returns for investors. Almost every small services company that went public during the Internet boom has gone bankrupt or come very close to it, including once-high fliers such as Breakaway Solutions, Scient, Viant, and Razorfish. The companies that went public did well in the short term for their owners on the IPO and secondary offerings but faded quickly.

I came away from this experience convinced that *a talented software services company should always remain profitable if it manages head count and expenses carefully.* This is why I feel that venture funding is often the "kiss of death" for an IT services firm. It is a form of artificial wealth. If a company were building a product that it could sell in volume, the rationale for outside funding would be different. NuMega, for example, needed outside funding or a wealthy partner in order to grow the business, as Compuware did successfully. Concentric could have grown its business and possibly survived had it gotten more funding. But in the case of IT services, the rationale for getting outside funding is to enable the company to hire employees and managers more quickly than bootstrapping would allow and to open more offices to be closer to potential customers. A pure software services and consulting firm can easily acquire too much overhead to survive the booms and busts of the business. Most services companies grow their revenues only as they grow their head count, and the bigger they become, the more projects and revenues they need to remain a viable business. Unlike hybrid solutions providers, software services firms may have no recurring revenues from customers unless they have built custom systems that require continual maintenance and significant periodic enhancements.

On my eight-point scale, NetNumina does fairly well. The management team was experienced and credible, and the company started in a reasonably attractive market, at least until 2001–2002. Its skill set and focus made the service offering reasonably distinctive. It started and remains a high-end niche company. NetNumina has not had much trouble finding customers, several of whom came from the previous company. But the business model is pure services, and there is not much flexibility. Consequently, there is little potential for a large payoff to investors, except for the brief moment during the Internet boom when NetNumina could have been acquired. As Sayeed and I discussed many times, scaling the company enough to go public would always be difficult if it maintained the focus on high-quality people and projects in which it had special expertise. In the middle of a boom, it seemed worth taking the risk of trying to grow fast with the market, and this is why NetNumina took in outside funding.

Unfortunately, the founders and holders of common stock and options will probably never see any money from this venture. The VCs all have preferred stock, so they will get their money back first. Given the low valuations for many IT services companies in the current climate (except for some high fliers, such as India's Infosys) and NetNumina's historical level of sales, the VCs will do well just to get their money back. The founders are now either gone or reduced to salaried executives.

Oneworld Software: A Niche That Wasn't

Oneworld Software (now part of Estarta Solutions, a company based in Jordan) was a software development contracting firm established by several MIT alumni in September 1997. (Full disclosure: I joined the advisory board of Oneworld in September 2000.) The initial offices were in Cambridge, Massachusetts, as well as Amman, Jordan, the hometown of the founder and CEO, Ennis Rimawi. The company eventually established development centers or offices in San Francisco, San Diego, and Beijing before running out of money and customers in September 2001. Rather than disappear completely, however, the board of directors sold the Jordan development center to some local investors, and this entity continued operating as Oneworld Jordan, with about 100 people. In the fall of 2002, Oneworld Jordan merged with another local company, Zeine Technological Applications, which also had about 100 employees. The new company received an investment from Microsoft of just under $5 million. Rimawi became the chairman and president (and later the CEO) of the merged company, named Estarta Solutions. Estarta inherited both the custom software focus of Oneworld and some software technologies for pattern recognition and messaging (SMS middleware) that Zeine had developed.[35]

Oneworld initially attracted my attention because it relied heavily on process management for software development. In addition, custom programming ventures rarely get the level of start-up funding this company received. Also, I felt that its niche strategy was flawed, and I tried to convince Rimawi, a former student of mine, to change it. I still believe the strategy was too limited, though the company did better than I expected.

Rimawi's original idea was to provide development services to software products companies, offering U.S.-based project management and design skills with low-cost software-programming labor from the Middle East and then China. Rimawi's background had been in automobile components manufacturing at Ford, where he had worked after graduating from MIT. Automobile companies routinely outsource 50 to 80 percent of their components, and increasingly they have come to use low-cost overseas suppliers. Rimawi believed that software products companies would eventually go the same way. It is true that large corporations routinely outsource a lot of their custom software development and IT management needs. Why wouldn't the Microsofts of the world do the same thing? Or (as turned out to be more common), why wouldn't start-ups and less able software products companies turn to outsourcing?

To make the strategy work, Oneworld cultivated its process management skills over the entire software development life cycle. Rimawi believed these skills would make it easy for Oneworld personnel to integrate with the development cycles of software products companies. In addition, the company hired several people from Sapient, an IT consulting firm that had developed excellent requirements generation techniques, and devised a similar process. As part of its attraction, Oneworld also offered clients a "fixed-price/fixed-time" contract. If its engineers were late and over budget in finishing their work, Oneworld absorbed the extra costs. This was impressive since industry data, which Oneworld heavily publicized, indicated that 75 percent of all software projects came in late or were cancelled. Oneworld also moved forward in projects gradually, from the design through development and deployments stages, and priced each phase separately while allowing customers to back out or renegotiate, as they chose.

In its first couple of years, the company was remarkably successful as technology spending boomed in the United States and abroad. Oneworld got customers such as Flash Communications (later acquired by Microsoft), Gray Peak (acquired by U.S. Web and then spun off to Opus 360), and 3Com (the router and modem company wanted a decision analysis system for new-product development projects). Oneworld's founders bootstrapped the venture and were cash-flow positive through early 1999, at which point it had grown to about fifty people.

Then, once again, the "kiss of death" appeared—VC funding for an IT services company. Oneworld initially got an infusion of $3.5 million, which Rimawi used to hire more people, particularly from Sapient and Cambridge Technology Partners, and open more offices. By May 2000, head count stood at 150 people, and Oneworld had new facilities in Beijing, San Diego, and San Francisco. Revenues were expanding at about 50 percent a quarter. To fund its expansion, the company raised an additional $15 million in early 2000 from Advent International, Citicorp Venture Capital, and New Horizons Ventures.[36] It finished the year with about $13 million in revenues and 350 employees.

From the fall of 2000, I argued that selling design and development services to software products companies was equivalent to focusing on "a niche that wasn't." The fact that Oneworld had large revenues as well as nearly $17 million in venture funding made me seem wrong. But software products companies, in my view, were in the business of designing and developing software products. The companies I knew well, such as Microsoft, Netscape, and Business Objects, had rarely if ever needed to outsource their core activity. The only exceptions I could think of were for some cases of porting a product to a little-used language or operating system platform, and these were not likely to be high-margin jobs. Microsoft and other software companies used contractors, but these were generally the equivalent of temporary workers used for low-priority projects or testing. It was becoming more common for software companies to establish overseas development centers, especially in India and China, but I saw that as being different from outsourcing to a third-party services firm. In any case, Rimawi was successfully growing the business. I encouraged him at least to cultivate a handful of technical programming specialties such as Java, wireless, the 64-bit Intel platform, or .NET applications that might give the company more leverage in getting projects. I also wanted it to go after nonsoftware companies—not a niche, but a mass market that clearly existed.

As the demand for custom programming services declined after 2000, Oneworld did scramble for customers and expanded its target list. The company brochure from June 2001 noted clients that now included not only software product vendors but also application service providers and "large IT organizations within the financial services, telecommunications, healthcare services, and manufacturing industries."[37] Oneworld's marketing materials also claimed that the company had "unique capabilities" based on its extensive experience in software development, ability to deploy software engineers at a moment's notice and have them work around the clock from a global network of offices and partners, and cultivation of several technical specialties, such as Java, wireless applications, new Microsoft platforms, and database technologies.[38]

Rimawi admitted in an interview for this book that Oneworld had not, in fact, managed to get much business from elite software products companies. Some clients were relatively large, such as MicroStrategy, Informatica, and Thomson Financial. Some, such as 3Com and Kyocera, were large hardware or systems companies making products that included software. But most clients were Internet or dot-com start-ups that were venture capital–backed and had little if any revenues. When the start-ups ran out of money and the larger firms started cutting back on their technology spending, Oneworld felt the impact. Things started to become especially tight late in 2000, when some 80 percent of the company's clients starting running out of money. Rimawi tried to get additional funding from his investors, but eventually the board of directors decided to close the offices and sell what was left of the company. Fortunately for Rimawi and about a hundred of Oneworld's employees, the merger with Zeine and the formation of Estarta gave them someplace to go.

Estarta's strategy is to sell development services in Jordan and the Middle East, where 70 percent of the company's business lies. The new company has offices in Amman as well as Qatar. It boasts the same technical specialties as Oneworld.[39] There are relatively few software products companies in the region, so this potential niche is no longer a target. Current customers are mainly government offices, telecommunications firms, and banks. The largest job at year-end 2002 was a government project in Qatar. Other clients included Saudi Telecom, Riyad Bank, and Aramex. Overall, the company seems to have enough customers and regional connections to succeed. The local media has praised Estarta as "one of Jordan's greatest merger stories," particularly because of the Microsoft connection.[40] The new company is well connected. Even the king of Jordan got involved by appealing directly to Bill Gates to make the investment.[41]

Looking back at Oneworld through my eight-point lens, there were some strengths in the company, but not many. The management team was strong in general process but lacked experience and credibility in the software business. The market for custom programming was booming in the late 1990s and 2000, but this was a temporary phenomenon. Oneworld did not have a viable niche and specialty service offering, as NetNumina did. The business model suggested labor-intensive custom programming for low-end jobs. It was not a scalable model and therefore was unlikely to lead to a significant payoff to investors. It is true that firms such as Infosys have done extremely well for investors, and Oneworld looked for a time as though it might become another elite outsourcing company, but it never quite crossed this chasm. Before the merger with Zeine, Oneworld had no skills to change this strategy either, such as product development. It also had a serious problem with the quality of many of its customers. Too many were fledgling Internet start-ups that did not have the resources to hire their own programmers, and in any case they ran out of money.

The basic idea that software products companies might take advantage of low-cost programmers overseas turned out to be right. However, companies such as Microsoft and Oracle tend to establish their own development subsidiaries rather than outsource, except for routine or labor-intensive projects. The strategy may work better for some other entrepreneurs in the future, although the world-class Indian software firms would seem to have an inside track on these kinds of programming jobs.

Cybergnostic: Scaling Up a One-Person Consulting Operation

Cybergnostic, based in Trumbull, Connecticut, is not a software services start-up in the sense of NetNumina or Oneworld/Estarta; it designs and runs communications networks. (Full disclosure: I served as an adviser to Cybergnostic during 1999–2001 and still retain some stock options in the company.) The original strategy had been to offer small and medium-sized firms the capability to rent rather than purchase wide-area network (WAN) and data center infrastructure more typical of larger firms, complete with expert staff and "24/7" technical support. Customers can get cheaper high-speed Internet access (T1 service) because Cybergnostic purchases higher-capacity (T3 lines) from phone companies and service providers such as World-Com, Verizon, and AT&T and then resells fractions of this capacity to small customers that would have to buy in larger increments on their own.[42]

Andrew Greenawalt, currently the CTO of Cybergnostic, founded the company in 1997. A graduate of the University of Massachusetts, Amherst, he had been working as a consultant and network designer at a small communications firm in Connecticut. He designed networks for voice, data, and Internet communications for a variety of clients, including Caldor department stores, Pace University, the Gartner Group, and Baylor Medical Center. He also worked for a time as the senior network engineer at Norwalk Hospital. It occurred to him that many medium-sized organizations needed the kind of technical consulting he provided as well as access to better networking services. Large service providers that owned the Internet backbone and telephone networks, such as AT&T, MCI, UUNET, and the local Bell operating companies, provided such services, but they generally ignored small and medium-sized enterprises, or their offerings were too expensive.

Greenawalt hired a small team to help grow the business. After doing some research, they concluded there were 10,000 to 20,000 small and medium-sized enterprises in the local Connecticut and adjoining New York area that needed wide-area networking services and did not have them.[43] Campbell Stras, a Brown University graduate with an MBA from the University of Rochester, who was also a veteran of Analog Devices and Shiva Corporation, took on the post of CEO and head of product marketing. (Stras left the company in fall 2001 and is currently vice president of marketing for Altaworks, a start-up selling performance management software for Web-based systems.) Greenawalt's brother Richard, a sales expert with a background in the insurance and construction industries, headed sales until leaving the company in spring 2001. An experienced IT data center and systems manager, Gail Beauchemin, became the director of operations.

Stras and I met at a venture capital meeting in New York City in mid-1999. After learning about the company, I concluded that they had found a viable niche. Cybergnostic was serving a certain type of customer better than the bigger network providers were doing at the time, and demand for Internet and telecommunications services was rising rapidly. On the customer front, it was impressive that Greenawalt had lined up some relatively large accounts: Fujicolor Processing, which had a growing network of manufacturing plants for providing film-processing services to Wal-Mart stores; and Mediacom, a rural cable TV aggregator that was growing fast and, by 2002, would become the ninth largest cable company in the United States. *Red Herring* magazine was sufficiently impressed with Greenawalt to compare him to Netscape founder Marc Andreessen and his Loudcloud venture for IT outsourcing.[44]

The key question for me when evaluating Cybergnostic was *Is this a business with real growth prospects or a large one-person consulting operation?* The challenge would be to get more customers like Fujicolor and Mediacom and service them adequately, without spending too much money. I can remember an early board meeting when we debated whether or not Greenawalt had been more "lucky" than "good" in getting these customers; if the offering was really so attractive, more customers should be signing on, and they weren't. I urged the Cybergnostic team to study and then try to replicate the process whereby Greenawalt had gotten such great customers. The company then started spending a lot of money on sales and marketing. A few more customers did sign on, but they still came much too slowly. As of early 2000, Cybergnostic had eighteen employees and only thirty customers, and expected revenues of about $2 million for the year. More worrisome was the fact that 80 percent of that revenue was coming from the two big customers: Fujicolor and Mediacom.[45]

Despite the paucity of customers, the management team had ambitious growth ideas. They wanted to build an infrastructure capable of handling hundreds and even thousands of customers as well as various types of networking services. The May 2000 business plan, for example, called for about $25 million in capital expenditures through 2003 and forecast that revenues would jump from $2.5 million in 2000 to $17 million in 2001 (based on the assumption that the company would have more than four hundred customers by this time) and $165 million in 2003.[46] The team wanted to raise money, and that is why they were attending VC meetings.

Cybergnostic managed to get a few hundred thousand dollars from angel investors, but it needed serious venture capital to implement these plans and compete with larger players. In May 2000, to raise more money and manage the growth of the company, the board brought in Brad Miller to become the new CEO. Miller was not from the industry, but he had business experience and training—a Columbia University MBA and a background in investment banking. He had also been COO of PRG, a supplier of entertainment technology products and services with over $300 million in revenue.

What happened to Cybergnostic's growth plans for 2001 is, by now, a familiar story. The demand for Internet-based networking services and outsourcing did not increase nearly as fast as expected. Established service providers became more aggressive in going after clients of different sizes. Cybergnostic had to change its strategy and grow more incrementally. Miller still managed to raise about $4 million in new money from Connecticut Innovations, Trident Ventures/Redstone7.com, and 1to1 Venture Partners. Cisco and Nortel also provided $1 million in lease financing for equipment.

In 2002, Cybergnostic made about $7.5 million in revenues with merely 22 employees. Revenues have increased eightfold since Miller joined the company, with roughly the same number of employees. And Cybergnostic has been profitable since December 2001 and should have about $4 million in cash by the end of 2003. The break-even revenue rate is about $500,000 per month. The revenue forecast for 2003 was between $10 million (the current twelve-month sales run rate) and $15 million. To double its revenues, Cybergnostic should have to invest only another half a million dollars or so since it already has the network infrastructure in place. Miller described his financial expectations: "At our current rate of growth, we should be generating over $20 million of recurring revenue and close to $10 million of pretax profit by year-end 2004."[47] So here is a modest success story, although its road was not so clearly marked.

Miller recounted in an interview for this book his view on the state of the company when he joined in mid-2000 and how the new strategy had evolved.[48] First, the management team examined how Greenawalt had gotten his two big customers. Miller concluded that "Andy had been somewhat lucky in landing Fujicolor and Mediacom, or at least lucky that these once-small customers grew so quickly. Between 1999 and 2001, all the company did was catch up to the growth provided by these clients." Miller also realized that Fujicolor and Mediacom had become Cybergnostic clients not through a direct sales effort but because they had been buying a new accounting package from another vendor and found that their networks were inadequate. This independent software vendor (ISV) knew Greenawalt and had recommended him as a network consultant. This history suggested a new strategy: *Partner with ISVs or other value-added resellers to get customers who want to buy new software but need a better network infrastructure and don't have the resources to go to high-priced service providers.* Over the next two years, about 75 percent of Cybergnostic's revenues came through partners. Miller observed, "There is an inflection point when people are willing to buy networking services, and that is usually when they are buying new software."

Another insight came from looking carefully at what types of *new* customers were coming to Cybergnostic. Through the end of 2000, it got only six new customers. One was a local community bank, the other a lumberyard, the third a car dealer. It occurred to Miller and other members of the management team that these types of customers represented vertical markets with similar networking needs. In order to differentiate themselves from larger competitors, they decided to specialize rather than continue trying to be a generalist provider of networking services for small and medium-sized firms.

The lumberyard also came through an ISV, Enterprise Computer Systems. The client wanted to buy new back-office software and needed better networking services. Enterprise approached Cybergnostic, and it landed the customer—the pattern repeated. As of early 2003, Enterprise was providing about $1.2 million a year in business to Cybergnostic. Miller noted, "Enterprise brings us in whenever the network is an obstacle to their sales, and it's usually an issue 50 percent of the time." Cybergnostic now has more than forty lumberyards as its customers, from all around the United States, and all through Enterprise Computer Systems, which takes a fee of 20 percent of the initial contracts. Miller estimates there are another three thousand lumberyards or construction supply firms in the United States that are potential customers.

The most successful vertical focus, though, has been providing networking security services to some of the ten thousand community banks around the United States. Cybergnostic even established a subsidiary, Perimeter Internetworking, to focus on their special security concerns.[49] Banks provided about 40 percent of Cybergnostic's revenues in 2002, compared to 20 percent for lumberyards and 40 percent for a variety of legacy customers, led by Fujicolor and Mediacom. Cybergnostic generally charges about $4,000 to $5,000 per month per bank, depending on its size and needs.

The first banking customer was New Haven Savings Bank, which wanted a secure Internet connection so that its employees could use the Web and still comply with government security regulations for financial institutions. At the time, Cybergnostic was selling mainly WAN services, with only a few security services. Cybergnostic agreed to build a secure network for the bank, with the idea that it could market the same service to other community banks around the country. This followed Greenawalt's original mantra for growing the business: "Build it once, sell it many times." To push the banking vertical, Miller hired a couple of sales specialists and lined up additional partners such as Enterprise that specialized in selling technology exclusively to banks. By early 2001, Cybergnostic had a total of twelve banking customers, all in Connecticut. By the end of 2002, it had sixty banking customers in fifteen states and were about to get a lot more after partnering with another firm that had a network of some three hundred banks, BISYS (symbol BSG on the New York Stock Exchange).

In looking back at what Cybergnostic has done, Miller feels that the company's story was mainly one of *adaptation and flexibility*— figuring out where the market should be, rather than trying to compete with the big service providers: "We had to get small to get big. We couldn't be all things to all people." He cut out layers of management and generalist salespeople and then focused on sales through partners within two or three verticals. As for the growth achieved in 2002, Miller saw this as simply replicating their early successes.

Cybergnostic also proves that *it is possible to expand a small-scale consulting operation, but at a cost.* When Greenawalt worked on his own as a network consultant, he made a profit. When he got Fujicolor and Mediacom as customers, he started to lose money because he had to move out of his basement, buy equipment, lease networking bandwidth, and hire staff. To service his new customers and grow, he also had to take in outside investors and bring in professional management.

Miller's arrival in May 2000 was probably the critical event that turned Cybergnostic from a small networking services operation into a profitable growth company. Not only did he raise sufficient money for investment, but he brought much-needed discipline to the sales process and expenditures. Miller also honed the vertical market focus, although it would take more than a year to figure out a workable strategy: "As in most cases, we were not smart enough to figure out what the right verticals were, so we stumbled upon them in the natural course of business. We were smart enough to recognize when we stumbled into a good thing." [50]

Looking at this venture through my eight-point lens, Cybergnostic was and remains an above-average investment opportunity. Its strengths were a competent management and technical team, a compelling offering for medium-sized firms, early demonstrations of customer interest, and credibility that came from having real customers early on and an experienced network engineer and consultant (Andy Greenawalt) leading the sales and technical efforts. The services have also been highly scalable, with only a modest investment. The strategy turned out to be relatively flexible in identifying the vertical-niche strategy. Perhaps most important, this start-up generates large *recurring revenues*. Cybergnostic is a fine example of the "asset management" or "bank" model. It was also fortunate that Cybergnostic did not raise so much venture capital that it expanded beyond its ability to make a profit (as in the cases of CDS and Oneworld).

The main negative associated with the company is the declining attractiveness of networking services. Demand still has not reached anticipated levels, and competition from a variety of service providers has increased. Stras had this comment on Cybergnostic, though he was referring more to the earlier days of the company: "The unique strength of the business model, the fact that customers get deeply locked into our service, mirrors what is considered to be a problem— slow revenue growth." [51] Cybergnostic's answer to this market problem has been the vertical focus and partnerships, both of which were working well in 2002–2003.

As for the potential payoff to investors, I had assumed when I first joined the advisory board that some larger network services provider would "roll up" Cybergnostic and combine its customer base and infrastructure with its own. This remains a possibility. Cybergnostic generates the funds it needs and probably will not try to become a public company unless management and the board decide to grow through acquisition—in which case it will probably require public capital.

HYBRID SOLUTIONS START-UPS

Investhink: Good Idea, Weak Implementation, Weaker Sales

My involvement with Investhink, located in London before liquidation in November 2002, goes back to January 1997. A Turkish entrepreneur named O. Emre Eksi, who had worked briefly as an international journalist and had had some success in the perfume business as well as in infrastructure development in Turkey (Bodrum International Airport and Hilltop Holiday Resorts), had been studying the market for financial investment tools for about a year. Eksi's lawyer in New York had learned of my interests and recommended he come speak with me about his idea for a new venture.

Eksi wanted to create a mass-market PC version of the Bloomberg workstation for active investors and financial advisers. The Bloomberg workstation (similar to one that Reuters offered) uses dedicated phone lines to bring together real-time prices of stocks and other financial products, enables trading on different exchanges, and facilitates analysis of various types of market information and data. But Eksi had a barely comprehensible sketch of a plan, no investors, no management team, and no partners. He had no programming skills. I told him I thought the idea made sense but advised him to make the system *Internet-based*. I also urged him to get help writing a more precise business plan, put a small team together, and then market the idea again.

About a year later, after I had all but forgotten about the visit, Eksi contacted me again. He had found a backer in London called Sigma Technology Management, a new incubator and investment vehicle for early-stage ventures, founded in December 1996 by Neil Crabb and Graham Barnet.[52] Eksi also found a partner in Sina Hakman, a childhood acquaintance who had become an accomplished IT consultant and the regional director for Microsoft software developer relations in Turkey. Together with Sigma, they refined the business plan and did the required market research. The company would create a PC workstation and an Internet portal that would aggregate information and Web-based tools for investors, as well as serve as a mechanism for financial services firms to sell products and services to users of the Web site. The company (then called World Wide Investing Network— Interactive Tools or "WINIT" for short) would make money from sales of advertising as well as from fees received from companies that sold products and services through the site.

I agreed to go to London to meet with the team at Sigma's offices, then in the Canary Wharf section of London. I was impressed with Hakman as well as Crabb (who had worked as an investment manager running technology portfolios and office computing systems for the Equitable Life Assurance Society, a large U.K. investment house). Eksi continued to be the driving force behind the idea. I was concerned that this was a very different venture from what he had done before. But he was remarkably passionate and determined. He had also put together the beginnings of a solid team—as well as convinced me to travel to London.

With Sigma, and investors that Sigma arranged, the new venture would eventually raise a total of £4.5 million (about $6.5 million) in two rounds. We incorporated the company (later renamed Investhink) in April 1999. Crabb took the post of nonexecutive chairman of the board. He was later succeeded by John Parcell, a former CEO of Reuters Information and a board member of the Reuters Group. Parcell joined the Investhink board in July 2000 and left in September 2002. Eksi served as the first president but eventually left the management team in January 2002 and continued as a board member until resigning in August 2002. Hakman took the post of CEO and later moved to COO when Andrew Delaney, who had been editor in chief at Waters Information Services and worked for several years at *The Wall Street Journal,* came on as chief content officer and then CEO. Michael McSweeney, another Reuters veteran, joined in 2001 and took over from Delaney as CEO. I joined the board of directors from the onset and received about 5 percent of the company's stock as a cofounder. Eksi and Hakman each received about 24 percent equity in the company. Sigma took an interest that eventually reached 29 percent.[53] (Full disclosure: I also joined the Sigma advisory board in 2000.)

The Investhink team worked for more than a year on the workstation and the portal, lined up an impressive list of major content providers in the United States, Europe, and the United Kingdom, and created an edited database of information on financial products. Most of the technology development and some of the content editing took place in Turkey, which saved considerable money compared to operating completely in London. A January 2000 article in *Inside Market Data* (a Waters Information Services publication) described how the new company was trying to become an "infomediary" that would "go a step further by adding the ability to purchase services through its interface, and by providing vendors with detailed information on how their products are being used."[54]

By the end of 2000, however, the company had to make a major change in its strategy. It became clear that the consumer portal and search engine for financial products and services were not going to generate much revenue. Investhink then shifted to offering a low-cost platform for midtier or small-scale financial services companies that wanted to provide investment tools, products, and information over the Web but did not have the resources to build a system or get access to content, or that just wanted a lower-cost alternative to Bloomberg and Reuters.

But Investhink was stretching its resources dangerously. Earlier in 1999, we had opened a New York office and hired an American team to launch a major U.S. marketing effort. Based on my experience with Customer Dialogue Systems, I strongly opposed opening the New York office and encouraged the company to focus on providing services and content to firms based in the United Kingdom and Europe, or even in Turkey, where we were trying to line up additional funding. I felt the U.S. market was much too crowded with providers of financial services and investor tools. I lost this argument as my colleagues on the board insisted that most potential users and the largest financial services firms were in the United States. Whether a venture in the United States would have succeeded or not became moot after the end of the Internet boom and the events of September 11, 2001. Investhink closed the New York office later in the fall of 2001, having spent well over a million dollars in the United States with no results.

Before wrapping up the company, Investhink refined its strategy one more time. The last sales efforts aimed at providing the low-cost Bloomberg-like workstations with a "content integration platform" to financial services vendors for their in-house use and mobile investment advisers, rather than to mass-market customers.[55] Unfortunately, though, Investhink acquired only three small paying customers. The first was Tullet & Tokyo Liberty, which signed on in April 2001. Tullet used an early version of the platform to distribute internal and third-party information to more than 1,000 of its customers, who were mainly independent financial advisers. Late in 2002, Investhink also did some consulting for the Dutch bank ABN AMRO and started a project with a financial technology company called Kinetech.

The customers were too few and too late. As the market for Internet-based stock investment deteriorated in 2001–2002, Investhink found it harder to make major deals with customers, especially as it started running out of money. Financial institutions worried that Investhink wouldn't be around to provide the services they required. In fact, much of Investhink's history involved coming tantalizingly close but never quite landing any major customer deals with firms that included (in the final days) Old Mutual, ABN AMRO, Dresdner Bank, UBS Warburg, and Morgan Stanley. The company also signed a partnership agreement with a better-funded U.S. start-up named Bang Networks, and together the two firms were about to land a wealthy customer when Investhink ran out of money.[56]

Sigma, which had gone public in April 2001 on the London Stock Exchange Alternative Investment Market, agreed to provide more funding if another major investor joined. No one came forward, and the board decided to dissolve the venture in December 2002 before the company accumulated any more liabilities. In three years of operations, Investhink had generated merely £36,240 in revenues (about $50,000) and lost a total of £4,160,358 (about $6 million). At its peak, Investhink had about twenty-five employees based in London, New York, and Turkey. At the end, it had thirteen employees, ten of whom would later continue under the auspices of a new company based on the Investhink technology and purchased by a few members of the management team for about $100,000 through the liquidation court.

The executives and salespeople always came up with a long list of reasons why financial institutions should buy the Investhink solution: It was neutral (i.e., not owned by a major financial institution or content vendor), powerful, and cheaper than the competition's. It was based on the most advanced and open Internet technologies and easily integrated with other solutions. But in the final analysis, these arguments were not convincing enough to potential customers. Investhink in the last year lacked the financial strength to convince customers it would still be around the next year. Negotiation cycles were taking six to nine months and usually ended in nothing or only small deals.

Equally important, from the beginning, Investhink focused mainly on *spending the money we had raised*. The team built general-purpose technology that we all thought would sell, rather than finding a few customers first and providing them with a specific or custom solution. It never had an experienced sales team that knew how to close deals. Part of this was related to hiring practices; the two main founders initially hired people they knew and felt comfortable with, rather than the best available people. It also turned out that the first set of senior executives was too inexperienced. Their backgrounds were as software engineer and journalist. The last CEO and chairman came from Reuters and had a far better handle on customer needs. They should have made a difference, but they also failed to land any major customers or line up new funding.

What did I learn from this venture—as a director and second-level founder? On the positive side, I learned firsthand how *a passionate entrepreneur with vision can bring people and money together to create something out of nothing.* At its peak, Investhink had a valuation of $30 million. On the negative side, I learned *how easily a good idea and good intentions can go awry.* A venture, if it is to succeed, needs constant attention—to strategy, plans, budgets, personnel, and, most important, potential customers. Especially in bad times, the market can change quickly. If a firm does not adapt quickly, conserve its resources, and find paying customers, it becomes extremely vulnerable to failure. And once a company appears financially weak, potential customers become even more reluctant to do business with it—the "catch-22" I mentioned in Chapter 5.

Timing and delays in implementation were also problems for Investhink. Had the team been able to roll out the original portal and workstation sooner, say in 1998, it might have had a successful company or at least sold the business for a profit. By the time it had a system running, the Internet boom was starting to collapse. It made the right decision to switch to a business-to-business technology offering, but this market proved to be extremely hard to crack in the deteriorating conditions. By the time Investhink had a new strategy and a low-cost solution that was complete, it was already early 2002.

From Eksi's point of view, the venture turned increasingly sour during 2001–2002 as the other members of the management team and the board largely brushed him aside. He kept trying to bring in new customers and partners, but he became increasingly emotional and isolated and eventually left. The bankruptcy outcome and its aftermath were also very unsettling for him. Eksi had invested a lot of personal time but came out with nothing (which is also true of Sigma and many other investors), even though a part of the company lives on.[57] From Sigma's point of view, though, Neil Crabb argued that there was little to be done about the outcome. Investhink had too many financial liabilities (in particular, the office lease) to continue as it was with so little revenue. Sigma was unwilling to put any more money into the company, given the weak market and the lack of any new investors.[58]

From Hakman's point of view, the New York venture was a big mistake, as were the lack of experienced sales and marketing people and the late decision to offer an enterprise solution. More important, though, he regretted the emphasis on spending money to build technology rather than working with specific customers: "Once the money is raised, you need to spend the money as you said you would. . . . If we had been cautious about spending money as we built up, we would have been in a much better position."[59]

My view of the central failure is that Investhink wasted too much time and money going after major customers in the United States that had little interest in getting technology and services from a British start-up. It should have been able to find local financial services firms that were late in getting onto the Web. Similarly to the CDS venture, the danger of having too grandiose a vision that overextends a start-up is especially clear in retrospect. But this is not so obvious when you are still enthusiastic about a technology and prospects for the future and you have cash to spend.

Looking back through the eight-point lens, Investhink was never more than an average venture. It could have worked out had the team arrived at the final offering earlier. But it took too long to figure out the right strategy and business model and revamp the solution. By early 2002, there was too much competition, including a low-end offering from Reuters and free information from portals such as Yahoo! and the Web sites of innumerable brokerages and asset management firms. Most seriously, though, the market for Web-based financial investment tools and services turned out to be very unattractive after 2001.

Marex: A Very Expensive Experiment

One of the most expensive miscalculations of a business model and customer-value proposition I know of firsthand occurred at a Miami-based start-up that became a public NASDAQ company, named Marex Technologies.[60] (Full disclosure: I served as a member of the board of directors of Marex for three months before resigning in

March 2002.) Marex was initially named Florida Marine Management when it was founded in 1992. This firm provided industry research reports, sold through Moody's. The company later changed its mission and in 1999 took on the name Marex, short for "Marine Exchange." The executive team then raised more than $52 million in equity financing from investors that included Brown Simpson Asset Management of New York City and Genmar Holdings, a billion-dollar boatbuilder with seven thousand employees headquartered in Minneapolis.[61] Marex also accumulated losses of more than $73 million ($42 million if noncash write-downs are excluded) against revenues of just $687,000 between 1997 and December 2002, when the company folded (Table 6-3). How the firm raised and lost so much money, with so little to show for it, is another story of a good idea gone bad due to uncontrolled spending, some bad luck, and too little probing of what customers wanted—and didn't want.

Marex's founder, David Schwedel, was a veteran boat racer and venture capitalist. He originally came up with the idea in 1992 of using standard telephone lines to link boatbuilders (there were some 1,200 in the United States at the time) with boat dealers (about 15,000) and component suppliers (more than 10,000).[62] The objective was to replace mail and faxes with an electronic data interchange (EDI) system, which users would pay for on a subscription basis. The idea proved too difficult to implement since most boatbuilders were small and didn't have modems in their offices. When the Web appeared in 1994, however, the CIO of the company, Roger Bauman, convinced Schwedel to make an Internet-based system, which evolved into a marketplace exchange. They began raising money and recruiting more people, including a Harvard MBA, Michelle Miller, who came on as COO and then president. Other experienced executives (Tim Richardson as CIO and Kenbian Ng as CFO) also joined the team. Marex's 10-K report described the company's strategy as of 1999:

> Marex.com, Inc. ("Marex.com" or the "Company") is a leading provider of business to business ("B2B") e-commerce solutions for the marine industry. We are developing a comprehensive set of procurement solutions for the automation of business transactions on the Internet among suppliers, boat builders, boat repairers, and dealers/distributors. . . . We began registering members for the Ex-

Table 6-3: Marex Financial Data, 1997–2002

(In thousands of dollars)

Fiscal year ended December 31	1997	1998	1999	2000	2001	2002*
Net sales	—	—	$7	$39	$623	$15
Costs and expenses:						
Cost of product sales	—	—	—	—	103	—
Product support and development	—	90	1,132	9,435	5,893	1,364
Selling and marketing	—	167	1,138	7,480	3,094	660
General and administrative	—	25	1,245	5,327	3,094	1,918
Impairment of software dev.	—	—	—	—	5,865	—
Stock-based compensation	—	—	—	848	476	469
Fair value of warrants	—	—	140	21,747	1,764	117
Total	—	$282	$3,655	$44,836	$20,667	$4,528
Loss from operations		(282)	(3,647)	(44,796)	(20,044)	(4,513)
Interest income and other expenses	(56)	(46)	98	1,350	416	100
Discontinued operations	(600)	(827)	(140)	—	—	(741)
Net loss	$(656)	$(1,155)	$(3,690)	$(43,446)	$(19,628)	$(5,154)
Cash and cash equivalents	29	350	3,434	19,624	4,479	479
Fiscal year-end employees	NA	NA	33	93	36	NA

* *2002 figures are through September.*

Source: *Marex 10-K and 10-Q reports, 2000–2001, available at www.sec.gov/cgi-bin/srch-edgar?text=marex&first=1996&last=2002&mode=Simple*

change in November 1998. The Exchange allows buyers to solicit quotes online from sellers for specific equipment, parts and supplies. Buyers are displayed the best prices available, which are updated on a real-time basis as bids are posted. Through the Exchange, we seek to provide a worldwide search capability to buyers for equipment, parts and supplies and create a lowest price forum for buyers to take advantage of spot market pricing of sellers' overstocked and available inventory.[63]

Between 1999 and 2001, Marex spent more than $16 million on software development and technology purchases and nearly $12 million on sales and marketing. The goal continued to be creation of an online marketplace, though the plan for generating revenues shifted to charging transaction fees on business going through the exchange. This revenue model then fell into disfavor as most e-commerce ventures that proposed to live on transaction fees were collapsing. The company returned to the idea of a subscription model, but it still had to finish the solution and line up users. Meanwhile, Marex executives continued to spend heavily on software technology that was not working and consultants that were not delivering, all from name-brand companies (Breakaway Solutions, Andersen Consulting, Vitria, Rightworks, Yantra, Moai, and Clarus). The company was also keeping twenty software developers on staff.

Finally, late in 2001, Marex came down to earth. Miller and other senior executives resigned, and Schwedel reasserted his authority as CEO. He downsized the staff from a peak of around 130 employees, switched strategies, and redirected the development team to create a simpler solution. The new goal was to give the communications software away to boatbuilders and suppliers, then charge supplier firms a monthly fee—$150 to $350, depending on the level of services—for using the software to communicate with boatbuilders. The new state-of-the-art Marex software, with some manual intervention, could even translate faxes and voice mail to Web-based forms.

I first learned about the company in August 2001, when Schwedel contacted me after another board member (who worked in the Boston area) recommended me for the board. I then met with Schwedel and interviewed other board members as well as reviewed technical specifications for the Marex system, a strategy presentation, and financial documents. My assessment was that, while the company had been badly out of control and wasted far too much money, it had survived the Internet bust and seemed about to launch a real business. I also thought it possible to market the same software and services to other verticals with similar characteristics, such as aircraft builders and construction firms—industries with a few large vendors supplied by many small suppliers. The new business model for Marex was different from the 1999 plan—it had become a hybrid solutions (software and services) company, rather than a producer and manager of an online marketplace. But the fundamental idea and target market remained the same. The business depended on providing a solution to small suppliers that had unsophisticated ways of communicating with their customers.

I agreed to become a director and stay on until the software was ready and we could determine whether or not Marex had a viable business. If the company did not generate significant revenues by spring of 2002, it would have to close anyway for lack of cash. Marex had a few hundred thousand dollars of guaranteed annual revenues from a new software subsidiary (purchased in October 2001) that provided IT systems to marinas, but there was no other income. Investors' patience was running out, and the company had already gotten a delisting notice from the NASDAQ authorities. The stock had fallen from a high of about $42 in early 2000 to a low of 26 cents.

Marex still had several things going for it. First was the personality of the founder. David Schwedel was and remains a *great* salesman. He had raised a lot of money, put together an ambitious management team, and had everything at stake in this venture. He demonstrated a deep understanding of the boatbuilding industry. Second, and potentially most valuable, Marex had a documented relationship with one of the largest boatbuilders in the world, Genmar. This firm had invested in Marex and promised to give Schwedel access to its list of 8,000 suppliers. There was some apparent tension in the relationship, and other large boatbuilders were not so comfortable with Marex given that Genmar had become a backer. But Schwedel was distancing Marex from Genmar financially and doing what he could to become a neutral player in the industry. The other major boatbuilder, Brunswick, had also expressed an interest in the Marex service. Third, I was told that early phone surveys had indicated a high level of interest in the service among boat suppliers—who would be the paying customers. Combined with the list of Genmar suppliers, Marex seemed a reasonable bet to achieve some level of success. Finally, the new software was within a month or so from being completed, so there was an end in sight to the cash burn.

Schwedel was continuing to cut head count and other expenses (such as by renegotiating the lease for office space). I calculated that Marex, with the overhead costs of December 2001, needed to get about four thousand companies to sign on at the basic service rate to make the company viable. This was a large number, but there were other verticals to explore, and the CEO was planning a large-scale marketing campaign in March. It was possible to reduce the break-even number by cutting employee head count further or raising the monthly fee.

Then the sales team actually tried to sell the new service. The first problem was that the Genmar list of 8,000 suppliers turned out to contain more like 2,500. Within a couple of weeks in March 2002, salespeople contacted 6,126 suppliers by telephone, primarily in the marine, aircraft, and construction industries. Only a few hundred firms agreed to pay the monthly fee. According to Schwedel, the sales team had called only 10 percent of the potential customers in the industry databases, but the initial reaction had been so dismal, the economy was so bad, and the company's cash was so short that he had concluded that the venture was too risky to continue.

A day before the March 2002 board meeting, Schwedel decided to let all the employees go, except for those at the recently acquired subsidiary, which was selling software and services at a profit, and another individual who was designing a telemetry product for tracking boats and other "mobile assets." Since I had agreed to help direct a software company, I resigned directly after the board meeting. Marex continued to operate through the end of 2002, but it sold the software support business in August 2002 and no longer had any revenues after that.[64] Also in the summer of 2002, Schwedel set up a joint venture using the Marex technology for pollution control monitoring.

Schwedel was remarkable in his flexibility and never-ending stream of ideas for the company. As he told *The Miami Herald,* "[Darwin] didn't say the strong survive. It's those that can adapt that can survive."[65] Schwedel continued to hope that the new telemetry product would become the equivalent of LoJacks for boats and other mobile assets, such as fleet trucks. He was still working on this idea in 2003. But nothing he did in 2002 was enough to salvage Marex. He finally resigned in December 2002, leaving the company's remaining assets to its major investor, Brown Simpson.[66]

Hindsight is twenty-twenty, of course, but it is still worth reflecting on what went wrong. One mistake was misplaced faith in the marketplace exchange and transaction-fee concept, but this was hard to evaluate during the late 1990s. Some Internet marketplace exchanges have survived, such as for auto parts and travel services. But most have not. A second mistake was the belief in a monthly service-fee concept. Providing an Internet-based service to unsophisticated suppliers in fragmented industries was an experiment worth trying, but how much was the service worth? Not enough companies were willing to pay a third party $150 a month without evidence that they would save at least as much. A third mistake was to put so much stock in the Genmar relationship and list of suppliers. The relationship was critical for raising money, but it did little to generate revenues, and the size of the list was badly exaggerated. But the biggest mistake was the *lack of control over spending,* both on software technology that took too long to get working and on sales and marketing efforts that brought too few results. Here the blame must go to the executive team as well as the board of directors. The story is similar to that of Investhink, but multiplied by several times. Most puzzling is how much money the company spent before determining that there were not enough customers for the business to be economically viable.

Looking at Marex through my eight-point lens suggests that this was just an average venture, except for the amount of cash burned. Marex also managed to go public, which most start-ups do not accomplish. But there was nothing outstanding about the idea, the market, the team, the business model, or the payoff potential.

What did I learn from this experience? There is an old saying: "If it seems too good to be true, it probably is." And this is what occurred: The Marex business model was simple: roll out the software and the service to Genmar's eight thousand suppliers, and then the money will roll in on a monthly basis, like a bank collecting interest on assets under management. *It was too good to be true.* A public company that, at its peak, was worth about $300 million in early 2000, of which Schwedel owned 27 percent, fell to virtually nothing in value by the end of 2002.

H5 Technologies: Build the Product and Customers Will Come—Perhaps

H5 Technologies (originally called ejemoni) started operations in March 2000 in San Francisco. The founders were two Wharton MBA students—Nicolas Economou and Jeff Kangas—and a former Bell Labs scientist and professor of computer science at Northern Illinois University named Joel Jeffrey. Kangas had decided to forgo finishing his MBA to start the company. Economou graduated but left a master's program at Harvard's John F. Kennedy School of Government to become an entrepreneur. (Full disclosure: I agreed to join the advisory board of the company in January 2001.)[67]

The basis for this start-up was a unique technology (analogous to digital "bar codes") that Jeffrey had invented. The bar codes made it possible to conduct very sophisticated searches without the need for matching keywords. An investment prospectus from January 2001 described the approach as a "(n)ovel technology so powerful, scalable, precise and versatile that it can become the de facto standard and *Lingua Franca* for characterizing and matching unstructured information, with the promise of multiple multi-billion dollar market opportunities." The company thought of its technology (initially called the "Universal Language Encoding System") as a potential horizontal play and described it as a new "standard for handling unstructured information"—a market that was five times larger than that for structured information, such as that for Oracle databases.[68]

My MIT colleague Ed Roberts became acquainted with Economou in late 1999 and signed on as an adviser early in 2000. So did another acquaintance of mine, Dr. John Seely Brown, the chief scientist at Xerox and director of Xerox PARC. The scientific advisory board, in addition to Seely Brown, included Mitchell Marcus of the University of Pennsylvania, an MIT Ph.D. in artificial intelligence who specialized in linguistic applications (and is widely regarded as one of the foremost computational linguists in the world); Daniel Hillis, another MIT Ph.D., who founded Thinking Machines and specialized in parallel computing; and H. Paul Zeiger, another MIT Ph.D. in electrical engineering, who had been head of the computer science department at the University of Colorado, where Jeffrey had done his doctorate.

In my mind, the fact that these individuals vouched for the technology gave the company instant technical credibility. The management ranks, though, were less impressive. Economou took on the job of CEO, but he was not experienced in the field of information management. He had worked at Asea Brown Boveri in project management and trade finance. Kangas took on the job of COO/CFO. He had been a consultant at PricewaterhouseCoopers and had a CPA before attending business school.

This was also a start-up that had money: a seed round and an A round of funding in 2000–2001 generated $12 million in investments and an additional $8 million in contingent commitments. The majority of the money came from a fairly small fund in New York rather than from a major venture capital firm. This arrangement had pluses (relatively little outside VC interference) and minuses (no large VC network to assist the firm as it tried to get customers and additional funding). Other early financial backers on a smaller scale included James Bidzos, the founder of VeriSign Software and vice chairman of RSA Security, and John Dean, chairman and then CEO of Silicon Valley Bank. Esther Dyson's monthly technology newsletter of March 2002 described how the company hoped to compete with its distinctive technology:

> H5's technology captures the "aboutness" of a document. Unlike traditional approaches, it requires no training on a set of documents by customers. A customer just starts feeding content into the system, and it produces category matches. Second, the H5 system classifies documents according to very fine distinctions, of the sort that typically only human beings have been able to make. . . . Not everyone needs this level of sophistication. Basic classification of news stories for a consumer portal, for example, can probably be handled by existing clustering solutions such as Autonomy. But many organizations today use human classifiers because no automated solution is good enough. . . . By representing the ways people actually talk about subjects, H5 comes closer than traditional approaches to what human classifiers do manually.[69]

To some extent, though, like firstRain, Jeffrey had developed a novel technology in search of an application. The company's initial business model called for giving away the software to anyone to generate a large number of "aboutness bar codes," which could easily be disseminated over the Internet in the form of encrypted XML tags. Then H5 hoped to charge for the decoding software. Who the customers would be was not clear initially, and this became more of a worry as time passed and more money went to R and D, salaries, and office expenses.

As in the case of SkyFire Technologies (see Chapter 2), I worried that a broad horizontal strategy might consume too many resources and not land any customers that *absolutely needed* this technology. Economou admitted that they had once thought they could be a solution for any type of precise digitized database search.[70] They later decided to concentrate on one vertical market: government information. When they looked at the most common market for data searches— general business information, such as provided by the International Data Group (IDG) or financial service or investment companies— they found that these vendors were not willing to pay much for a tool to categorize information because their customers were not willing to pay much for content. In the media and investment worlds, digitized information had become a commodity, and there were good enough basic search tools (such as using keywords or pattern-matching techniques) for most user needs. So they were getting offers for deals of tens of thousands of dollars rather than millions of dollars, which they were hoping to base on sales of seats. Government intelligence was different, especially after September 11, 2001. In particular, they hoped that a new allocation of funds by the U.S. Congress for antiterrorist intelligence research would fund more precise and sophisticated ways of searching enormous databases. We can see this strategic evolution in how H5 packaged its product and service offerings. The Web site in August 2003 described its primary vertical focuses as government agencies and litigation support.[71]

At some level, H5 sold products. One was H5 InScribe. This automated the assignment of customer-defined categories, what the company generically called "subject descriptors," for text-based information and replaced manual tagging. The other main product was H5 Atlas, which offered search and document-filtering capabilities. But the company was really offering a hybrid solution because the H5 technology was not completely automated. Though H5 tools replaced manual classifiers, before that was possible, company experts had to do up-front manual work to create information representations for individual fields of knowledge. To do this knowledge representation work, H5 hired Ph.D.s and other highly trained people in areas ranging from philosophy and linguistics to history. I must admit to being surprised at how labor-intensive this preparatory work was. However, whereas H5 required a significant up-front investment in knowledge representation, it could reuse the knowledge hierarchies with different customers—as long as it focused on similar vertical markets.

Through January 2002, H5 had raised a total of $12 million, but the collapse of the Internet bubble and the U.S. stock markets had severe repercussions for the company. The main New York investor was unable to meet its remaining funding commitments, and this caused the withdrawal of the other contingent commitments. Another disappointment was the postponement and possible cancellation of a multimillion-dollar annual deal with a major U.S. intelligence agency that the company had worked on for months. This was unfortunate because, in the due diligence process, the government evaluation found that H5's solution significantly outperformed competing technologies that were tested as well as the average accuracy achieved by humans. With funding running out and no customers, H5 downsized its staff but still had thirty-two executives and employees who were living from paycheck to paycheck. Economou reduced the monthly burn rate to about $200,000 by the end of 2002, down from about twice that at the beginning of the year.

One mistake Economou realized too late was how to fund development until the company had paying customers or more venture backing. He created a large engineering team to build the software and another large team to create the information classifications. The result was that H5 spent most of its cash to finish a working product before it got any customers. The team had initially believed that, because competing solutions already existed, a start-up had to approach customers with a working product to be competitive. Normally, I would say this strategy is correct, but a company still has to have enough money on hand to pay rent and salaries, as well as market and sell the product. In this field, it turned out that sophisticated government customers had the ability to evaluate new technologies in their early stages and needed to see only a working prototype. A better approach would have been to conserve cash, build enough of the core engine and knowledge base to create prototypes, close at least one deal with a major customer, and then finish the product. At least, this is how Economou would have liked to proceed in retrospect.

Fortunately, unlike CDS, Concentric, Investhink, and Marex, this story is not yet over. Economou raised $2 million in early fall 2002 to keep the company afloat. Then, in February 2003, Draper Fisher Jurvetson closed a $6.5 million funding round, and in May 2003 H5 signed a contract with the General Services Administration, which will make it easier for government agencies to buy and use H5 software.[72] There were also several sales deals in the pipeline that H5 expected to conclude with different U.S. intelligence agencies. In this vertical, the long-term hope was to establish H5's digital bar codes as a new platform for classifying content in digitized text.

Based on the eight-point lens, H5 still seems like a good bet but clearly not a sure thing. Its strength is a unique technology and credibility, given its technical advisers and financial backers. There is also customer interest. But it is not clear how attractive the market is or how scalable the business model is since there is a great deal of labor involved in creating the knowledge hierarchies. The hybrid solution is fairly complex and not very flexible, though H5 can reduce the classification work by focusing on one or two vertical markets and reselling the solution to different customers.

The big question for this company remains one of *differentiation:* Is the H5 solution sufficiently superior to existing software and manual alternatives to generate paying customers and high price points? Another key question is, Can H5 deploy its solution in other domains such as insurance fraud detection or litigation support, where automated tools and human analysts are inadequate or too slow and costly? To become a public company and bring a significant return to investors, H5 will have to grow its revenues by developing customers not only in the intelligence community but in other verticals as well.

WRAP-UP COMMENTS

The stories of these ten start-ups provide a number of ideas on how to succeed and how to fail in the software business. Many elements have to converge to produce a large payoff to investors. Of all the ventures, only one (NuMega) has been an unqualified success, and five have ended in bankruptcy. In good times, more of these firms would probably have survived. But in bad times for venture investments and public offerings, such as in 2001–2003, only firms with a compelling product (like NuMega's), distinctive service capabilities (like Cybergnostic's and NetNumina's), and compelling but flexible technologies and business strategies (like firstRain's and H5's) seem to have a better-than-average chance of becoming viable businesses (Table 6-4). This is also an above-average sample given that in general nine out of ten start-ups fail.

Is software entrepreneurship different from entrepreneurship in other businesses? I think the answer is both yes and no. For software products companies, the potential for economies of scale is probably greater than in any other area except for digital content businesses, though publishing comes close. Software also offers many opportunities to develop services and hybrid solutions. The number of possible segments in the software business is limited only by the human imagination. Managing software development projects, whether you create a product, service, or hybrid solution, can pose extraordinary problems as well. Customer Dialogue Systems, Investhink, and Marex in particular burned through far too much money developing general-purpose technology without having enough specific customers.

Because software is a technology with almost unlimited applica-

Table 6-4: Evaluation of Ten Software Start-ups

Key: ✓+ = very good (2 points), ✓ = neutral (1 point), ✓− = weak (0 points)

	NuMega	CDS	Concentric	firstRain	NetNumina	Oneworld	Cybergnostic	Investhink	Marex	H5
1. Management team	✓+	✓	✓+/✓	✓+	✓+	✓	✓+/✓	✓	✓	✓
2. Attractive market	✓+/✓	✓+/✓	✓	✓	✓	✓		✓	✓/✓−	✓
3. Compelling offering	✓+	✓+/✓	✓	✓+/✓	✓+/✓	✓	✓+	✓	✓	✓+
4. Customer interest	✓+	✓+	✓	✓+/✓	✓+	✓+/✓	✓+/✓	✓	✓	✓+/✓
5. Credibility	✓+	✓+	✓	✓+	✓+	✓	✓+	✓	✓	✓
6. Business model	✓+	✓−	✓	✓	✓	✓−	✓+	✓	✓	✓+
7. Flexibility	✓	✓−	✓	✓+	✓	✓	✓+/✓	✓	✓	✓
8. Payoff potential	✓+/✓	✓	✓	✓	✓	✓	✓+/✓	✓	✓	✓
Total score	**14**	**8.5**	**8.5**	**12**	**11.5**	**6.5**	**13**	**8**	**7.5**	**10.5**
Average	✓+	✓	✓	✓+/✓	✓+/✓	✓−	✓+/✓	✓	✓	✓/✓+

Rank Order	Score	Business Model
NuMega	14	Products
Cybergnostic	13	Services
firstRain	12	Products
NetNumina	11.5	Services
H5	10.5	Hybrid
CDS	8.5	Products
Concentric	8.5	Products
Investhink	8	Hybrid
Marex	7.5	Hybrid
Oneworld	6.5	Service

tions, entrepreneurs need to acquire a deep understanding of a particular end market in order to know what to build and how to sell it. This means they need to get firsthand knowledge or hire people with the knowledge they need. At the same time, venture capitalists and analysts must somehow develop a similar expertise in end markets in order to be more than dilettantes when evaluating business plans and proposals. Overwhelmingly, though, the biggest problem may be how to get a really good reference customer that will be a company's big break. This is a form of chasm crossing. Sales momentum and real revenues are required to avoid falling into the abyss of failed start-ups.

I will also repeat my observation that venture funding can be the kiss of death for some start-ups—particularly software services firms, but also hybrid solutions companies. When companies raise a lot of outside money, the overwhelming tendency is to spend it. Often this is essential to creating a company. But sometimes it encourages a firm to expand its head count and overhead commitments or its marketing plans to levels it cannot sustain.

7

Conclusion:

The "Ideal" Versus "Realistic" Software Business

The hardest part of writing this book has been to generalize about the "ideal" or "best" model for ongoing software businesses as well as software start-ups. There are so many variables to consider. In most industries, there is rarely one best way to do anything; it usually depends on the circumstances or the particular resources and capabilities available to a firm, as well as what its customers want and how its competitors behave. Nonetheless, I have argued from the first chapter that managers, programmers, and entrepreneurs have a choice in business models. Moreover, they can often look into their own potential futures because we usually know what the pattern of evolution is, at least for enterprise software companies.

To summarize: There are *products companies* at one end of the strategy spectrum, *services companies* at the other end, and *hybrid solutions companies* in between. Products companies in enterprise software also tend to evolve into hybrid solutions providers and even into primarily services and maintenance companies. Where is the best place to be? Again, that depends, but we can think about the question in terms of the basic characteristics as well as the strengths and weaknesses of the different models.

Characteristics of the Three Models

I noted in Chapter 2 that the primary focus of software products companies, in good times and bad, is to sell a *fully standardized product*—packaged software. I have also called this "the printing press model" because replicating software packages is similar to printing money or books. There are potentially enormous economies of scale and profit margins, at least in good economic times. Venture capitalists usually prefer start-ups that have the potential to become products companies because, if they hit it right, they can make such enormous returns on their investments. So there is real money in this business model. I have talked a lot about Microsoft in this and other books, of course, but much more modest firms (Adobe, Intuit, Business Objects) are also good examples of this type of business model. Even a modest products company such as Netscape, which had a limited life span as an independent firm, earned more than *$10 billion* for its investors.

The primary focus of software services companies, again, in good times and bad, is to sell *services, broadly defined,* mainly to other firms. Services range from consulting and systems integration to product customization and maintenance of custom systems. Services companies may also derive part of their revenues from software products that drive some or all of their services. Even pure IT services companies, such as PricewaterhouseCoopers, EDS, Cap Gemini Ernst & Young, and Accenture, or the IT divisions of IBM, Fujitsu, and Hitachi, usually rely on in-house packages or reusable design frameworks to provide most of the functionality in the custom systems they build and maintain for individual clients.

The primary focus of hybrid solutions companies is to sell a mixture of products and services, with maintenance upgrades or special product enhancements that must be supported in the future. Often these companies have not been able or *do not want* to productize their technology fully. Or they might have trouble getting new customers and have to rely on sales to an existing customer base. Whatever the reason, for hybrid solutions providers, making a sale and using the technology requires considerable attention to individual customers for consulting, customization, implementation, training, and integration with other software systems, as well as maintenance or enhancements over time. Although I have called this a separate business model, many enterprise software companies will pass through the hybrid solutions stage on the journey from being a products company to becoming a services and maintenance company—like it or not.

Hybrid solutions or software services companies that sell custom and semicustom solutions also resemble what I have called the "bank" or "asset management" business model in contrast to the printing-press model of software products companies. Firms that build hybrid or custom systems have an installed base of users that rely heavily on long-term contracts for services and upgrades. These contracts generate recurring revenues, much as assets on deposit in a bank generate a recurring stream of interest. In addition to IT services organizations, companies such as PeopleSoft and SAP are now in or close to this category because the vast majority of their revenues come from services and maintenance contracts rather than software license fees (new-product sales). IBM, with its base in hardware, is perhaps the best example of a hybrid solutions provider. IBM is also unusual in that it now has large e-business and open-systems consulting operations that are decoupled from its hardware and software product sales.

Although the transition toward services and maintenance is probably inevitable for most enterprise software companies, I have also argued that hybrid companies need to select a strategic orientation: Do they want to sell mainly products or mainly services and maintenance contracts? Can they decouple services from product sales? The reason to choose is that organizational capabilities vary considerably for products companies and services companies. Some enterprise software companies remain in a hybrid sales pattern more or less permanently, depending on the nature of their technology. Nonetheless, hybrid companies can easily get stuck in the middle between products and services and do neither well.

For many firms, the distinction among the three business models is really a life-cycle story: They place more emphasis on products or services, or on hybrid solutions, depending on the development stage of the company and its products and customers. As software products mature and the user base ages, companies sell fewer new software license fees to new customers and more services and maintenance contracts to existing customers. Unless they revitalize their product offerings and place a renewed emphasis on selling new products to new customers, firms will undoubtedly see services and maintenance become an increasingly larger part of their business—again, like it or not. Financial analysts and investors also dislike this transition in the business model of a software company because of the lower profit margins made from services. My view, however, is that services and maintenance revenues can be as much a sign of financial strength as a sign of weakness.

Different Strengths and Weaknesses

The software products company is a growth model especially well suited to good times for technology spending. Sometimes these virtual printing presses come out with compelling products that become "killer apps" such as Lotus 1-2-3, Microsoft Office, or Netscape Navigator that sell in the millions and tens of millions of copies. Sometimes the companies create platforms that other companies build products and services around (such as Windows from Microsoft, WebSphere from IBM, WebLogic from BEA Systems, Acrobat from Adobe, and enterprise databases from Oracle). Often the killer apps become popular because of positive "network externalities" driven by platform compatibility, the availability of compelling complements, and bandwagon effects.

In these cases of killer apps and popular platforms, the potential economies of scale, growth opportunities, and profit margins are enormous. The danger, though, is that software products may become commodities over time and drop in price or sales volume when markets become saturated, low-priced competing products emerge, or bad economic times set in. In particular, unless there is strong patent protection, a software company that packages its technology to become "off the shelf" and conform to open standards may expand its market but may also face competition from other firms that introduce similar products at lower prices or even for free.

Products are a business model of "high highs and low lows." Some companies, such as Microsoft, have tremendous financial performance over long periods of time. But even Windows is now subject to copying at some levels and is becoming a commodity of sorts (note the growing popularity of Linux and the challenge posed by a Windows-compatible version of Linux called "Lindows"). Other companies, such as Netscape, may be one-hit or short-term wonders. They can enter the business with a bang and grow at lightning speed but then disappear or decline with barely a whimper, except from disaffected investors. Still other companies (such as Siebel, with 70 percent of the CRM market) may dominate their segments but then find that new-product sales collapse as customers reach a saturation point and low-priced competitors jump into the market.

Hybrid solutions—sold either by former "pure" products companies or by services companies that build custom or semicustom information systems—seem to offer a more stable approach to revenues. They may be better suited to the ups and downs of technology spending. But hybrid solutions also fit the business model of products firms well along in their life cycles—that is, beyond the stage of having a "killer app." The best feature of this type of company is that, properly managed, it seems easier to keep it profitable. The existing customer base provides a steady stream of revenues for services and maintenance upgrades.

Enterprise software companies that have complex products requiring extensive customization or implementation work are the best examples of hybrid solutions firms. SAP and Oracle fit nicely into this category, but the products side of their business is still subject to low-priced commodity competition. Microsoft has entered the ERP market by acquiring Great Plains and Navision. It also has SQL Server and other database products. Indian companies such as Infosys build inexpensive semicustom solutions with their own technology and low-priced labor. Nonetheless, hybrid software businesses should provide a very stable level of growth and profitability if they can cultivate strong client relationships and devise useful but "sticky" solutions that are difficult to dislodge. The only caveat I have here is that hybrid solutions companies require a daunting set of technical and organizational capabilities. They need the skills of both products companies and services companies, and that combination can be hard to master.

Different Capabilities

Software products companies create products, of course. This means that they should organize not around compartmentalized functions, such as design, programming, testing, and marketing, but around *product teams* that target specific competitors or customer segments. Unless they are in very small niche markets, these kinds of companies usually focus on product development for general users in their market. Enterprise software products companies also need to cultivate skills of incremental innovation in new features for product upgrades that generate maintenance revenues.

Software services companies create relationships with individual customers. They may build technologies that look like products or can be packaged in some way, but generally they cater to the needs of individual clients. They need excellent skills in client management as well as project management. To be most efficient, they need to learn how to leverage technology and knowledge gained in one project to other projects without compromising customer confidentiality. Software services firms are technical consulting firms, so they need all the skills of consultants plus many of the skills of a software company.

Hybrid solutions companies have the biggest challenge. They must learn how to package software technology to meet the needs of more than one user. But they must also learn to customize each product without spending too much money and cultivate a relationship with *each* customer. Software factories or factory-like IT organizations in the United States, Japan, and India have sought this balance and done reasonably well in achieving economies of scope across multiple projects and customers. A structured development process that maximizes reuse and standardization is helpful here, but it is not so easy to implement or advisable for all companies in all situations. Nonetheless, software businesses, whether they are more oriented toward one-of-a-kind projects or hybrid solutions, can still manage software development systematically by emphasizing common principles of design, development, testing, and project management, as well as instituting some measures to promote reusability of designs and code.

Along with what capabilities to cultivate and when in the lifecycle of the business to cultivate them, managers, programmers, and entrepreneurs always need to *balance structure with flexibility*. This is perhaps most obvious in strategy during the early stages of a firm and in software development during early stages or periods of technical change. Software projects of more than a handful of people always need some way to coordinate complex tasks and come to an end within a predicable window. At the same time, members of software projects and company executives need to be flexible enough technically to react quickly to unforeseen problems, unforeseen opportunities for innovation, and unanticipated changes in the marketplace.

At the strategy level, most companies need to go through a process of trial and error before they figure out what works. So, over time, managers, programmers, and entrepreneurs need to think about and constantly prepare for change, both subtle and obvious. The rates of change are much faster in some segments of the software business and at certain points in time—such as in the early days of the mainframe computer as well as the PC and the World Wide Web. But change driven by technological innovation is inherent in the software business and much less predictable than many entrepreneurs and venture capitalists would have us believe.

IDEALISM VERSUS REALISM

Now, to think about what might be the *best* business model for a software company, I find it helpful to reflect again on the questions I posed at the beginning of Chapter 2. If some answers seem much "better" than others in the sense of probably leading to a more profitable or more rapidly growing business, then there is hope of finding "one best" model:

- Do you want to create mainly a *products* company or a *services* company?
- Do you want to sell to *individuals* or *enterprises, mass* or *niche* markets?
- How *horizontal* (broad) or *vertical* (specialized) is your product or service?
- Can you generate a *recurring revenue stream* that will endure in good times and bad?
- Will you target mainstream customers, or do you have a plan to avoid "the chasm"?
- Do you hope to be a *leader, follower,* or *complementor*?
- What kind of *character* do you want your company to have?

Given its financial history, it is probably not surprising that I believe the "ideal" software business looks very much like Microsoft. I also can cite Adobe, Intuit, and Business Objects—software products companies. I will throw in my lot—for the moment—with VCs who believe that the "ideal" is mainly a products company that can fully exploit its high gross margins by selling to mass markets. I don't care if the products are for individuals at home or at work, or for the general needs of enterprises. Small and medium-sized firms more closely resemble mass markets with minimal customization requirements, so I would prefer smaller rather than larger enterprises as customers, but I am not rigid on this point because large enterprises generally will pay higher prices for software. It follows that the ideal software business targets horizontal markets because these are generally larger than vertical niches and present more opportunities for economies of scale, growth, and large payoffs to investors.

One problem with this ideal model is that software products companies going after volume markets have to "cross the chasm" into the world of mainstream, conservative users, and this will require coming up with rock-solid quality and a "whole-product solution" that includes technical support and documentation. A second problem is that there are no guaranteed recurring revenues. However, the ideal software company should also be a platform leader. Like Microsoft, Intuit, and Adobe, it should be able to generate a stream of new releases and use some technical tricks, such as subtle incompatibilities, to encourage users to upgrade on a regular basis or sell new licenses on a multiyear subscription basis. A platform leader should be able to sell new versions of its main products in both good times and bad because so many other firms have incentives to keep selling their complementary products and services. The ideal company will have its own complements business as well to make sure there is a demand for new versions of the platform, just as Microsoft drives new sales of each generation of Windows with new generations of Office. Finally, the ideal software business will maintain high standards of credibility with customers, partners, competitors, and government authorities by recognizing revenues properly, delivering products when it says it will, and obeying antitrust laws.

But here is where I depart from many members of the VC community: *How common is this ideal software company? And how sustainable is this business model?* Although I need to collect more data on more firms for a longer period of time, my experience tells me that, one, the ideal model is too uncommon to be a good filter for investments. And two, it doesn't seem to last for long. It is true that platform leaders with monopoly market positions such as Microsoft's or specialty products such as Adobe's can stay on top for a very long time. But they are rare. So what is the most realistic strategy for a software company? I believe that *hybrid solutions sold to enterprises—*

the business model that combines products and services—are a realistic goal for a software company that does not have a hit product or a dominant platform to sell.

Hybrid solutions combine the best and the worst of both worlds. They can do all the things that an ideal software products company would do. They can create best-selling products and reap the benefits of scale economies, rapid growth, and high profit margins. But they can also provide services to complete their product offerings and benefit from this part of the business as well—maybe doubling or tripling their total revenues over time. The services (such as customization and integration work) also tend to fend off copying and commoditization. The services tied to products generate recurring revenues that are generally more stable than new-software license fees. Services and maintenance revenues tied to product sales will decline if product sales decline, but with a lag that can help a software business survive temporary downturns in the marketplace and continue to invest in new-product development as well as in expanding services. The worst part of the model is the skill set needed to manage a hybrid solutions business, but we know what the challenges are.

THE NEXT CHASM TO CROSS

As I conclude this book, I find myself thinking about what are the most important things I have learned over nearly two decades of studying the software business and surviving the boom and bust of the Internet era. What last thoughts would be most useful if I were a software manager, programmer, or entrepreneur staking a bet on the *future* of this exciting but volatile business?

First, we should always remember that bubbles are just that— bubbles. They expand and then burst. It follows that good times for technology-based companies must return. The question is when and at what level, not if. Software companies, whether they are products companies, services companies, or something in between, will once again be exciting places to work in and exciting investments to make. And for some people, they will always be exciting topics to study.

Second, history provides some guidelines for thinking about the future. For example, software applications today seem to have relatively few hardware limits; they appear to be limited mainly by human imagination, with some minor constraints imposed by real-world factors such as users' habits and costs. Since human creativity is so vast in potential and computer hardware is still evolving in leaps and bounds, it would be foolish to think of software technology as being mature. The historical examples I cited in Chapter 3 suggest that *most new opportunities for software entrepreneurs come with new hardware or computing platforms and niche applications, often for new platforms.* This observation tells me to watch for new software opportunities at the forefront of hardware innovation and platform evolution. Over the next decade, then, we should look carefully at new products and services generated for new devices and see how well they might take advantage of novel software technologies, including networking and communications technologies. The current buzzwords include mobile broadband (i.e., wireless multimedia), peer-to-peer functionality (like the controversial Napster technology for exchanging music files), and Web services, but other new software technologies will continue to appear every year or two.

Finally, I recall something from the days when I was studying Microsoft intensively a decade ago. I learned at the time that Bill Gates and other people in the PC industry realized, long before I did, that there is another chasm for software companies to cross. That chasm is to *the truly novice user*—the 5 billion or so people in the world who do not own a computer. The computing devices now available include not only PCs but also Web-enabled cell phones (look out for Nokia and Symbian!), personal digital assistants (but I expect PDAs to be transitional devices and become absorbed into cell phones), handheld computers (small devices that may evolve as temporary substitutes and complements for PCs), video-game machines (a potential home computer platform), and set-top TV boxes (another potential home-computer platform, though its ties to the TV will probably limit its usefulness). No doubt other devices will appear that someone has yet to imagine. So my final thought is that, even in the year 2003, we are still in the early stages of what has already been a remarkable ride for so many people, with the highest of highs and the lowest of lows—the business of software.

Appendix

Appendix Table 1: Business Objects Income Statement Analysis, 1993–1997

(In thousands of dollars)

Fiscal year ended December 31	1993	1994	1995	1996	1997
Revenues:					
Software licenses	$11,563	$24,306	$48,782	$64,241	$ 78,478
Services and maintenance	2,540	5,881	11,824	20,686	35,775
Total	*$14,103*	*$30,187*	*$60,606*	*$85,137*	*$114,253*
% License fees	82%	81%	80%	76%	69%
% Services and maintenance	18%	19%	20%	24%	31%
Growth rates—total:	—	114%	101%	40%	34%
Licenses	—	110%	101%	32%	22%
Services and maintenance	—	132%	101%	75%	73%
Costs and expenses:					
Cost of software licenses	944	1,466	2,107	3,235	3,773
Cost of services and maintenance	724	1,619	4,044	6,780	13,107
Gross margins:					
Software licenses	91.8%	94.0%	95.7%	95.0%	95.2%
Services and maintenance	71.5%	72.5%	65.8%	67.2%	63.4%
Other costs (% of revenues):					
Sales and marketing	54.9%	53.5%	50.6%	58.8%	59.6%
Research and development	16.7%	14.2%	13.3%	12.5%	12.3%
General and administrative	13.2%	11.4%	9.4%	8.7%	9.7%
Total costs and expenses	$11,947	$23,900	$44,443	$68,074	$ 93,241
Operating income	$ 488	$ 3,202	$10,012	$ 7,048	$ 4,132
Operating profit rate	*3.5%*	*10.6%*	*16.5%*	*11.6%*	*3.6%*
Net income	$ 230	$ 2,377	$ 8,048	$ 5,160	$ 2,877
Net profit rate	*1.6%*	*7.9%*	*13.3%*	*6.1%*	*2.5%*

Source: *Compiled from Business Objects, Form 10-K, 1997, and company data.*

Appendix Table 2: Business Objects Income Statement Analysis, 1998–2002

(In thousands of dollars)

Fiscal year ended December 31	1998	1999	2000	2001	2002
Revenues:					
Software licenses	$108,761	$153,747	$220,845	$249,594	$243,955
Services and maintenance	58,133	87,896	128,089	166,200	$210,844
Total	*$166,894*	*$241,643*	*$348,934*	*$415,794*	*$454,799*
% License fees	65%	64%	63%	60%	54%
% Services and maintenance	35%	35%	37%	40%	46%
Growth rates—total	46%	45%	44%	19%	9%
Software licenses	39%	41%	44%	13%	−2%
Services and maintenance	62%	51%	46%	30%	27%
Costs and expenses:					
Cost of software licenses	3,272	4,297	2,569	2,155	3,102
Cost of services and maintenance	23,899	35,467	53,101	63,497	71,489
Gross margins:					
Software licenses	97.0%	97.2%	98.8%	99.1%	98.7%
Services and maintenance	58.9%	59.6%	58.5%	61.8%	61.1%
Other costs (as % of revenues):					
Sales and marketing	53.4%	48.8%	48.0%	49.0%	49.0%
Research and development	11.6%	11.1%	11.7%	13.3%	16.5%
General and administrative	8.5%	6.8%	6.2%	5.8%	6.46%
Amortization, acquisitions	$ 1,254	$3,143	$ 4,254	$ 4,492	—
Total operating cost	$123,946	$164,387	$234,239	$287,649	$332,492
Operating income	$ 15,777	$ 37,492	$ 59,025	$ 62,493	$ 47,716
Operating profit rate	*9.5%*	*15.5%*	*16.9%*	*15.0%*	*10.5%*
Net income	$ 10,287	$ 23,780	$ 42,403	$ 44,878	$ 40,580
Net profit rate	*6.1%*	*9.8%*	*12.2%*	*10.8%*	*8.9%*
Year-end employees	977	1,321	1,888	2,226	2,166
Average employees	867	1,149	1,605	2,057	2,196
Annual sales/employee	$192,000	$210,000	$217,000	$202,000	$207,000

Source: *Compiled from Business Objects, Form 10-K, 1998-2001, and press release on 2002 fourth quarter revenues, 1/29/03.*

Appendix Table 3: i2 Technologies Income Statement Analysis, 1992–1996

(In thousands of dollars)

Fiscal year ended December 31	1992	1993	1994	1995	1996
Revenues:					
Software licenses	$ 218	$3,073	$ 8,562	$18,711	$50,855
Services and maintenance	1,705	1,582	2,936	7,235	25,487
Total	*$1,923*	*$4,655*	*$11,498*	*$25,946*	*$76,342*
% license fees	11%	66%	75%	72%	67%
% services and maintenance	89%	34%	25%	28%	33%
Growth rates—total:	—	142%	147%	126%	194%
Software licenses	—	310%	179%	119%	172%
Services and maintenance	—	−7%	86%	146%	252%
Costs and expenses:					
Cost of software licenses	1	9	26	65	2,896
Cost of services and maintenance	763	948	1,333	3,814	15,315
Gross margins:					
Software licenses	99.5%	99.7%	99.7%	99.7%	94.3%
Services and maintenance	55.2%	40.0%	54.6%	47.3%	39.9%
Other costs (% of revenues):					
Sales and marketing	16.3%	21.5%	32.9%	33.2%	37.5%
Research and development	14.2%	14.0%	14.4%	15.7%	19.2%
General and administrative	25.0%	16.1%	10.5%	14.0%	8.8%
Total costs and expenses	$1,833	$3,360	$ 7,993	$20,177	$68,221
Operating income	$ 90	$1,295	$ 3,505	$ 5,733	$ 8,121
Operating profit rate	*4.7%*	*27.8%*	*30.5%*	*22.2%*	*10.6%*
Net income	$ 56	$ 815	$ 2,186	$ 3,774	$ 6,092
Net profit rate	*2.9%*	*17.5%*	*19.0%*	*14.5%*	*8.0%*

Source: *i2 Technologies, Form 10-K, 1996.*

Appendix Table 4: i2 Technologies Income Statement Analysis, 1997–2002 (Restated)

(In thousands of dollars)

Fiscal year ended December 31	1997	1998	1999	2000	2001	2002
Revenues						
Software licenses	$141,766	$235,219	$228,907	$ 216,222	$ 196,383	$ 88,629
Contract software	0	0	4,140	116,877	304,531	527,755
Services and maintenance	80,010	135,978	219,316	339,441	374,428	291,992
Total	*$221,776*	*$371,197*	*$452,083*	*$ 672,540*	*$ 875,342*	*$ 908,376*
% License fees	64%	63%	51%	32%	22%	10%
% Contract software	0%	0%	1%	17%	35%	58%
% Services and maintenance	36%	37%	48%	51%	43%	32%
Growth rates—total:	191%	67%	22%	49%	30%	4%
Software Licenses	179%	66%	−3%	−5%	−9%	−45%
Contract software	—	—	—	2823%	161%	73%
Services and maintenance	214%	70%	61%	155%	10%	−22%
Cost and expenses:						
Cost of software licenses	2,746	10,089	12,493	18,947	27,257	2,976
Cost of contract software	—	—	133,810	42,482	76,374	157,820
Cost of services and maintenance	48,422	79,198	2,802	218,464	247,305	131,884
Gross margins:						
Software licenses	98.1%	95.7%	95.4%	91.2%	86.1%	96.6%
Contract software	—	—	−3,132%	63.7%	74.9%	70.0%
Services and maintenance	39.5%	41.8%	98.7%	35.6%	34.0%	15.3%
Other costs (as % of revenues):						
Sales and marketing	34.8%	34.7%	43.0%	56.4%	46.2%	21.9%
Research and development	25.9%	25.2%	29.3%	32.5%	33.0%	19.1%
General and administrative	11.3%	10.3%	11.8%	13.4%	12.4%	7.2%
Amortization, acquisitions	9,306	7,618	3,285	1,738,390	3,128,852	26,379
Restructuring and other charges	—	—	5,100	94,574	4,489,797	149,588
Total costs and expenses	$219,921	$357,455	$537,256	$ 2,801,175	$ 8,771,809	$ 905,982
Operating income/loss	$ 1,855	$ 13,742	$(85,173)	$(2,128,635)	$(7,896,467)	$ 2,394
Operating profit rate	*0.8%*	*3.7%*	*—*	*—*	*—*	*0.26%*
Net income loss	$ (1,752)	$ 10,387	$(50,664)	$(2,027,519)	$(7,718,862)	$(898,932)
Net profit rate	*—*	*2.8%*	*—*	*—*	*—*	*—*
Year-end employees	1,006	2,244	2,800	6,000	4,800	2,960 est.
Average employees	716	1,625	2,522	4,400	5,400	3,880 est.
Annual sales/employee	$310,000	$228,000	$179,000	$ 153,000	$ 162,000	$ 234,000

Source: *i2 Technologies, Form 10-K, 1997–2002.*

Appendix Figure 1: Products and Services/Maintenance Actual Revenue

Business Objectives

Siebel

PeopleSoft

i2

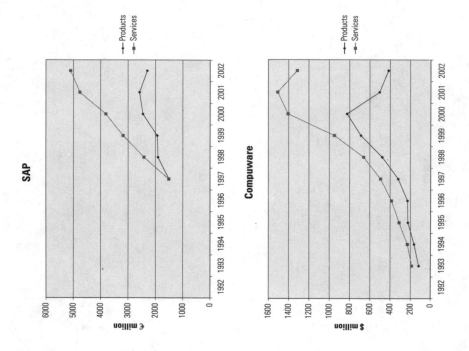

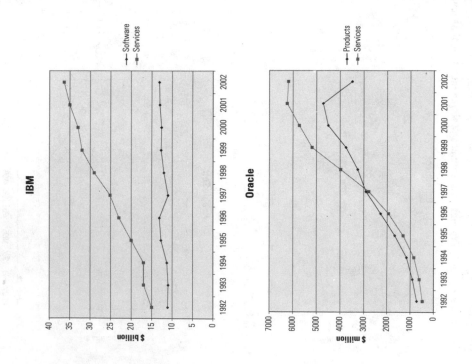

Appendix Figure 2: Growth Index Comparisons, 1999–2002

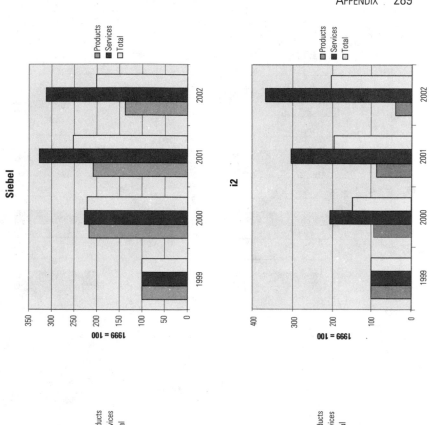

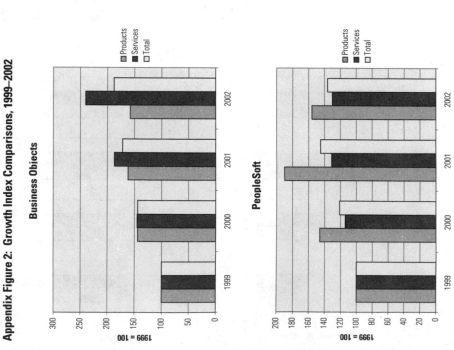

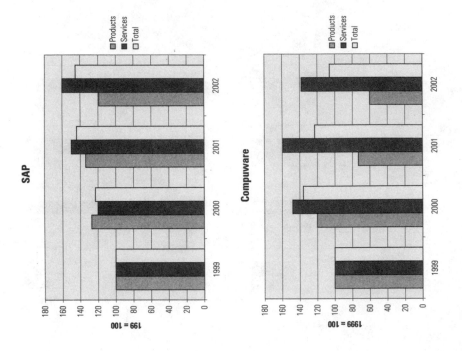

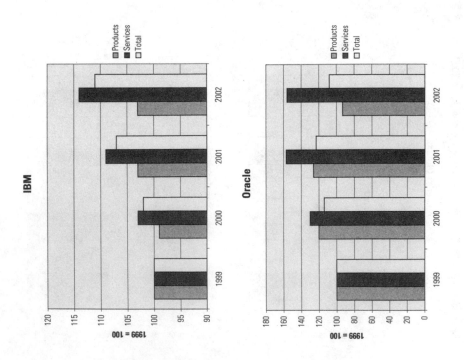

Appendix Table 5: *Software Magazine*'s Top Fifty Software Companies (2002)

(In millions of dollars)

Company	Software and Services Revenues	Main Software Business Area
1. IBM	$47,895	Middleware, application servers, Web servers
2. Microsoft	24,666	Operating systems/applications
3. Electronic Data Systems	21,543	IT services, outsourcing, consulting
4. Accenture	13,348	IT services, outsourcing, consulting
5. Oracle	10,860	Databases, applications
6. Computer Sciences Corporation	10,524	IT services, outsourcing, consulting
7. Compaq	7,747	IT services, outsourcing, consulting
8. PricewaterhouseCooper	7,481	IT services, outsourcing, consulting
9. Cap Gemini Ernst & Young	7,455	IT services, outsourcing, consulting
10. NTT Data	6,460	IT services, outsourcing, consulting
11. SAP	6,454	E-business applications, services, tools
12. Unisys	6,018	Storage management
13. NEC	5,892	Other
14. Computer Associates	4,190	Infrastructure, network management, performance
15. Sun Microsystems	4,015	Application development, testing, lifecycle tools
16. Getronics	3,675	IT services, outsourcing, consulting
17. Cisco	3,567	Infrastructure, network management, performance
18. NCR	3,197	Data warehouse, query tools, OLAP
19. Lockheed Martin	2,879	Other
20. Atos Origin	2,691	IT services, outsourcing, consulting
21. EMC	2,532	Storage management
22. Apple	2,276	Operating systems
23. Hewlett-Packard	2,261	IT services, outsourcing, consulting
24. Affiliated Computer	2,064	IT services, outsourcing, consulting
25. Siebel Systems	2,048	Customer relationship management
26. PeopleSoft	1,971	Enterprise resource planning
27. Sungard Data Systems	1,929	Financial applications
28. Compuware	1,836	Application development, testing, lifecycle tools
29. Fiserv	1,818	Application service provider
30. DST Systems	1,660	IT services, outsourcing, consulting
31. CSK Corp.	1,655	IT services, outsourcing, consulting
32. Logica	1,603	IT services, outsourcing, consulting
33. Amdocs	1,534	Other
34. Veritas	1,492	Storage management

(continued)

Appendix Table 5: *Software Magazine's* Top Fifty Software Companies (2002)

(In millions of dollars)

Company	Software and Services Revenues	Main Software Business Area
35. Cadence Design	1,430	Computer-aided design tools
36. BMC	1,376	Other
37. Hitachi	1,358	Other
38. Intuit	1,262	Financial applications
39. Adobe	1,230	Other
40. Misys	1,225	Financial applications
41. Perot Systems	1,205	Infrastructure, network management, performance
42. SAS Institute	1,130	Business intelligence
43. Corporate Software	1,077	IT services, outsourcing, consulting
44. Novell	1,040	Infrastructure, network management, performance
45. Samsung	1,032	Infrastructure, network management, performance
46. Symantec	1,011	Security, antivirus, policy management
47. Reynolds & Reynolds	1,004	IT services, outsourcing, consulting
48. i2 Technologies	986	Supply chain management, factory planning
49. VeriSign	984	Security, antivirus, policy management
50. BEA	976	Middleware, application server, web server

Source: *www.softwaremag.com/SW500_2002 (accessed June 27, 2003).*

Appendix Table 6: Microsoft Income Statement Analysis, 1998–2002

(In millions of dollars)

Year ended June 30	1998	1999	2000	2001	2002
Revenues	$15,262	$19,747	$22,956	$25,296	$28,365
Operating expenses (as % of revenue):					
Cost of revenue	16	14	13	14	18
Research and development	17	15	16	17	15
Sales and marketing	19	16	18	19	19
General and administrative	3	4	5	3	5
Total operating expenses	$ 57	$ 49	$ 52	$ 54	$ 58
Operating profit rate	*43%*	*51%*	*48%*	*46%*	*42%*
Net profit rate	*29%*	*39%*	*41%*	*29%*	*28%*
Average employees	24,643	29,315	35,377	43,390	49,050
Annual sales per employee ($1000)	$ 619	$ 674	$ 649	$ 583	$ 578

Source: *Microsoft Corporation, Form 10-K, 1999–2002.*

Appendix Table 7: Software Magazine Top 100 Companies by Sector (2002)

Systems and Infrastructure Software Products = 29
- Infrastructure/systems management (5)
- Development tools/languages (5)
- Security (4)
- Computer-aided design and manufacturing tools (4)
- Middleware/connectivity/application servers (3)
- Storage management (3)
- Operating systems (3)
- Wireless (2)

Services = 28
- IT services/consulting (23)
- E-business services (4)
- Application service provider (ASP) (1)

Enterprise Application Products = 23
- Enterprise resource planning (ERP) (6)
- Customer relationship management (CRM) (5)
- Financial (4)
- Business intelligence (3)
- Vertical applications (2)
- Database and data warehouse/query/OLAP* (2)
- Collaboration/project management (1)

Other Products and Services = 20

* OLAP = *online analytical processing software.*

Source: *Constructed from data in www.softwaremag.com/SW500_2002 (accessed June 27, 2003).*

Appendix Table 8: SAP Product Offerings (2003)

MySAP Functional Solutions	MySAP Business Maps	Services
Business intelligence	Aerospace and defense	Global support
Customer relationship management	Automotive	Consulting
Enterprise portals	Chemicals	Custom development
Financials	Consumer products	Hosting
Human resource management	Engineering, construction and operations	Ramp-up
Marketplace	High-tech	Tools and technology
Mobile business	Industrial machinery and components	
Product life cycle management	Mill product	
Supplier relationship management	Mining	
Supply-chain management	Oil and gas	
Netweaver (hosted solutions)	Pharmaceuticals	
	Retail	
	Service management	
	Financial services	
	Health care	
	Higher education	
	Insurance	
	Media	
	Professional services	
	Public sector	
	Service providers	
	Telecommunications	
	Utilities	

Source: *www.sap.com (accessed June 27, 2003)*

Appendix Table 9: Microsoft's Product and Service Offerings (2002)

Desktop Applications
- Microsoft Office (Word, Excel, PowerPoint, Access)
- Other (Project [project management], Visio [diagramming])
- Great Plains [accounting suite, including Dynamics, Solomon, eEnterprise]
- bCentral [small-business Internet services portal]

Desktop Operating System Platforms
- Windows XP [replacement for Windows 95/98, using NT/2000 code base]
- Windows 2000 Professional
- Windows NT Workstation
- Windows Millennium (Me) [upgrade to Windows 98]
- Windows 98 [upgrade to Windows 95]

Enterprise Software and Services
- Windows 2000 Server, Advanced Server, and Datacenter Server [upgrade to Windows NT Server]
- Microsoft .NET servers (SQL Server, Exchange Server, Application Center, Biztalk Server, Commerce Server, Content Management Server, Host Integration Server, Internet Security and Acceleration Server, Microsoft Operations Manager, Mobile Information Server, SharePoint Portal Server).
- Other servers (Small Business Server, Systems Management Server)
- Developer tools and services (Visual Studio.Net, Visual C++, Visual C#, Visual Basic, Visual InterDev, Visual J++, Visual Studio, Visual FoxPro)
- Enterprise services (consulting and support)

Consumer Software, Services, and Devices
- Xbox [video game console]
- MSN Internet access
- MSN network services
- PC and online games
- Learning and productivity software (Encarta, Bookshelf, My Personal Tutor, Microsoft Works, Microsoft Money, Microsoft Picture It! Publishing, Microsoft Streets & Trips)
- Mobility (wireless) and embedded systems (Pocket PC operating system, Microsoft Mobile Explorer, Microsoft Smartphone/Stinger platform, Windows CE, Windows NT Embedded, Microsoft Mobile Information Server)

Consumer Commerce Investments and Other
- HomeAdvisor (online real estate service)
- Expedia, Inc. (online travel service)
- CarPoint (online automotive service)
- Microsoft IntelliMouse
- Microsoft Natural Keyboard
- Microsoft Sidewinder (game controllers and joysticks)
- Microsoft Press

Source: *Microsoft Corporation, 2002 Annual Report, pp. 16–19.*

Appendix Table 10: Oracle's E-Business Suite and Product Descriptions (2003)

1. *Marketing Products:* Marketing, Trade Management (2)
2. *Sales Products:* TeleSales, Sales Online, Sales Offline, Incentive Compensation, iStore, Quoting, Configurator, iPayment (8)
3. *Service Products:* TeleService, iSupport, Field Service, Mobile Field Service, Wireless Option for Service, Advanced Scheduler, Depot Repair, Complex Maintenance, Repair, and Overhaul, Service Contracts, Interaction Center (12)
4. *Contracts:* Service Contracts, Sales Contracts, Project Contracts, Lease Management (4)
5. *Finance Products:* Activity-Based Management, Assets, Balanced Scorecard, Cash Management, Collections, Financial Analyzer, Financials Intelligence, General Ledger, Global Consolidation System, Internet Expenses, iReceivables, Payables, Property Manager, Receivables, Sales Analyzer, Treasury, Risk Management (17)
6. *Human Resources Products:* Core Human Resources, Advanced Benefits, HR Intelligence, Oracle iLearning, Payroll, Self-Service HR, Time & Labor, Training Administration, Learning Management, iRecruitment, Oracle Tutor (11)
7. *Supply Chain Management Products:* Product Development, Advanced Planning, Procurement, Manufacturing, Order Fulfillment, Exchanges, Supply Chain Intelligence (7)
8. *Order Fulfillment Products:* Order Management, Advanced Pricing, Configurator, Release Management, Warehouse Management, Global Order Promising, Mobile Supply Chain, Transportation (8)
9. *Projects Products:* Internet Time, Project Billing, Project Contracts, Project Costing, Project Resource Management (5)
10. *Procurement:* iProcurement, Sourcing, Purchasing, iSupplier Portal, Purchasing Intelligence, Exchanges (6)
11. *Asset Management Products:* Finance, Human Resources, Projects, Supply Chain Management (4)
12. *Manufacturing Products:* Discrete, Process, Flow, Shop Floor Management, Warehouse Management, Manufacturing Scheduling, Manufacturing Intelligence, Product Development Exchange (8)
13. *Learning Management:* Core Human Resources, Advanced Benefits, HR Intelligence, Oracle iLearning, Payroll, Self-Service HR, Time & Labor, Training Administration, Learning Management, iRecruitment, Oracle Tutor (11)

Source: *www.oracle.com/applications/crm/marketing/index.html?content.html (accessed January 21, 2003).*

Appendix Table 11: Infinium Software Income Statement Analysis, 1997–2002

(In thousands of dollars)

Fiscal year ended December 31	1997	1998	1999	2000	2001	2002
Revenues:						
Software licenses	$29,781	$ 40,704	$ 32,437	$ 20,473	$ 10,363	$ 10,700
Services and maintenance	56,861	73,490	89,568	72,261	63,707	55,992
Total	$86,642	$114,194	$122,005	$ 92,734	$ 74,070	$ 66,692
% License fees	34%	36%	27%	22%	14%	16%
% Services and maintenance	66%	64%	73%	78%	86%	84%
Growth rates—total:	21%	32%	7%	−24%	−20%	−10%
Software licenses	23%	37%	-20%	−37%	−49%	3%
Services and maintenance	19%	29%	22%	−19%	−12%	−12%
Costs and expenses:						
Cost of software licenses	5,070	7,210	14,518	7,101	8,157	1,582
Cost of services and maintenance	22,400	32,330	40,389	31,563	19,304	16,873
Gross margins:						
Software licenses	83%	82%	55%	65%	21%	85%
Services and maintenance	61%	56%	55%	56%	70%	70%
Other costs (as % of revenues):						
Sales and marketing	35%	32%	33%	39%	37%	26%
Research and development	19%	17%	16%	23%	22%	15%
General and administrative	9%	8%	12%	17%	22%	11%
Total operating costs and expenses	$88,715	$115,790	$128,696	$111,682	$ 87,239	$ 53,640
Write-offs of in-process R and D	6,846	11,196	—	—	—	
Operating income	(150)	148	(4058)	(12,844)	(13,147)	13,052
Operating profit rate	—	0.1%	—	—	—	20%
Losses from discontinued operations	—	—	—	8,112	13,469	—
Net income	$ 113	$ 101	$ (2,360)	$(27,816)	$(24,332)	$ 15,561
Net profit rate	0.1%	0.1%	—	—	—	23%
Year-end employees	549	658	608	541	344	302
Average employees	?	604	633	575	443	323
Annual sales/employee		$189,000	$193,000	$161,000	$167,000	$206,000

Source: *Infinium Software, Form 10K, 1997–2001, and company information for 2002.*

Appendix Table 12: IBM Income Statement Analysis, 1992 and 1997–2002

(In millions of dollars)

Fiscal Year ended December 31	1992	1997	1998	1999	2000	2001	2002*
Revenues:							
Hardware	$33,800	$ 36,630	$36,096	$37,888	$37,777	$33,392	$ 27,456
Services	15,000	25,166	28,916	32,172	33,152	34,956	36,360
Software	11,100	11,164	11,863	12,662	12,598	12,939	13,074
Other	4,700	5,548	4,792	4,826	4,869	4,579	4,296
Total	$64,500	$ 78,508	$ 81,667	$ 87,548	$ 88,396	$ 85,866	$ 81,186
Revenue breakdown							
% Hardware	52%	47%	44%	43%	43%	39%	34%
% Services	23%	32%	35%	37%	38%	41%	45%
% Software	17%	14%	15%	14%	14%	15%	16%
% Other	8%	7%	6%	6%	5%	5%	5%
Costs:							
Hardware	—	$ 23,473	$ 24,653	$ 27,591	$ 27,038	$ 24,137	$ 20,015
Services	—	18,464	21,125	23,304	24,309	25,355	26,797
Software	—	2,785	2,260	2,240	2,283	2,265	2,040
Other	—	3,177	2,757	2,859	2,342	2,237	2,052
Total	—	$ 47,899	50,795	55,994	56,342	54,084	50,904
Gross margins:							
Hardware	—	36%	32%	27%	28%	28%	27%
Services	—	27%	27%	28%	27%	27%	26%
Software	—	75%	81%	82%	82%	82%	84%
Total	—	39%	38%	36%	36%	37%	37%
Expenses (R and D, G&A, etc.)	—	$ 21,511	$ 21,832	$ 20,172	$ 20,890	$ 20,829	$ 22,760
Operating profit rate	—	12%	11%	13%	13%	13%	9%
Net profit rate	—	8%	8%	9%	9%	9%	7%
Year-end employees	302,000	269,465	291,067	307,401	316,303	319,876	315,889
Average employees	—	255,040	280,266	299,234	311,852	318,090	317,883
Annual sales/employee	—	$307,826	$291,391	$292,574	$283,454	$269,942	$255,396

* IBM's revenues declined in 2002 and the percentage of hardware sales declined at least in part due to sale of its data storage business to Hitachi Data Systems for approximately $2.05 billion.

Source: *IBM Corporation, Annual Report.*

Appendix Table 13: Red Hat Financials Statement Analysis, 2000–2003

(In thousands of dollars)

Fiscal Year ended in February	2000	2001	2002	2003
Revenues:				
Subscriptions	$ 25,352	$ 45,498	$ 42,300	$ 48,592
Services	$ 17,075	$ 35,334	$ 36,610	$ 42,334
Total	*$ 42,427*	*$ 80,832*	*$ 78,910*	*$ 90,926*
Growth rate	—	91%	−2%	15%
Revenue breakdown:				
% Subscriptions	60%	56%	54%	53%
% Services	40%	44%	46%	47%
Costs and expenses:				
Cost of subscriptions	13,773	14,660	9,887	9,121
Cost of services	9,064	20,485	18,628	22,341
Gross margins				
Subscriptions	46%	68%	77%	81%
Services	47%	42%	49%	47%
Other costs (as % of revenues)				
Sales and marketing	57%	56%	45%	37%
Research and development	29%	23%	26%	25%
General and administrative	57%	44%	28%	20%
Total costs and expenses	$ 63,503	$140,996	$ 185,444	$ 97,525
Net loss	$(42,427)	$(86,715)	$(140,216)	$ (6,599)
Year-end employees	435	735	634	566
Average employees	—	585	685	600
Annual sales/employee	—	$138,000	$ 115,000	$152,000

Source: *Red Hat, Form 10-K (media.corporate-ir.net/media_files/NSD/RHAT/reports/ 10-K2003.pdf).*

Appendix Table 14: Preliminary Data from Global Software Process Survey

		India	Japan	USA	Europe and Other	Total
Projects		24	27	31	22	104
Architectural specs	% Yes	83.3	70.4	54.8	72.7	69.2
Functional specs	% Yes	95.8	92.6	74.2	81.8	85.6
Detailed designs	% Yes	100	85.2	32.3	68.2	69.2
Code generation	% Yes	62.5	40.7	51.6	54.5	51.9
Design reviews	% Yes	100	100	77.4	77.3	88.5
Code reviews	% Yes	95.8	74.1	71.0	81.8	79.8
Subcycles	% Yes	79.2	44.4	54.8	86.4	64.4
More than 1 beta	% >=1	66.7	66.7	77.4	81.8	73.1
Pair tester	% Yes	54.2	44.4	35.5	31.8	41.3
Pair programming	% Yes	58.3	22.2	35.5	27.2	35.3
Daily builds	% Beginning	16.7	22.2	35.5	9.1	22.1
	% Middle	12.5	25.9	29.0	27.3	24
	% End	29.2	37	35.5	40.9	35.6
Regression test on each build	% Yes	91.7	96.3	71.0	77.3	83.7
Output*	Median	209	469	270	436	374
Defects†	Median	.263	.020	.400	.225	.150

* Output = New Lines of Code/(average staff × calendar duration)

† Defects = Number of defects reported in the 12 months after implementation/1000 source lines of code, adjusted for projects reporting fewer than 12 months of data.

Source: M. Cusumano, A. MacCormack, C. Kemerer, and B. Crandall, "Software Development Worldwide: The State of the Practice," IEEE Software, November–December, 2003, 28–34.

Appendix Table 15: Some Emerging Software Technologies and Businesses

Year	Business or Technology
1997	Internet telephony and video conferencing
	Java-based solutions
	Artificial intelligence applications
	Audio and video streaming
	Electronic payment systems
	Internet-based groupware
1998	MPEG and peer-to-peer sharing applications
	Open-source software
	E-commerce services
	Voice-recognition
	Virtual reality modeling language
	Intelligent agents
	Enterprise applications hosting
1999	Bluetooth
	Wireless Application Protocol (WAP)
	JINI
	XML (Extensible Markup Language)
	CORBA (Common Object Request Broker)
	M-commerce business models
	Electronic auctions
2000	Web services
	Home networking
	Handheld devices
	Supply-chain management
2003	Mobile software for Web phones
	Grid computing
	Microsoft platform evolution
	Web services
	AI applications for user interface, learning, speech, vision, etc.
	Software development outsourcing
	Tools and techniques for organizational learning

Source: *Student presentation materials from "The Software Business," Subject 15.963/15.358, MIT Sloan School of Management, fall 1997–fall 2000 and spring 2003.*

Notes

CHAPTER 1: THE BUSINESS OF SOFTWARE: A PERSONAL VIEW

1. Frederick P. Brooks, Jr., *The Mythical Man-Month: Essays on Software Engineering* (Reading, Mass.: Addison-Wesley, 1975), 4.
2. Interview with Chris Peters, former vice president, Microsoft, April 12, 1993, cited in Michael A. Cusumano and Richard W. Selby, *Microsoft Secrets: How the World's Most Powerful Software Company Creates Technology, Shapes Markets, and Manages People* (New York: Free Press/Simon & Schuster, 1995), 210.
3. See Michael A. Cusumano, *The Japanese Automobile Industry: Technology and Management at Nissan and Toyota* (Cambridge, Mass.: Harvard University Press, 1985).
4. There was considerable media coverage of this press conference. See, e.g., Jacob Schlesinger, "Japan Makes Strides in Software Design: 'Factory' Approach Contrasts with U.S. Production," *The Wall Street Journal,* February 8, 1991, A7; Neil Gross, "Now Software Isn't Safe from Japan," *Business Week,* February 11, 1991, 84; Neil Gross, "Rails That Run on Software: Thanks to Hitachi, There's Never a Hitch on Japan's Bullet Train," *Business Week,* Quality 1991 Special Issue, 84.
5. The data from the survey can be found in Michael A. Cusumano and Chris F. Kemerer, "A Quantitative Analysis of U.S. and Japanese Practice and Performance in Software Development," *Management Science* 36, no. 11 (November 1990): 1384–1406, as well as Michael A. Cusumano, *Japan's Software Factories: A Challenge to U.S. Management* (New York: Oxford University Press, 1991), 456–467.
6. I am referring to *Microsoft Secrets* as well as two other books. See Michael A. Cusumano and David B. Yoffie, *Competing on Internet Time: Lessons from Netscape and Its Battle with Microsoft* (New York: Free Press/Simon & Schuster, 1998), and Annabelle Gawer and Michael A. Cusumano, *Platform Leadership: How Intel, Microsoft, and Cisco Drive Industry Innovation* (Boston: Harvard Business School Press, 2002).

7. See Cusumano and Selby, *Microsoft Secrets,* 4–6.
8. Business Objects, Annual Report 2001, 4 (www.businessobjects.com).
9. Author's interview with Bernard Liautaud, CEO of Business Objects, June 21, 2002. Subsequent references to the Liautaud interview refer to this date.
10. Ibid.
11. "The Best Entrepreneurs," *Business Week,* January 8, 1996, 63.
12. Business Objects, Form 10-K, U.S. Securities and Exchange Commission, Washington, D.C., December 31, 1997, 19.
13. "The Stars of Europe: Entrepreneurs," *Business Week,* June 17, 2002, 77.
14. "Time Digital Top 25," *Time,* October 14, 2002, online edition (www.time.com/time/europe/magazine/2002/1014/timedigital/15-11.html).
15. See i2 Technologies, Inc., Form 10-K, U.S. Securities and Exchange Commission, Washington, D.C., December 31, 1996, 2.
16. See Dean A. Yuliano, "i2 Founder Takes Lead in Tough Times," *The Wall Street Journal,* May 15, 2002.
17. I calculated this number by dividing revenues into costs, excluding the listed nonrecurring charges. See Appendix Table 4.
18. i2 released its 2002 annual report in July 2003 and restated financial results for 1999–2001 as well as quarterly reports in 2002. See i2 Technologies, Inc. Form 10-K, U.S. Securities and Exchange Commission, Washington, D.C., December 31, 2002. For the discussion of contract revenue see p. 55.
19. See "55 Percent of i2 Reference Customers Have Not Achieved Positive ROI, Says Independent Study," *Business Wire,* June 13, 2003 (www.businesswire.com).
20. The Dell story is recounted on i2's Web site at www.i2technologies.com/Home/Customers/index.html (accessed January 22, 2003).
21. Eliot Spagat, "i2 Technologies to Cut Jobs in Move to Reach Profitability," *The Wall Street Journal,* November 14, 2002, online edition (http://online.wsj.com/article_email/0.,.,SB1037295179917115348.00.html).
22. i2 Technologies, Inc., *i2 Annual Review 2001* (www.i2.com/investor/2001/shareholders.cfm), accessed October 15, 2002.

CHAPTER 2: STRATEGY FOR SOFTWARE COMPANIES: WHAT TO THINK ABOUT

1. Michael A. Porter, *Competitive Strategy* (New York: Free Press, 1980) and *Competitive Advantage* (New York: Free Press, 1984); Richard J. Foster, *Innovation: The Attacker's Advantage* (New York: Summit, 1986); Clayton Christensen, *The Innovator's Dilemma* (Boston: Harvard Business School Press, 1997).
2. Early versions of this and other sections can be found in my column for the *Communications of the ACM,* from February 2002.
3. For a good discussion of the services-versus-products debate in software and other industries, see Satish Nambisan, "Why Service Businesses Are Not Product Businesses," *MIT Sloan Management Review* 42, vol. 4 (Summer 2001): 72–80.
4. Author's interview with William Gerraughty, former CFO, Infinium Software, April 19, 2002.

5. Author's interview with Ann Marie Monk, former chief counsel, Infinium Software, June 25, 2003. My thanks also to Ann Marie for help in drawing up Table 2-1.

6. This breakdown is also supported by the McKinsey study of software companies. See Detlev J. Hoch et al., *Secrets of Software Success* (Boston: Harvard Business School Press, 1999), 36, n. 14.

7. There are some interesting similarities and differences between my three business models and the "delta" framework of system lock-in, total customer solutions, and best product. See Arnoldo C. Hax and Dean L. Wilde, *The Delta Project: Discovering New Sources of Profitability in a Networked Economy* (New York: Palgrave, 2001).

8. Siebel Systems, Annual Report 2001, 10.

9. My thanks to Professor Fernando Suarez of London Business School for this observation.

10. See http://globalservices.fujitsu.com.

11. SAP, Form 20-F, Washington, D.C., U.S. Securities and Exchange Commission, December 31, 2001, 20.

12. Oracle Corporation, Form 10-K, U.S. Securities and Exchange Commission, Washington, D.C., May 31, 2003, 18, 71.

13. Ibid., 4.

14. See 2002 Siebel financial data at www.siebel.com/downloads/about/news_events/press_releases/pdf/siebel_2002_04_earnings.pdf (accessed February 1, 2003).

15. Elise Ackerman, "Software Rebel: Marc Benioff's Radical Business Model Is Winning Converts," *San Jose Mercury News,* December 19, 2002, online edition (www.bayarea.com/mld/bayarea/business/4700073.htm). See also the company Web site at www.salesforce.com.

16. See the SAP annual reports and financial data for 2002 at www.sap.com.

17. Microsoft Corporation, Annual Report 2001, p. 26.

18. Calculated from company data summarized in www.softwaremag.com/SW500_2000/index.cfm.

19. Standard & Poor's, *Industry Surveys, Computers: Software* 170, no. 4 (January 24, 2002).

20. Alexander Blunt & Seth Shafer, "Computer Software," (www.hoovers.com/industry/snapshot/profile/0.3519.13.00.html), accessed May 12, 2002.

21. Cited in Iwata Akio, *Sofutouea gyokai handobukku* [Software Industry Handbook] (Tokyo: Toyo Keizai, 2002), 189.

22. Hoch et al., *Secrets of Software Success,* 38, n. 20. See also "Hoover's Online Profiles 676 Companies in the US(?) Software Industry in 2001" at www.hoovers.com/industry/snapshot/companies/1.3516.13.00.html.

23. "Nokia v Microsoft: The Fight for Digital Dominance," *The Economist,* November 23, 2002, 61–63.

24. Hoch et al., *Secrets of Software Success,* 36, n. 14.

25. Michael A. Cusumano and Richard W. Selby, *Microsoft Secrets* (New York: Free Press/Simon & Schuster, 1995), 362–364, 367–368.

26. Mylene Mangalindan, "IBM Wrests Database Market Lead from Oracle as Sector Consolidates," *The Wall Street Journal,* May 7, 2002, online edition (www.wsj.com).

27. Cusumano and Selby, *Microsoft Secrets,* 445–447.
28. For a discussion of SAP's growth strategy, see Georg von Krogh and Michael A. Cusumano, "Three Strategies for Managing Fast Growth," *MIT Sloan Management Review* 42, no. 2 (Winter 2001): 57–59.
29. See Microsoft Corporation, Form 10-Q, U.S. Securities and Exchange Commission, Washington, D.C., December 31, 2002, 10. The data I am referring to here are for the new categories Microsoft is using for fiscal 2003: Client, Server Platforms, and Information Worker (which is primarily Office).
30. SkyFire Technologies, Executive Summary, March 2001, 6
31. Cusumano and Selby, *Microsoft Secrets,* 389–397.
32. Jim Kerstetter, Steve Hamm, and Andrew Park, "Larry's One-Man Show," *Business Week,* March 25, 2002, 64–66.
33. See i2 Technologies, "i2 Announces Final Second Quarter 2002 Results," company press release, July 16, 2002 (www.i2.com/investors/); and Alorie Gilbert, "i2 Board Member Resigns," C/NET News.com, October 1, 2002 (news.com.com/2100-1017-960362.html?tag=cd_mh).
34. See J. Timmons, *New Venture Creation* (Burr Ridge, Ill.: Irwin, 1998), 14.
35. von Krogh and Cusumano, "Three Strategies," 53–61.
36. Cusumano and Selby, *Microsoft Secrets,* 43–50.
37. See, e.g., Richard P. Rumelt, *Strategy, Structure and Economic Performance* (Boston: Harvard Business School Press, 1974 and 1986), and "Diversification Strategy and Profitability," *Strategic Management Journal* 3 (1982): 359–369.
38. Infinium customers typically spent about 30 to 50 percent less on services relative to software license fees compared to the averages in the ERP industry. See http://infinium.www.conxion.com/solutions/corpover.pdf (accessed July 18, 2002).
39. Infinium, "Infinium Software Elects Bob Pemberton President and Chief Executive Officer," company press release, July 14, 1999 (www.infinium.com/news-events/news-releases/release.asp?ReleaseID=93).
40. Infinium, "Infinium Board of Directors Names James E. McGowan President and Chief Executive Officer," company press release, February 9, 2001 (www.infinium.com/news-events/news-releases/release.asp?ReleaseID=96).
41. Infinium, "Infinium Reports $0.25 Earnings per Share for the Second Quarter of Fiscal Year 2002," company press release, April 22, 2002 (www.infinium.com/news-events/news-releases/release.asp?ReleaseID=139).
42. IBM, "IBM Transforms Mid-Market eServer with Integrated Software, On/Off Capacity by the Day," company press release, January 20, 2003 (www.916.ibm.com/press/prnews.nsf/jan/AF26BF608A4C2E1B85256CB4004FB992), accessed January 21, 2003.
43. See Michael E. Porter, "From Competitive Advantage to Competitive Strategy," *Harvard Business Review,* May 1987, 43–59.
44. SSA Global Technologies, "SSA Global Technologies Completes Acquisition of Infinium Software, Inc.," company press release, December 20,

2002 (http://ogs.ssax.com/www_asp/news/news_info.asp?id=81) (accessed January 21, 2003).

45. Rebecca Buckman, "Microsoft's Plan for Its Office Suite Stirs Debate over Growth Prospects," *The Wall Street Journal,* March 12, 2002, online edition; and Hiawatha Bray, "Microsoft's New Software Policy Leaves Many Customers Fuming," *The Boston Globe,* August 7, 2002, C3.

46. Geoffrey A. Moore, *Crossing the Chasm* (New York: HarperCollins, 1991).

47. Carl Shapiro and Hal R. Varian, *Information Rules* (Boston: Harvard Business School Press, 1999).

48. See Michael A. Cusumano and David B. Yoffie, *Competing on Internet Time: Lessons from Netscape and Its Battle with Microsoft* (New York: Free Press/Simon & Schuster, 1998), 234–239, for an analysis of how Netscape managers viewed their transition process.

49. See, e.g., Porter, *Competitive Advantage,* 164–200.

50. Andrew S. Grove, *Only the Paranoid Survive* (New York: Currency Doubleday, 1996).

51. Annabelle Gawer and Michael A. Cusumano, *Platform Leadership: How Intel, Microsoft, and Cisco Drive Industry Innovation* (Boston: Harvard Business School Press, 2002).

52. Richard S. Rosenbloom and Michael A. Cusumano, "Technological Pioneering and Competitive Advantage: The Birth of the VCR Industry," *California Management Review* 29, no. 4 (Summer 1987): 51–76; Michael A. Cusumano, Yiorgos Mylonadis, and Richard S. Rosenbloom, "Strategic Maneuvering and Mass-Market Dynamics: The Triumph of VHS over Beta," *Business History Review* 66 (Spring 1992): 51–94.

53. Gary Jacobson and John Hillkirk, *Xerox: American Samurai* (New York: Macmillan, 1986), especially 141–152.

54. Paul Freiberger and Michael Swaine, *Fire in the Valley: The Making of the Personal Computer* (New York: McGraw-Hill, 1984); Robert X. Cringeley, *Accidental Empires* (New York: HarperBusiness, 1992), 182–208.

55. See www.intuit.com and 10-K filings with the SEC.

56. See Michael A. Cusumano and David B. Yoffie, *Competing on Internet Time: Lessons from Netscape and Its Battle with Microsoft* (New York: Free Press/Simon & Schuster, 1998).

57. See www.investopedia.com/terms/g/gaap.asp.

58. Infinium Software, Form 10-K, U.S. Securities and Exchange Commission, Washington, D.C., fiscal year ended September 30, 2001.

59. See, e.g., Craig Stedman, "Users Worry as Baan's Woes Rise," *Computerworld,* January 10, 2000, and Kathleen Ohlson, "Baan's Future in More Doubt After 1999 Loss Widens," July 18, 2000, online edition (www.computerworld.com).

60. "Peregrine Software Inflated Revenue over Years," August 20, 2002 (www.nbcsandiego.com/news/1642615/detail.html); Peregrine Systems, "Peregrine Systems Receives Approval of First-Day Motions in Volun-

tary Chapter 11 Reorganization Case," company press release, September 25, 2002 (www.peregrine.com/us/News/PressReleases/2002/PR_2002-09-25.htm).

61. See Stacey Cowley, "SEC Expands CA Accounting Probe," *Computerworld*, May 15, 2002, online version (www.computerworld.com). See also Gillian Law, "Report: SEC Questions Former CA Employees," *Computerworld*, November 25, 2002, online version.

62. Author's telephone interview with Bob Cirabisi, vice president of investor relations, Shannon Lapierre, corporate communications manager, and Bob Lamm, vice president of corporate governance, May 22, 2003.

63. Cusumano and Yoffie, *Competing on Internet Time*, 89–221.

64. For a more specific discussion of this argument, see Michael A. Cusumano, "That's Some Fine Mess You've Made, Mr. Gates," *The Wall Street Journal*, April 5, 2000, A26.

CHAPTER 3: SERVICES, PRODUCTS, AND MORE SERVICES: HOW SOFTWARE BECAME A BUSINESS

1. This historical sketch is based on Martin Campbell-Kelly and William Aspray, *Computer: A History of the Information Machine* (New York: Basic Books, 1996), particularly 87–92, 183, 196. Also see Steve Lohr, *Go To: The Story of the Math Majors, Bridge Players, Engineers, Chess Wizards, Maverick Scientists, and Iconoclasts—The Programmers Who Created the Software Revolution* (New York: Basic Books, 2001), 3–6. For a book-length history of the software industry that will shortly become the standard reference, see Martin Campbell-Kelly, *A History of the Software Industry: From Airline Reservations to Sonic the Hedgehog* (Cambridge, Mass.: MIT Press, 2003). I prepared this chapter before seeing the page proofs of Campbell-Kelly's new book, although this chapter does draw heavily on prior work by Campbell-Kelly.

2. Martin Campbell-Kelly, "Development and Structure of the International Software Industry, 1950–1990," *Business and Economic History* 24, no. 2 (Winter 1995): 82.

3. See Michael A. Cusumano, *Japan's Software Factories* (New York: Oxford University Press, 1991), 119–160, for a detailed analysis of the SDC software factory.

4. Campbell-Kelly, "Development and Structure," 83, and Campbell-Kelly and Aspray, *Computer*, 157–180, 223–225.

5. See Kenneth Flamm, *Creating the Computer: Government, Industry, and High Technology* (Washington, D.C.: Brookings Institution, 1988), especially Appendix Table A-3.

6. Flamm, Appendix Table A-4; Richard N. Langlois and David C. Mowery, "The Federal Government Role in the Development of the U.S. Software Industry," in *The International Computer Software Industry: A Compative Study of Industry Evolution and Structure*, ed. David C. Mowery (New York: Oxford University Press, 1996), 53–85.

7. Detlev J. Hoch et al., *Secrets of Software Success* (Boston: Harvard Business School Press, 1999), 38. Also see Elmer C. Kubie, "Recollections of the First Software Company," *IEEE Annals of the History of Computing* 16, no. 2 (1994): 65–71.

8. Campbell-Kelly, "Development and Structure," 84–86.
9. Thomas Haigh, "Software in the 1960s as Concept, Service, and Product," *Business and Economic History* 24, no. 2 (Winter 1995): 5–13.
10. For a discussion of this application, see JoAnne Yates, "Application Software for Insurance in the 1960s and Early 1970s," *Business and Economic History* 24, no. 1 (Fall 1995): 123–134.
11. Campbell-Kelly, "Development and Structures," 89–90.
12. Watts S. Humphrey, "Software Unbundling: A Personal Perspective," *IEEE Annals of the History of Computing* 24, no. 1 (January–March 2002): 59.
13. Ibid., 59–62.
14. Ibid., 60–63; Burton Grad, "A Personal Recollection: IBM's Unbundling of Software and Services," *IEEE Annals of the History of Computing,* vol. 24, No. 1 (January–March 2002): 64–71.
15. Grad, p. 70.
16. Campbell-Kelly and Aspray, *Computer,* 204.
17. Humphrey, "Software Unbundling," 61.
18. Amdahl, founded by former IBM design engineer Gene Amdahl in 1970, became a subsidiary of Fujitsu in 1974. It provided the Japanese company with IBM-compatible know-how. It was renamed Fujitsu IT Holdings in 2002.
19. For these financial details, see the SAP annual report at www.sap.com/company/investor/reports/ar_onlin/2001/financials/income.htm.
20. See Jay Greene, "Microsoft: How It Became Stronger than Ever," *Business Week,* June 4, 2001, 77, and Microsoft Corporation, "Microsoft to Acquire Navision," company press release, May 7, 2002 (www.microsoft.com/presspass/press/2002/may02/05–07NavisionPR.asp), accessed January 24, 2003.
21. JoAnne Yates, "Co-evolution of Information Processing Technology and Use: Interaction Between the Life Insurance and Tabulating Industries," *Business History Review* 67 (Spring 1993): 1–51.
22. The following discussion is based primarily on Campbell-Kelly and Aspray, *Computer,* 109–138.
23. See Franklin Fisher, James McKie, and Richard Mancke, *IBM and the U.S. Data Processing Industry* (New York: Praeger, 1983), 15–17.
24. Campbell-Kelly and Aspray, *Computer,* 131–132.
25. Ibid., 137–138.
26. Ibid., 199–200.
27. Frederick P. Brooks, *The Mythical Man-Month: Essays on Software Engineering* (Reading, Mass.: Addison-Wesley, 1975).
28. Campbell-Kelly, "Development and Structure," 200–203. Also on IBM's contributions in software, see Cusumano, *Japan's Software Factories,* 88–97.
29. Campbell-Kelly and Aspray, *Computer,* 222–226.
30. This sketch of IBM under Gerstner is based on Steve Lohr, "He Loves to Win. At I.B.M., He Did," *The New York Times,* March 10, 2002, sec. 3, pp. 1, 11.
31. See also Spencer E. Ante, "For Big Blue, the Big Enchilada," *Business Week,* October 28, 2002, 58–59.

32. Louis V. Gerstner, Jr., *Who Says Elephants Can't Dance? Inside IBM's Historic Turnaround* (New York: HarperBusiness, 2002), 137, 140.
33. Ibid., 142–145.
34. My thanks to Professor Fernando Suarez of London Business School for first making this observation.
35. Amy Harmon, "Microsoft Loses a Round to Rival Sun," *The New York Times,* December 24, 2002, C1; and Lyle Denniston, "Microsoft Ordered to Install Sun's Java," *The Boston Globe,* January 22, 2003, C2.
36. Erick Schonfeld, "This *Is* Your Father's IBM, Only Smarter," *Business 2.0,* May 2002, 55.
37. Spencer Ante and David Henry, "Can IBM Keep Earnings Hot?" *Business Week,* April 15, 2002, 58–60.
38. Steve Lohr and Jonathan D. Glater, "I.B.M. to Purchase Consulting Group for $3.5 Billion," *The New York Times,* July 31, 2002, A1.
39. Steve Lohr, "The New Leader of IBM Explains His Strategic Course," *The New York Times,* October 31, 2002, C5.
40. See www.rational.com/corpinfo/services.jsp and www.rational.com/corpinfo/index.isp?SMSESSION=NO (accessed December 31, 2002).
41. For PCs and the Internet, a good basic reference is Campbell-Kelly and Aspray, *Computer,* 233–300. Also on PCs, see Robert X. Cringely, *Accidental Empires* (New York: HarperBusiness, 1993). For Internet entrepreneurs, see Robert Reid, *Architects of the Web* (New York: Wiley, 1997).
42. This section is based mainly on Campbell-Kelly and Aspray, *Computer,* 249–258.
43. See Campbell-Kelly and Aspray, *Computer,* 277, for CP/M sales data.
44. See Campbell-Kelly, "Development and Structure," 260, for market data. Microsoft historical data can be found in Michael A. Cusumano and Richard W. Selby, *Microsoft Secrets: How the World's Most Powerful Software Company Creates Technology, Shapes Markets, and Manages People* (New York: Free Press/Simon & Schuster, 1995), 3.
45. Stephen Manes and Paul Andrews, *Gates: How Microsoft's Mogul Reinvented an Industry—and Made Himself the Richest Man in America* (New York: Doubleday, 1993), 91–92, reproduce Gates's letter, which was published in *Computer Notes* in February 1996.
46. See Tim Berners-Lee, *Weaving the Web: The Past, Present, and Future of the World Wide Web by Its Inventor* (London: Orion Publishing, 1999).
47. See Ashlee Vance, "Judge Blocks Napster Sale," *Computerworld,* September 3, 2002, online edition www.computerworld.com/government topics/government/legalissues/story/0.10801.73961.00.html). *Computer world* has a special site devoted to its Napster articles. See www.computerworld.com/news/special/pages/0.10911.1411.00.html. Also see Amy Kover, "It's Back. But can the New Napster Survive?" *The New York Times,* August 17, 2003, C4; D. C. Denison, "Napster Files for Chap. 11, Hopes to Speed Relaunch," *The Boston Globe,* June 4, 2002, D1, and Matt Richtel, "Turmoil at Napster Moves the Service Closer to Bankruptcy," *The New York Times,* May 14, 2002 (www.nytimes.com). Post-Napster sites can be found at www.afternapster.com/# (accessed June 22, 2003).

48. See www.priceline.com for details. Financial reports are available through clicking on the Investor Relations link on the main Web site.
49. See www.valueclick.com for details. The 2002 results are estimates from the 2002 third-quarter SEC filing and a press release detailing fourth-quarter results.
50. www.opensource.org/docs/history.html (accessed April 10, 2002).
51. www.opensource.org (accessed April 10, 2002).
52. Campbell-Kelly and Aspray, *Computer,* 192–193.
53. www.opensource.org/advocacy/faq.html (accessed April 10, 2002).
54. wwws.sun.com/software/star/staroffice/6.0/ (accessed August 18, 2003).
55. See Paul Abrahams, "Microsoft to Reveal Code for Windows Free," *Financial Times,* January 15, 2003, 18, and Steve Lohr, "Microsoft to Share Code to Fight 'Open' Software," *International Herald Tribune,* June 16, 2003, 11 (from *The New York Times*).
56. See Eric von Hippel, "Innovation by User Communities: Learning from Open-Source Software," *MIT Sloan Management Review* 42, no. 4 (Summer 2001): 82–86.
57. www.vasoftware.com (accessed June 22, 2003).
58. Caldera International, Inc., Form 10-K, U.S. Securities and Exchange Commission, Washington, D.C., October 31, 2002, 35. See also www.caldera.com/company (accessed June 22, 2003).
59. See Glyn Moody, *Rebel Code: Inside Linux the Open Source Revolution* (Cambridge, Mass., Perseus, 2001), 202; and Michael A. Cusumano, "A Brighter Future: Mozilla and Open Sourcing Redux," *Computerworld,* November 1, 1999, online edition (www.computerworld.com).
60. Moody, 127–130.
61. Ibid., 205–213.
62. See press releases at http://ir.seo.com/releases.cfm (accessed June 22, 2003). See also Todd R. Weiss, "AIX Users Unworried About SCO's Unix Offensive Against IBM," *Computerworld,* June 20, 2003 (www.computerworld.com).

CHAPTER 4: BEST PRACTICES IN SOFTWARE DEVELOPMENT: BEYOND THE SOFTWARE FACTORY

1. An excellent recent overview is Steve McConnell, *Rapid Development* (Redmond, Wash.: Microsoft Press, 1996).
2. See Michael A. Cusumano, *Japan's Software Factories: A Challenge to U.S. Management* (New York: Oxford University Press, 1991).
3. See Cusumano, *Japan's Software Factories,* for the history, except for Microsoft's encounter with factory concepts introduced by Charles Simonyi. For the latter story, see Robert X. Cringely, *Accidental Empires* (New York: HarperBusiness, 1992), 108–113.
4. Cusumano, *Japan's Software Factories,* 388–420, contains an analysis of several Japanese government–sponsored and cooperative R-and-D efforts in software technology, as well as a brief discussion of the U.S. responses. Also see Michael A. Cusumano, "Competitiveness of the U.S. Software Industry: Hearing Before the Committee on Commerce, Science, and Transportation," Washington, D.C., U.S. Government Printing Office, November 13, 1991, 5–14.

5. Watts Humphrey, *Managing the Software Process* (Reading, Mass.: Addison-Wesley, 1989).

6. See the SEI Web site at www.sei.cmu.edu/cmm.

7. See Stanley A. Smith, "Software Development in Established and New Entrant Companies: Case Studies of Leading Software Producers," unpublished M.S. thesis, Management of Technology Program, MIT, June 1993.

8. http://interactive.sei.cmu.edu/Features/1999/June/Background/Back ground.jun99.htm (accessed May 9, 2002).

9. See, for example, the classic article by Michael E. Fagan, "Design and Code Inspections to Reduce Errors in Program Development," *IBM Systems Journal* 15, no. 3 (1976): 182–211.

10. See Michael A. Cusumano and Richard W. Selby, *Microsoft Secrets: How the World's Most Powerful Software Company Creates Technology, Shapes Markets, and Manages People* (New York: Free Press/Simon & Schuster, 1995), 13–19.

11. Interview with Dave Maritz, at the time test manager, MS-DOS/Windows, Microsoft Corporation, April 15, 1993. Quoted in Cusumano and Selby, *Microsoft Secrets,* 18–19.

12. See examples in Steven C. Wheelwright and Kim B. Clark, *Revolutionizing Product Development* (New York: Free Press, 1992).

13. See Victor R. Basili and Albert J. Turner, "Iterative Enhancement: A Practical Technique for Software Development," *IEEE Transactions on Software Engineering* SE-1, no. 4 (December 1975): 390–396; Barry W. Boehm, "A Spiral Model of Software Development and Enhancement," *IEEE Computer,* May 1988, 61–72; and Mikio Aoyama, "Concurrent-Development Process Model," *IEEE Software,* July 1993, 46–55.

14. See, for example, Kent Beck, *Extreme Programming Explained: Embrace Change* (Reading, Mass.: Addison-Wesley, 1999).

15. See Winston W. Royce, "Managing the Development of Large Software Systems," *Proceedings of IEEE WESCON,* August 1970, 1–9.

16. See Wheelwright and Clark, *Revolutionizing Product Development,* as well as, e.g., Glen L. Urban and John R. Hauser, *Design and Marketing of New Products* (Englewood Cliffs, N.J.: Prentice Hall, 199?).

17. See in the particular the memo describing the meeting and its outcome by Chris Mason, "Zero-Defect Code," internal Microsoft memo, June 20, 1989, quoted in Cusumano and Selby, *Microsoft Secrets,* 43.

18. See also Marco Iansiti, "Microsoft Corporation: Office Business Unit," Harvard Business School, Case Study no. 9-691-033, 1994.

19. For the Navigator/Communicator development story, see Michael A. Cusumano and David B. Yoffie, *Competing on Internet Time: Lessons from Netscape and Its Battle with Microsoft* (New York: Free Press/Simon & Schuster, 1998), 156–221.

20. G. Pascal Zachary, *Show-Stopper* (New York: Free Press/Simon & Schuster, 1994); Cusumano and Selby, *Microsoft Secrets,* 223.

21. This section relies on material, initially from *Microsoft Secrets,* in Michael A. Cusumano and Richard W. Selby, "How Microsoft Builds Software," *Communications of the ACM* 40, no. 6 (7 June 1997): 53–62.

22. See Michael A. Cusumano, *The Japanese Automobile Industry: Technology and Management at Nissan and Toyota* (Cambridge, Mass.: Harvard University Press, 1985).

23. Cusumano and Yoffie, *Competing on Internet Time*, 222–297; Michael A. Cusumano and David B. Yoffie, "Software Development on Internet Time," *IEEE Computer*, Special Issue on Software Engineering and Management, October 1999, 2–11.

24. Interview with Max Morris, program manager, Internet Applications and Client Division, Microsoft, October 31, 1997. Cited in Cusumano and Yoffie, *Competing on Internet Time*, 250.

25. I am indebted to Frances Paulish of Siemens in Germany for providing a transcript of a presentation I gave at the company in March 2001. This transcript was the basis for this section on implementation strategies and subtleties.

26. Cusumano and Yoffie, *Competing on Internet Time*, 194.

27. Cusumano, *Japan's Software Factories*, 187–188.

28. Jim Kerstetter, Steve Hamm, and Andrew Park, "Larry's One-Man Show," *Business Week*, March 25, 2002, 64–66.

29. Cusumano, *Japan's Software Factories*, 264–265.

30. Michael A. Cusumano and Kentaro Nobeoka, *Thinking Beyond Lean: How Multiproject Management Is Transforming Product Development at Toyota and Other Companies* (New York: Free Press/Simon & Schuster, 1998), 43, 47, 97.

31. Carliss W. Baldwin and Kim B. Clark, *Design Rules: The Power of Modularity* (Cambridge, Mass.: MIT Press, 2000); Karl T. Ulrich and Steven D. Eppinger, *Product Design and Development* (New York: McGraw-Hill, 1995).

32. Alan MacCormack, "Microsoft Office 2000," Harvard Business School, Multimedia Case Study no. 9-600-023, 2000.

33. Cusumano and Yoffie, *Competing on Internet Time*, 181.

34. Ibid., 186.

35. Frederick P. Brooks, Jr., *The Mythical Man-Month: Essays on Software Engineering* (Reading, Mass.: Addison-Wesley, 1975); Tom DeMarco and Timothy Lister, *Peopleware: Productive Projects and Teams* (New York: Dorset, 1987).

36. DeMarco and Lister, *Peopleware*, 44–46.

37. Also see a more detailed treatment of software teams in Michael A. Cusumano, "How Microsoft Makes Large Teams Work like Small Teams," *MIT Sloan Management Review* 39, no. 1, (Fall 1997): 9–20.

38. Cusumano and Selby, *Microsoft Secrets*, 45.

39. Brier Dudley, "Ballmer's Heaping Plate: Implications of Microsoft's Executive Changes," *The Seattle Times*, April 8, 2002, online edition http://seattletimes.nwsource.com/htm/mondaytechnology/134432996_micromanagement08.htm.

40. Stephen Manes and Paul Andrews, *Gates: How Microsoft's Mogul Reinvented an Industry—and Made Himself the Richest Man in America* (New York: Doubleday, 1993), 316.

41. A good account of Microsoft's encounters with IBM during the OS/2 development is the recollections of Steve Ballmer, currently Microsoft's

CEO, in "Triumph of the Nerds," a documentary video produced by the Public Broadcasting System.

42. Cusumano and Selby, *Microsoft Secrets,* 363.

43. Barry W. Boehm, "Software Engineering," *IEEE Transactions on Computers,* C-25, 12, reproduced in Edward N. Yourdon, ed., *Classics in Software Engineering* (New York: Yourdon Press, 1979).

44. Michael A. Cusumano, "Objectives and Context of Software Measurement, Analysis, and Control," in D. Rombach et al., eds., *Experimental Software Engineering Issues: Critical Assessment and Future Directions* (Berlin: Springer-Verlag, 1993), 54.

45. Cusumano and Selby, *Microsoft Secrets,* 329–348, for additional details.

46. Ibid., 360–384.

47. A first version of the international data is analyzed in Pearlin Cheung, "Practices for Fast and Flexible Software Development," unpublished master's thesis, Department of Electrical Engineering and Computer Science, MIT, June 2002.

48. The pilot survey was first analyzed in Sharma Upadhyayula, "Rapid and Flexible Product Development: An Analysis of Software Projects at Hewlett Packard and Agilent," unpublished master's thesis in System Design and Management, MIT, June 2001.

49. See Michael Cusumano, Alan MacCormack, Chris Kemerer, and Bill Crandall, "Software Development Worldwide: The State of the Practice," *IEEE Software,* forthcoming November-December 2003, 28–34.

50. See Alan MacCormack, Chris Kemerer, Michael Cusumano, and Bill Crandall, "Trade-offs between Productivity and Quality in Selecting Software Development Practices," *IEEE Software,* September/October 2003, 78–85.

51. See Michael A. Cusumano and Chris F. Kemerer, "A Quantitative Analysis of U.S. and Japanese Practice and Performance in Software Development," *Management Science* 36, no. 11, November 1990.

52. This data is from the Web site of India's National Association of Software and Service Companies, www.nasscom.org. Also see Devesh Kapur and Ravi Ramamurti, "India's Emerging Competitive Advantage in Services," *Academy of Management Executive* 15, no. 2 (2001), reprinted in *IEEE Engineering Management Review* 30, no. 2 (2002): 44–55.

53. See Michael Cusumano, "Made in India: A New Sign of Software Quality," *Computerworld,* (February 28, 2000, available at www.computerworld.com).

54. Mark Paulk, "List of Maturity Level 4 and 5 Organizations," May 2002 (www.sei.cmu.edu/cmm/high-maturity/HighMatOrgs.pdf).

55. Victor Basili and Gianluigi Caldiera, "Improve Software Quality by Reusing Knowledge and Experience," *MIT Sloan Management Review* 37, no. 1 (Fall 1995): 55–64.

56. Sarala Ravishankar et al., "Insights from MIEL: Optimizing a Software Organization," unpublished presentation, Motorola India Electronics Ltd., SEPG 99, Bangalore, India, 1999.

57. I also learned on my visit that India's largest software company, Tata Consultancy (also an SEI Level 5), had used *Japan's Software Factories*

as a key input for its facilities, especially for its Y2K work, and had used *Microsoft Secrets* as a guide for iterative development projects.

58. Ravishankar et al., "Insights," 86–87.

59. D. Wiggins et al., "Trends for the Indian and Chinese Software Industries," Gartner Group, Strategic Planning Research Note, SPA-16-6118, June 7, 2002, 2.

60. Infosys Technologies Annual Report 2002, 78 (www.infosys.com/investor/reports/annual/Infosys_AR_2002.pdf).

61. www.infosys.com/investor/reports/quarterly/2002-2003/Q4/US_GAAP_fs.pdf (accessed June 24, 2003).

62. Infosys Technologies, "Infosys Technologies Announces Results for the Quarter Ended December 31, 2002," U.S. GAAP press release, January 10, 2003 (http://infosys.com/investor/reports/quarterly/2002-2003/Q3/US_gaap_pr.pdf).

63. www.infosys.com/consulting/value.asp (accessed February 25, 2003).

64. www.infosys.com/consulting/gdm.asp (accessed February 25, 2003).

65. Cusumano, *Japan's Software Factories*, 443–444. The quotation is from Bruce Arden, ed., *What Can Be Automated?* (Cambridge, Mass.: MIT Press, 1980), 797.

CHAPTER 5: SOFTWARE ENTREPRENEURSHIP: ESSENTIAL ELEMENTS OF A SUCCESSFUL START-UP

1. I wrote a column on the subject. See Michael A. Cusumano, "Web Start-ups: A Wave of Creativity or Mediocrity?" *Computerworld*, July 5, 1999, available at www.computerworld.com.

2. www.akamai.com.

3. See Edward B. Roberts, *Entrepreneurs in High Technology: Lessons from MIT and Beyond* (New York: Oxford University Press, 1991).

4. John Nesheim, *High Tech Startup* (New York: Free Press/Simon & Schuster, 2000), 1–3.

5. Linda Himeltein, "VCs Turn the Screws," *Business Week*, May 27, 2002, 82–83.

6. Michael Porter, *Competitive Strategy* (New York: Free Press/Simon & Schuster, 1980), 3–33.

7. Andrew S. Grove, *Only the Paranoid Survive* (New York: Currency/Doubleday, 1996), 30.

8. Roberts, *Entrepreneurs in High Technology*, 185.

9. See, e.g., Henry Mintzberg, "Crafting Strategy," *Harvard Business Review*, July–August 1987, pp. 66–75.

10. Quoted in Michael A. Cusumano and David B. Yoffie, *Competing on Internet Time: Lessons from Netscape and Its Battle with Microsoft* (New York: Free Press/Simon & Schuster, 1998), 27.

11. Quoted in ibid., 22.

CHAPTER 6: START-UP CASE STUDIES:
SOFTWARE PRODUCTS, SERVICES, AND HYBRID SOLUTIONS

1. Details of the NuMega story, in addition to my own recollections, are from an e-mail correspondence with Jim Moskun, December 19, 2002, commenting on an early sketch of the NuMega case.
2. Author's interview with Jim Moskun.
3. Ibid.
4. www.compuware.com.
5. www.mindreef.com.
6. www.polarisventures.com/who/bio_t_herring.html and www.expresiv.com/index.html.
7. www.rational.com.
8. E-mail correspondence with Yannick Loop, December 18, 2002.
9. Some company information remains available on the Web at www.e-unlimited.com/stockholm/techsector/download/3%20eCRM%20article.pdf.
10. Michael Cusumano, "2001 Follow-up Report for Customer Dialogue Systems," submitted to Yannick Loop and the board of directors, March 1, 2001, 4–5.
11. Karen J. Bannan, "Concentric Visions: Making It Easy to Customize Rich Media," June 2002, *EContentMag.com* (www.ecmag.net/bs4/2002/bannan6_02.html) (accessed August 22, 2002).
12. For a discussion of the benefits and limits of the Concentric application as used at Nikon, see Zachary Rodgers, "Flash Factory: Nikon Brings the Eye Candy In-House," TurboAds.com, March 13, 2002 (www.turbo ads.com/case_studies/2002features/c20020313.shtml) (accessed August 22, 2002).
13. Jennifer Mears, "Start-up Aims to Keep Users of Rich Media out of the Poorhouse," *Network World,* October 29, 2001, (www.nwfusion.com/news/2001/1029apps.html) (accessed August 22, 2002).
14. E-mail correspondence with Garth Rose, January 14, 2003.
15. E-mail correspondence with Garth Rose, January 14, 2003.
16. Author's interview with Ron Schreiber, managing director, Seed Capital Partners, a Softbank affiliate, December 7, 2002.
17. E-mail correspondence with Garth Rose, January 14, 2003.
18. Written comments on this manuscript from Ed Roberts of MIT, received January 27, 2003, who reviewed the company as a member of the I-Group Hotbank advisory board.
19. Interview with Gaurav Rewari and Navaid Farooqi, December 26, 2002.
20. firstRain, Inc., "firstRain Executive Overview," internal company document, December 2000, 1.
21. E-mail from Navaid Farooqi, December 1, 2000.
22. firstRain, Inc., "firstRain Closes $11 million Series A Funding Round," company press release, October 15, 2001 (www.firstrain.com/en/news/archive/default.asp#).
23. firstRain, Inc., "Nobel Laureate Michael Spence Joins Board of firstRain," company press release, March 26, 2002 (www.firstrain.com/en/news/archive/default.asp#).

24. See www.firstrain.com/en/cust/default.asp (accessed December 12, 2002).

25. See, e.g., Nadine Heintz, "Software Startup firstRain Is on a Roll," *Worth Magazine,* July–August 2002, online edition www.worth.com/content_articles/display/articles.cfm?id=04%CFTVY%2A%3C7%21R%2BB%3BVEQ%3FNE%23%221Z%0A&tid=&eaID=1862).

26. www.firstrain.com/en/products/default.asp (accessed December 22, 2002).

27. "FirstRain," *Venture Reporter,* October 2002, online edition (www.firstrain.com/en/news/media/images/venture_reporter_122002.pdf).

28. Author's interview with J. P. Singh, December 26, 2002.

29. Gaurav Rewari et al., "A Review of Key Performance Indicators for firstRain, July 2001–November 2002" board presentation, 3.

30. Author's interview with Imran Sayeed, chairman of the board, NetNumina Solutions, November 25, 2002.

31. www.netnumina.com/company/history; see the timeline for July 1998.

32. NetNumina Solutions, "NetNumina and Raincastle Winners for 1999 MIMC Awards," company press release, November 9, 1999 (www.netnumina.com/news/press/releases/00110999.html).

33. See the NetNumina Web site for details on these awards at www.netnumina.com/news/press/releases.

34. Author's interview with Imran Sayeed, November 25, 2002.

35. Details on these events come from author's interview with Ennis Rimawi, chairman, Estarta Solutions, November 22, 2002.

36. www.oneworldsoftware.com/about_inv.html (accessed December 15, 2002).

37. A description of Oneworld's service offerings and capabilities can be found in Oneworld Software Solutions, "Services Description," June 20, 2001, www.oneworldsoftware.com, company brochure, PDF format (accessed December 15, 2002), 3.

38. Ibid., p. 5.

39. www.estartasolutions.com/FocusAreas.htm (accessed December 15, 2002).

40. Natasha Twal, "Merging Necessary for International Competitiveness— IT Experts," *Jordan Times,* October 1, 2002, online edition (www.estartasolutions.com/Images/Jordan%20Times%20(Economy%20Section)2.htm) (accessed December 15, 2002).

41. Francesca Sawalha, "Microsoft Announces Estarta, First of a Kind Investment in Region," *Jordan Times,* May 21, 2002, online edition (www.estartasolutions.com/Images/x8.jpg) (accessed December 15, 2002).

42. www.cybergnostic.com/aboutUs.asp (accessed January 1, 2003).

43. This market number comes from former COO Campbell Stras, in comments via e-mail on an early draft of this case write-up, January 1, 2003. A later business plan, however, noted that there were some 1.5 million small and medium-sized firms that could be target customers for the company. See Cybergnostic, "Confidential Business Plan," internal company document, May 2000, 3.

44. Steve Silverman, "Cybergnostic Takes on Loudcloud," *Red Herring*, December 28, 2000 (www.redherring.com/vc/2000/1228/vc-ltr-dealflow 122800.html).
45. Comments, by Campbell Stras, January 1, 2003.
46. Cybergnostic, "Confidential Business Plan," 3, 23.
47. Email correspondence with Brad Miller, January 3 and 23, 2003.
48. Interview with Brad Miller, January 3, 2003. Subsequent references and quotes from Miller refer to this interview.
49. www.perimeterco.com (accessed January 1, 2003).
50. E-mail correspondence with Brad Miller, January 3 and 23, 2003.
51. Comments by Campbell Stras, January 1, 2003.
52. For details on Sigma today, see www.sigmatech.co.uk/public_html/index.html.
53. Details on the company are from a memo by Baker Tilly, " 'Investhink Limited: Directors' Report and Statement of Affairs,' December 5, 2002." This document was prepared by Baker Tilly, an accounting firm in charge of the liquidation proceedings.
54. Angela S. Wilbraham, "Investhink to Launch New Data Search Engine with Delaney on Board," *Inside Market Data*, January 17, 2000 (from text circulated to Investhink personnel by e-mail by Andrew Delaney, January 18, 2000).
55. Baker Tilly, " 'Investhink Limited.' "
56. www.bangnetworks.com.
57. E-mail correspondence with O. Emre Eksi, January 26–28, 2003, and interview, January 29, 2003.
58. E-mail correspondence with Neil Crabb, January 24, 2003.
59. E-mail correspondence with Sina Hakman, January 30, 2003.
60. See www.marex.com and NASDAQ symbol of MRXX, before delisting in mid-2002. The over-the-counter symbol as of December 2002 was OTCBB—MARX.
61. Marex Technologies, "Marex Announces Resignation of David A. Schwedel," *PR Newswire*, December 16, 2002; Marex.com, Inc., Form 8-K, U.S. Securities and Exchange Commission, Washington, D.C., March 3, 2000, 28; www.genmar.com.
62. This discussion relies on e-mail correspondence and comments on the draft from David Schwedel, January 28, 2003.
63. Marex.com, Inc., Form 10-K, U.S. Securities and Exchange Commission, Washington, D.C., March 23, 2000, 1.
64. Marex.com, Inc., Form 10-Q, U.S. Securities and Exchange Commission, Washington, D.C., November 14, 2002.
65. Bea Garcia, "Marex Shifts Focus to Pollution Monitoring," *The Miami Herald*, August 5, 2002, online edition (www.miami.com/mld/miami herald/business/columnists/bea_garcia/3790375.htm) (accessed January 22, 2003).
66. Marex Technologies, "Marex Announces Resignation of David A. Schwedel," *PR Newswire*, December 16, 2002.
67. This write-up benefited from e-mail comments from Nicolas Economou on December 26, 2002, and January 23, 2003, in response to an early draft.

68. "ejemoni Investment Opportunity," internal company document, January 7, 2001.
69. Esther Dyson and Kevin Werbach, "Back to the Frontier: The 2002 PC Forum Roundup," *Esther Dyson's Monthly Report Release 1.0* 20, no. 3 (March 21, 2002) (www.h5technologies.com/press/Release1.pdf) (accessed December 20, 2002).
70. Interview with Nicolas Economou, 6/21/02.
71. www.h5technologies.com/solutions/solutions.html (accessed August 18, 2003).
72. www.h5technologies.com/press/pressRel.html (accessed June 26, 2003).

Index

Accenture, 8, 97, 191, 261, 273
  start-ups and, 224, 226, 228
  strategies and, 26–27, 32, 34, 44
accounting practices, 79–81, 189
acquisitions, *see* mergers and
    acquisitions
Adobe, 36, 87, 218
  business models and, 273, 275,
    278–79
  strategies and, 25, 27, 34–36,
    43–44
Agilent Technologies, 181, 183
Allen, Paul, 12, 111, 205, 210
Amazon.com, 117, 119
Amdahl, 93–94
Ampex, 72
Andersen Consulting, *see* Accenture
Andreessen, Marc, 12, 114–15, 164,
    205, 210, 213, 248
AOL, 74, 103, 117, 164
Apache, 77, 104, 107, 121–23
Apple Computer:
  and history of software business,
    109–11, 113, 115
  products of, 48, 68–69, 75, 77–78,
    113, 115, 145, 159
  software development and, 145,
    152, 159, 164, 189
  start-ups and, 216–18
  strategies and, 34, 52, 68–69, 72,
    75, 77–78
applications software:
  development of, 133–34, 137,
    144–45, 150–52, 156–57,
    161–62, 166, 168–69, 176, 178

future and, 280–81
and history of software business,
    94–100, 102–4, 109–11, 116–17,
    122, 127
start-ups and, 200–202, 204,
    206–7, 209–11, 215, 217,
    230–31, 233–36
Applied Data Research (ADR), 91
Arden, Bruce, 193
Arner, Michael, 56
Aspray, William, 99–100
Asset Sciences, 226
AT&T, 79, 120, 132, 181, 218,
    247

Baan, 3, 80–81, 96
Ballmer, Steve, 83, 172
Basili, Victor, 186–87
BEA Systems, 76–77
  and history of software business,
    114–15
  start-ups and, 230, 238–41
  strategies and, 74, 76
  WebLogic of, 74, 77, 275
Beecher, Bill, 21–22
Be Free, 118–19
Bell Labs, 130, 212, 264
Berners-Lee, Tim, 11, 114, 122
Bloomberg, 253, 255
Bluetooth, 201, 214
Boeing, 96, 189, 218
Borland, 59, 237–38
Brady, Greg, 20, 22
brands, branding, 17, 39, 105, 118,
    209

Brooks, Frederick, 2–3, 101
builds, 144, 150, 152, 158–59, 162,
    164, 166–67, 177–78, 181
business models, business plans,
    xv–xvii, 1–2, 4, 270–80
    best, 272, 278–79
    early growth and profit potential
        shown in, 208–9
    and history of software business,
        107, 111, 116–17, 119, 126
    software development and, 129,
        189, 277
    start-ups and, 195–97, 199–200,
        202, 208–12, 215–16, 218, 222,
        228, 232–33, 242, 246, 248,
        252–53, 258–61, 264, 266, 268,
        270–73
    strategies and, 25–26, 28–29, 31,
        47, 67, 84–85, 272, 274, 277–78
Business Objects, xvi, 11–22, 117, 289
    business models and, 273, 278
    case study on, 13–18
    comparisons between i2
        Technologies and, 19–21
    finances of, 3, 13–17, 21, 35,
        283–84, 287
    software development and, 13,
        16–18, 181
    start-ups and, 14–17, 196, 205,
        215, 221, 223, 230, 244
    strategies and, 27, 30, 33–35,
        37–38, 40, 42–44, 60, 70, 74
Business Week, 16–17

Caldera Systems, 122–23
Cambot, Jean-Michel, 14
Campbell-Kelly, Martin, 99–100
Canon, 65, 72
Capabilities Maturity Model (CMM),
    135–36, 147, 180, 186, 188–90
Cap Gemini Ernst & Young, 97, 273
    strategies and, 26, 32, 34, 44
chasm, 278–81
    business models and, 278–79
    in future, 280–81
    leaping and accelerating across,
        70–71
    start-ups and, 216, 222, 246, 271
    strategies and, 25, 67–71, 85
China, 192, 242–44
choice, 31–32
Cisco Systems, 115
    software development and, 185,
        189
    start-ups and, 199, 218, 249

Clark, Jim, 12, 205, 210
commitment, 175
commoditization, 232
    business models and, 275–76, 280
    and history of software business,
        97, 111
    strategies and, 38–39, 46, 49, 84
company character, 278
    customer confidence and, 81–82, 85
    and industry leadership and
        responsibility, 82–83
    revenue recognition and, 79–81, 85
    strategies and, 25, 78–83, 85
Compaq, 34, 65, 164
competition, competitors,
        competitiveness:
    and author's involvement with
        software business, 8–9
    business models and, 272, 275–76,
        279–80
    and history of software business,
        86, 92, 96, 98–100, 102–4,
        120–21, 124, 126
    i2 Technologies and, 21–22, 37–39
    software development and, 128,
        136, 139, 149, 156, 161–62, 166,
        173, 188, 191
    start-ups and, 203–7, 209–10,
        215–16, 218–22, 225, 227–28,
        230, 235, 238, 240, 250–52, 256,
        258, 267–68
    strategies and, 24, 30, 32, 36–39,
        47–48, 52–53, 55, 59, 62, 67,
        69–74, 76–78, 82–83, 85
complements, complementors, 98
    business models and, 275, 278–79
    start-ups and, 204, 216, 236
    strategies and, 25, 32, 71–72,
        74–78, 82–83, 85
Computer Associates (CA), 81, 91, 95,
    116
Computer Sciences Corporation, 34,
    90
Computer Usage Company, 90
Compuware, 116, 288, 290
    start-ups and, 219–20, 241
    strategies and, 30–31, 34–38,
        41–45, 61
Concentric Visions, 215, 229–33, 237,
    241, 268
consultants, consulting, 189
    business models and, 273–74, 277
    and history of software business,
        96, 104, 106–8, 116
    i2 Technologies and, 19, 21

start-ups and, 205–6, 209, 212–15,
    223–25, 231–32, 239–42,
    246–48, 250–52, 261, 265
strategies and, 31–32, 34, 39,
    42–44, 46, 48, 51, 64, 79–80
continuous process and product
    improvement, 178–80
Crabb, Neil, 253–54, 257–58
creativity, 196, 281
    focus, 154–57
    software development and, 130,
        132–33, 154–57, 163, 166–67
credibility, 128, 279
    start-ups and, 207–8, 222, 224,
        228, 236, 238, 246, 252, 265,
        268, 270
    strategies and, 70–71, 81–82, 85
Crossing the Chasm (Moore), 67–71,
    98
Cullinane Software, 95
Customer Dialogue Systems (CDS),
    215, 222–28, 252, 255, 258,
    268–70
customer relationship management
    (CRM) software, 39, 74, 236,
    276
customers, xvi, 1–5, 7, 9, 11, 20–32
    business models and, 272–80
    Business Objects and, 13–17
    enterprise, *see* enterprises
    in good vs. bad times, 23, 27–28,
        30, 37
    and history of software business,
        91–92, 94, 96–113, 116–19, 121,
        125–26
    i2 Technologies and, 20–22, 37
    software development and, 130–31,
        133, 135, 138, 141–42, 152, 156,
        159–62, 164–65, 168, 173, 177,
        179–80, 183–84, 190–92
    start-ups and, 195–97, 199, 202–9,
        214, 216, 218, 222–29, 232–52,
        255–59, 261–71
    strategies and, 24–29, 31–32,
        34–42, 44, 46–53, 55, 57–75,
        77–83, 85
Cybergnostic, 216, 246–52, 269–70

databases:
    business models and, 275–76
    Business Objects and, 13–15, 60
    and history of software business,
        91, 95, 105, 115–17, 126
    software development and, 135–36,
        152

start-ups and, 205, 230, 238, 245,
    254, 263, 265–67
strategies and, 32, 48, 50, 52–53,
    59–60
debugging, 144, 147, 151–52, 154,
    157–59, 162, 169, 177
    start-ups and, 215, 217–19
Defense Department, U.S., 101, 120,
    135, 229
Dellarocas, Chris, 201
Dell Computer, 21, 65, 72, 164,
    189
DeMarco, Tom, 171
development, *see* research and
    development; software
    development
DeWitt, Charles, 20
Digital Equipment Corporation
    (DEC), 8, 89, 94, 102–3, 126
Digital Research, 102, 109
documentation, 279
    software development and, 137–38,
        140–41, 144, 153–54, 162–63,
        165, 179, 182, 190
    strategies and, 50, 55
Doerr, John, 213–14
duplicating, 60–61
Dyson, Esther, 266

Early Adopters, 67–68
Early Majority, 67
e-business, 59, 189, 274
    and history of software business,
        87, 104, 106, 115–19
    stages of, 116–19
    start-ups and, 196, 200, 215–16,
        231, 237–39, 259–61
Eckert, John, 99
economies of scale:
    and business models, 273, 275,
        279–80
    and history of software business,
        87, 116, 119
    and start-ups, 209, 269
    and strategies, 32, 43–44, 48, 58,
        84
economies of scope, 32, 166–67, 187,
    209, 277
Economou, Nicolas, 264–66, 268
EContentMag.com, 229–30
EDS, 90, 116, 273
    strategies and, 26, 34, 46
Eksi, O. Emre, 253–54, 257
Electronic Delay Storage Automatic
    Calculator (EDSAC), 88

Electronic Numerical Integrator and
    Computer (ENIAC), 88, 99
Ellison, Larry, 2, 52
employment, employees, 2–3, 8, 12
  Business Objects and, 17–18
  and history of software business,
      90, 99, 101, 103, 107, 110, 124
  i2 Technologies and, 20, 22, 33, 37
  software development and, 142–43,
      189
  start-ups and, 200, 209, 218,
      222–23, 226, 228–29, 233, 237,
      239–42, 244, 248–49, 251,
      256–57, 259, 261–63, 267–68
  strategies and, 32–34, 37, 39–42,
      45–46, 51, 54–55, 61, 73, 78, 81,
      83
  see also engineering, engineers;
    management, managers;
    programming, programmers
engineers, engineering, 16
  and history of software business,
      89, 92, 100–101
  software development and, 129–31,
      133–37, 141, 149–50, 152,
      156–57, 165–67, 169–71, 175,
      177, 185–91, 193
  start-ups and, 217–18, 226–27,
      230–33, 235, 243, 245, 247, 252,
      257, 265, 268
  strategies and, 59, 82
Enterprise Computer Systems, 250–51
enterprise resource planning (ERP)
    software, 19, 276
  and history of software business,
      95–97, 116–17, 126
  strategies and, 30, 39–42, 52–53,
      60–62, 80
enterprises:
  business models and, 272–80
  differences between individual
      customers and, 49–51
  and history of software business,
      94–97, 102, 111, 114, 125–27
  software development and, 136–37,
      153, 162, 189–90
  start-ups and, 200, 202, 209, 212,
      230–32, 237–39, 247, 258
  strategies and, 24, 27–29, 31, 34,
      39–42, 45, 47–55, 57, 64–66, 70,
      75, 78–79, 84–85
entrepreneurship, entrepreneurs,
    xv–xvii, 3–5, 7, 13–17
  business models and, 272, 277–78
  Business Objects and, 14–17, 20, 22

future and, 280–81
  and history of software business,
      86–91, 93–95, 102, 108–14,
      116–17, 119–20, 123–26
  i2 Technologies and, 19–20, 22
  software development and, 136,
      161, 163, 185, 188
  strategies and, 25, 39, 47, 49, 55,
      68, 79, 83
  see also start-ups
Estarta Solutions, 242, 245–46
Europe, 10–12, 17
  and history of software business,
      90, 95–96
  software development and, 129,
      171, 181–82, 184–85, 188–89,
      191
  start-ups and, 222–24, 226–27,
      254–55
  strategies and, 46, 54–55, 77
Extreme Programming (XP), 148, 178,
    181–82

Fanning, Shawn, 118
Fidelity Investments, 181, 189
  start-ups and, 218, 226, 239–40
financial metrics, 33–36
firstRain, 215, 233–36, 266, 269–70
flexibility, 6, 98, 277
  software development and, 129–30,
      134, 145–46, 157, 163, 172, 183
  start-ups and, 210–11, 222, 233,
      235–36, 242, 251, 263, 268–70
followers, 25, 71–72, 278
France, 11, 14, 17, 20, 90
free software, see open-source
    software
Fujicolor Processing, 248–51
Fujitsu, 8–9, 11, 273
  and history of software business,
      90, 93–94, 97
  software development of, 133–34
  start-ups and, 195, 218
  strategies and, 32, 34

Gartner Group, 52
Gates, Bill, 2, 12, 69, 73, 102, 281
  and history of software business,
      111–13, 121
  software development and, 172–73,
      177
  start-ups and, 203, 205, 210, 213,
      246
Gawer, Annabelle, 72, 75–77
General Electric (GE), 90, 99, 132

Genmar Holdings, 259, 262–64
Germany, 10–11, 95, 107, 223
Gerstner, Lou, 102–8
globalism:
  and history of software business,
    96, 113, 116, 125
  software development and, 159,
    171, 181–92
  start-ups and, 201, 245
  strategies and, 46–47, 60
  see also Europe; specific countries
Global Software Process Survey, 301
granulating, 60
Great Britain, 254–56, 258
Great Plains Software, 42, 78, 97, 276
Greenawalt, Andrew, 247–52
Greenawalt, Richard, 247
Grossman, Frank, 216–18, 220–21
Grove, Andy, 71, 204

Hakman, Sina, 253–54, 258
Herring, Tom, 218–21
Hewlett-Packard (HP), 12, 218
  and history of software business,
    94, 102, 107–8
  software development and, 173–74,
    181, 183, 185
  strategies and, 52, 65
H5 Technologies, 216, 264–70
High Tech Startup (Nesheim), 198
Hitachi, 8–9, 11, 32, 195, 273
  and history of software business,
    90, 93–94, 97, 106
  software development and, 133–34,
    180–81, 192
horizontal market niches:
  business models and, 278–79
  Business Objects and, 13–16
  and history of software business,
    90, 95–97, 109–10, 126
  start-ups and, 203–4, 216, 233,
    265–66
  strategies and, 24, 53–59, 76–77,
    84–85
Humphrey, Watts, 92, 135
hybrid solutions, hybrid solutions
    companies, xvi–xvii, 1, 4, 6,
    272–77
  best business model and, 279–80
  capabilities of, 277
  characteristics of, 273–75
  comparisons between bank model
    and, 29, 84, 274
  as compelling, 205–6
  future and, 280

and history of software business,
  96–97, 111, 124, 127
i2 Technologies and, 21, 29
products companies in becoming,
  36–43, 84
software development and, 134,
  161
start-ups and, 195, 205–6, 214,
  216, 224, 228, 232–33, 253–71
strategies and, 26, 28–29, 31, 33,
  36–43, 84

IBM, xvi, 6–8, 11–12, 16, 135–36,
  288, 290, 299
  business models and, 273–75
  and history of software business,
    86–87, 89–111, 113–16, 120–21,
    123–24, 126–27
  services and, 102–8
  software capability limits of,
    101–2
  software compatibility and, 93–95
  software development and, 128,
    130, 133, 135, 141, 145, 149–50,
    152, 163, 174–75, 181, 185–86,
    191, 193
  start-ups and, 195, 210, 216–19,
    222, 238
  strategies and, 30–32, 34, 37–38,
    41, 46, 49, 52, 54, 61–64, 69–71,
    74, 76–78, 92–94, 127
  whole-product solution and,
    98–100, 103–4
IBM, products of:
  AS/400, 61–63
  Consolidated Functions Ordinary
    (CFO), 91, 96
  eServer iSeries, 61, 63
  1401, 99–100
  OS/2, 75, 78, 105, 111, 145, 152,
    174–75, 218
  OS/360, 6, 91–92, 101, 128, 130,
    163
  System/360 family, 91, 93, 100
  System/370 family, 93
  WebSphere, 74, 77, 104, 108,
    123–24, 275
IBM Global Services, 46, 104, 186
I-Group Hotbank, 229–30, 232
incremental architecture evolution,
  168–69
India, 209
  business models and, 276–77
  i2 Technologies and, 13, 22
  outsourcing to, 185–92

India (*cont.*)
    software development and, 129,
        133, 181–82, 185, 188–92,
        233
    start-ups and, 233, 235, 240, 242,
        244, 246
    strategies and, 32, 34
infinite defect loops, 150–53, 163,
    178
Infinium Software, 215, 221, 298
    strategies and, 61–65, 79
Information Rules (Shapiro and
    Varian), 69–70
Informix, 15, 52, 95, 218
Infosys, 32, 276
    software development and, 181,
        186, 188–92
    start-ups and, 209, 242
infrastructure, infrastructure software:
    investing in, 175–76
    start-ups and, 196, 200–202, 204,
        209, 215, 233–35, 246–50,
        252–53, 255
    strategies and, 48, 62, 81
initial public offerings (IPOs),
    197–98, 200, 209, 212, 220, 237,
    241
Innovators, 67
Inside Market Data, 254–55
integration, 46
    business models and, 273, 280
    and history of software business,
        106, 125
    software development and, 138,
        140–41, 144, 147, 149, 151,
        153–54, 162, 164, 166, 168,
        173–74, 178
    start-ups and, 216, 236–37, 243,
        255–56
    strategies and, 50–51, 54, 60, 64,
        67, 77
Intel, 151
    and history of software business,
        95, 102, 109, 111
    start-ups and, 199, 217–18, 234,
        244
    strategies and, 65, 69, 71–72, 74,
        76–77
Internet, 9, 11, 278
    Business Objects and, 13, 17
    future and, 280–81
    and history of software business,
        87, 89, 104–5, 108, 112–21,
        126–27
    i2 Technologies and, 19–21

software development and, 128,
    133, 144–45, 153, 159–60,
    163–64, 182, 189–90
start-ups and, 196–201, 204–5,
    207, 209–10, 212–14, 221,
    225–27, 229–35, 238–42,
    245–49, 251, 253, 255–59, 261,
    263, 266–67
strategies and, 31, 47, 50, 55–56,
    60, 63, 66, 70, 73–74, 77–78, 84
Intuit:
    business models and, 273, 278–79
    strategies and, 34, 65–66, 73–74
Invensys PLC, 80, 96
Investhink, 216, 253–58, 264, 268–70
investment, investors, 11–12, 279–80
    business models and, 273, 275–76,
        279
    and history of software business,
        98, 107, 119
    software development and, 130,
        136, 175–76, 185, 190
    start-ups and, 196–99, 202–3,
        206–9, 211–14, 217, 219–20,
        222–23, 225–34, 236, 239,
        241–46, 249, 251–59, 262–69
    strategies and, 31, 33, 45–47, 56,
        59, 62, 68, 78, 80
    see also venture capitalists
i2 Technologies, xvi, 13, 285–87, 289
    case study on, 19–22
    finances of, 3, 19–22, 26–27, 29,
        33, 35, 37–38, 43, 285–86
    software development and, 189
    start-ups and, 205, 209, 215, 221
    strategies and, 26–27, 29–31,
        33–40, 43–44, 59–61, 70

Japan, 6–12, 18, 72, 229, 277
    and history of software business,
        90, 96–97, 101
    software development and, 11–12,
        129–30, 132–36, 145, 147,
        165–66, 171, 177–82, 184–89,
        191–93
    strategies and, 32, 46
Jeffrey, Joel, 264–66
Johnson & Johnson, 60, 239–40
Jordan, 242, 245–46
Joy, Bill, 213
Justice Department, U.S., 83, 92–93

kaizen, 178
Kangas, Jeff, 264–65
Katz, Roberta, 211

Kemerer, Chris, 181, 184
Kildall, Gary, 102, 109
Knapp, Chris, 56

Laggards, 67
large firms, 47, 50, 52, 94, 125
Late Majority, 67–68
leaders, leadership:
　business models and, 278–79
　in industry, 82–83
　in markets, 52, 71–74
　platforms and, 32, 36, 69, 71–72,
　　74–78, 82, 85
　strategies and, 25, 32, 52–53, 69,
　　71–77, 82–83, 85
Liautaud, Bernard, 13–18, 20, 203,
　205
licenses, license fees, 167
　business models and, 274, 279–80
　Business Objects and, 15, 17, 43
　and history of software business,
　　93–94, 96, 122, 124–25
　i2 Technologies and, 19–21, 33,
　　38
　perpetual, 51
　site, 93
　start-ups and, 225, 230, 232, 235
　strategies and, 27–28, 31–36,
　　38–45, 49–50, 61, 64, 66, 69, 79,
　　81
life cycle models, 26
Linux, 214, 275
　and history of software business,
　　104, 107, 121–25
　strategies and, 48–49, 52, 76–78
Lisbonne, Bob, 169–70
Lister, Timothy, 171
Lizza, Fred, 62–63
Loop, Yannick, 222–23, 228
Lotus, 59, 105, 110, 113, 152, 275
　start-ups and, 218
　strategies and, 73, 78
Lucent, 3, 185, 189, 218

McGowan, Jim, 62–63
maintenance, maintenance fees, 241
　business models and, 273–77, 280
　Business Objects and, 16, 38, 40,
　　42, 44
　in good vs. bad times, 23, 28, 37
　and history of software business,
　　93, 96, 101, 104
　i2 Technologies and, 21, 38, 40
　recurring revenues generated by,
　　64–65

software development and, 131,
　133, 144, 154, 162, 165, 190
strategies and, 27–31, 33–42,
　44–46, 49–51, 54–55, 64–67, 74,
　79–81, 84
management, managers, xv–xvi, 1–10,
　16–22, 277–80
　business models and, 272, 277–78,
　　280
　Business Objects and, 13–14,
　　16–18, 22
　and history of software business,
　　86, 92, 100–101, 103, 105, 107,
　　113, 116, 118, 123–25
　i2 Technologies and, 19–22
　of knowledge and people, 142–43
　panic, 203, 226
　of projects, 137–38, 152–54, 157,
　　173–76, 187–88, 191, 193, 209,
　　240, 243, 277
　of risks, 164–65
　software development and, 128–35,
　　137–39, 142–48, 152–54,
　　156–57, 159–66, 169–76,
　　178–80, 183, 186–88, 190–91,
　　193
　start-ups and, 195–96, 199, 202–3,
　　206, 209–10, 216–23, 226,
　　228–30, 232–41, 243, 246–54,
　　256–57, 261–62, 265, 270
　strategies and, 25, 31–32, 47, 50–51,
　　55, 58–60, 62, 68–69, 79–85
　of teams, 171–73
　technology vs., 5–7
Manugistics, 38–39
Marex, 216, 258–64, 268–70
Maritz, Dave, 146–47, 161
markets, marketing, xvi, 2–7, 9,
　11–17, 65
　business models and, 275–79
　Business Objects and, 13–17, 43
　in Europe, 11–12
　and history of software business,
　　86–87, 90–92, 94–100, 102–3,
　　107–14, 118–19, 122–23,
　　125–27
　i2 Technologies and, 19, 22, 37, 43
　leaders in, 52, 71–74
　segmentation of, *see specific market
　　segments*
　software development and, 129–30,
　　132, 136–40, 143–45, 149,
　　152–53, 156–57, 159, 161–63,
　　165–66, 169–70, 173, 177,
　　183–84, 191, 193

markets, marketing (*cont.*)
　start-ups and, 197, 202–9, 211–12,
　　216–22, 236, 239–48, 250–53,
　　255–71
　strategies and, 24–25, 29–34,
　　37–39, 43, 45–63, 67–78, 82–85
mass markets:
　business models and, 278–79
　and history of software business,
　　95, 98, 108, 110–14, 119
　software development and, 129,
　　162, 169, 173, 177, 191
　start-ups and, 219, 226, 244, 253,
　　255
　strategies and, 24–25, 32, 42,
　　46–49, 51–54, 58, 67–71, 73, 75,
　　77–78, 85
Matsushita, 72, 74, 181
Mauchly, John, 99
Mediacom, 248–51
medium-sized firms, 279
　and history of software business,
　　97, 125
　software development and,
　　137–44
　start-ups and, 246–47, 250, 252,
　　255
　strategies and, 47, 50, 52
mergers and acquisitions, 6, 13, 276
　and history of software business,
　　91, 95–97, 99, 102–3, 105–8,
　　118–19, 122, 125
　and i2 Technologies, 19–21
　and start-ups, 197–98, 209, 216,
　　219–20, 222, 226, 230–31, 237,
　　240–46, 252, 263
　and strategies, 42, 44, 47, 52,
　　62–63, 73–74, 78, 80
MicroPro, 72–73, 110
Microsoft, xvi, 2–3, 6, 12, 14–16, 21,
　　281, 293
　antitrust problems of, 9, 73, 77, 83,
　　107
　and author's involvement with
　　software business, 9–10, 14, 18
　business models and, 273, 275–76,
　　278–79
　Business Objects and, 14, 16
　and history of software business,
　　87, 94–95, 98, 102–16, 121–24,
　　126
　software development and, 128–29,
　　132, 136, 139, 141, 143–60,
　　162–64, 166–82, 185, 188–89,
　　192–93

　start-ups and, 199, 205, 210–11,
　　218–20, 230, 237–38, 242–46,
　　253
　strategies and, 25, 27, 31–32,
　　35–36, 42–43, 46, 48–50, 52–59,
　　61–78, 82–83
Microsoft, products of, 296
　Access, 52, 152, 169
　BASIC, 109, 111
　DOS, 12, 15–16, 50, 66, 71, 75–76,
　　102, 111, 113, 145, 150, 152,
　　169, 176, 218
　.NET, 9, 76–77, 145, 163, 244
　Excel, 50, 58–59, 64, 73, 144–45,
　　152, 166, 168–69
　Internet Explorer, 78, 83, 115, 123,
　　145, 153, 160
　Money, 73
　MSN, 42, 117, 173
　NetMeeting, 160
　Office, 21, 36, 50, 52–53, 55, 58,
　　66, 70–72, 145, 157, 166,
　　168–69, 219, 275, 279
　PowerPoint, 58–59, 166, 169
　SQL Server, 52, 70–71, 230, 276
　Visual Basic, 219
　Windows, 12, 15–16, 30, 32, 36,
　　42, 47–48, 50, 52, 55, 57, 59,
　　62–63, 65–66, 69–78, 82–83, 94,
　　104, 107, 113, 115–16, 121,
　　123–24, 128, 139, 144–47,
　　150–51, 153, 159, 164, 169,
　　173, 177, 179, 218–21, 230, 275,
　　279
　Word, 50, 58–59, 65–66, 73, 110,
　　144–45, 150–52, 162, 166,
　　168–69
Microsoft Secrets (Cusumano and
　　Selby), 14, 144, 150, 154, 157,
　　172
MicroStrategy, 233
Middle East, 242–43, 245–46
middleware, 115, 204–5, 215–16,
　　237–39, 242
milestone technique, 152, 154–57,
　　159–60, 162, 164, 174, 181
Miller, Brad, 249–52
Miller, Michelle, 259, 261
Moore, Geoffrey, 49, 67–71, 85, 98
Moskun, Jim, 216–18, 220–21
Motorola, 49, 109, 190–92
　in India, 181, 186–88, 190–91
　software development and, 136,
　　181, 186–88, 192
　start-ups and, 195, 218

MP3, 118
Mythical Man-Month (Brooks), 2, 101

Napster, 118, 200, 214, 281
NASDAQ, 13, 20, 122, 188, 197,
    258, 262
National Aeronautics and Space
    Administration (NASA), 173, 187
National Center for Supercomputer
    Applications (NCSA), 114–15,
    122
Navision, 97, 276
NEC, 8, 11, 181, 193, 195
    and history of software business,
        90, 97
    software development of, 133–34
Nesheim, John, 198
NetNumina Solutions, 215–16,
    236–42, 246, 269–70
Netscape, xvi, 9, 12, 18
    business models and, 273, 275
    and history of software business,
        107, 113–15, 117, 121, 123
    software development and, 136,
        139, 144, 152, 159–60, 163–64,
        166–67, 169–70, 175–76,
        178–80
    start-ups and, 205, 210–11, 213,
        218, 226, 244, 248
    strategies and, 60, 70, 73–74, 78,
        83
Netscape, products of:
    Communicator, 152, 164, 169–70,
        226
    Mosaic, 115, 122, 213–14
    Navigator, 12, 78, 83, 121, 123,
        152, 164, 169–70, 211, 226, 275
New Haven Savings Bank, 251
New York Times, 104, 212
niches, niche markets, 281
    business models and, 276, 278–79
    differences between mass markets
        and, 51–53
    and history of software business,
        86, 90, 94–97, 119, 126
    start-ups and, 208, 236, 241–46,
        248
    strategies and, 24, 46–49, 51–53,
        61, 63, 67–70, 75, 85
Nokia, 49, 56, 94, 109, 181, 195, 281
North Atlantic Treaty Organization
    (NATO), 130–31, 171
Novell, 69, 78, 124, 230
NuMega Technologies, 30, 44,
    215–22, 228, 238, 241, 269–70

Olsen, Ken, 89
on-demand computing, 108
one best development process, 161–62
Oneworld Software, 216, 242–46,
    252, 270
Only the Paranoid Survive (Grove), 71
Open Environment Corporation
    (OEC), 237–38, 241
open-source software, xvi, 49, 214,
    274
    and history of software business,
        87, 104–6, 115, 118, 120–25,
        127
    start-ups and, 237–39
operating systems:
    business models and, 275, 279
    and history of software business,
        91–94, 96, 100–102, 104–5, 107,
        109, 111, 113, 115–16, 120–26
    software development and, 128,
        130, 133, 135, 138–40, 144–47,
        149–53, 156–57, 159, 163–64,
        166, 169, 173–77, 179
    start-ups and, 210, 215, 217–21,
        244
    strategies and, 32, 48–50, 52–57,
        61–63, 65–66, 68–72, 74–78,
        82–83
Oracle, 2–3, 6, 20–21, 288, 290
    business models and, 275–76
    Business Objects and, 13–15
    E-Business Suite of, 59, 297
    and history of software business,
        95, 104, 107–8, 121
    software development and, 165,
        185
    start-ups and, 218, 230, 233, 246,
        265
    strategies and, 29–31, 34–38,
        41–44, 47, 52–53, 59, 61, 68, 78
outsourcing:
    and history of software business,
        94–95, 110–11
    software development and, 129,
        133, 185–92
    start-ups and, 224, 243–44, 246,
        248–49
    strategies and, 44–45

Palm, 32, 94, 207
    strategies and, 56–58, 74, 76–78
Parcell, John, 254
partners, partnerships, 279
    and history of software business,
        93–94, 96

partners, partnerships (*cont.*)
  start-ups and, 206, 208, 217,
    219–20, 224, 226, 228, 231, 245,
    250–53, 256–57, 263
  strategies and, 46, 49, 54, 76, 78,
    82–83
Payre, Denis, 14–17, 205, 223
PC hardware, emergence of, 109–11
PC Magazine, 218
PC software:
  development of, 133–34, 141–42,
    144–53, 163, 165
  and history of software business,
    109–14, 119
  start-ups and, 210, 217, 221
peer-to-peer technology, 118, 281
  start-ups and, 200, 214
Pemberton, Robert, 61–63
PeopleSoft, 96, 274, 287, 289
  strategies and, 26–27, 29–31,
    34–40, 42–44, 47, 59, 62
Peopleware (DeMarco and Lister),
    171
Peregrine Systems, 81
Peters, Chris, 6, 153, 172, 175
Platform Leadership (Gawer and
    Cusumano), 75–77
platforms, platform issues, 16,
    279–81
  business models and, 275, 279–80
  complementors and, 75–78
  and history of software business,
    87, 91, 93, 96, 104–5, 108–14,
    121, 123, 126–27
  leaders and, 32, 36, 69, 71–72,
    74–78, 82, 85
  software development and, 128,
    134, 139, 151, 157, 173
  start-ups and, 207, 210, 216,
    244–45, 255, 268
  strategies and, 32, 36, 49, 53–57,
    59, 61–63, 69, 71–72, 74–78, 82,
    85
Porter, Michael, 24, 71, 203–4
price, prices, pricing, 5, 15
  business models and, 275–76,
    279
  and history of software business,
    91–94, 103, 113
  i2 Technologies and, 38–39
  start-ups and, 196–97, 203–4, 212,
    231, 235, 240, 260, 269
  strategies and, 36–39, 48, 58–59,
    63, 66, 68–70, 73, 80, 83
Priceline.com, 118–19

PricewaterhouseCoopers (PWC), 97,
    107, 191, 265, 273
  strategies and, 26–27, 32, 34, 44
productivity, 2, 8
  software development and, 131,
    175, 181, 183–85
  strategies and, 33–36, 44, 67
products, *see* software products,
    software products companies
profit, profits, profitability, 1, 3, 5–6,
    8–9, 11–14
  business models and, 273, 275–76,
    278, 280
  Business Objects and, 13–14, 17,
    19, 21, 43–44
  and history of software business,
    95, 98, 100, 103, 106–7, 112,
    119, 122–25
  i2 Technologies and, 21–22, 44, 59
  software development and, 128,
    189
  start-ups and, 197–98, 200, 203–4,
    208–9, 211, 214, 219, 224,
    226–28, 239, 241, 249, 251–52,
    257, 263
  strategies and, 29, 31–36, 39–46,
    48, 50–51, 53, 55–56, 59, 62–65,
    70–71, 73, 78, 84–85
programming, programmers, 1, 3–5,
    7–13, 22, 280
  business models and, 272, 276–78
  in Europe, 10–12
  and history of software business,
    86–88, 90–91, 94, 100–102, 104,
    109, 113, 117, 120–21, 123, 125
  software development and, 130–34,
    137, 142, 145–47, 150, 153, 156,
    159–63, 166–67, 169, 171–72,
    174–76, 178–84, 187–89,
    191–93
  start-ups and, 205, 209–10,
    213–14, 217–19, 221–22, 224,
    229–30, 243–46, 253
  strategies and, 25, 47–48, 55, 57,
    68, 79, 83
project discipline, 175–76

quality assurance (QA), 130, 140–42,
    161, 165, 176–80, 187–88, 190

Rational Software, 108, 219, 222
Razorfish, 116, 230–31, 241
RCA, 90–93, 99
Red Hat, 122, 124–25, 300
Red Herring, 248

research and development:
  and history of software business,
    98–99, 103, 125
  and i2 Technologies, 22, 59
  and start-ups, 206, 225, 228,
    266–68
  and strategies, 32–33, 37, 43, 45,
    48, 50–51, 59, 67–68, 72, 77, 80,
    83
  see also software development
Reuters, 218, 253–55, 257–58
revenues, 19–23
  business models and, 273–80
  Business Objects and, 13–16, 21,
    27, 33–34, 38, 43–44
  deferred, 66
  in good vs. bad times, 23, 25,
    27–28, 33, 37
  and history of software business,
    90, 95–96, 98, 105–8, 113, 117,
    119, 122–26
  i2 Technologies and, 19–22, 26–27,
    29, 33, 38, 43
  recurring, 25, 31, 51, 63–67, 73,
    98, 106, 113, 126, 216, 249, 252,
    274, 278–80
  software development and, 144,
    186, 189
  start-ups and, 199, 203, 208–9,
    216–18, 220, 222–23, 225,
    227–29, 231–35, 237–41,
    244–45, 248–52, 256,
    258–64
  strategies and, 25–31, 33–47,
    49–52, 54–56, 62–67, 73–74,
    79–81, 84–85
Rewari, Gaurav, 233, 235
Rimawi, Ennis, 242–43, 244–45
risks:
  software development and, 137–38,
    156, 163–65, 192
  start-ups and, 209, 242, 263
  strategies and, 27, 77–78
Roberts, Ed, 198, 232, 265
Rose, Garth, 230–32
Roxio, Inc., 118

SABRE, 89
SAGE, 88, 101
sales, selling, salespeople, 1–6, 12–17,
    19–37
  business models and, 273–74, 276,
    278–80
  Business Objects and, 13–17, 27,
    42–43

and history of software business,
    87, 91–93, 95, 97–98, 100,
    104–5, 107, 110–12, 114,
    116–19, 123–27
  i2 Technologies and, 19–22, 27, 37,
    43
  software development and, 137–38,
    140, 144, 153, 160, 186
  start-ups and, 196, 202, 207–9,
    211, 214, 216–25, 227, 231, 236,
    239–42, 244–45, 247–52,
    256–60, 262–64, 267–71
  strategies and, 24–37, 39–55,
    58–69, 72–74, 78–85
SAP, 3, 11–12, 21, 288, 290
  business models and, 274, 276
  and history of software business,
    96–97, 107, 117
  products of, 55, 117, 295
  strategies and, 26–27, 29–31,
    34–43, 46, 52–55, 58–61,
    84
Sapient, 116, 243–44
Sayeed, Imran, 237–38, 240–42
scaling, 60–61
Schreiber, Ron, 232
Schwedel, David, 259, 261–64
SCO Group, 122, 124
scope of the firm, 75–76
Securities and Exchange Commission
    (SEC), 16, 20, 38, 78–79, 81
Selby, Richard, 9, 14, 129, 144, 150,
    154, 157, 172, 174–75
servers:
  and history of software business,
    104–5, 108, 114–16, 121–23,
    126
  software development and, 166,
    173
  start-ups and, 204, 210–11, 215,
    226, 230, 234–35
  strategies and, 55–57, 60, 70–71,
    74, 78
services, see software services,
    software services companies
Shapiro, Carl, 69–70
Sharma, Ken, 19–20, 205
Sidhu, Sanjiv, 19–20, 22, 205
Siebel Systems, 3, 234, 276, 289
  software development and, 179,
    181
  strategies and, 29–31, 34–40,
    42–44, 74
Sigma Technology Management,
    253–54, 256–58

Singh, Jaswinder Pal, 233, 235
SkyFire Technologies, 56–58,
     207
  start-ups and, 215, 234, 266
small firms, 47, 52, 97, 279
  start-ups and, 246–50, 261
software, software business:
  author's involvement with, 7–10,
     14, 18
  failures in, 2–4
  functions performed by, 2, 6–7
  generalizations about, 10–13
  history of, 86–127
  pirating of, 112
  successes in, 2–6
  uniqueness of, 1–3, 7
software development, xv–xvi, 1–4,
     8–9, 11–13, 20, 128–93
  business models and, 129, 189, 277
  Business Objects and, 13, 16–18,
     181
  common problems and solutions in,
     130–44
  factory approach to, 11–12,
     129–30, 132–36, 145, 147, 149,
     165–66, 171, 177–78, 180,
     184–88, 192–93, 277
  implementation strategies and
     subtleties in, 161–80
  international comparisons in,
     181–85, 188, 191
  outsourcing of, 129, 133, 185–92
  SEI and, 129, 134–36, 139, 161–62,
     180, 182, 184–85, 187–89, 193
  start-ups and, 139–40, 164, 170,
     200, 215–16, 223–27, 229–30,
     233, 235, 243, 246, 261–62
  synch-and-stabilize approach to,
     xvi, 6, 129, 144–60, 164, 167,
     173–74, 177–78, 181, 183, 185,
     188, 191, 193
  waterfall approach to, 129, 134,
     141, 145, 149, 151–52, 168, 173,
     177, 181–83, 188, 190–92
Software Development Magazine, 219
Software Engineering Institute (SEI),
     xvi, 6, 101
  software development and, 129,
     134–36, 139, 161–62, 180, 182,
     184–85, 187–89, 193
Software Magazine, 34, 47, 238,
     291–92, 294
software products, software products
     companies, xv–xvii, 1–5, 7–9,
     11–75, 267–81

  in becoming services or hybrid
     companies, 36–43, 84
  best business model and, 278–80
  bundling of, 53, 58–60, 65, 78, 81,
     85–87, 91–94, 104, 109, 111,
     124
  Business Objects and, 13–18, 42–44
  capabilities of, 276–77
  characteristics of, 273–75
  comparisons between printing press
     model and, 28–29, 51, 84,
     273–74
  compatibility of, 66, 75, 92–95,
     100, 139
  as compelling, 205–6
  definition of, 36
  flexibility in, 210–11
  future and, 280–81
  in good vs. bad times, 23, 27,
     29–30, 37, 46
  history of, 86–117, 120–27
  i2 Technologies and, 19–22, 29–30,
     37–39, 59–60
  recurring revenues generated by,
     65–67
  services vs., 24–46, 84
  standards dynamics and, 68–71
  start-ups and, 195–96, 200–212,
     214–36, 253, 255, 261–64,
     267–71
  strategies and, 24–75, 77–78, 80–85
  strengths and weaknesses of,
     275–76
  suites of, 53, 58–60, 66, 139, 219,
     230–31, 238
  too much growth and diversification
     in, 60–63
  types of, 55
  upgrading of, 65–66, 80, 84, 93, 98,
     113–14, 207, 273–74, 277, 279
  see also software development
software services, software services
     companies, xv–xvii, 1, 3–5, 9, 11,
     272–81
  best business model and, 278–80
  Business Objects and, 16, 27, 38,
     42–44
  capabilities of, 277
  characteristics of, 273–75
  comparisons between bank model
     and, 28, 84, 274
  as compelling, 205–6
  definition of, 26
  flexibility in, 210
  future and, 280–81

in good vs. bad times, 23, 27–28, 30, 37
history of, 86–87, 90–93, 96–98, 100, 102–8, 111–20, 122–27
i2 Technologies and, 19, 21, 27, 38
products companies in becoming, 36–43, 84
products vs., 24–46, 84
recurring revenues generated by, 64–65
software development and, 128, 130, 144–45, 161, 173, 186, 189
start-ups and, 195–96, 200, 203–6, 208–10, 214–16, 231–33, 235–70
strategies and, 24–50, 54, 61, 63–68, 71, 74–75, 79–80, 82–85
strengths and weaknesses of, 276
Sony, 72, 74
SSA Global Technologies, 63, 80, 96
Standard & Poor's, 46, 239
standards, standardization:
    business models and, 275, 277
    and history of software business, 96, 115, 126
    software development and, 131, 133–34, 166
    strategies and, 68–71, 74–75
start-ups, xvi–xvii, 6–7, 24, 195–273
    Business Objects and, 14–17, 196, 205, 215, 221, 223, 230, 244
    case studies on, 215–71
    essential elements of successful, 200–212
    and history of software business, 95, 102, 110, 116, 118–19, 125
    i2 Technologies and, 19–20
    normal state of affairs for, 197–200
    predicting success vs. failure of, 196–202, 213–14
    software development and, 139–40, 164, 170, 200, 215–16, 223–27, 229–30, 233, 235, 243, 246, 261–62
    see also entrepreneurship, entrepreneurs
Stras, Campbell, 247, 252
strategies for software companies, xv–xvi, 24–85
    and business models, 25–26, 28–29, 31, 47, 67, 84–85, 272, 274, 277–78
    and company character, 25, 78–83, 85
    and complementors, 25, 32, 71–72, 74–78, 82–83, 85
    and customers, 24–29, 31–32, 34–42, 44, 46–53, 55, 57–75, 77–83, 85
    and followers, 25, 71–72, 278
    and history of software business, 92–94, 96–98, 100, 104–8, 121, 127
    and leaders, 25, 32, 52–53, 69, 71–77, 82–83, 85
    and markets, 24–25, 29–34, 37–39, 43, 45–63, 67–78, 82–85
    and products vs. services, 24–46, 84
    and profits, 29, 31–36, 39–46, 48, 50–51, 53, 55–56, 59, 62–65, 70–71, 73, 78, 84–85
    and recurring revenues, 25, 31, 51, 63–67, 73
    and sales, 24–37, 39–55, 58–69, 72–74, 78–85
    and software development, 161–80
    and start-ups, 195, 203, 210–11, 226–27, 232, 235–36, 240, 243, 246–47, 249–50, 252, 255, 257–61, 266–69
    and unbundling, 92–94, 127
Subramaniam, Sundar, 229–30, 237
Sun Microsystems, 12
    and history of software business, 94, 104, 107, 115, 121, 126
    products of, 121, 213
    software development and, 181, 185
    start-ups and, 234, 238
    strategies and, 48, 52, 78
Sybase, 15, 52, 95, 218, 240
Symbian, 32, 49, 76, 94, 281
System Development Corporation (SDC), 8, 88, 132
systems software, 48, 86–91, 93–94, 109–11, 126

technical support:
    business models and, 273, 279
    and history of software business, 96, 98, 122–23
    software development and, 130, 137–38, 162, 180
    start-ups and, 207–8, 219, 247
    strategies and, 50–51, 55, 64, 66, 68, 82

technology, technologies:
disruptive, 24
emerging, 302
and history of software business,
89–90
leaders in, 72–74, 85
management vs., 5–7
software as, 1, 4–7, 10, 12, 14,
111
strategies and, 47, 76
terrorism, 255, 267
Thompson, John, 105
Time, 17
Toshiba, 8–9, 11, 97, 133–34,
166–67
Toy, Michael, 170
training, 100, 273
software development and, 130–31,
134, 142, 186
start-ups and, 209, 223, 229,
231–32, 235
strategies and, 39, 43, 45–46,
50–51, 54, 64, 79
Tullet & Tokyo Liberty, 255
Turkey, 253–56

United States, 17, 46, 277
generalizations about software
business in, 10–12
and history of software business,
94–96
software development and, 129,
134–35, 159, 171, 181–82,
184–86, 188–89, 191, 193
start-ups and, 226–27, 242–44,
254–56, 258
UNIVAC, 99, 120
UNIX, 32, 139, 213, 217
and history of software business,
104, 114–16, 120–21, 123–24,
126
strategies and, 48, 52, 77–78
Upside, 218

ValueClick, 119
Varian, Hal, 69–70
venture capitalists (VCs):
business models and, 273,
278–79

start-ups and, 195–200, 202–3,
209, 211–13, 217, 221–22,
228–31, 233–34, 239, 241–42,
244–45, 247–49, 259, 265,
269–71
strategies and, 33, 46–47, 56
vertical market niches, 13–14
business models and, 278–79
Business Objects and, 13, 16
and history of software business,
90, 94–96, 110, 126
start-ups and, 203–4, 216, 239–40,
250–52, 261–62, 266–68
strategies and, 24, 51, 53–55,
57–59, 61, 84–85
videocassette recorders (VCRs), 72,
74–75
VisiCalc, 73, 110
vision statements, 153–56, 159, 164,
172
von Krogh, Georg, 60
von Neumann, John, 88

Wall Street Journal, The, 22, 254
Wang, 216–18
Waters Information Services,
254–55
What Can Be Automated? (Arden),
193
Whirlwind, 88–89
whole-product solutions, 279
and history of software business,
98–100, 103–4, 126
strategies and, 49, 67–71, 85
wireless applications, 56–57, 213,
215, 233–36, 245, 281
WordPerfect, 51, 59, 73, 78, 110, 113,
152, 177
working in parallel, 157–58
World Wide Web, *see* Internet

Xerox, 63, 72, 113, 181, 213
start-ups and, 218, 265

Yoffie, David, 170, 213
Y2K, 19–20, 62

Zeine Technological Applications,
242, 245–46

About the Author

Michael A. Cusumano (B.A. Princeton, Ph.D. Harvard) is the Sloan Management Review Distinguished Professor at MIT's Sloan School of Management. Professor Cusumano is one of the world's leading experts on the computer software industry. He has served as a director or adviser to a dozen software companies and has consulted for some fifty major firms throughout the world, including Alcatel, AOL, AT&T, Business Objects, Cisco, Ericsson, Fiat, Fujitsu, General Electric, Fidelity, Hitachi, i2 Technologies, IBM, Intel, Lucent, Motorola, NASA, NEC, Siemens, Texas Instruments, and Toshiba. Professor Cusumano has served as editor in chief and chairman of the MIT *Sloan Management Review* and written articles for *The Wall Street Journal, Computerworld,* and *The Washington Post.* He is author or coauthor of six books, including *Competing on Internet Time, Thinking Beyond Lean,* and *Microsoft Secrets,* all published by Free Press, and most recently *Platform Leadership* (HBS Press, 2002).